"I would highly recommend this book to preservice and in-service K–12 teachers, other educators, and researchers interested in second language education. Tedick and Lyster provide a much-needed research-based presentation of pedagogical practices to enhance language development in dual language and immersion classrooms. Their clear definitions, specific strategies and instructional models, and self-assessment tools add a significant layer of depth to our understanding of how to teach two languages in dual language and immersion classrooms. This book provides important implications for program design, curriculum, and instructional practices in dual language and immersion programs to significantly improve language learning and teaching. Buy it today and use it tomorrow!"

— *Kathryn Lindholm-Leary, Professor Emerita, Child and Adolescent Development, San Jose State University, USA*

"Tedick and Lyster have drawn on decades of research and experience to produce this remarkable book. The authors' deep knowledge of classroom practices and their respect for teachers' creativity and hard work are reflected on every page. From reviewing research findings to providing guidance for lesson planning and pedagogy, the book is comprehensive, original, and practical. It will become a foundational text for teacher education and professional development in immersion and dual language education."

— *Patsy Lightbown, Distinguished Professor Emerita, Education, Concordia University, Canada*

South Academy of International Languages
8300 Nations Ford Road
Charlotte, NC 28217
P: 980-343-5815
F: 980-343-5854

SCAFFOLDING LANGUAGE DEVELOPMENT IN IMMERSION AND DUAL LANGUAGE CLASSROOMS

This book introduces research-based pedagogical practices for supporting and enhancing language development and use in school-based immersion and dual language programs in which a second, foreign, heritage, or indigenous language is used as the medium of subject-matter instruction. Using counterbalanced instruction as the volume's pedagogical framework, the authors map out the specific pedagogical skill set and knowledge base that teachers in immersion and dual language classrooms need so their students can engage with content taught through an additional language while continuing to improve their proficiency in that language. To illustrate key concepts and effective practices, the authors draw on classroom-based research and include teacher-created examples of classroom application. The following topics are covered in detail:

- defining characteristics of immersion and dual language programs and features of well-implemented programs
- strategies to promote language and content integration in curricular planning as well as classroom instruction and performance assessment
- an instructional model to counterbalance form-focused and content-based instruction
- scaffolding strategies that support students' comprehension and production while ensuring continued language development
- an approach to creating cross-linguistic connections through biliteracy instruction
- a self-assessment tool for teachers to reflect on their pedagogical growth

Also applicable to content and language integrated learning and other forms of content-based language teaching, this comprehensive volume includes graphics to facilitate navigation and provides Resources for Readers and Application Activities at the end of each chapter.

The book will be a key resource for preservice and in-service teachers, administrators, and teacher educators.

Diane J. Tedick is Professor of Second Language Education at the University of Minnesota. Her research interests include student language development in immersion classrooms, content-based language instruction, and immersion/dual language teacher education and professional development. She provides professional development experiences for immersion and bilingual teachers in the US and internationally. She has co-edited two books on immersion, both published by Multilingual Matters: *Pathways to Multilingualism: Evolving Perspectives on Immersion Education* (2008) and *Immersion Education: Practices, Policies, Possibilities* (2011). She has twice received the US Paul Pimsleur Award for Research in Foreign Language Education, in 2013 with co-recipient Laurent Cammarata, and in 2016 with Tara Fortune.

Roy Lyster is Professor Emeritus of Second Language Education at McGill University, Montreal. His research examines content-based second-language instruction and the effects of instructional interventions designed to counterbalance form-focused and content-based approaches. He was co-recipient with colleague Leila Ranta of the 1998 Paul Pimsleur Award for Research in Foreign Language Education and was presented with the Robert Roy Award by the Canadian Association of Second Language Teachers in 2017. He is the author of a module called *Content-Based Language Teaching* published by Routledge in 2018, and two books: *Learning and Teaching Languages Through Content* published by Benjamins in 2007 and *Vers une approche intégrée en immersion* published by Les Éditions CEC in 2016.

ROUTLEDGE SERIES IN LANGUAGE AND CONTENT INTEGRATED TEACHING & PLURILINGUAL EDUCATION

Series Editors: Angel M.Y. Lin and Christiane Dalton-Puffer

Scaffolding Language Development in Immersion and Dual Language Classrooms
Diane J. Tedick and Roy Lyster

For a full list of titles in this series, please visit: www.routledge.com/Routledge-Series-in-Language-and-Content-Integrated-Teaching--Plurilingual-Education/book-series/CITPE

SCAFFOLDING LANGUAGE DEVELOPMENT IN IMMERSION AND DUAL LANGUAGE CLASSROOMS

Diane J. Tedick and Roy Lyster

Routledge
Taylor & Francis Group

LONDON AND NEW YORK

First published 2020
by Routledge
2 Park Square, Milton Park, Abingdon, Oxon OX14 4RN

and by Routledge
52 Vanderbilt Avenue, New York, NY 10017

Routledge is an imprint of the Taylor & Francis Group, an informa business

British Library Cataloguing in Publication Data
A catalogue record for this book is available from the British Library

Library of Congress Cataloging in Publication Data
Names: Tedick, Diane J., author. | Lyster, Roy, author.
Title: Scaffolding language development in immersion and dual language classrooms / Diane J. Tedick and Roy Lyster.
Description: New York, NY: Routledge, 2020. |
Series: Clil and plurilingual education |
Includes bibliographical references and index.
Identifiers: LCCN 2019041898 (print) | LCCN 2019041899 (ebook) |
ISBN 9781138369986 (hardback) | ISBN 9781138369993 (paperback) |
ISBN 9780429428319 (ebook)
Subjects: LCSH: Immersion method (Language teaching) |
Education, Bilingual. | Language arts–Correlation with content subjects.
Classification: LCC P53.44 .T44 2020 (print) | LCC P53.44 (ebook) |
DDC 418.0071–dc23
LC record available at https://lccn.loc.gov/2019041898
LC ebook record available at https://lccn.loc.gov/2019041899

ISBN: 978-1-138-36998-6 (hbk)
ISBN: 978-1-138-36999-3 (pbk)
ISBN: 978-0-429-42831-9 (ebk)

Typeset in Bembo
by Deanta Global Publishing, Services, Chennai, India

To immersion and dual language teachers everywhere.

CONTENTS

ACKNOWLEDGMENTS

This book was motivated by the many immersion and dual language (ImDL) teachers we have worked with and observed over the years. We express our heartfelt thanks to those who have opened their classrooms to us and shared their work. The commitment, dedication, professionalism, and enthusiasm of ImDL teachers to bring their students into the world of bi- and multilingualism inspires us every day. We especially thank all the teachers who allowed us to showcase their work throughout the book and who are identified accordingly in the many Teacher Spotlight capsules featured throughout.

We are indebted to the following individuals, who spent considerable time and effort to read earlier versions of book chapters to provide us with constructive and insightful feedback: Susan Ballinger, France Bourassa, Carrie Grabowski, Laurent Cammarata, Karita Mård-Miettinen, Corinne Mathieu, and Stacey Vanden Bosch. We are also grateful to peer reviewer Michelle Haj-Broussard for her thorough review of the book manuscript and her excellent feedback. The insightful comments we received from all these individuals helped to keep us on track!

Our collaboration with many colleagues over the years has inevitably had a tremendous impact on this book, and we express our gratitude to the many supportive people who have shared their vision of ImDL education with us and helped us shape ours. Specifically, we would like to acknowledge the contributions of the following individuals:

- The ImDL unit and module/lesson plan templates presented in Chapters 7 and 8 are based on much earlier templates developed by Tara Fortune and Diane Tedick, which have evolved considerably over the years. We also thank Tara for the acronym IRI (indigenous language revitalization immersion). Indeed, Tara's voice and ideas are certainly present in this book, given the number of years that Tara and Diane have worked together.

- Stacey Vanden Bosch led us to the "norms for collaboration" presented in Chapter 8.
- Thanks to Ana Llinares for checking the accuracy of the Spanish used in Appendices A, B, and C.
- The self-assessment rubric in Appendix D is based on the "DLI-Specific Formative Assessment of Teaching Rubric," which was developed by Diane Tedick and Corinne Mathieu for a University of Minnesota preservice licensure program in elementary education with a focus on ImDL. Development of the original rubric was supported by funds from the US Department of Education's National Professional Development grant program. The design of the adapted rubric in Appendix D benefitted from input from Mike Bostwick, who helped to pilot parts of it with the English immersion teachers at Katoh Gakuen Elementary School in Numazu, Japan.

Finally, we express our heartfelt gratitude to Angel Lin and Christiane Dalton-Puffer for inviting us to inaugurate this new Routledge Series in Language and Content Integrated Teaching & Plurilingual Education. They also provided us with outstanding feedback, leading to revisions that considerably improved the book.

INTRODUCTION

We were motivated to write this book by the growing interest around the world in teaching additional languages through subject-matter content as a means to provide opportunities for students to develop proficiency in more than one language. Our specific focus is on the development of minority (non-English) languages in Canadian and US programs that offer at least 50% of subject-matter instruction through the medium of a second, foreign, heritage, or indigenous language. We aim to offer guidance to teachers and other educators working in and with these contexts by drawing upon our experiences as teachers, teacher educators, and researchers in the field of bilingual, immersion, and dual language education, as well as on the expertise of teachers, researchers, and teacher educators with whom we have worked. This introduction addresses the following questions:

- Who is this book for?
- How did we get here? (the current state of immersion and bilingual education in Canada and the US)
- Why the focus on minority-language development?
- What's next?
- What special features does the book offer?

Who is this book for?

The primary target audience for this book is preservice and in-service K–12 teachers in additive bilingual, immersion, and other dual language programs in the Canada and the US. It will also be of interest to others, such as teacher educators and curriculum or program coordinators and administrators of such programs. Although the main target audience is Canadian and US educators, we hope that immersion educators outside these contexts may also find this book useful.

The focus of this book is on enhancing *non-societally dominant* or *non-English* languages in Canada and the US—for instance, French, German, Japanese, Mandarin, Ojibwe, and Spanish—in K–12 classrooms. Nevertheless, concepts and practices are applicable to other content-based instructional settings, such as sheltered English as a second language (ESL) in the US or Canada and English immersion, English-medium instruction, and content and language integrated learning (CLIL) in Europe, South America, and Asia. The majority language in most countries comprising these latter areas, of course, is *not* English. Instead, English and other non-dominant languages are typically referred to as "foreign" languages in Asia, Europe, and South America.

How did we get here?

The umbrella term that is used around the globe for programs that utilize at least two languages as media of school-based instruction is **bilingual education**. Bilingual education has existed around the world for millennia, and it has surfaced in different national contexts as a result of many different factors (Baker & Wright, 2017). In the US, bilingual education emerged initially within the historical context of immigration (in the 18th and 19th centuries) and in more contemporary forms within the context of political movements such as civil rights and educational equality, as well as language policies in the 1960s (Baker & Wright, 2017; Ovando, 2003).

There are many types of bilingual education programs, as each is influenced by the sociolinguistic and cultural contexts in which it occurs. Programs have different learner audiences, different languages (with different sociolinguistic statuses), and different goals (Christian & Genesee, 2001). Baker and Wright (2017) and Baker and Jones (1998) propose two broad categories of bilingual programs—strong and weak—based on their primary aims or goals. Strong bilingual programs lead to **additive** bilingualism (Lambert, 1980), allowing students to acquire a new or second language (L2) at no expense to their first or home language (L1). Weak bilingual programs lead to **subtractive** bilingualism, that is, loss of one's home language as a result of learning an L2 (Lambert, 1980). For instance, US transitional bilingual programs, which are designed for students whose home language is not English, often lead to subtractive bilingualism for learners. Their goal is to provide temporary (two or three years) support in students' home language while they learn English so that, ultimately, they can be mainstreamed into regular English-medium education.

✍ KEY CONCEPTS

Additive bilingualism refers to acquisition of a second language at no expense to the first language. *Subtractive bilingualism* refers to the loss of one language on the road to learning another.

Bilingual programs are also driven by political agendas. Baker and Jones (1998) explain that those falling into the weak category are assimilationist in nature; they aim to assimilate immigrant learners into mainstream society. Strong forms of bilingual education, in contrast, strive to maintain different linguistic groups and to create cultural pluralism and multiculturalism within the society. Second-language acquisition research has also long established that *children can acquire new languages while still developing their first* (Lightbown & Spada, 2013), and this can effectively occur when languages are learned through subject-matter instruction.

An example of a strong, additive bilingual program is **language immersion education**, which was born in Canada in the 1960s amidst the backdrop of the rising significance of French in the province of Quebec (e.g., Genesee, 2015). A group of anglophone (English-speaking) parents in St. Lambert, a suburb of Montreal, were concerned that their children were not acquiring much proficiency in French in the traditional "core" French programs. They wanted a more effective way to develop their children's bilingualism and were also motivated by a desire to ensure that their children would be able to compete in the job market in Quebec, where French was about to become the official language of the workplace. They enlisted the expertise of local academics at McGill University, namely Wallace Lambert and Richard Tucker, and sought their advice and support for developing an alternative model—a "language bath" or immersion program in which all subject-matter instruction would occur initially in the children's L2 (French).

Lambert and Tucker embarked on a longitudinal evaluation of the "St. Lambert experiment," as the first immersion program came to be known (Lambert & Tucker, 1972), and the rest, as they say, is history. The success of the program, with respect to students' academic achievement and their acquisition of French (at no expense to their English-language development), led to the introduction of French immersion programs across Canada. These programs continue to grow, with a 52% increase in French immersion enrollment between 2003 and 2013 (Government of Canada, 2018). Today over 425,000 students study in several types of immersion in every Canadian province and two of its three territories (Canadian Parents for French, 2017).

The Canadian immersion success story also led to the establishment of immersion programs in French and other languages in the US and around the world. The following program examples (to name just a few) received direct inspiration from Canadian French immersion:

- Spanish immersion in the US (Culver City, California, in 1971; Campbell, 1984) and, today, immersion in over 20 languages;
- Swedish immersion in Finland (Björklund, 1997);
- Immersion in Australia in multiple languages (Johnson & Swain, 1997);
- Estonian immersion for Russian-speaking students in Estonia (Mehisto, 2015);
- English immersion in Japan (Bostwick, 2001) and in Brazil (French, 2019).

As immersion education emerged in Canada in the 1960s, across the border in the US contemporary forms of bilingual education for immigrants materialized. A bilingual program developed in 1963 at Coral Way Elementary School in Miami-Dade County, Florida, is credited with bringing about the rebirth of bilingual education (after bilingual programs for early immigrants to the US fell out of favor at the start of the 20th century due to rising fear of immigrants and their cultures) (González, 1979; Ovando, 2003). It was founded by Cuban exiles who thought their stay in the US was temporary and who wanted school support in developing their children's native Spanish and in teaching them English. It was not until 1968 that the federal role in bilingual education for minority-language students became a reality with the appropriation of the Bilingual Education Act (see *Resources for Readers* below). Both strong and weak forms of bilingual education were introduced throughout the 1960s and 1970s. Developmental or maintenance bilingual education is a strong, additive form, as its long-range purpose is to ensure the continued development and maintenance of children's L1 or home language while they learn English. As explained briefly above, transitional bilingual programs—still prevalent today—are weak, subtractive models. Early US bilingual legislation was transitional and deficit oriented in its emphasis; in other words, this legislation positioned immigrant learners as having a deficit because they did not know English, although they already spoke an L1 and were becoming proficient in an L2. This federal emphasis led to a much greater focus on the development of transitional programs at that time. Surprisingly, still today there are some who perceive bilingualism as a deficit—even highly educated adults. They mistakenly believe that bilingualism may lead to language delays. On the contrary, research suggests that the human brain is wired to be bi- or multilingual (e.g., National Academies of Sciences, Engineering, and Medicine, 2017; Paradis, Genesee, & Crago, 2011).

Before we introduce different models of immersion, bilingual, and dual language education, it is important to discuss the distinction between minority and majority languages in Canada and the US. Context is critically important.

Contexts of minority-majority languages in Canada and the US

The US and Canada have very different histories and thus have different orientations to minority and majority languages. Despite controversy around the terms "minority" and "majority" language (e.g., Shohamy & Ghazaleh-Mahajneh, 2012), we use these labels when it is important to distinguish between the two learner groups and languages in society. English is clearly the de facto majority language of the US because it is the societally dominant language. However, it is not legally the official language of the country. In fact, the US has no official language, although since the passage of the Native American Languages Act of 1990, Native American languages do have explicit federal recognition, and in some states, such as Alaska and Hawaii, indigenous languages have official status.

In contrast to the US, Canada is an officially bilingual country, with French and English having co-official status at the federal level. This means that French and English have equal status in services provided by the Canadian government, with Canadians having the right to receive federal services in the official language of their choice.

According to the latest census data (Statistics Canada, 2017), 58% of Canada's population of 35 million claim English as their L1, and 21% claim French as their L1. Whether these official languages are considered minority or majority languages depends on the context. In the province of Quebec, where 79% of its population of 8 million claim French as their L1 and only 9% claim English, French is officially recognized as the majority language and English the minority language. In the provinces and territories outside Quebec, where 73% of the population claim English as their mother tongue and only 4% claim French, English is considered the majority language and French the minority language.

What is important to understand is that the French immersion programs falling under the umbrella of immersion and dual language education (ImDL) programs presented in Figure I.1 (see next section) are not housed in French-language (i.e., francophone) schools but, rather, in schools designated as English speaking (i.e., anglophone). French-language schools outside Quebec are designed for French-language minority communities and thus for children whose home or heritage language is French. The ImDL programs that are the primary target of this book are housed in English-language schools, including French immersion programs as well as bilingual (50/50) programs such as those in the province of Alberta offered in a range of international languages. Throughout the book, we refer to all non-English languages that are not societally dominant as minority languages, even when referring to French immersion in Quebec and also to indigenous languages, given their status relative to that of English in the North American context.

⚓ KEY CONCEPTS

Because the focus of this book is on ImDL programs in the US and Canada, when we refer to the *majority language* we are referring to English. When we refer to the *minority language* we are referring to the program's non-English language of instruction. All ImDL programs engage students in both languages, but *majority-language students* are those whose primary or home language is English, while *minority-language students* are those whose primary or home language is the program's non-English language of instruction. In addition, some students who enroll in these programs are simultaneous bilinguals. Students whose primary or home language is neither of the languages of instruction will be referred to as third-language (L3) speakers.

Dual language education

As the introductory section makes clear, the term "bilingual education" has been used historically in the US to refer only to programs developed for minority-language students, such as students whose home language is Spanish. In the 1990s and early 2000s, this term became highly politicized, and anti-bilingual education initiatives took hold in some states. It was about this time that the designation "dual language education" emerged as an alternative and more inclusive way to describe a range of additive bilingual programs serving both minority- and majority-language students (Tedick, 2015).

Four strong, additive bilingual program types fall under the ImDL umbrella (Figure I.1). They are *"one-way" foreign-/second-language immersion* (as developed in Canada), *"two-way" immersion*, *"one-way" developmental bilingual education*, and *indigenous-language revitalization immersion*. Thomas and Collier (2012) explain that "one-way" refers to programs that serve *one* language group receiving their schooling through their home language and an additional language. Two-way programs serve *two* language groups—each having one of the program languages as their home language. Key features that correspond to all four models as well as each model's unique characteristics are explained in Chapter 1.

FIGURE I.1 ImDL program models (adapted from Howard, Olague, & Rogers, 2003)

One-way foreign-/second-language immersion programs (such as French immersion in Canada) mainly serve a relatively homogeneous student population of majority-language students. Today, one-way programs are less homogeneous, as demographics have shifted. It is increasingly common to find Spanish home language students enrolled in one-way Spanish immersion programs in the US, for example, or French home language children in French immersion programs in Quebec in cases where one of their parents or siblings had attended an English-language school in Canada. In addition, some third-language (L3) students—those who speak a home language other than English and the partner language of the program—also attend one-way programs.

One-way developmental bilingual programs also primarily serve a linguistically homogeneous student population of minority-language students. In the US, these programs mostly enroll Spanish home language students and, increasingly, Spanish/English simultaneous bilinguals (i.e., bilinguals from birth).

Two-way immersion programs are an amalgam of one-way immersion and developmental bilingual programs, as they intentionally target a combined student audience of minority- and majority-language students. They also enroll some L3 learners. Interestingly, the bilingual program established in Miami-Dade County, Florida in 1963 is also credited with being the first two-way immersion program in the US (although it was not labeled as such at the time) (Christian, 2011; Fortune & Tedick, 2008; Ovando, 2003). The school welcomed both Spanish-speaking learners of English and English-speaking learners of Spanish, the linguistically mixed student population that characterizes two-way programs.

Two-way immersion is primarily a US phenomenon. However, this model has been launched in other countries. For example, Estonia has recently introduced two-way programs (Russian/Estonian), and Switzerland has a French/German two-way program in Biel/Bienne. As previously mentioned, in the province of Quebec, some French immersion programs serve significant numbers of French home language students (nearly 40% in some cases) (Lyster, Collins & Ballinger, 2009), although the programs are not referred to as two-way.

Indigenous-language revitalization immersion programs serve children with indigenous ancestry and aim to revitalize endangered indigenous languages and cultures. Most are one-way, but there have been two documented two-way programs (both in Navajo-Diné in Arizona). Indigenous language immersion programs arose in North America in the 1980s as deliberate efforts to bring back endangered indigenous languages. In the US, the first program, established in Hawaii, was hard won, because teaching through the medium of Hawaiian had been declared illegal in the early 1900s (Wilson & Kamanā, 2001). Today, the Hawaiian Islands boast 20 Hawaiian immersion programs serving Grades K–12. Other states have also introduced indigenous language revitalization immersion programs—Alaska, Minnesota, and Oklahoma, to name a few. Canada offers programs in Kanien'kéha (the Mohawk language), Mi'kmaq, and Cree.

Immersion and dual language education (ImDL)

In the previous section, we described the four program models falling under the ImDL umbrella. One might ask why we include "immersion" in the title of this book and the language used throughout if "dual language" education encompasses immersion programs. We find using "dual language education" alone to be problematic for a variety of reasons.

In the US context, dual language education is often used as a synonym for two-way immersion (see, for example, Baker & Jones, 1998; Lindholm-Leary, 2012). Additionally, we find that only those programs serving minority-language students are typically associated with dual language education. US educators working in one-way immersion and indigenous language revitalization immersion often do not perceive their programs as dual language models. Similarly, educators working in two-way and developmental bilingual programs—those programs that serve minority-language students—do not typically perceive their programs as immersion programs.

Utah, a US state that has significant state-level support for the development of ImDL programs, proposed "dual language immersion" as an inclusive term (Leite & Cook, 2015), and it has been adopted by many across the US. Nevertheless, we find that, like dual language education, it is also often interpreted as meaning two-way immersion. Moreover, we find dual language education and dual language immersion to be terms used nearly exclusively in the US. They are not commonly used in Canada or other parts of the world.

Because we want this book to be inclusive of all additive bilingual programs and to reach an international audience, we have chosen to use both immersion and dual language education. Our definition for these programs appears below. In Chapter 1, we explore the goals of ImDL programs and describe their characteristics in more detail.

 KEY CONCEPT

Immersion and dual language education programs are forms of additive bilingual education serving minority- and majority-language students that provide subject-matter instruction in a second, foreign, heritage, or indigenous language for extended periods of time with intentional development of language, literacy, and academic skills in at least two languages (including the societal majority language) as well as cultural understanding.

Why the focus on minority-language development?

Research has shown that, while ImDL programs support academic achievement, they may not be reaching their potential when it comes to minority-language development for both majority- and minority-language speakers enrolled in the programs. Studies have shown that the minority-language development of majority-language learners in these programs often lacks grammatical accuracy, lexical specificity, and sociolinguistic appropriateness when compared with the language that native speakers produce. Some studies of two-way programs have also pointed to underdeveloped proficiency in Spanish among minority-language students. A more detailed overview of the research on target language outcomes in ImDL programs appears in Chapter 1. We focus on minority-language development in this book because of the benefits afforded to individuals who achieve high levels of bilingualism and biliteracy and because English-language development is not the challenge in contexts where English is the societally dominant language.

The benefits of bilingualism and biliteracy

Underdeveloped minority-language proficiency is problematic if students are to reap the benefits of bilingualism and biliteracy. This is the case for minority-language and majority-language students as well as students with indigenous ancestry.

Research affirms that the development of high levels of proficiency and literacy in the home language is critical for minority-language learners when it comes to their academic and societal success and their proficiency and literacy in English (e.g., Thomas & Collier, 2012). Bilinguals who use both their languages frequently—in the home, in the community, and in the workplace—and who have high levels of biliteracy are more likely to (a) pursue undergraduate degrees, (b) obtain higher-paying, professional jobs in the workforce, and (c) have more opportunities for professional advancement (Porras, Ee, & Gándara, 2014; Santibañez & Zárate, 2014). Minority-language students also benefit personally from developing their languages to high levels. Doing so allows them to maintain strong connections to families and communities. As de Jong (2011) puts it, "Language plays an important role in socializing children into the linguistic and cultural norms of a community" (p. 30).

Majority-language learners also benefit most when they develop high levels of bilingualism and biliteracy. Knowing other languages in addition to English will benefit them in many ways—potentially professionally (if they attain high enough levels of bilingualism and biliteracy), and personally through international travel, deeper understanding of diverse cultures, and communication with others both face to face and via the Internet (e.g., Hamayan, Genesee, & Cloud, 2013), as well as access to information and distinctive viewpoints that are only available from knowing other languages and their cultures (National Standards Collaborative Board, 2015). In today's globalized world, being able to communicate in more than one language represents a significant advantage.

Students with indigenous or First Nations ancestry who have the opportunity to learn through their ancestral language do better academically and are more likely to stay in school than peers schooled in English only (McCarty & Lee, 2014; Slaughter, 1997; Wilson & Kamanā, 2011). Learning the indigenous language can support children's identity and self-efficacy development, sense of well-being, and self-esteem (Hakuta, 2001).

English-language development is not the challenge

We also focus on minority-language development because English-language development and literacy are not at issue for students in ImDL programs. Studies have compared the English-language development of students enrolled in one-way and two-way programs that devote more instructional time to the minority language and less to English (at least initially) with those that devote approximately 50% to each language throughout the duration of the program. They have found no difference in English-language achievement despite less exposure to English (e.g., Christian, Genesee, Lindholm-Leary, & Howard, 2004; Genesee, 1981; Lindholm-Leary, 2001).

It is believed that ImDL students' extended exposure to and development of the minority language has additive effects on their English-language development (Genesee & Lindholm-Leary, 2013). Additionally, in Canada and the US, students are exposed to and use a great deal of English outside the classroom and school environment.

Moreover, studies have consistently shown that students in ImDL programs, *regardless of L1 background*, prefer to use English during instructional time in the minority language (e.g., Broner, 2000; Fortune, 2001; Hernández, 2015; Potowski, 2004). English use is especially prevalent and persistent as students advance in grade level. The challenge is to encourage students to keep using the minority language so that they develop high levels of bilingualism and biliteracy.

In the decades of work that we have done as ImDL teachers, researchers, and teacher educators, we have spent many hours in classrooms. Our experience, in addition to the significant research evidence, is that the challenge in ImDL programs is to develop the minority language; hence our focus for this book.

What's next?

This book is divided into four parts. In **Part I** we set the stage by establishing the foundations of ImDL. In **Chapter 1** we return to the four program types that fall under the ImDL umbrella (Figure I.1). We summarize the varieties and main characteristics of the four models to show how they are similar and different. We describe the underlying goals and summarize the research-based outcomes corresponding to those goals. We also describe the defining characteristics that all ImDL programs have in common. **Chapter 2** summarizes key features that characterize well-implemented programs.

Part II provides a research-based rationale for bringing in more of a focus on language across the ImDL curriculum and outlines the key features of counterbalanced instruction, the pedagogical framework that guides the book. **Chapter 3** summarizes the research that explains students' underdeveloped minority language and introduces counterbalanced instruction. **Chapter 4** describes and exemplifies the CAPA (contextualization, awareness, practice, and autonomy) model, a framework for designing instruction that integrates content (meaning) and language (form). This framework strengthens students' meta-linguistic awareness and invites them to use the target language purposefully through guided practice, which leads to autonomous use. To illustrate the model, we share several teacher-developed examples of instructional sequences.

 **KEY CONCEPT**

Counterbalanced instruction involves systematic integration of content (meaning) and language (form) in teaching and learning.

Part III focuses on the key role that scaffolding plays in ImDL pedagogy. In **Chapter 5** we first outline verbal, procedural, and instructional scaffolding as they relate to both language comprehension and language production. Through examples from actual classroom interactions, we then explore questioning techniques and follow-up strategies that encourage student language production. In **Chapter 6** we address the pivotal role of corrective feedback during teacher-student interaction. Corrective feedback represents another way for teachers to integrate a focus on language into their instructional practices. We introduce teachers to various types of oral corrective feedback, review the research on the effectiveness of corrective feedback, and explain some of the different patterns observed in student responses to corrective feedback. Using extracts from actual classroom interaction, the chapter helps teachers to learn to avoid ambiguous feedback and strive for clarity in feedback provision.

Curriculum planning and assessment are addressed in **Part IV**. **Chapter 7** and **Chapter 8** work in tandem to introduce readers to detailed instructional design templates for developing content-based and language-focused curriculum. We provide guidance on how to write effective learning objectives for content and language and how to differentiate objectives and tasks for diverse student audiences. The concepts described in these chapters are illustrated by a teacher-developed unit plan and a detailed series of lessons made available in appendices. In **Chapter 9** we focus on instructional design for biliteracy development. We describe the complex concept of biliteracy and explore a variety of approaches to biliteracy instruction appropriate for ImDL classrooms. We discuss teacher collaboration and bilingual read-aloud projects as one approach to enhancing cross-linguistic connections. In **Chapter 10** we focus on both student and teacher performance assessment. We introduce readers to a number of key concepts related to assessing students' language use and content learning. In particular, we emphasize a classroom-based tool called the Integrated Performance Assessment (IPA) (Adair-Hauck, Glisan, & Troyan, 2013). The IPA involves a series of three inter-related tasks that assess students' content understanding and language use in relationship to the interpretive mode (reading or listening), the interpersonal mode (spontaneous oral interaction with a partner), and the presentational mode (speaking or writing for an audience). In another appendix, we share a teacher-developed IPA to illustrate concepts throughout the chapter. We also briefly describe teacher performance assessment and unveil a self-assessment rubric that can be used by ImDL teachers to assess their ability to put into practice the pedagogical strategies emphasized in this book.

In the **Conclusion**, we provide a synthesis of the instructional approaches advocated throughout the book and highlight their potential to engage L2 learners with language across the curriculum.

What special features does the book offer?

To facilitate navigation throughout the book and to highlight important concepts connected to the main text, we include the following features.

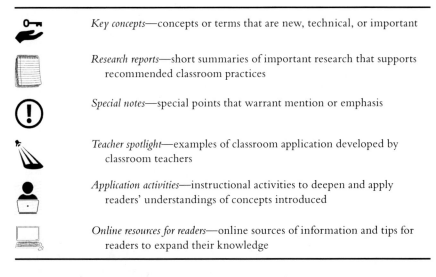

Key concepts—concepts or terms that are new, technical, or important

Research reports—short summaries of important research that supports recommended classroom practices

Special notes—special points that warrant mention or emphasis

Teacher spotlight—examples of classroom application developed by classroom teachers

Application activities—instructional activities to deepen and apply readers' understandings of concepts introduced

Online resources for readers—online sources of information and tips for readers to expand their knowledge

Online resources for readers

General ImDL program design and support

Several organizations offer extensive and outstanding web-based resources to support ImDL program design and implementation.

Canadian Association of Immersion Professionals (CAIP)/Association canadienne des professionnels de l'immersion (ACPI): www.acpi.ca/

Center for Advanced Research on Language Acquisition (CARLA) Immersion Projects: http://carla.umn.edu/immersion/index.html

Center for Applied Linguistics (CAL): www.cal.org

CAL's bilingual and dual language education resources: www.cal.org/areas-of-impact/en
glish-learners/bilingual-and-dual-language-education

CAL's directory of dual language programs: http://webapp.cal.org/duallanguage/

CAL's archived two-way immersion website: www.cal.org/twi/

US legislation regarding bilingual education and bilingual learners

For more information on current US education legislation, the Every Student Succeeds
Act (ESSA): www.ed.gov/essa?src=ft

For detailed policy on English learners (minority-language students) within the current
Title III of ESSA: www2.ed.gov/policy/elsec/leg/essa/essatitleiiiguidenglishlearners
92016.pdf

PART I

What is immersion and dual language education?

The purpose of Part I is to lay the foundation for understanding and distinguishing between the main immersion and dual language (ImDL) program models and to outline characteristics that define them and correspond to their implementation. The premise is that, despite the different contexts in which these programs are offered and the different student audiences they serve, ImDL programs have much in common, and there is much to be gained by exchange of ideas and practices. Chapter 1 describes in detail the four ImDL program models that fit under the ImDL umbrella presented in the Introduction. It identifies the goals of these programs and summarizes the research-based outcomes aligned with these goals. The chapter also outlines the defining characteristics of ImDL programs and discusses ImDL program model similarities and differences. Chapter 2 expands educators' understanding of ImDL programs by describing in detail 14 inter-related characteristics that define well-implemented programs. These characteristics are organized into five categories: program leadership and design, teachers, families and community, curriculum and instruction, and assessment and accountability.

1

FROM GOALS AND OUTCOMES TO PROGRAM MODELS AND CHARACTERISTICS

In the Introduction, we presented the four immersion and dual language (ImDL) program models that are emphasized in this book. In this chapter, we describe these models and their goals, outcomes, and characteristics in greater detail. Educators must be knowledgeable about these issues to be able to serve as strong advocates for ImDL programs in their communities. We address the following questions:

- What are the goals of ImDL education and the research-based outcomes in relationship to those goals?
- How does English-language development compare with minority-language development in ImDL programs?
- What defining characteristics do all ImDL program models have in common?
- How are the ImDL models similar and different?

Prelude: The importance of learning other languages and the complexity of what to call them

Parents who want to provide their children with opportunities for becoming bilingual through school-based programs are opting in increasing numbers for ImDL programs. Reasons abound for children of the 21st century to move beyond the limitations of monolingualism and to become bilingual or even multilingual. Knowing two or more languages opens a world of possibilities when it comes to social and cultural interaction. It provides opportunities to interact with more people and to come to understand nuances of other cultures. When they are able to communicate in two or more languages, people's lives are personally enriched as they develop new perspectives. Some research has shown, for example, that people experience themselves as different people when they speak different languages (Koven, 1998). Knowing more than one language can also improve an individual's competitiveness in the job market and can open up new career opportunities. Indeed, knowing two or more languages enriches one's life in myriad ways; it helps young learners meet the challenges and enjoy the benefits of globalization. This is why ImDL programs have so much potential to open doors for students and to contribute to their becoming citizens of the world.

Knowing more than one language, however, is simply the norm for many people, and, in that sense, getting there should be a fairly straightforward process, given the right conditions. However, even in the case of strong willpower and the best of ImDL programs, obstacles to fully engaging with other languages remain, one of which is the social status of the target language and the opportunities it affords for its use. That is, the higher status of a majority language often militates against using and maintaining a minority language, unless measures are taken to level the playing field, which is a promising possibility in ImDL programs that target both languages. This is why we have opted to make clear distinctions throughout this book between majority and minority languages.

To be specific, and as explained in the Introduction, throughout this book we will be using the term *majority language* to refer to the societally dominant language: English in the US and most parts of Canada. The term *minority language* will be used to refer to non-English languages in the US and Canada, including indigenous languages and others that may not otherwise be thought of as "minority" languages, such as Chinese, German, or Japanese. Although languages such as Chinese, German, or Japanese are also referred to as *foreign languages* in the US and Canada, we refer to non-English languages of instruction in US and Canadian schools as minority languages in order to underscore their status relative to English in the US and Canada—a status that adds considerably to the challenge of learning and maintaining non-English languages in the US and Canada.

We acknowledge this as a potential source of confusion for readers from contexts outside the US and Canada, where the target language of many ImDL programs is English, a language which, in those contexts, is considered neither a majority nor a minority language but, rather, a foreign language. We ask those readers to consider our use of *minority language* to be equivalent to *second or foreign languages* in their contexts and to understand that we cannot refer to Spanish in the US or French in Canada as a "foreign" language. Although we use the term second language (L2) throughout where appropriate, it too proves problematic because, in the US, many students in two-way immersion programs have Spanish (a minority language) as their L1, not their L2, and are learning English as their L2. However, as explained later and substantiated by research, their English-language development fares rather well in these programs. Of greater concern in ImDL programs is the development of high levels of academic proficiency in the minority language—by both minority-language and majority-language students. Furthermore, many teacher resources are available that support the English-language development of English L2 learners, whereas little is available to support minority-language development by both minority-language and majority-language students. It is this gap that our book aims to fill. Because our primary focus is on ImDL programs in the US and Canada, our goal is to provide support for teachers in scaffolding the non-English languages of their programs, which we refer to throughout as minority languages.

Goals and outcomes of ImDL education

All ImDL program models share three fundamental goals. These goals have been referred to as the "ABCs" of ImDL by Tara Fortune of the Center for Advanced Research on Language Acquisition (CARLA, University of Minnesota). The ABCs of ImDL education are:

- **Academic achievement** in both languages (appropriate to the grade level);
- **Bilingualism and biliteracy** in a minority, indigenous, or foreign language and the societal majority language;
- **Cultural and intercultural competence** or understanding.

This section presents each of the three goals—academic achievement, bilingualism and biliteracy, and cultural and intercultural competence—by summarizing student outcomes associated with each goal as revealed by research on ImDL education conducted over the past 50 years.

Academic achievement

The first major goal of ImDL programs aims for age-appropriate academic achievement (achievement in mathematics, reading/language arts, science, etc.) in *both* program languages. The majority of studies, especially those conducted in the US, report only on academic achievement outcomes as measured in English, not the minority language. Decades of research done in these contexts has consistently shown that, *in the long term*, both majority- and minority-language ImDL students in all types of programs perform on a par with or above students schooled only through English on standardized achievement measures administered in English (e.g., Genesee, 1987, 2004; Lapkin, Hart, & Turnbull, 2003; Lindholm-Leary, 2001; Steele et al., 2017; Thomas & Collier, 2012; Turnbull, Lapkin, & Hart, 2001).

These academic achievement results are also consistent with respect to learner differences, such as ethnic background, socioeconomic status (SES), and special education needs (Fortune with Menke, 2010; Genesee & Fortune, 2014). Such factors typically place students at risk for low academic achievement. Research on such learners compares their performance with that of non-ImDL students having similar demographics or other risk factors. In a detailed review of studies related to at-risk learners, Genesee and Fortune (2014) conclude that ImDL programs "can be effective with a wide range of students, including students with characteristics and backgrounds that may put them at risk" (p. 204). And these at-risk students benefit from developing bilingualism and biliteracy—skills that will bring advantages to them in society. Yet, Genesee and Fortune are careful to caution readers that there is an urgent need for more research on at-risk students in ImDL.

Related to academic benefits are cognitive benefits. Studies focused on students in the process of developing bilingualism, such as ImDL students, have pointed to greater cognitive flexibility (Bruck, Lambert, & Tucker, 1976), non-verbal problem-solving skills (Bamford & Mizokawa, 1991), and executive control (Bialystok & Barac, 2012). Executive control refers to a set of cognitive abilities that permit humans to plan, think flexibly, and control their attention and behavior (National Academies of Sciences, Engineering, and Medicine, 2017). However, a number of reports have shown that the results of some of these studies have not been replicated in other contexts. There are myriad reasons for this; for example, there are many different types of bilingualism (simultaneous, sequential, etc.), and bilingualism is but one factor that affects brain function. What we do know at this time is that cognitive benefits for developing bilinguals appear to accrue over time, in relationship to the level of L2 proficiency attained (Bialystok & Barac, 2012; Hamayan et al., 2013). This notion suggests some support for Cummins's (1981) hypothesis that a certain threshold of proficiency may be necessary before cognitive benefits emerge. These benefits notwithstanding, we recommend that ImDL programs not "sell" their programs on the basis of cognitive benefits but instead emphasize other benefits associated with bilingualism—such as the fact that bilingualism affords more opportunities to communicate with others, which, in turn, brings forth many personal and potentially professional advantages.

Bilingualism and biliteracy

The second major goal of ImDL education is bilingualism and biliteracy in a minority, indigenous, or foreign language (e.g., Chinese, French, Hmong, Japanese, Spanish, or Yup'ik) and the societal majority language (English). ImDL students' English-language development has been the focus of much research since the inception of ImDL programs in the 1960s. The research findings have consistently shown that, in the long term, both majority- and minority-language ImDL students' English-language development ranges from equivalent to superior to that of non-immersion students irrespective of program type (e.g., Genesee, 2004; Lindholm-Leary, 2001; Slaughter, 1997). We address this topic in more detail later in this chapter.

There is thus a clear consensus that ImDL education has no negative effects on students' academic achievement and no negative effects on their English-language development. But what about students' development in the non-English language?

Given the greater amount of time in the curriculum devoted to the minority language, ImDL students develop higher levels of proficiency in the minority language than do students studying the language as a regular subject in a foreign-language program (e.g., for one period per school day). For example, a large-scale study conducted by the Center for Applied Second Language Studies (CASLS, 2013) compared the language proficiency scores (reading, writing, and speaking) of students schooled through immersion (in Chinese, French, Japanese, and Spanish) with those of students who studied those same languages in non-immersion foreign-language classrooms. The majority of high-school students were ranked in the American Council on the Teaching of Foreign Languages (ACTFL)'s (2012a) Novice range after four years of non-immersion foreign-language study, whereas virtually all students enrolled in ImDL programs throughout elementary and secondary school performed in ACTFL's Intermediate range, and many were at Advanced levels.

Studies comparing ImDL students' proficiency in the minority language with that of native speakers of the minority language have also revealed positive outcomes, as well as some that fall short of expectations. For example, in comparison with native speakers of French of the same age, research has characterized French immersion students' proficiency in French in two ways (Harley, Cummins, Swain, & Allen, 1990):

1. high levels of comprehension abilities as measured by tests of listening and reading comprehension;
2. high levels of communicative ability, but with lower-than-expected production skills in terms of grammatical accuracy, lexical variety, and sociolinguistic appropriateness.

More specifically, still in comparison with native speakers of French of the same age, Harley et al. found that French immersion students performed similarly on measures of *discourse competence*. Discourse competence is the ability to understand and produce language *coherently* and *cohesively*. An example of coherence in discourse is the accurate use of pronouns to refer to characters, objects, and locations when telling a story. Examples of discourse cohesiveness include the accurate use of conjunctions and adverbs to make logical connections—such as temporal sequencing and cause-effect relationships—between clauses and sentences.

In contrast to their native-like levels of discourse competence, French immersion students were much less proficient on most grammar aspects, which included verb and preposition usage. Students in this study also fell short of native speakers of French of the same age on measures of *sociolinguistic competence*, which is the ability to vary one's language according to social context, ranging from informal language use in informal contexts to more formal uses of language in formal contexts. Specifically, French immersion students used significantly fewer markers of politeness and formality, such as formal second-person pronouns (i.e., singular *vous*) and conditional verb forms to soften requests.

What emerges from this early research on Canadian French immersion programs can be summed up by Genesee's (1994) description of majority-language students' development of the minority language as "linguistically truncated, albeit functionally effective" (p. 5). More specifically, Harley (1994) character-ized immersion students' oral production of the minority language as contain-ing phonologically salient, high-frequency lexical items, along with syntactic patterns that are congruent with English, but lacking in the less salient mor-phosyntactic features, which are incongruent with English or not crucial for getting one's meaning across (more on this in Chapter 3). We hasten to add, however, that overcoming these shortcomings through compensatory instruc-tion has proven effective and has thus motivated the pedagogical approach we describe throughout this book.

Similarly to Canadian French immersion studies, US studies have shown that majority-language students in one-way immersion programs in alphabetic lan-guages typically develop near-native levels of reading and listening proficiency in the minority language. However, recent research on US immersion programs in languages such as Mandarin Chinese and Japanese has shown that, although students achieve good scores in listening comprehension, they demonstrate rather low levels of reading comprehension in these languages. For example, Burkhauser et al. (2016) found that Grade 8 students in a partial (50:50) Japanese program were at the Intermediate Low to Mid level in reading, and Grade 8 students in a partial Chinese program only achieved Novice Mid to High levels in reading. Fortune and Song (2016) examined the proficiency of Grade 5 early total Mandarin immersion students and reported that over half of the students were rated at Intermediate Low or higher in reading, but 44% were still per-forming in the Novice range. These outcomes suggest that partial programs may not provide enough instructional time in the minority language (particularly Mandarin Chinese) for students to achieve grade-level reading skills.

Like their Canadian counterparts, majority-language students in US one-way immersion programs produce spoken and written language that lacks gram-matical accuracy. Moreover, their language is typically not sociolinguistically appropriate (see Tedick & Wesely, 2015 for a review), and their vocabulary can be underdeveloped (e.g., Fortune & Tedick, 2015). Most US studies on the lan-guage development of one-way immersion students have been done in Spanish or French programs, but teachers representing programs in a wide range of languages, including indigenous languages such as Hawaiian or Ojibwe, share anecdotally that immersion students' minority-language development is far from optimal.

Research on two-way immersion programs in the US has shown that English L1 students continue to perform better in English than in Spanish, while Spanish L1 students tend to develop more balanced oral and written proficiencies in both languages. However, some Spanish L1 students have been shown to become dominant in English (Fortune, 2001) and to develop certain grammatical inac-curacies in Spanish, their home language (e.g., Potowski, 2007; Tedick & Young, 2016). Again, most of the research has been done in Spanish/English programs, but anecdotal evidence indicates that L1 speakers of other minority languages in two-way immersion, such as Hmong, also develop some grammatical inaccuracies in their home language.

Moreover, researchers and teachers alike have noted that students in "early" ImDL programs (beginning in kindergarten or Grade 1) appear to reach a plateau in their minority-language development around the same time that (a) more English instruction is introduced into the curriculum and (b) pre-adolescents and adolescents increasingly use English to communicate among themselves in class. For example, the plateau effect was evident in Fortune and Tedick's (2015) study of one-way Spanish immersion programs in the US, which showed that the oral proficiency in Spanish of students in Grade 8 was not significantly different from that of students in Grade 5. In fact, Grade 8 students' proficiency was not statistically different from that of Grade 2 students in the areas of oral fluency, grammar, and vocabulary. Only in terms of listening comprehension did the Grade 8 students outperform Grade 2 students. This suggests that the lack of progress in minority-language development might be a result of the decrease in both exposure to and use of the minority language, specifically in contexts where the majority language is English.

It is important to point out, however, that much of the research indicating that students communicate in the minority language with functional effectiveness but in non-target-like ways in terms of grammatical structure, lexical choices, and sociolinguistic expression has been done in comparison with native speakers of the same age. The comparison with native-speaker peers might not seem fair, given that the goal of ImDL programs is not to expect native-like proficiency in all aspects of both target languages. Thus, as Day and Shapson (1996) suggested, "we may want to have different standards in certain areas of communicative competence than those attained by native-speakers of the language" (p. 98). However, they attributed the lower-than-expected proficiency levels in the minority language not to instructional or learning constraints inherent in ImDL education but, rather, to attitudinal and pragmatic factors. They stated that immersion students have "no strong social incentive to develop further toward native-speaker norms" (p. 95) because of their success in communicating with one another and with the teacher.

In ImDL classrooms, however, the minority language is not only a communication tool for interacting with the teacher and peers, but also a means for cognitive growth and academic success. Met (2008) sums it up as follows:

> Because language is at the heart of schooling and, because in immersion, language plays an even greater role than in other classrooms, immersion educators must be ever mindful of language, its role in the development of literacy and its influence on academic literacy. (p. 49)

As students progress through the grades, "they are increasingly required to manipulate language in cognitively demanding and context-reduced situations that differ significantly from everyday conversational interactions" (Cummins,

2000, p. 69). The need to improve ImDL students' abilities in the minority language is thus not for the purpose of attaining native-like levels of proficiency but, rather, for enhancing their ability to engage with the type of complex language that is key to school success and characteristic of the academic literacy of which formal accuracy is an integral part. The premise underlying this book is that reasonably high expectations need to be set with respect to ImDL students' proficiency in the minority language, aiming not only for functional communicative skills in the minority language but also for high levels of bilingual proficiency that have the potential to open many doors—socially, professionally, culturally, and academically.

Finally, it is important to acknowledge that some students who attend ImDL programs speak a home language that is neither English nor the program's minority language. For example, Canadian French immersion programs enroll learners who speak other languages in the home (e.g., Arabic, Mandarin, or Punjabi), although English is likely to be a shared common language outside the home and possibly in the home as well. The same occurs in US ImDL programs, which enroll learners with other home languages such as Russian, Somali, or Tagalog, to name a few. ImDL programs typically do not offer support for home languages besides English and the partner (minority) language of the school. Nevertheless, studies have shown that ImDL programs are effective for these "third language (L3) learners" in terms of academic achievement (e.g., de Courcy, Warren, & Burston, 2002), proficiency in the program's languages (e.g., Mady, 2015), and identity development (Rolstad, 1997). Swain, Lapkin, Rowen, and Hart (1990) found that L3 learners who were literate in their home languages had a language learning advantage relative to L3 learners who were not. They reported that this advantage persisted regardless of oral proficiency in the home language, SES, or the distance between languages (e.g., Spanish and French versus Spanish and Mandarin). This means that ImDL teachers should encourage L3 students to maintain their home language and can be supportive of endeavors to develop literacy skills in the home language without fearing that such endeavors might interfere with progress in the school's two languages of instruction.

Cultural competence

Cultural competence is a broad term that encompasses intercultural competence and cross-cultural competence. Intercultural competence entails the capacity to function in appropriate ways between cultures, to think and act appropriately, and to be able to communicate and interact with people from different cultural backgrounds either abroad or in one's home environment. In essence, it represents interaction between culturally different people. Cross-cultural competence involves the ability to make comparisons across cultures. What is meant by cultural competence varies somewhat depending upon the particular student group being served by an ImDL program. For example, majority-language students in one-way and two-way immersion programs are expected to develop an understanding of and appreciation for the culture of the target language group and their own culture(s). In developmental bilingual and two-way immersion programs, the development of biculturalism, or a positive identity with the home culture and that of the majority-language community, is crucial for minority-language students (Cloud, Genesee, & Hamayan, 2000). Revitalization of traditional cultural values and practices and reclamation of indigenous cultural identity are at the heart of indigenous immersion programs (Wilson & Kamanā, 2011). Whereas cultural revitalization tends to be front and center in indigenous-language revitalization immersion programs, the goal of cultural competence tends to be more elusive in one-way and two-way programs. It has received much less attention from scholars and practitioners alike than the goals of academic achievement and bilingualism, in part because it is very difficult to define and measure.

Studies conducted in the 1980s and 1990s reported that one-way foreign-/ second-language immersion students in the early grades have quite positive attitudes toward representatives of the minority language group, but as they become older their attitudes are less positive (Genesee, 1987; Snow, 1990). Age appears to be a factor. At least according to these early studies, children prior to the age of 10 or 11 seem to be prime candidates for attitudinal benefits, but it becomes more challenging to maintain those positive attitudes after puberty. Also focused on one-way contexts, Corbaz (2006) explored whether US Grade 4 French and Spanish immersion students displayed higher levels of intercultural sensitivity than non-immersion students. He used the Miville-Guzman Universality-Diversity Scale (Miville et al., 1999) to measure features of intercultural sensitivity across three subscales:

1. diversity of contact sought out with others;
2. relativistic appreciation of oneself and others;
3. a sense of connection with the large society/humanity as a whole (i.e., comfort with differences).

Corbaz found that immersion girls had significantly higher levels on the second and third subscales than non-immersion girls. There were no significant differences for the first subscale or between the immersion and non-immersion boys. Corbaz suggested that girls may benefit more from participating in immersion than boys in the area of intercultural sensitivity. Another study of one-way immersion in the US found that middle-school immersion students' motivation to continue learning through the minority language may be influenced by sustained and meaningful exposure to the culture(s) of the minority language (e.g., school-supported travel abroad with home stays) (Wesely, 2010). This finding suggests that ImDL programs would be wise to expose learners to such experiences (see also Wesche, 1993).

Studies involving students in two-way immersion settings have reported that they are stronger in areas relating to intercultural competence relative to students in regular (English-medium) settings (see Feinauer & Howard, 2014, and Tedick & Wesely, 2015, for reviews). Other studies with two-way immersion students have shown that they value having classmates from different linguistic and cultural backgrounds, and that such positive attitudes persist among students after they leave the program (Feinauer & Howard, 2014, for review). A study conducted with secondary two-way immersion students found that Latinx students in these programs identify as bicultural but Anglo students do not, even though they report having sensitivity to other cultures (Bearse & de Jong, 2008).

With respect to Hawaiian immersion students, Slaughter (1997) reported that their attitudes toward Hawaiian language and culture were more positive than those of a similar class of non-immersion students, while they also had a positive attitude toward English. Moreover, they were more positive about their identity as "part-Hawaiian" and "part other" (e.g., Japanese or Portuguese) than they were about identity as "Americans."

These findings from research on cultural sensitivity, cross-cultural knowledge, and intercultural communicative competence suggest that ImDL programs have the potential to meet this third goal. The bottom line is that students participating in all forms of ImDL education should be able to interact appropriately and respectfully with individuals from diverse cultures both at home and internationally. They should also be able to engage in cross-cultural comparisons. However, more studies are sorely needed.

Defining characteristics of ImDL programs

As explained in the Introduction, four program models fall under the "immersion and dual language education" umbrella. All ImDL programs share three defining characteristics, which we identify next. These should be thought of as *non-negotiables*; in other words, without these features, a program ceases to be an ImDL program.

Additive bilingualism and biliteracy

All the program models that we emphasize in this book are designed to foster additive bilingualism and biliteracy. The expectation is that majority-language speakers will reach the same level of proficiency in English as they would through English-medium schooling. Thus, in the long run, they acquire a second, minority, indigenous, or foreign language at no expense to their English-language development. Minority-language students with a home background in the program's non-English language maintain and continue to develop their proficiency in this language while acquiring the societal majority language—English.

The additive nature of ImDL differentiates these programs from other L2-medium programs that do not ensure the ongoing development and maintenance of the L1. With this in mind, it is important not to be misled by program names. For example, so-called "structured English immersion" programs for minority-language students became prevalent in California when anti-bilingual legislation was passed in 1998, which has since been repealed (see *Resources for Readers* at the end of this chapter). But "structured English immersion" represents a misappropriation of the term "immersion." As stated by Lambert (1984):

> [One-way] immersion programs were not designed or meant for ethno-linguistic groups in North America that have some language other than English as the main language used in the home. To place such children in an initially all-English instructional program would be to misapply the immersion process in a harmful, subtractive way. Their personal identities, their early conceptual development, their chances of competing or succeeding in schools or in occupations, and their interest in trying to succeed would all be hampered by an immersion-in-English program. (p. 26)

So-called "structured English immersion" programs are not immersion programs at all. They are *submersion* programs. The difference is additive bilingualism. In these programs, minority-language students are taught only through English. They don't have an opportunity to learn through the home language or to acquire literacy skills in the L1 at school. Therefore, "structured English immersion" is fundamentally subtractive in nature. In contrast, in one-way second-/foreign-language immersion programs, English becomes a formal part of the curriculum. English-speaking students learn through the medium of the second or foreign language—French, Mandarin, or Spanish—but also learn through English. The point at which English is introduced varies according to the program model, as explained later.

Subject-matter instruction in the minority language

ImDL programs are *subject-matter driven*. They teach the same curriculum that other English-medium schools offer, and they are responsible for meeting the same academic learning standards or outcomes as other schools in the state or province. The emphasis on academic subject matter in the ImDL curriculum distinguishes ImDL programs from other types of educational programs or experiences that might be called "immersion" (in addition to "structured English immersion" described above). Some examples (adapted from Fortune & Tedick, 2008) include:

- using only the second (or indigenous or foreign) language to communicate while explicitly teaching *about* the language;
- providing intensive short-term residential experiences that use the second language exclusively to teach communicative language skills and cultural understanding (e.g., language camps);
- offering intensive learning abroad opportunities where students attend language and culture classes to develop language proficiency.

Learning a language through subject-matter instruction is more effective than learning a language in non-immersion settings such as foreign-language classrooms, many of which are known to have "limitations in quantity and quality of exposure" (Muñoz & Spada, 2019, p. 235). Based on her review of research on content-based instruction at both primary and secondary levels, Lightbown (2014) concluded that content-based language instruction is effective and motivating and can promote advanced levels of proficiency.

From a learning perspective, one of the most attractive features of ImDL programs is their increased exposure to and engagement with the minority language. In addition to more time on task, the effectiveness of these programs has been attributed to their being content driven, which provides a motivational basis for purposeful communication and a cognitive basis for language learning. That is, the depth of processing required for learners to engage with subject matter taught through the minority language is believed to move minority-language development forward. At the same time, however, engagement with content learned through the minority language is insufficient on its own to ensure the high levels of proficiency required to continue engaging with increasingly complex subject matter. As Swain (1988) argued, "not all content teaching is necessarily good language teaching" and, thus, it needs to be "organized to enhance L2 learning" (p. 68). Therefore, students and teachers in these programs need to understand and accept that content learning must go hand in hand with language learning—systematic attention must be paid to language if students are to acquire high levels of bilingualism. This is the case even for minority-language students in two-way immersion and developmental bilingual programs, with respect to not only their English acquisition but also their continued development of the minority language. We describe how to support language development throughout the remainder of the book.

 SPECIAL NOTE

In ImDL language doesn't just "take care of itself"—learning language requires focus and specific effort.

Extensive exposure to the minority language

Finally, ImDL programs are by definition language intensive; that is, they offer a great deal of exposure to the minority language through content instruction. Their purpose is to *immerse* students in the target language for extended periods of time. To this end, programs must provide *at least* 50% of core subject-matter instruction through the medium of a second, foreign, heritage, or indigenous language throughout the primary school years (K–Grade 5/6) and ideally through Grade 12.

In secondary continuation programs, two or more subject areas must be taught through the minority language for the program to be considered an immersion program (Christian, 2011; Fortune & Tedick, 2008). Although it can be challenging to maintain continuation programs in Canadian French immersion, efforts to do so are common. In contrast, in the US, strong secondary (middle- and high-school) continuation programs are rare, especially at the high-school level (Grades 9–12). One reason for the challenge is that it is difficult to find teachers who are licensed in secondary content areas and who have the requisite proficiency in the minority language to teach cognitively demanding content through the medium of that language. Another is that scheduling becomes more complex at the secondary level, because students have more curricular choice and thus take many different kinds of classes. Additionally, students and parents become convinced that taking more classes in English at the secondary level will better prepare students for post-secondary studies undertaken in English.

ImDL program model variations

The foregoing section described the defining features that all ImDL programs have in common. This section goes further in illuminating the various models of ImDL education: one-way second-/foreign-language immersion (hereafter IMM), two-way immersion (TWI), developmental bilingual education (DBE), and indigenous-language revitalization immersion (IRI).

First, these programs vary by language and available linguistic resources. A wide range of languages are taught in ImDL programs. In Canada, French is by far the most common minority language offered in IMM programs, although others, such as Spanish, are also taught. In the US, Spanish is the most common language of IMM, DBE, and TWI programs, but many other languages are also offered, such as French, Hmong, Mandarin, Russian, and Vietnamese, to name a few. A wealth of language resources are available for some languages, such as Spanish and French, but sorely lacking for others, such as Hmong and Vietnamese.

Canada offers IRI programs in Cree, Mi'kmaq, and Mohawk. Although there is no record of the total number of IRI programs or the number of indigenous languages being revitalized through immersion across the US, the majority of US IRI programs are in Hawaiian. Other endangered languages, such as Navajo (Diné), Ojibwe, Cherokee, and Yup'ik, are also being revitalized through immersion. We would be remiss if we did not acknowledge some of the special challenges faced by IRI programs that are not experienced by IMM, DBE, and TWI programs in modern world languages. In most cases, indigenous languages have no external country to promote them (Wilson & Kamanā, 2011). They also lack the vocabulary used in academic settings and books; consequently, indigenous communities must establish linguistic committees or councils to create new vocabulary and to establish written grammar rules. IRI programs typically lack resources such as university-educated individuals who are proficient in the languages and traditions to serve as teachers, administrators, and curriculum developers (McCarty & Watahomigie, 1999). Perhaps the greatest challenge of all is that indigenous communities are consistently up against the decline of their proficient native-speaker base (Wilson & Kamanā, 2011). This is especially difficult given that most, if not all, IRI programs rely on elders as linguistic and cultural resources. Doing so is necessary because nearly all IRI teachers are L2 learners of the language or raised by L2 learners of the language. Despite these challenges, the determination of indigenous peoples to reclaim their languages and cultures is strong, and more and more communities are turning to immersion as a significant part of their language-preservation efforts. An encouraging sign in Canada is the government's commitment to increasing funding available for the revitalization and preservation of indigenous languages in response to the Calls to Action put forth by the Truth and Reconciliation Commission of Canada (2015).

In addition to varying by language and language resources, ImDL programs also differ with respect to student population, program onset, level of exposure to or amount of instructional time in the minority language, language of initial literacy instruction, and type of setting. These variations are summarized in Table 1.1 and discussed further in the following sections. Whereas variations in instructional practices are also to be expected across these different program models, what they share is the need for effective approaches to scaffolding the minority language in ways that support students in learning both subject-matter content and the minority language.

Student population

Although all ImDL programs were originally conceived to serve particular student populations (Table 1.1), today they attract populations representing much more linguistic and cultural diversity. For example, ImDL programs enroll many ethnic minorities who may speak different varieties of English or the partner language of the program. Many, if not most, of the minority-language students in TWI have been born in the US and are simultaneous bilinguals (e.g., de Jong, 2016; Escamilla et al., 2014). Students' languages and their language varieties need to be acknowledged and valued in ImDL classrooms and programs. Dagenais (2008) has described the importance of critical language awareness activities in linguistically diverse ImDL programs. She argues that when students are offered the opportunity to attend systematically to the range of languages and cultures represented among their classmates and communities, a more inclusive learning environment may be fostered. This sensitivity to language varieties notwithstanding, it is imperative that ImDL students be exposed to and expected to develop "standard" and academic varieties of English and the minority language if they are to be successful in school and beyond.

TABLE 1.1 ImDL program variations

Program type	Student population	Program onset	Amount of exposure	Language of initial literacy instruction	Type of setting
IMM	• designed originally for majority-language speakers • currently serve students with more linguistic diversity (including students who speak the minority language of the program as well as L3 learners)	US and Canada: • "early": preschool, kindergarten, or Grade 1 Canada: • "middle" or "delayed": Grade 4 • "late": Grade 7	• "total" or "full": 100% of subject-matter instruction in the minority language in Grades K–2 or 3 (sometimes higher) with gradual increase of English • "partial" (50:50 or bilingual): 50% in each program language from onset and throughout duration • secondary continuation programs: at least two subject matters in the minority language; strong programs offer at least 50%	• early, total programs: initial literacy instruction in the minority language • partial (50:50): in English or the minority language or both simultaneously (two literacy blocks per day, one in each language)	• single track (immersion center or whole-school model) • dual track (strand or stream within larger English-medium school)
TWI, DBE	• TWI—combine minority-language and majority-language speakers (1:1 ratio ideal or at least 1/3 of each language group) who remain integrated for instruction • DBE—minority-language speakers • currently serve students having linguistic and ethnic diversity (simultaneous bilinguals, dialect variation, L3 learners)	• preschool, kindergarten, or Grade 1	• 90:10: 90% subject-matter instruction in the minority language, 10% in English for first few years of program with gradual increase of English • 50:50: 50% in each program language from onset and throughout duration • other variations (e.g., 80:20, 70:30) • secondary continuation programs: at least two subject matters in the minority language; strong programs offer at least 50%	• initial literacy instruction *should* occur in the minority language in programs serving minority-language students • 90:10 (80:20, etc.): initial literacy instruction typically occurs in the minority language • 50:50: initial literacy is typically taught in both languages simultaneously (two literacy blocks per day, one in each language)	• single track (whole-school model) • dual track (strand or stream within larger English-medium school)

(Continued)

TABLE 1.1 Continued

Program type	Student population	Program onset	Amount of exposure	Language of initial literacy instruction	Type of setting
IRI	• typically enroll students with indigenous or First Nations ancestry (most one-way, but two TWI programs documented in Arizona [Navajo])	• "early": infancy or preschool	• "total" or "full": 100% of subject-matter instruction in the indigenous language in PreK–3 (sometimes higher) with gradual increase of English • some 50:50: 50% in each program language from onset and throughout duration • secondary continuation programs: at least two subject matters in the indigenous language; strong programs offer at least 50% (few secondary programs offered)	• early, total programs: initial literacy instruction in the indigenous language • 50:50: initial literacy is typically taught in both languages simultaneously (two literacy blocks per day, one in each language) • lack of written materials often causes programs to introduce English literacy earlier	• single track (whole-school model) • dual track (strand or stream within larger English-medium school) • many housed in buildings on reservations and receive support from elders and entire Native community

As Table 1.1 indicates, TWI programs serve a combined student population of minority-language and majority-language speakers. A 1:1 ratio of minority- to majority-language students is ideal, but at least one-third of each language group (i.e., a 2:1 ratio) has been recommended (e.g., Howard et al., 2018). Moreover, it is critical that all TWI students remain integrated for instruction in both program languages. Integration "contributes to the development of positive inter-group relationships" between the linguistic groups (de Jong & Howard, 2009, p. 85) and is essential when it comes to academic achievement outcomes.

 SPECIAL NOTE

Keeping linguistic groups integrated for instruction in both program languages is key in TWI.

Indeed, in all ImDL programs, students should be integrated for instruction. As aptly stated by Thomas and Collier (2012), "By keeping students together and intentionally building a classroom and school community that respects and values all students, social and cultural relationships are transformed" (p. 119).

Program onset

ImDL programs vary by the grade level at which the program begins. As Table 1.1 shows, the US and Canada offer "early" programs, which begin in preschool, kindergarten, or Grade 1, and in the case of IRI, as early as infancy. Canada also offers "middle" or "delayed" programs, which begin in Grade 4, and "late" programs (Grade 7). In delayed and late programs, students study the minority language as a subject prior to receiving subject-matter instruction in that language when the IMM program begins. Although one might assume that early exposure leads to better L2 outcomes, some Canadian research has shown that late immersion students can perform as well as students in early total programs with respect to L2 proficiency (Genesee, 1981). Some studies have pointed to the importance of pedagogical factors in the success of late immersion students. For example, Stevens (1983) compared two late French immersion programs, one in which students spent 80% of their school day learning subjects in French and the other in which students had only 40% of their school day in the L2. The second group performed as well as the first on several L2 measures. Stevens identified a variety of key pedagogical factors that appeared to influence the L2 outcomes of the second program: it was activity based, permitted individualization, and gave students choice in what they would study and how they would meet curricular competences.

Amount of exposure

ImDL programs also differ in terms of amount of exposure to the minority language. Total or full IMM programs offer 100% of subject-matter instruction in the early grades—typically from PreK to Grades 2 or 3. English may be introduced in the curriculum during the second half of Grade 2, the early part of Grade 3, or even later. Instructional time in English gradually increases, so that by the end of the elementary years approximately 50% of instructional time is allocated to each language. Partial (50:50) programs provide 50% of instruction in each of the program languages from the beginning and for the duration of the program. Programs typically distribute different subject areas between the two program languages, although literacy and language arts should be taught in both languages throughout the elementary grades. Sometimes programs offer a subject area, such as science, in both languages and alternate curricular units by language (for example, a unit on growth of living things in Portuguese followed by a unit on animal classification in English, followed by another unit in Portuguese, and so on).

DBE and TWI programs can be 50:50 or provide more minority-language exposure. The model offering the most exposure is referred to as the 90:10 model, with the first number representing the percentage of instructional time in the minority language and the second the percentage of instructional time in English. There are more variations within DBE and TWI than within IMM or IRI models. Some programs begin with 70–80% of instructional time in the minority language with the remainder in English.

Importantly, studies have shown that students in 50:50 IMM programs are not at an advantage when it comes to English-language development, even though they receive more instructional time in English over the long term. However, they *are* at a *dis*advantage when it comes to proficiency attainment in the minority language. Studies have shown that students in total or 90:10 ImDL programs outperform students in 50:50 programs when it comes to minority-language proficiency (Christian et al., 2004; Genesee, 1987, 2004; Lindholm-Leary, 2001).

Regarding English-language arts and reading for minority-language students, there can be short-term advantages for 50:50 programs, but those advantages disappear by upper elementary grades (Christian et al., 2004). When administrators discover that minority-language students are not performing at grade level in English on Grade 3 standardized tests, they should not panic. It's important to trust the model, based on the research evidence. In well-implemented programs (see Chapter 2), minority-language students have proven to do at least as well in English by upper elementary or middle-school grades as students being schooled only in English.

 SPECIAL NOTE

More time in English doesn't mean better English! In the long run, ImDL students do at least as well in English-language development as students in 50:50 programs and those who learn only in English.

Whether minority-language students are in DBE or TWI, it's imperative that programs be designed to go beyond Grade 5 and that parents make a long-term commitment to the program. This is because results from longitudinal studies of well-implemented DBE and TWI programs have shown that minority-language students' achievement reaches that of native English speakers' average performance by Grade 6 in TWI and by Grade 8 in DBE (Thomas & Collier, 2012). Their reading achievement *surpasses* that of average English speakers in the upper middle- and high-school grades. Thus, both DBE and TWI programs are the strongest school-based program options for minority-language students as long as they are well implemented (see Chapter 2) and maintain instruction in the minority language through the middle-school grades and, ideally, beyond.

Because of the revitalization goal, many IRI programs are of the early, total variety, beginning with 100% of instruction in the indigenous language at the preschool level (sometimes starting in infancy) and, when possible, continuing into the early grades, while later introducing English in the curriculum (Grade 3 or after). The Kanien'kéha immersion program in Kahnawà:ke, Quebec, offers full immersion in the Mohawk language from Nursery through Grade 4; students then continue their elementary schooling in Grades 5 and 6 in English. Some 50:50 programs also exist. For instance, a school district in southwest Alaska adopted a 50:50 model for some K–6 programs, which previously had offered Yup'ik-medium instruction only through Grade 2 (Siekmann, Webster, Samson, & Moses, 2017). Other IRI programs become 50:50 quite early on. May (2013) reported that in one of the Navajo programs all instruction occurred through Navajo in the early grades (preK–Grade 1), but the program became 50:50 by Grade 2. In contrast, some Hawaiian programs do not formally introduce English in the curriculum until Grade 5, and one program maintains all subject courses in Hawaiian through Grade 12, except for the subject of English language/language arts (Wilson & Kamanā, 2011).

Strong ImDL secondary-level continuation programs maintain at least 50% of instructional time in the minority language throughout the program. It should be noted, however, that in both the US and Canada it is not uncommon to see a significant decrease in minority-language instructional time even as early as Grade 6. And, unfortunately, some ImDL programs do not even continue past the elementary years. The challenge is a lack of certified and highly proficient teachers as well as curricular materials (especially in indigenous and less common languages such as Hmong).

Language of initial literacy instruction

ImDL programs that begin early and offer more exposure to the minority language typically introduce literacy initially through the minority language. Students are able to transfer their literacy knowledge and skills to English once they begin learning in English in Grade 2 or later. For example, students transfer knowledge of sensory-motor skills (the spatial and directional skills involved), common writing system features (sound–symbol correspondence), comprehension strategies (using picture and context clues), study skills, and habits and attitudes (Cloud et al., 2000). The more similar the two languages are (e.g., French and English), the more positive the transfer is. Yet, positive transfer occurs in the more general skills noted earlier even with languages having very different writing systems, such as Chinese and English. Non-transferable skills will need to be taught separately. For example, learners of Chinese must learn how to identify radicals within characters. Learners of Spanish and English will need to understand that, while Spanish has just five vowel sounds or phonemes, English has many more (and that number varies depending upon the variety of English— whether American or Australian, for example—not to mention the differences that exist within these varieties!).

Initial literacy instruction in 50:50 models may occur in English or the minority language, or in both languages simultaneously. This means that students receive formal literacy instruction in both languages beginning in kindergarten, but without translation; in other words, students have two literacy classes each day (one in English and one in the minority or partner language). Beeman and Urow (2013) and Escamilla et al. (2014) explain that a simultaneous approach should not provide students with two unrelated literacy classes based on teaching literacy to monolinguals, but, rather, should be approached from a biliteracy perspective. We will return to this topic in Chapter 9.

A significant challenge faced by IRI programs (or programs in less common languages such as Hmong) is lack of written materials, which may lead to an earlier introduction to English literacy than if more materials were available in the indigenous language. Some initiatives have supported IRI programs through organized materials development. For example, Siekmann et al. (2017) describe a collaborative project to design Yup'ik language and cultural materials linked to academic content for Yup'ik early total and 50:50 programs. They reported that the teachers involved generally felt more comfortable writing books for the younger grades, as books for higher grades required higher levels of proficiency, especially in written Yup'ik, and more complex grammar. To compensate, they "worked closely with elders, the linguistic and cultural knowledge bearers, to create authentic and appropriate representations of Yup'ik culture" (p. 8). Similarly, some Hmong ImDL teachers are engaging in writing materials for use in their programs (Rao, 2019).

Type of setting

ImDL programs also vary by type of setting, specifically whether the program is a single-track (i.e., immersion center or whole-school model) or dual-track program (i.e., a strand or stream within a larger English-medium school). A number of Canadian studies have examined different aspects of single- and dual-track settings for French immersion programs (see Doell, 2011 and Genesee, 1987, for summaries). Some studies compared student outcomes and showed that single-track students outperformed dual-track students in subject areas and in listening and reading comprehension in both French and English, oral production, and French-language arts. Other studies that explored stakeholder perspectives reported that, in single-track programs, teachers and students were more pleased with available resources and support services. The perception is that, in single-track programs, students are exposed to more French and are encouraged to use French more even outside classrooms. Nevertheless, one study, which examined only dual-track IMM programs, identified advantages of this setting, including student exposure to diversity, development of cultural tolerance, elimination of neighborhood cliques, and benefits of keeping community schools open (Crawford, 1995).

Most DBE and TWI programs are of the dual-track variety in the US (de Jong, 2014; Lindholm-Leary, 2001). Some studies have shown that dual-track TWI programs can undermine efforts to equalize the status of program languages and maintain key program principles (e.g., de Jong & Bearse, 2014; Palmer, 2007).

It is important for all ImDL dual-track programs to be connected to the overall school community and for there to be positive collaboration and interaction between the two programs in the school. Some practical recommendations (most adapted from Guimont, 2003 and Howard & Christian, 2002) include the following:

- During the planning phase, offer an informational session about ImDL to all stakeholders to encourage them to voice concerns and/or to vote on whether to launch the program.
- As the ImDL program grows (adding a grade level each year), be mindful of staffing issues. It's better to rely on teacher retirements than to displace teachers who have worked in the school for many years.
- Build a sense of community among staff members and establish overarching academic goals and behavioral expectations for the whole school. Plan for other cohesion-building factors such as having a school mascot or song that applies to the whole school.
- Have specialists (art, physical education, and music teachers) include a focus on the minority (partner) language and culture(s).
- Partner each ImDL classroom with an English-medium classroom to work on joint projects and to socialize.
- Schedule common planning time for ImDL and English-medium teachers at each grade level.
- Ensure that all school committees have representation from both programs.
- Display a clear presence for both programs on the school website and on the building's external signage.

Summary

In this chapter, we have described the goals and defining characteristics of ImDL programs. We have also described the four program model variations that fall under the ImDL umbrella, specifically with respect to their languages and linguistic resources, student population, program onset, amount of instructional time in the minority language, language of initial literacy instruction, and type of setting (single or dual track). In Chapter 2, we continue this foundational information by identifying features that represent well-implemented programs.

Application activity 1

To aid in developing critical language awareness among your students, have them create their own language biography booklets. On the first page of the biography booklet, have them draw their "language story." They should begin with a picture of themselves (or a circle with their name in it) in the middle of the page. Surrounding that picture, they should write the names of family members and others they interact with on a frequent basis outside school. Have them draw lines between themselves and each person. On each line, they should write the language they use with that person—for example, if Maite (see Figure 1.1) uses Spanish with her dad and if he uses Spanish with her, she should draw a line with two arrows—one pointing to dad and one to Maite. Alternatively, if she uses one language with a family member and the family member uses another, there should be two separate lines with arrows pointing in opposite directions (Figure 1.1).

On subsequent pages of the booklet, ask students to write the language story depicted in their picture to describe what languages they use and with whom. Or, you can tailor this activity to learners who aren't able to write much yet. For example, you can provide the following questions (or others that you create) on subsequent pages, and students can answer them. Or, they can dictate answers and the teacher can write their responses in the booklet.

1. What language(s) do you speak?
2. What language(s) can you understand (but not speak)?
3. What do your languages look like? Write the same word in all the languages you know or can understand (get help from family members if you need it).
4. What language(s) have you heard but can't understand or speak or can understand or speak just a little or some (about a few topics but not many)?
5. What language(s) have you seen but can't read or speak or can read or speak just a little or some?

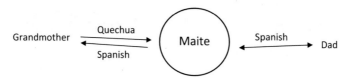

FIGURE 1.1 The start of Maite's language story

Application activity 2

Educators are asked questions or need to field uninformed comments about ImDL all the time—from parents, community members, school district representatives, and complete strangers! It's important that you are able to respond confidently and accurately as you advocate for these programs in your community. The following questions were developed originally for use in CARLA "Immersion 101" summer institutes at the University of Minnesota by Maureen Curran-Dorsano, Amy Egenberger (both former IMM teachers), Tara Fortune, and Diane Tedick. We have also used them in our professional development courses. Based on what you've learned in the Introduction and Chapter 1, develop a two- or three-minute response for one or more of the following questions. Remember to use lay language and refrain from too much educational jargon. You may need to read some of the papers we cite in this chapter to ensure your response is thorough and well informed by the research.

Common questions and comments about ImDL

1. What is this immersion/dual language thing about anyway?
2. Why would anyone choose to send their kid to a school where they don't speak English (or other majority language) all the time?
3. If kids already speak Spanish, why would you send them to a two-way immersion school where they'll use Spanish most of the time? How will they ever learn English?
4. Wouldn't a child who has difficulty with a language or learning disorder be better off in a regular (English-medium) school?
5. Why would you send your child to an Ojibwe (or other indigenous-language) immersion school? Native children have trouble succeeding academically so wouldn't it be better if they just learned in English? English is what they really need, after all.
6. We need to put more English (or other majority-language) instruction into the curriculum earlier on. I'm worried about test scores and I'm quite sure the kids' English (majority-language) development and reading will improve if we spend more time in English.
7. If Spanish immersion works so well for kids who speak English at home, English immersion (in the US) should work just as well for kids who speak Spanish at home, right?
8. We can support our two-way immersion program at the K–5 level, but beyond that there are no guarantees.
9. Second-graders from the neighborhood school are already reading chapter books, and my French immersion second-grader can't read any books in English (majority language) yet. How do I convince my mother-in-law that her grandchild WILL learn how to read in English just as well as the other kids?
10. I was really excited to learn that my niece got into a Chinese immersion program. She'll be completely bilingual by Grade 5!

🖥 Online resources for readers

Benefits and myths of bilingualism

Check out this extensive, searchable database that identifies and provides research evidence for 700 reasons to study other languages: www.llas.ac.uk/700reasons/700r easons.html

In a videotaped interview by LinguaHealth (2012), Brenda K. Gorman provides an interesting and accessible discussion about the myths of bilingualism in children. Check out the video on YouTube: www.youtube.com/watch?v=LVYhpCprtzQ&t=10s

Program design

See Howard and Christian's (2002) *Two-Way Immersion 101* at www.cal.org/twi/pdfs/two-way-immersion-101.pdf

See the updated 2018 *Guiding Principles for Dual Language Education*. This set of guiding principles can be purchased or downloaded for free: www.cal.org/twi/guidingprinciples.htm

Language policies

For information on California's Proposition 227, see www.lao.ca.gov/ballot/1998/227_06_1998.htm and ballotpedia.org/California_Proposition_227,_the_%22English_in_Public_Schools%22_Initiative_(1998)

For information on California's Proposition 58, the legislation that repealed Proposition 227, see https://ballotpedia.org/California_Proposition_58,_Non-English_Languages_Allowed_in_Public_Education_(2016)

IRI resources

For a list of indigenous languages in North America, see the online Catalogue of Endangered Languages, available at endangeredlanguages.com

The Yup'ik materials created by the university-school collaborative project described by Siekmann et al. (2017) are available for download at www.uaf.edu/pe/materials

2

CHARACTERISTICS OF WELL-IMPLEMENTED IMMERSION AND DUAL LANGUAGE PROGRAMS

In the last chapter, we presented the defining characteristics, program variations, and foundational principles of immersion and dual language (ImDL) education. In this chapter, we identify features that characterize well-implemented programs. We address the following questions:

- What key features reflect a well-implemented ImDL program?
- What is "translanguaging" and why is establishing separate instructional spaces for program languages in ImDL classrooms recommended?

Introduction

Chapter 1 described the defining features, or "non-negotiables," of ImDL education—features that are common across ImDL programs and without which they would not be ImDL programs. It also discussed how ImDL program models vary. In this chapter, we present characteristics that represent a strong implementation of ImDL programs. de Jong (2011) reminds ImDL educators that "merely choosing a program design (e.g., two-way immersion) will not guarantee positive outcomes—schools must also pay close attention to the quality of program implementation" (p. 163).

Research that points to the benefits of ImDL education is typically based on outcomes associated with "well-implemented" programs. Researchers have reported that the higher the quality of implementation, the stronger the outcomes of ImDL programs (Genesee, Lindholm-Leary, Saunders, & Christian, 2006; National Academies of Sciences, Engineering, and Medicine, 2017; Thomas & Collier, 2017). Features corresponding to strong ImDL program implementation have been described by others in the field. For example, the *Guiding Principles of Dual Language Education* (Howard et al., 2018) include seven research-based strands that reflect the main dimensions of program design and implementation. Each strand is divided into a number of principles, which are further divided into key points, and each key point is accompanied by progress indicators that programs can use for planning and reflection.

Most Canadian provinces provide some guidance for effective implementation of their French immersion programs. For example, Alberta has a *Handbook for French Immersion Administrators* (Alberta Education, 2014) and, for French immersion teachers, Manitoba published *La langue au cœur de l'immersion française: une approche intégrée dans la pédagogie immersive* (Government of Manitoba, 2016). In the US, some states have also established criteria that correspond to strong program implementation. For example, the state of Louisiana, known primarily for its French immersion programs (but now offering programs in other languages such as Spanish and Mandarin), passed state legislation in 2011 that outlines a process by which ImDL programs can be certified by the state (Legislature of Louisiana, 2011). It involves meeting specific criteria as stipulated in the legislation, which, in essence, defines standards for ImDL programs, or characteristics of well-implemented programs. The process is intended to assist and support schools in establishing and maintaining high-quality, highly effective ImDL programs (see Haj-Broussard, 2018, for more details).

Drawing from the *Guiding Principles* as well as other resources and our experiences, this chapter highlights characteristics that are especially critical for well-implemented programs. As depicted in Figure 2.1 and elaborated on throughout the chapter, we identify 14 characteristics of well-implemented ImDL programs distributed across five categories: program leadership and design; teachers; families and community; curriculum and instruction; and assessment.

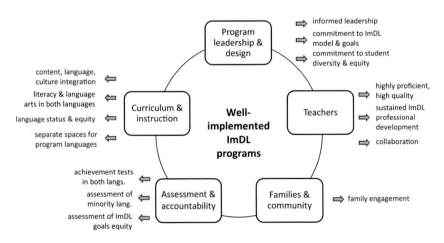

FIGURE 2.1 Characteristics of well-implemented programs

Program leadership and design

1. *Strong, informed leadership*

Studies have shown that successful schools are led by effective leaders (e.g., Herman et al., 2017). Well-implemented ImDL programs have strong, informed leadership that demonstrates knowledge about the research base, program models, and characteristics of ImDL programs (e.g., Howard et al., 2018; Thomas & Collier, 2017). Such leaders develop and communicate a school-wide shared vision for the program and for the promotion of bilingualism and biliteracy and ensure that there is a plan to bring that vision to fruition. Hunt (2011) maintains that having a clear, unified mission that is derived from a school-wide commitment to ImDL education is key to the ongoing success of ImDL programs. Effective leaders, having sought out and availed themselves of ImDL-specific preparation, are well informed about ImDL education, second language development, research that underlies ImDL programs, and ImDL-specific instructional practices, and they make sure that their decisions are grounded in research. They support collaborative and shared leadership and decision-making, seeing their role as working *with* teachers to lead the program. Such collaboration implies that they have trust in their teachers (and vice versa) (Hunt, 2011). Strong ImDL leaders ensure access to high-quality curriculum, cultivate language proficiency, and promote sociocultural integration (Scanlan & López, 2012, cited in Menken, 2017), and they establish close relationships with families and communities. They strive for flexibility so that program structures can conform as needed to changing program and student needs (Hunt, 2011). They fundamentally trust that ImDL works, and can thus push against policies that privilege English and serve as strong advocates for their students and the program within the school board or district and the community.

It is a significant bonus if the principal and/or other school leaders and employees are bilingual in the program's languages. It's ideal when a school hires bilingual special education teachers, speech-language pathologists, administrative staff (such as school secretaries), and other support staff such as cafeteria workers and so on. Strong ImDL leaders also advocate for support from the school district or board and strive to ensure that the program is equitably and sufficiently funded (Howard et al., 2018; Thomas & Collier, 2017).

Effective leaders advocate for ImDL programs to continue beyond the elementary level. Principals in middle and high schools that house secondary continuation programs (which, by default, are dual-track programs) need to understand the basic principles of ImDL education. They understand, for example, that at least two subject courses must be taught in the minority language for the program to qualify as ImDL, and they advocate for more than two, ideally maintaining at least 50% of subjects taught in the minority language through the secondary years. They work with secondary teachers to tackle the challenge of scheduling subject-matter classes taught in the minority language so that students can take them during a coherent block of time rather than intermittently with classes taught in English (to the degree possible). Principals in middle and high schools need to understand the unique needs that ImDL teachers have and advocate for ImDL-specific professional development and resources for their teachers. Often teachers whose training was for non-immersion foreign-language teaching are hired to teach ImDL language arts classes at the secondary level. They and their subject-matter licensed colleagues (math, science, and social studies educators) teaching in the ImDL program need professional development to learn how to work most effectively with ImDL students. Moreover, when secondary continuation programs are offered, knowledgeable leaders at the school district level should work to ensure program articulation across schools—from elementary to middle school to high school.

2. Commitment to the program model and goals

Well-implemented ImDL programs maintain a strong commitment to program model characteristics and goals (Howard et al., 2018; Thomas & Collier, 2017). It should be clear that the program strives for the three goals: academic achievement at or above grade-level standards in both languages, additive bilingualism and biliteracy, and cultural competence. In addition, model-specific characteristics should be observable within the program; for example, leaders ensure that in two-way immersion (TWI) programs learners remain *integrated* for all instruction (see Chapter 1). The entire school staff should fully understand the research-based rationale behind the defining characteristics and other program features, and program leaders must make sure that these features are apparent in ImDL classrooms and the program at large. This is equally important in dual-track models, including secondary continuation programs. Non-ImDL teachers in these schools should support use of the minority language by teachers and students in the hallways, the cafeteria, and the teachers' lounge. They should understand how important and beneficial bilingualism is and support the ImDL program's efforts in maintaining high standards for minority-language use and development inside and outside the classroom.

A recent newspaper article highlighted the importance of maintaining a commitment to the program model (Huicochea, 2016). It summarized the preliminary results of an audit of TWI programs in the Tucson Unified School District (TUSD), conducted by Rosa Molina, executive director of the Association of Two-Way & Dual Language Education in the US. The pressure for students to perform well on state-mandated achievement tests administered in English led teachers to deviate from Spanish instruction when students struggled to understand concepts. Molina was quoted as saying:

> The walk through of (dual language) classrooms showed significant weaknesses at the intermediate and middle school levels … It appeared that both the teacher practices and the students' use of language had been significantly compromised by the lack of fidelity to the program model, pressure to perform in English and very low expectations for students to achieve high levels of Spanish proficiencies in reading, writing and oracy. (para. 8)

After the audit, TUSD indicated a commitment to identifying and administering a Spanish-language assessment aligned with state requirements and instituting ImDL-specific professional development for teachers to help them maintain commitment to the program model. They also considered following Molina's recommendation to seek an exemption from Arizona state law, which stipulates that only students who are already proficient in English are eligible to participate in two-way immersion programs. In accordance with this law, Spanish speakers in Arizona are placed in English-only classrooms until they acquire enough English proficiency to participate in ImDL programs. State lawmakers thereby prohibit Spanish-dominant learners from participating in the very programs that are most likely to lead to their English-language development and academic success! ImDL stakeholders and advocates need to push back against such misinformed and discriminatory state-wide language policies.

Leaders should also establish program-level policies, such as a policy for "lateral entry" of students. In other words, leaders must ensure that students entering the program after Grade 1 (or even the first semester of Grade 1) have an acceptable level of proficiency in the minority language so that they can succeed in the program. Admitting students with no proficiency in the minority language after Grade 1 can undermine program goals and be linguistically, academically, and emotionally challenging for such students. One of the difficulties reported by Tucson dual language teachers with respect to staying true to the program model was the need to accommodate enrollment of English-speaking students with no Spanish proficiency after Grade 1. One of the criteria that Louisiana requires in its state ImDL certification process is a written policy outlining conditions and processes for entry into and exit from the program (Haj-Broussard, 2018).

Similarly, in ImDL secondary continuation programs, it is not uncommon to include heritage speakers of the minority language who did not participate in the elementary ImDL program. This practice is acceptable as long as the heritage speakers have a high enough level of proficiency in the minority language—both orally and with regard to literacy. Proficiency in English also is ideal but not necessary, as being able to learn some subjects through the medium of the home language will allow minority-language proficient heritage students to keep pace in those subjects as they acquire English. Typically, heritage students entering at the secondary level have benefitted from formal schooling in their home language and thus are already literate in that language, so they will very likely acquire English more quickly.

3. Commitment to student diversity and equity

ImDL program staff in well-implemented programs ensure that the program welcomes and is appropriate for a wide range of learners, including children from diverse ethnic, linguistic, socioeconomic, and developmental backgrounds. This is important for all programs, but perhaps especially one-way second-/foreign-language immersion programs, which can run the risk of being labeled "elitist" if they cater only to White middle or upper-middle class students. We recommend that these programs strive to recruit students such that the diversity of their student population mirrors that of other schools in the same district or school board.

Well-implemented ImDL programs institute "school policies and [classroom] practices that reflect respect for and affirm students' and teachers' diversity of linguistic and cultural experiences and beliefs" (de Jong, 2011, p. 175). Students thrive socially, linguistically, and academically when they feel validated for what they know and are given opportunities to build on that knowledge. They are more likely to participate actively during instruction and apply themselves linguistically and academically when their identities are affirmed (Cummins, 2001). de Jong (2011, p. 176) suggests that

- educators include and represent different languages, cultures, and experiences in the mission statement, school plans, textbook adoption, and family engagement activities;
- administrators value cross-cultural differences and foster the development of positive social relationships among students from diverse linguistic, racial, cultural, and socioeconomic backgrounds;
- teachers meaningfully include students' lived experiences in classroom activities and provide students with opportunities to "represent and explore multiple identities."

In addition, well-implemented ImDL programs have teachers and other staff that are committed to educational equity and incorporate equitable practices at all levels (Howard et al., 2018). Equity is critical in programs that serve and integrate students with different backgrounds. Howard et al. (2018, p. 11) characterize teachers and staff members who are committed to equity as those who:

- believe that all children can learn;
- demonstrate awareness of diverse learner needs;
- are trained in sociocultural understanding;
- use multiethnic and multicultural curricular materials;
- integrate students' cultural values into the classroom;
- celebrate and encourage the use of all home language varieties; and
- invite students to think critically and engage in learning activities that promote social justice.

Teachers

4. Highly proficient, high-quality teachers

It has been long established that teachers are the most important school-level factor impacting student achievement. Well-implemented ImDL programs employ teachers who are *highly proficient* in the language(s) of instruction and technically qualified to teach the subject area(s) (e.g., Fortune & Tedick, 2008; Howard et al., 2018; Swain & Johnson, 1997). Teachers in ImDL programs are not always bilingual, but they should have a high level of proficiency in the language(s) they use to teach.

When it comes to language proficiency, just how proficient is "highly proficient"? The 2018 *Guiding Principles* (Howard et al., 2018) propose that ImDL teachers need "native or native-like proficiency in the language(s) in which they teach" (p. 91). Language proficiency, however, is often determined at the local school level when a teacher is hired. In general, it can be challenging to find a sufficient number of ImDL teachers with native or near-native proficiency. Some schools have a hiring process that includes having applicants teach a lesson in the minority language, and some require official language proficiency ratings. They also often require formal study in the minority language for non-native speakers. Principals should become aware of options available to them for assessing teachers' language proficiency. In the US, the American Council on the Teaching of Foreign Languages (ACTFL), the professional organization for foreign-language teachers, offers proficiency testing in speaking and writing.

In the US, some states require a minimum level of proficiency to teach in an ImDL program. Utah, for example, requires a minimum of "advanced-mid" according to the ACTFL Guidelines (2012a). The Guidelines are comprised of holistic rubrics with 11 levels ranging from "novice low" to "distinguished," and they describe what individuals can do with language in the four modalities—listening, speaking, reading, and writing—in real-world situations that are spontaneous (non-rehearsed). Another scale used to describe language proficiency was developed by the Council of Europe (2001). The Common European Framework of Reference for Languages (CEFR) was designed to provide a framework to aid in the development of language curriculum and learning materials and for assessing language proficiency. The CEFR describes six levels of language proficiency (from A1 to C2) with an additional three "plus" levels (B1+, B2+, and A2+). A B2 ("advanced-mid") (ACTFL, n.d.) is the minimum level of proficiency needed for ImDL teachers, and higher levels are preferred. Aligned with the CEFR levels are the *Diplôme d'études en langue française* (DELF) for French and *Diploma de estudios en lengua española* (DELE) for Spanish. These can also be used for assessing teacher proficiency. See additional information towards the end of this chapter.

Regarding the language proficiency of French immersion teachers in Canada, the Canadian Association of Immersion Professionals (ACPI, 2018) recently confirmed in its final report of a Canada-wide consultation that "no formal tests governing entry into the profession are systematically required" (p. 19). Moreover, given the continued growth of French immersion programs in Canada, which exceeds the number of qualified immersion teachers, ACPI also noted that "it is not uncommon for a school board to hire individuals who are not qualified teachers, are not immersion professionals, or do not speak French" (2018, p. 19). Because it can be so challenging to find qualified teachers having the necessary level of proficiency in the minority language in both the US and Canada, some school administrators compromise on teachers' language proficiency.

However, it's important not to compromise! When teachers have lower levels of proficiency it will be difficult for them to provide the necessary input and feedback that students need to develop proficiency in the minority language.

(!) SPECIAL NOTE

Administrators—it is important to hire teachers with high levels of proficiency. If your teachers lack proficiency it will be impossible for them to get students to develop high levels of proficiency in the minority language.

Teachers—it is your responsibility to maintain high levels of proficiency in the language(s) you use for instruction. Use the minority language as much as possible within and outside the school, read in that language, travel abroad to practice use of the language with others (as much as possible), etc.

Like program leaders, teachers also need to be knowledgeable about the ImDL program model and research base as well as ImDL-specific pedagogical practices. They must understand how ImDL education works and adhere to practices that align with program goals and principles. Fundamentally, high-quality teachers care about their students and are committed to ensuring their learning. They are also dedicated to continually improving their own proficiency in the minority language and acquiring knowledge about teaching and ImDL education specifically.

5. Sustained, ImDL-specific professional development

ImDL teachers are responsible for making academic content comprehensible to students who are learning through the medium of a second language while at the same time developing student proficiency and literacy in that language. ImDL teaching requires a unique knowledge base and pedagogical skill set (e.g., Cammarata & Tedick, 2012; Lyster, 2007; Tedick & Fortune, 2013), yet many ImDL teachers graduate from teacher preparation programs that do not prepare them specifically for ImDL contexts. Thus, continued professional development is critical for ImDL teachers, even those who have had some ImDL-specific preparation. In well-implemented ImDL programs, teachers are afforded opportunities for ImDL-specific professional development (Howard et al., 2018; Tedick & Fortune, 2013). Whenever possible, professional development should be sustained, as it is more likely to then become a part of teachers' daily practices (e.g., Dana, 2010). Professional development activities should engage teachers in reflection and critical thinking so that they can continuously examine and improve their classroom practices.

This book is designed to serve as a teacher preparation or professional development guide for ImDL teachers. It provides background to build teachers' ImDL knowledge base and illustrates a range of pedagogical practices that we hope will become part of their teaching repertoires, including the use of optimal input for acquisition, multiple opportunities for student output, and cooperative grouping strategies. In Chapter 10 we introduce a self-assessment rubric that can be used by teachers to assess their own performance and to challenge themselves to improve in specific areas in which they are lacking. The development of mastery in ImDL-specific pedagogical practices is a process that requires considerable time, practice, reflection, and feedback. To that end, this rubric can be used as a powerful professional development tool for practicing teachers.

6. Teacher collaboration

Research affirms that teacher collaboration has positive effects on teachers and student achievement: "Student achievement gains are greater in schools with stronger collaborative environments and in classrooms of teachers who are stronger collaborators" (Ronfeldt, Farmer, McQueen, & Grissom, 2015, p. 512). Collaboration among ImDL teachers is a strong sign of a well-implemented program and is important for a variety of reasons. For example, teachers share responsibility for instructional outcomes and student grouping when they plan collaboratively (Howard et al., 2018). Collaboration can help to ensure curricular coherence, particularly between the English and minority-language portions of the instructional day. Thomas and Collier (2017) identified teacher collaboration, specifically among partner teachers at the elementary level who teach the same group of students but through different languages (i.e., English and the non-English language), as a key feature of well-implemented programs, and emphasized the need for teachers to appreciate and value each other. When partner teachers collaborate thoughtfully, they have the potential to strengthen connections across languages and content areas. We illustrate how this can be done in Chapter 9.

Research on teacher collaboration specifically in ImDL contexts has been conducted for the most part at the elementary level. However, teacher collaboration at the secondary level is equally important, but might not necessarily involve collaboration between the language arts teachers of each program language, unless, of course, the ImDL students are indeed required to take language arts in both languages. An obstacle to collaboration at the secondary level stems from scheduling that does not necessarily place all ImDL in the same classes; this can be an obstacle because teacher collaboration benefits students the most when teachers of the same group of students are able to make links between their classes. However, in cases at the secondary level where the language arts teacher and a content teacher are teaching more or less the same group of ImDL students through the minority language, an ideal opportunity for teacher collaboration can be seized upon. For example, the language arts teacher can incorporate texts from a content area (e.g., history or science) to focus on from a language and discourse perspective rather than using texts unrelated to content areas. Moreover, the connections between a language arts class and a content class can be thematic rather than linguistic, in order to create curricular coherence and thus to serve as a source of motivation for students.

Here we provide an example of theme-based cross-curricular collaboration at the secondary level with a view to illustrating the potential links in a high-school French immersion program between content areas (science and history classes) and also language arts classes in both target languages (from Lyster, 2018). Thematic connections were proposed between novels studied in English-language arts and French-language arts—Charles Dickens's *A Tale of Two Cities* and Victor Hugo's *Les Misérables*—given that they were published at almost the same time (1859 and 1862, respectively). In the history class, students might study either the French revolution or the effects of 19th-century industrialization on social conditions. In the science class, the focus could be on the molecular forces at play behind the steam power that gave rise to the proliferation of factories during the industrial revolution. The coordination of such an integrated curriculum, of course, requires concerted efforts by all stakeholders, but the benefits for students' language development and content knowledge are promising.

Finally, teacher collaboration has also been found to be a key ingredient in effective professional development for ImDL teachers. In a study exploring ImDL teacher perceptions of the impact that ImDL-specific professional development experiences had on their practice, Tedick and Zilmer (2018) found that teacher collaboration was important in helping teachers to come to deeper understandings of concepts they were learning through professional development experiences.

Families and community

7. Family engagement

Parent involvement or engagement has been identified as one of the most crucial aspects influencing student achievement in schools (e.g., Henderson & Mapp, 2002). There is strong and growing evidence of the relationship between family engagement, school improvement, and increased student outcomes (Wood & Bauman, 2017). Parent engagement is "a school-community process designed to bring or construct an open relationship between school personnel and the parent community in support of the student's social and academic development" (Olivos, Ochoa, & Jiménez-Castellanos, 2011, p. 11). Engagement with minority-language families and communities is perceived as a powerful way to make schools more equitable, culturally responsive, and collaborative (e.g., Olivos, 2006). According to Olivos et al., engagement involves (a) building welcoming and trusting relationships; (b) building leadership skills; (c) creating spaces of belongingness and awareness of how to navigate the school system; and (d) promoting cultural, social, and linguistic diversity and inclusion (p. 11).

Engagement is two-way (initiated by both school personnel and parents), active, and ongoing. Thus, educators working in well-implemented ImDL programs intentionally build equitable and socially respectful relationships among students and families (and between educators and families). They ensure that families are engaged and informed and play integral roles in their children's education (Cloud et al., 2000; Howard et al., 2018).

Howard et al. (2018) and Shannon (2011) address the challenges that can arise in programs that serve children with different linguistic, cultural, and ethnic backgrounds and socioeconomic statuses. Studies have shown that high-status parents (typically middle to upper-middle class) tend to participate in the education of their children by exercising their privilege or "cultural capital" (Bourdieu, 1986), which refers to the social assets an individual has (level of education, style of speech and dress, etc.). In contrast, low-status parents often lack cultural capital and thus tend to defer to schools, to avoid direct involvement, and not to advocate for their children (e.g., Weininger & Lareau, 2003). The concept of cultural capital has been used in part to explain the school achievement disparities between certain groups of children. In her work with TWI programs, Shannon (2011) has found that this distinction between high- and low-status parents persists.

Different levels of parent/family engagement and issues related to equity among learners and families will likely emerge in TWI programs as well as any ImDL program that attracts a diverse student population. School leaders and teachers must be prepared to confront such issues head-on. Research affirms that schools can promote positive relationships between all families and the school, which, in turn, can lead to higher levels of engagement (e.g., National Academies of Sciences, Engineering, and Medicine, 2017). Howard et al. (2018) point to a number of strategies used by well-implemented ImDL programs to engage families, including the following:

- Approach families from a strength-based perspective; that is, understand that all families have many strengths to help their children, and show respect for parents' cultural and linguistic practices and customs.
- Provide a welcoming environment, for example by hiring bilingual staff, including in the front office, and being flexible in scheduling school meetings and events.
- Implement culturally and linguistically responsive services, such as translating materials and information into the languages spoken by families.
- Provide adult education programs to teach families how to support their children's development at home and give parents guidance about how to navigate the school system.
- Use technology such as texting to send families regular tips on supporting the language development of young children in their home languages.

Other strategies have also been identified. For example, Gareth Zehrbach (2006), former principal at Nuestro Mundo Community School (a two-way program) in Madison, Wisconsin, noticed that the Latinx, Spanish-speaking parents were not involved in meetings of the Site Leadership Council, a group formed to give parents a greater voice in school decision-making. School leaders decided to conduct meetings only in Spanish, and Zehrbach found the funds to purchase translating equipment to allow simultaneous translation into English. Once this shift occurred, Spanish-speaking parents' attendance at the meetings increased and they began to participate more. They reported feeling more at ease and appreciated efforts to include them. Moreover (and much to the surprise of the school leaders), there was no negative feedback from the monolingual English-speaking parents; instead, they responded positively. Creative solutions such as this one can have a profound impact on school-family relationships and can ensure that families have a voice in the educational process.

ImDL programs are also advised to have a designated bilingual family liaison who understands families' needs in the community and knows how to address these through family/parent education (Howard et al., 2018). The importance of establishing strong connections with ImDL families and engaging them as partners in supporting student learning cannot be overestimated. Educators who spend the time to forge these connections and partnerships are inevitably likely to see better outcomes when it comes to student engagement and achievement.

Curriculum and instruction

8. Integration of content, language, and culture in the curriculum

ImDL programs, by their very definition, are subject-matter-driven programs. They are responsible for teaching the regular school curriculum and meeting the same academic standards that have been set by the state or province. The curriculum must be developmentally appropriate and challenging for learners both cognitively and linguistically (e.g., Fortune & Tedick, 2008; Hamayan et al., 2013). There is much evidence from both research and teachers' daily experiences that the primary focus of ImDL programs is indeed on subject-matter content. Teachers and students are held accountable for teaching and learning the content through standardized testing and other measures; thus, content learning typically represents administrators' and parents' greatest concern.

The primacy of content learning in ImDL programs notwithstanding, to be effective as a language learning approach, well-implemented ImDL programs must also be language attentive. This means that there needs to be *systematic* attention to language development throughout the program. Research affirms that programs have greater difficulty in addressing language development (see Chapter 3). Language objectives should form an important part of curriculum planning (see Chapters 4 and 8). Oral and written language and literacy should be developed across the entire curriculum so that students can acquire the academic language related to the content and build both content knowledge and language proficiency across the curriculum (e.g., Hamayan et al., 2013; Howard et al., 2018; Lyster, 2007, 2016).

Just as content and language objectives are important drivers of ImDL curriculum, so too should cultural, intercultural, and/or cross-cultural objectives be considered essential to ImDL curriculum development (Hamayan et al., 2013; see also Chapter 8). This attends to the third goal, that of cultural competence. It should include many opportunities for students to learn about their own and other cultures in non-stereotyped ways and to develop a sense of their own and others' identities (e.g., Howard et al., 2018). This is especially important as ImDL programs increasingly enroll students from a range of socioeconomic, ethnic, racial, cultural, and linguistic groups. Many, if not most, Canadian and US schools tend to represent mainstream (often White, middle-class), Eurocentric cultural values and norms. Some teachers may be familiar with and proficient in these cultural frames, but less familiar with the specific cultural norms or orientations of their students. They must become familiar with their students' cultural characteristics, and, in so doing, they will enhance the efficacy of their instruction and their students' success (Cloud et al., 2000). One way to accomplish this is through *culturally responsive teaching*, which refers to an approach to pedagogy that acknowledges the importance of including students' cultural frames of reference in all aspects of their learning. Gay (2018) offers eight characteristics to describe culturally responsive teaching:

1. *Validating*—it affirms the prior experiences, cultural knowledge, performance styles, and frames of reference of diverse learners.
2. *Comprehensive and inclusive*—it develops "intellectual, social, emotional, and political learning by using cultural resources to teach knowledge, skills, values, and attitudes" (p. 38); it focuses on both minority and majority students, "but for different reasons and in different ways" (p. 39).
3. *Multidimensional*—it embodies curricular content, classroom climate, learning context, student-teacher relationships, instructional strategies, classroom management, and performance assessments.
4. *Empowering*—it supports students in being more successful learners and better human beings; teachers have high expectations and support students in reaching them, and students must believe they can succeed and be willing to work hard to achieve mastery.
5. *Transformative*—it "develops social consciousness, intellectual critique, and political and personal efficacy in students so that they can combat prejudices, racism, and other forms of oppression and exploitation" (p. 42).
6. *Emancipatory*—it releases students' learning from mainstream, Eurocentric ways of knowing and enables students to find their own voices and to become active participants in shaping their learning.

7. *Humanistic*—it promotes "being open, receptive, and respectful to the viewpoints, thoughts, experiences, and perceptions of self and others, including a willingness to critique them; learning from and relating to members of one's own and other cultures, races, ethnicities, and social classes; exploring and honoring the differences of self and others; recognizing that people view the world and life through different lenses; and actively promoting equality and social justice" (pp. 44–45).

8. *Normative and ethical*—it makes explicit how and why mainstream education is influenced by and representative of Eurocentric culture, perspectives, and experiences and emphasizes that incorporating cultural diversity into education for diverse students is "both the normal and the right thing to do" (p. 45).

Approaching ImDL teaching with a culturally responsive frame of reference can help students to develop strong ethnic or cultural identities and self-esteem. Feinauer and Howard (2014) assert that "a strong sense of one's own cultural identity is a first important step in developing intercultural sensitivities and cross-cultural competences" (p. 260). Thus, targeting identity development through culturally responsive teaching can help ImDL educators approach the third goal of ImDL education: cultural competence.

 TEACHER SPOTLIGHT

María Francisca Reines, a Grade 1 teacher in a DBE program in Minneapolis, engaged her Latinx learners in a very meaningful, culturally responsive activity. First, they read *"René tiene dos apellidos"* (*René Has Two Last Names*) by René Colato Laínez. It tells the story of a Salvadoran boy who comes to the US. To shorten his name, his teacher removes one of his two last names. After discussing the book and naming conventions in Latin America and among Latinos in the US, Francisca and her students co-constructed a rap to the tune of "In my feelings—Kiki, do you love me" by Canadian rap artist, Drake. The lyrics to their rap are below.

Oye, soy latino	Hey, I'm Latino
tengo dos apellidos	I have two last names
nunca, nunca me los quites	Never, never take them away from me
Uno es de mi papi	One is my dad's
y el otro	and the other
el otro es de mi mami	the other is my mom's

While holding up signs with their names, Francisca's class shared the book and performed their rap song in front of the whole school and their families during a school-wide assembly.

Published curricula and other materials that are purchased for ImDL programs do not typically integrate content, language, and culture. Teachers need specific guidance in how to create curriculum units and instructional sequences to do just that (see subsequent chapters). Well-implemented ImDL programs ensure that the curriculum is designed to represent all three program goals by integrating content, language, and culture.

9. Language arts and literacy instruction in both languages

Well-implemented ImDL programs provide high-quality language arts and literacy instruction in *both* languages. Students need intensive instruction in literacy and content areas to develop high levels of biliteracy. Reinforcement of content and literacy concepts across languages ensures vocabulary development and concept understanding at deeper levels. Although offering high-quality language arts and literacy instruction in both languages seems straightforward on the surface, it can be challenging to implement given time limitations and lack of minority-language resources and materials. For example, 50:50 programs divide instructional time evenly between the two languages. Given the need to teach all components of the regular school curriculum (mathematics, science, social studies, language arts, and literacy) as well as specialized areas (art, computers and media, music, and physical education), it can be difficult to set aside sufficient time for high-quality literacy and language arts instruction in both languages. In the 50:50 "Utah model," which is being implemented in a number of states in the US, only 15% of instructional time is devoted to minority-language literacy and language arts instruction in Grades 1–3, whereas 35% is devoted to literacy and language arts instruction in English (Utah Dual Language Immersion, 2018). Instructional time allocation improves for Grades 4–6, in which 25% of the time is dedicated to literacy and language arts instruction in each language. This model has limitations, because language arts and literacy instruction deserve equal instructional time in each language throughout the program.

In ImDL secondary continuation programs, language arts instruction is often provided by teachers who were prepared as foreign-language teachers. It is important that they learn how to work effectively with ImDL students. They need to embed their language arts and literacy instruction within meaningful content, and avoid teaching language arts or grammar in a decontextualized way. We provide frameworks for doing so in Chapters 4, 7, and 8.

Lack of high-quality minority-language resources and materials can lead programs to devote more instructional time to literacy and language arts instruction in English. Well-implemented programs spend the time, money, and effort to equip teachers with materials (texts, videos, audio-recordings, computer software, games, etc.) in the minority language. This certainly presents a challenge for indigenous languages and other languages, such as Hmong, for which materials and resources are very limited. Efforts must be devoted to developing materials for programs in these languages—through appropriation of grant funds to support such endeavors and organization of curriculum development projects, such as the Yup'ik language and cultural materials development project described briefly in Chapter 1.

Ideally, literacy and language arts lessons in the minority language and majority language should be related. In other words, teachers in well-implemented programs understand that biliteracy development is fundamentally different from developing literacy in just one language, and they take this into account during curriculum planning, instruction, and assessment. Through teacher collaboration and other approaches, they help learners make connections across languages and make frequent cross-lingual comparisons. They observe how students' literacy development in one language is related to their development in the other and approach instruction from this perspective. We return to this topic and describe a range of biliteracy instructional strategies in Chapter 9.

10. Language status and equity

ImDL programs that are well implemented view all instructional languages and speakers of different languages as having equal status and adopt practices to promote this stance. In the US and parts of Canada, however, where the English language and Anglo-European culture are associated with high status, other languages and cultures are systematically attributed a lower status, even though such differences in status between languages are socially constructed and do not exist "in any absolute sense" (Cloud et al., 2000, p. 21). There are powerful and hidden forces at play within the community, school, and classrooms that can undermine the value and importance of the minority language. Some institutional practices—such as decisions leading to program design and assessment strategies that favor English—risk communicating to students that English matters more. "The power of English as the dominant language in US society [and in parts of Canada] and its immediately perceived economic, educational, and political benefits [are] difficult to counter and [require] constant vigilance about issues related to linguistic equity" (de Jong, 2011, p. 211).

At the classroom level, some teachers may convey low expectations for the quantity and quality of student minority-language use. Still other teachers may express negative attitudes toward minority-language students' use of non-standard language varieties of their home language; in these cases, students will feel insecure about their home language and may opt for English instead if its use seems less likely to be negatively judged. In this regard, even though learning the standard varieties of both languages of instruction is the ultimate goal of ImDL programs, teachers need to embrace non-standard varieties as intrinsic to students' identities and thus their self-esteem. Non-standard varieties also serve as essential resources in students' literacy development, as they gain awareness of the differences between varieties, moving toward the standard variety for school-based literacy practices while maintaining the non-standard variety for home and social purposes. It is important for minority-language students who speak a non-standard variety to reap the benefits not only of bilingualism in both school languages but also of their "bidialectalism" in the minority language. ImDL programs are well suited to developing students' appreciation of linguistic diversity. Andersson and Trudgill (1990, p. 179) characterized language variation as a rich topic for class discussion with far-reaching benefits:

> Most children are already very aware of language variety and language attitudes when they come to school, and they find it a fascinating topic for classroom discussion. Teachers who are prepared to take an open-minded, unprejudiced attitude towards the varieties of language spoken by their pupils will be the ones who also succeed best in fostering and developing children's linguistic interests and abilities.

Studies have demonstrated how minority languages can be devalued in ImDL and other school programs. Heller (1996) found that only standard forms of French and English were accepted in a French language minority high school in Toronto where Franco-Ontarian students struggled with the stigmatization of their language variety, with many hoping to be transferred to an English-medium school. Similarly, in a TWI Grade 6 language arts classroom in Texas the teacher did not accept non-standard varieties of Spanish. Students "did not understand why their form of Spanish was unacceptable in the classroom and preferred to use English to avoid being corrected" (McCollum, 1999, p. 123). Hernández (2015) reported that the low status of Spanish relative to English in two 90:10 TWI programs in southern California led to (a) all students preferring to use English even during instructional time in Spanish, (b) English-speaking students dominating conversations when interacting with Spanish speakers in small groups, and (c) Spanish speakers conforming to English when English speakers shifted to English during interaction. Furthermore, Hernández observed and teachers confirmed that:

- There was tension between Spanish and English speakers, particularly in upper grades, where they lacked respect for each other and English speakers refused to work with Spanish speakers.
- Teachers permitted students to engage in a great deal of code-switching (often privileging English).
- The school district emphasized English with their focus on English instruction and standardized test results.
- Upper-grade Spanish materials were typically far too complex for both groups of learners—they lacked sufficient proficiency in Spanish to extract meaning from the texts.

Results from these studies are troubling. It is imperative for ImDL educators to counter these societal and educational realities by engaging in specific strategies to equalize the status of two languages and cultures within the program and individual classrooms. A number of educators and scholars have offered a wealth of ideas for equalizing the status of the two languages in ImDL programs. In Tables 2.1 and 2.2 we list several of the ideas that have been shared by Fortune and Tedick (2003), Hernández (2015), Unger (2001), and others. Ideas are offered for both administrators (Table 2.1) and teachers (Table 2.2).

TABLE 2.1 Administrator strategies for equalizing the status of the minority language in ImDL programs

- Do not compromise on teacher language proficiency! Hire teachers who are highly proficient in the minority language, and, as much as possible, make hiring choices to expose students to varieties of the language from different geographic locations.
- Purchase and/or develop high-quality materials in the minority language and ensure that the media center/library is stocked with a robust collection of minority-language books, videos, posters, music, etc.
- Ensure that the program includes standardized testing in the minority language whenever possible (not just English); both students' academic achievement and proficiency in the minority language should be assessed systematically and consistently.
- Ensure that the program's mission statement includes support for the minority language/culture.
- Determine a time in the program (e.g., January, Grade 1 or before) when the program officially recognizes and celebrates students' initiation and membership into the "minority-language speaking community" of the school.
- Privilege the minority language throughout the single-track school through signage, a strong website presence, etc. (for example, post signs in the minority language only and provide visitors with a handout of translations as needed); find ways to privilege the minority language in dual-track programs (a strong website presence, a separate "wing" for the ImDL program, etc., teaching the whole school a minority language or cultural practice such as a "word of the week").
- Conduct whole-school activities in the minority language (public address announcements, special assemblies, award ceremonies, and parent and staff meetings [providing simultaneous translation]).
- Educate parents about the positive benefits of being bilingual and teach them ways to support students' home language development (e.g., reading to their child in the home language) and development in the minority language (e.g., listening to their child read in the minority language).
- Adopt a "language use charter" for the program that stipulates expectations for minority-language use (e.g., the expectation that bilingual teachers will model use of the minority language within the school).
- Ensure that all communications sent home are provided in both program languages (particularly for TWI and DBE programs).
- Increase awareness of the subtle ways that the minority language can be devalued.

TABLE 2.2 Teacher strategies for equalizing the status of the minority language in ImDL programs

- Continuously work on your proficiency to ensure that you are exposing students to optimal input.
- Maintain high expectations for the quantity and quality of the minority language that students produce.
- Expect students to show different strengths in both their languages and avoid seeing minority-language or other students from a "deficit" perspective.
- Embrace students' non-standard language varieties as valuable and appropriate in some contexts and expand on these repertoires so that they come to include more standardized forms of the minority and majority languages.
- Be careful not to place minority-language speakers in "service" or interpreter roles for English speakers (see Valdés, 1997).
- Elevate the status of the minority language in the classroom by inviting guest speakers from minority-language speaking communities, exposing students to the minority language on an international level (as far as possible), and connecting to minority-language social media or Internet projects
- Develop lessons and activities that both assess and proactively address perceptions and attitudes about the minority language.
- Maintain clear and separate spaces for the instructional languages, and consistently expect students to use the minority language during instructional time in that language (as developmentally appropriate).
- Assess and report on minority-language growth systematically and with consistency in formal and informal ways.
- Provide parents with regular updates on their child's academic and linguistic development, including feedback on their child's use of the minority language in the classroom, and invite their support of this.
- Establish and maintain ongoing connections with "sister schools."
- In TWI programs, differentiate language objectives for L1 speakers and L2 learners of the minority language to ensure that L1 speakers are consistently being challenged to grow their proficiency.
- Showcase student work in the minority language throughout the school and in the community.
- Increase awareness of the subtle ways that the minority language can be devalued.

 TEACHER SPOTLIGHT

Language commitment contract

To increase the status of Spanish and to encourage student use of Spanish at all times during Spanish instructional time, Spanish immersion teachers at Minnewashta Elementary School in Minnetonka, Minnesota, have their students sign a pledge to speak only in Spanish. The pledge was developed by a team of teachers and shared by Kirsten Rue. Written only in Spanish for the students, the pledge is also signed by students' parents and the teacher.

> *Prometo hablar en español en nuestro salón*
> *en cada momento y con cada persona,*
> *cuando sea fácil, cuando sea difícil,*
> *cuando me divierto y cuando trabajo.*
> *Prometo ser un buen ejemplo y ayudar a los demás.*
> *Pues, sé que cuanto más practico, más aprendo.*
> *¡Español, eh!*
>
> [I promise to speak in Spanish in our classroom
> at every moment and with every person,
> when it's easy, when it's difficult,
> when I'm having fun and when I'm working.
> I promise to set a good example and help others.
> I know that the more I practice, the more I'll learn.
> Spanish, eh!]

In sum, issues related to language status are critically important in ImDL classrooms. Educators need to be hyper-aware of how both languages are being positioned in the program and need to incorporate strategies to privilege the minority language as much as possible. Cloud et al. (2000) sum up this issue as follows:

> The status of the two languages being learned and of the cultures associated with those languages is important for creating additive bilingual environments in [ImDL] programs. … *If educators behave, explicitly or implicitly, in ways that favor English and Anglo-European culture, they undermine students' motivation to learn the other language which, in turn, reduces program effectiveness.* The same is true for cultural aspects of the program. (p. 21, italics added)

11. Separate instructional spaces for program languages

As should be clear from the previous section, by definition, a minority language does not share equal status with English in societies where English is the majority language. A tried and tested way for ImDL programs to mitigate this imbalance is to maintain separate instructional spaces for both program languages in order to protect and to expect use of the minority language in at least one of them. It is important to note that maintaining separate spaces for each instructional language does not involve attempts to keep the languages separate in the students' minds. Indeed, students will naturally rely on the linguistic resources that they have at their disposal even when expected to use one language or the other. Moreover, this practice does not preclude cross-linguistic pedagogy. On the contrary, we advocate cross-lingual connections while maintaining separate spaces for each language, as we illustrate throughout this book.

Since their inception, ImDL programs have created such separate instructional spaces for ImDL teachers and students to use the minority language exclusively and consistently. Describing (one-way) Canadian French immersion programs, Lambert (1984) explained: "From the first encounter immersion teachers use only the target language" (p. 11). Similarly, among four defining characteristics of TWI programs, Lindholm (1987) stipulated "periods of instruction during which only one language is used" (p. 5). She pinpointed sustained monolingual lesson delivery as an essential factor for supporting program effectiveness, as it was an instructional practice known to promote language acquisition better than "language mixing" (p. 6).

Thus, establishing minority-language spaces (by teacher, time of day, subject area, or classroom context) has long been a program design strategy used in both Canadian and US ImDL programs. From the beginning of the program, students are encouraged to use the minority language as much as possible, with the understanding that they can and will use English until they have sufficient exposure to and some ability to use the minority language. In two-way programs the same applies for minority-language speakers during instructional time in English; in other words, they will use their home language during English instructional time until they are able to use English. It is important to note that although the primary goal is to use approaches in ImDL contexts to encourage students' extensive minority-language use, exceptions can and will arise. For example, if a child becomes injured or is having an emotional crisis, it is imperative for the teacher to accept and use the language that is most comforting and familiar to the child. Moreover, it is never acceptable for a teacher to punish a child for using English. Teachers must use their best judgment and knowledge of the child to encourage use of the minority language in ways that are not off-putting or harmful to the child's affect. Such exceptions notwithstanding, establishing and maintaining separate spaces for program languages in ImDL programs is considered a "non-negotiable" by many (e.g., Ballinger, Lyster, Sterzuk, & Genesee, 2017; Fortune & Tedick, 2008, 2019; Thomas & Collier, 2012).

Nevertheless, strict adherence to maintaining separate spaces for each program language in ImDL programs has been under debate in recent decades. In this section, we describe some of the theory and research that has brought this practice into question and then offer a rationale for maintaining this key principle in ImDL classrooms.

There are relatively new theoretical arguments about what language is and how bilinguals process, develop, and communicate in their languages. Languages are seen as dynamic, inter-related, and interactive systems of meaning making. It is now perceived as beneficial, possibly even essential, for bi- or multilingual individuals to exploit the relationship between and among their languages. Against this backdrop, scholars have begun to promote the use of "translanguaging" in ImDL and other classrooms, particularly those serving minority-language students. Translanguaging is the use of two or more languages to construct meaning, shape experience, and develop understanding and knowledge

(Baker & Wright, 2017; García, 2009). It reflects the idea that an individual's whole linguistic repertoire functions as one integrated system. In other words, the theory holds that the two languages of a bilingual are not separate linguistic systems but, rather, one unified system. Bilinguals have *one* lexicon, *one* phonology, and *one* morphosyntactic system, and they select from this single system based on the communicative needs they have (García, 2009; García & Li Wei, 2014; Otheguy, García, & Reid, 2015). It should be noted, however, that this notion has been critiqued by some scholars. Notably, MacSwan (2017) has posited an "integrated multilingual model," arguing that multilinguals have both shared and discrete grammatical resources.

 KEY CONCEPT

Translanguaging refers to bilinguals' or multilinguals' complex and strategic ways of using two or more languages to make meaning, gain understanding and knowledge, and shape experience.

 RESEARCH REPORT

The origins of "translanguaging"

The concept of "translanguaging" derives originally from the work of Cen Williams, a Welsh teacher educator. In the 1980s he used the term *traws-ieithu* in Welsh to describe a pedagogical strategy; namely, the planned, systematic use of two languages for teaching and learning within a lesson in Welsh-English bilingual programs in Wales (Williams, 1996). It was observed in and recommended for use in *secondary-level* classrooms. It entailed teachers providing subject-matter input in one language (English) and then requiring pupils to produce output in the other language (Welsh). The idea was to help students to take up deeper, more complex processing of information and to push them to develop more cognitively complex ideas in the weaker language (often Welsh). Williams (2002) maintained that

> translanguaging is more appropriate for children who have a reasonably good grasp of both languages, and may not be valuable in a classroom when children are in the early stages of learning and developing their second language. It is a strategy for retaining and developing bilingualism rather than for the initial teaching of the second language.
>
> *(Lewis, Jones, & Baker, 2012, p. 644)*

The term "translanguaging" was borrowed from Williams, and its meaning was changed and expanded by US scholars, notably García (2009). Since then, translanguaging as theory, pedagogy, and practice has taken the fields of applied linguistics and language education by storm. There are countless books, chapters, and articles on this topic, and a growing number of research studies, although none, to our knowledge, show that translanguaging advances minority-language development in ImDL classrooms.

Translanguaging proponents argue that because translanguaging is a typical social practice among bilinguals, it should be encouraged and capitalized on in ImDL classrooms. Many contend that maintaining separate spaces for instructional languages represents a monolingual bias that doesn't accurately reflect the dynamic nature of bilingualism (e.g., García, 2009; Palmer & Martínez, 2013; Sánchez, García, & Solorza, 2018). Thus, they argue that translanguaging theory and translanguaging practice among bilinguals should be translated into translanguaging pedagogies.

Much of the North American literature on translanguaging focuses on minority-language students learning in situations where their language use practices are marginalized in school or society (Fortune & Tedick, 2019). It emphasizes the importance of supporting these students' bilingual identities and socioemotional well-being and also the promotion of educational equity and social justice through schooling. On a number of important theoretical points, we agree with translanguaging advocates (see Ballinger et al., 2017; Fortune & Tedick, 2019). We agree, for example, that:

- Bilinguals are not two monolinguals in one.
- Languages are not completely discrete systems but, rather, overlap and evolve over time and with contact.
- Bilingualism is an asset to be nurtured and developed in schools.
- A bilingual's two languages are always available irrespective of their use of one language or the other at any given moment.
- Code-switching is a normal, highly rule-governed language use practice among bi- or multilinguals.
- Welcoming children's languages (including their non-standard linguistic varieties) in classroom settings is important, as it affirms their linguistic and cultural identities.
- Cross-linguistic comparisons and connections facilitate the development of bilingualism and biliteracy and are an important component of ImDL teaching and learning.

Despite our agreement with translanguaging advocates on the theoretical points listed above, we question how this theory gets translated to classroom pedagogy in ImDL contexts. A number of scholars have published papers and books promoting the use of translanguaging pedagogies and providing guidance in how to effectively implement them in ImDL classrooms and other settings (e.g., García,

Johnson, & Seltzer, 2017; Sánchez et al., 2018). Others have lauded teachers' and students' translanguaging practices observed in studies conducted in bilingual and TWI classrooms (e.g., García, 2011; García-Mateus & Palmer, 2017; Hamman, 2018; Palmer, Martínez, Mateus, & Henderson, 2014). Such practices include teachers' use of language mixing and concurrent translation and student use of whichever language they prefer during classroom instruction. We wonder if such practices and pedagogies are wise, particularly when it comes to minority-language development in ImDL programs in contexts where English is the societal majority language. We also find that ImDL educators are confused by the support for translanguaging that is so prevalent in the literature, at conferences, and, increasingly, in professional development offerings.

Therefore, we raise concerns about the use of the majority language (English) during instructional time in the minority language in ImDL classrooms. In English-dominant contexts such as those in the US and many parts of Canada, the high status of English as a societal majority language and global language makes development of a minority language challenging for all learners. Therefore, we offer a number of counter-arguments to translanguaging pedagogies:

1. Based on decades of research on the academic achievement and language proficiency outcomes of ImDL students, there is strong support for ImDL programs that have historically created separate spaces for instructional languages (e.g., Burkhauser et al., 2016; Lindholm-Leary & Genesee, 2014, for review; Steele et al., 2017).
2. Research in the 1970s and 1980s that compared outcomes from bilingual kindergarten classrooms maintaining separate spaces for instructional languages with those engaging in concurrent translation and other language mixing reported that those maintaining separate spaces had more equitable distribution of languages (Legaretta, 1977) and greater gains in L2 oral comprehension and communicative competence in both L1 (Spanish) and L2 (English) (Legaretta, 1979), and promoted greater L2 learning (Wong-Fillmore, 1982). See Fortune and Tedick (2019) for discussion.
3. Despite the fact that ImDL students develop relatively high levels of minority-language proficiency, there are significant shortcomings in their linguistic development (see Chapters 1 and 3). Canadian studies have revealed limitations in the French L2 proficiency of majority-language immersion students (see Lyster, 2007, for review). Similarly, US research has reported underdeveloped minority-language proficiency for majority-language ImDL students (e.g., Burkhauser et al., 2016; Fortune & Ju, 2017; Tedick & Young, 2016). Studies have also reported underdeveloped minority-language proficiency among minority-language students (Spanish speakers) in TWI programs (e.g., Potowski, 2004; Tedick & Young, 2016) as well as a shift in language dominance to English (Fortune, 2001). It is unlikely that increased use of English through translanguaging will improve the minority-language proficiency outcomes among ImDL students.

4. Studies have reported a plateau effect in L2 proficiency by upper elementary grades (Fortune & Tedick, 2015; Hart, Lapkin, & Swain, 1991) and difficulty for students to exceed upper-intermediate levels by Grade 8 (Burkhauser et al., 2016). Again, increased use of English through translanguaging is not likely to erase this plateau effect.

5. Studies have shown that, regardless of home language background, ImDL students prefer using English (e.g., Ballinger & Lyster, 2011; Fortune, 2001; Harley, 1992; Hernández, 2015; Potowski, 2004), and their preference for English increases as they advance in grade level. Ballinger et al. (2017) suggest that "there may be a link between increased English use and slowed rates of minority-language development [i.e., the plateau effect]" (p. 42). The status of English as the majority global language may be strongly linked to students' motivation to use English (Ballinger et al., 2017; Hernández, 2015).

6. A key feature of ImDL programs is that they offer overt support for continued development and maintenance of English. Research on the English-language development of ImDL students suggests that there is already sufficient time devoted to majority-language (English) instruction in ImDL programs.

7. Second language acquisition research has long established that learners need extensive input in and practice using the minority language if they are to achieve high levels of proficiency (Ballinger et al., 2017).

8. ImDL programs are based on the premise that teachers adapt instruction and modify their language in ways that support students as they learn subject matter through a language they know only partially (Ballinger et al., 2017). Because ImDL teachers have at their disposal a wide range of such scaffolding strategies (see Chapter 5), they do not need to rely on use of the majority language as a scaffold during minority-language instruction.

9. In the context of French immersion in Canada, Ballinger et al. (2017) argued that, "when learners are encouraged to draw on features from the majority language during class time allocated to the minority language, this practice can replicate, rather than resolve, an existing societal language imbalance" (p. 46). Indeed, in a recent study in a Grade 2 two-way classroom, Hamman (2018) observed:

> the practice of engaging in translanguaging was not equally distributed across students or across languages. This unequal distribution impacted how students were positioned in the classroom, particularly in relation to their academic and linguistic expertise, and generated a more English-centered classroom. (p. 37)

Hamman observed far fewer examples of students using Spanish during instructional time in English than the other way around.

10. There is a fundamental lack of empirical evidence showing that increased use of English during minority-language instructional time will benefit students' minority-language development or bilingual proficiency (Ballinger et al., 2017; Fortune & Tedick, 2019).

Many of the research findings reported above run counter to the idea that inviting more use of the majority language (English) during minority-language instructional time in ImDL classrooms will lead to greater proficiency in the minority language (Fortune & Tedick, 2019). Translanguaging theory has merit, and we support attempts to identify pedagogical approaches to help bilingual learners make connections between and among their languages. Yet, we raise questions about how to enact this support pedagogically and whether translanguaging practices and pedagogies are appropriate for all bilingual learners in every program context. The high status in the US and Canada of English as a societal majority language and as a global language makes the development of minority languages challenging—for both minority- and majority-language learners. Thus, we concur with Ballinger et al. (2017) in concluding that, "until empirical evidence supports increased use of English in [ImDL classrooms], crosslinguistic approaches that maintain a separate space for the majority language may represent ideal pedagogical practices in these contexts" (p. 32). Well-implemented programs maintain separate space for the minority language while simultaneously incorporating ways to forge cross-lingual connections. A number of cross-linguistic approaches that adhere to language separation in ImDL classrooms have been found to be successful in supporting students' minority-language development. These are described in detail in Chapter 9.

Assessment and accountability

12. Program-level achievement testing in both languages

Well-implemented programs are committed to selecting valid and reliable instruments to assess student achievement in both languages (Howard et al., 2018; Thomas & Collier, 2017). Programs should rely on a wide range of data sources for program evaluation and improvement (Howard et al., 2018). Distributing such assessments allows the program to engage in continuous evaluation of academic achievement outcomes. It is important for assessment to occur in both program languages. As research has reported, there may be a lag in reading and language arts achievement in English in early, total one-way immersion programs for majority-language learners because there is no formal literacy and language arts instruction in English in the early years of the program. Assessing students' achievement in the program's minority language provides a way to inform parents, administrators, and school district leaders how students are performing in the primary language of instruction. If a child is at grade level in the minority language, we can predict that he or she will be at grade level in English after English has been formally introduced in the curriculum. This outcome has been reported in previous research (e.g., Genesee, 1987).

Likewise, research has shown that minority-language students in two-way and developmental bilingual programs begin to perform like average English L1 students on reading by Grades 5–7. This means that their reading scores in English are likely to be below average for most of the elementary years of the program. Thus, when assessments are also offered in the minority language, and students are performing at grade level in that language, we can predict (based on previous research findings and their performance in the minority language) that eventually they will catch up to their English-speaking peers (e.g., Thomas & Collier, 2012). Without assessment data in the minority language, programs may have more difficulty convincing school district leaders that the program is effective. They may be pressured to introduce more English earlier in the program or to eliminate the ImDL program altogether (Lindholm-Leary, 2012). Additionally, some have argued that if minority-language students cannot show their academic knowledge on tests due to their limited proficiency in English, the test results are invalid because the tests cannot accurately demonstrate what the students know (Howard et al., 2018). It should also be emphasized that student performance on standardized achievement measures should only form part of an overall picture of program effectiveness.

13. Program-level assessment of minority-language development

ImDL programs that are well implemented have a systematic process in place to assess and report student progress in their development of the minority language. This is the case for their English-language development, which is assessed through standardized reading, writing, and language arts assessments. In addition, in the US, many school districts require a separate annual assessment of English-language proficiency for all minority-language students, including those enrolled in ImDL programs. Students' development of the minority language, however, is often neglected in ImDL programs.

In Canada, many French immersion students are opting to have their French-language proficiency assessed by means of the DELF, but this is done on a voluntary basis. The examinations for the DELF are often administered by school boards or provincial ministries. The actual diplomas are issued by the French Ministry for National Education in France and are recognized internationally. The different proficiency levels are based on the previously mentioned CEFR. See Rehner (2018) for a report on how the DELF and CEFR are having a positive impact on teachers' classroom practices. As mentioned earlier, a similar measure, the DELE, is available in Spanish. See *Resources for Readers* at the end of the chapter.

In the US, the Center for Applied Linguistics (CAL) has developed instruments that are designed to assess students' oral language proficiency: for example, the Early Language Listening and Oral Proficiency Assessment (ELLOPA) (preK–Grade 2), the Student Oral Proficiency Assessment (SOPA) (Grades K–8), and the CAL Oral Proficiency Exam (designed specifically for Grade 5–8 ImDL programs). These assessments are available in Chinese, English, French, German, Japanese, Russian, and Spanish. They entail having a trained interviewer who interviews pairs of students with a set of pre-determined tasks that increase in difficulty. The tasks can be modified to align with the curriculum of specific programs (see Fortune & Tedick, 2015, for detailed description of the assessment tools). CAL offers on-site workshops on how to use these assessments, so teachers and other school staff can be trained to administer the assessments and rate students' oral proficiency using provided rubrics reliably. CAL is also currently developing a web-based course for assessing children's Chinese-language development using the SOPA. It's important to understand that it is not necessary to assess the oral proficiency of every student in the program each year. ImDL programs should develop a systematic approach to oral language assessment. For example, the oral proficiency of a representative sample of students in Grades K, 2, and 4 might be assessed in the middle of the year and again at the end of the year. What's important is that the program is able to gauge the progress students are making in their oral minority-language development to inform classroom instruction and program-level policies and practices.

Some ImDL programs have used other assessments, such as the STAMP 4Se (Standards-Based Measure of Proficiency), which assesses student proficiency in the four modalities—listening, speaking, reading, and writing. It is available in 11 languages from Avant Assessment. Another assessment, developed by ACTFL, is the AAPPL (ACTFL Assessment of Performance Toward Proficiency in Languages). The AAPPL assesses student performance in relationship to the three communicative modes (interpersonal speaking and listening, presentational writing, and interpretive listening and reading) (see Chapters 7 and 10 for more description of the communicative modes). It is available in 13 languages and is designed for foreign-language students in Grades 5–12. ACTFL claims that the interpersonal speaking and listening portion may also be appropriate for ImDL students in earlier primary grades. It should be noted that these measures were designed for students learning languages in non-immersion foreign-language programs. Howard et al. (2018) maintain that ImDL assessments should test content and literacy in the minority language "rather than testing world language objectives" (p. 74). Indeed, assessment of ImDL students' minority-language proficiency should be aligned with the goals of ImDL programs. ImDL students learn language through learning the regular school curriculum. Therefore, they may be less likely to be able to demonstrate how well they can use language if tasks focus on typical foreign-language curricular content.

Escamilla and colleagues (2014) make the case for using parallel measures in program languages to assess biliteracy development. For reading, they specifically recommend two assessments developed by Celebration Press: the *evaluación del desarrollo de la lectura* (EDL2) for Spanish and the developmental reading assessment (DRA2) for English. Both assessments measure comparable reading behaviors in the areas of reading engagement, oral reading fluency, accuracy, and comprehension. For writing they recommend a "side-by-side" approach. Students write essays on similar (but not the same) topics in each language, and teachers are taught to look at student writing in both languages side by side so as to be able to get a more complete picture of how students are developing their writing skills across both their languages.

14. Classroom-level assessment of student performance

In well-implemented programs, classroom-level assessments are integrated to examine student performance in relationship to content, language, and culture objectives (Cloud et al., 2000; Hamayan et al., 2013). Teachers should use a combination of formative and summative as well as informal and formal assessment strategies to gather information about student learning of content and culture as well as their development of the minority language. In particular, teachers should emphasize performance assessment to examine students' language development. In Chapter 10 we introduce an especially powerful performance assessment, which involves three integrated tasks that assess students' content knowledge and language development concurrently.

Cloud et al. (2000, pp. 141–144) maintain that effective classroom-based assessment is

- linked to instructional objectives and methods;
- designed to optimize student performance;
- developmentally appropriate;
- based on performance criteria that are clearly defined and communicated to students;
- authentic;
- ongoing;
- planned.

Teachers should share classroom assessment results on a frequent basis with parents and partner teachers so that student learning and progress are monitored and so that students' successes can be celebrated.

Summary

In this chapter, we described what characterizes well-implemented programs. We discussed in detail 14 characteristics in five categories (see Figure 2.1). In the following chapter, we make an argument for integrating a stronger focus on the minority language across the ImDL curriculum and introduce key features of counterbalanced instruction, the pedagogical framework that guides this book.

Application activity 1

Explore issues related to language status in your program. In what ways is English or the minority/partner language privileged or not? Take pictures of signage, resources in the media center, screenshots of your school's website, etc. to support your observations. Develop a set of recommendations for enhancing the status of the minority language in the school/program environment. This might be presented in a PowerPoint® presentation that could be used for staff development or at a meeting with administrators. To prepare for this activity, read *"Equalizing the status of both languages in a dual immersion school"* by Megan Unger, a Grade 1 TWI teacher in Minneapolis: http://carla.umn.edu/immersion/acie/vol5/Nov2001_EqualStatus.html.

 Application activity 2

Consider the characteristics that we've described for well-implemented programs. How does your program measure up against these characteristics? What is your program doing well? What areas need improvement? First, consider what you can do at the classroom level. Then consider the areas that need program-level attention. Choose one or more of those areas and develop a set of action steps you would recommend to program leaders and your teaching colleagues. Share them with your principal and try to lobby for change. For example, if your program is not currently assessing student proficiency in the minority language, take some time to explore various assessment tools and recommend two or three tools to your principal with a clear rationale for choosing it and details about what it might cost and what the process would entail.

 Online resources for readers

Program leadership and design

Program design

See the updated 2018 *Guiding Principles for Dual Language Education.* This set of guiding principles can be purchased or downloaded for free: www.cal.org/twi/guidingprinciples.htm

Commitment to student diversity and equity

At the Center for Advanced Research on Language Acquisition (CARLA) website there are some excellent resources related to struggling learners in ImDL programs: http://carla.umn.edu/immersion/learners.html

Teachers

Teacher collaboration

The Edutopia website offers excellent tips for teacher collaboration: www.edutopia.org/
practice/teacher-collaboration-matching-complementary-strengths

Families and community

Family engagement

Working Together: School, Family & Community Partnerships—this website was developed
as a toolkit for New Mexico school communities and provides a wealth of resources
designed to strengthen connections between schools, families, and communities as
they work together in partnerships to support student success across all grade levels:
www.cesdp.nmhu.edu/toolkit/index.asp

The University of Minnesota *Dual Language and Immersion Family Education* project includes
a series of four workshops for ImDL parents and families that were developed to
educate, engage, and empower families in order to enrich the educational experience
of ImDL learners. They were designed specifically for TWI and developmental
bilingual education (DBE) programs (programs enrolling minority-language
students) but can be adapted for other ImDL models. Workshop materials for parent
educators and additional family resources (provided in English, Hmong, and Spanish)
are available at the site: http://carla.umn.edu/immersion/parentinfo/index.html

The archives of CARLA's *ACIE Newsletter* provide some excellent "Points for Parents"
and "Best Practices" articles showcasing ideas on how to engage parents and families
in ImDL programs: http://carla.umn.edu/immersion/acie/#bp

Curriculum and instruction

Integration of content, language, and culture

CARLA's *CoBaLTT website* provides fully developed units and lessons (some for ImDL)
that integrate content, language, and culture: http://carla.umn.edu/cobaltt/lesson
plans/search.php

Language status and equity

The *Teaching Tolerance* website offers many classroom activities and materials to support
multicultural education: www.tolerance.org/

Culture for Kids is a terrific resource to support multicultural learning experiences for
children: www.cultureforkids.com/

Assessment and accountability

Proficiency testing

ACTFL Oral Proficiency Interview: www.actfl.org/professional-development/assess
ments-the-actfl-testing-office/oral-proficiency-assessments-including-opi-opic
DELF for French: www.delfdalf.fr/index-en.html
DELE for Spanish: www.dele.org/

Student achievement testing

Some achievement tests are available in Spanish in the US, such as *Logramos* or *Aprenda 3*.

Logramos Tercera Edición parallels the scope and sequence of the Iowa Assessments. It measures achievement in Spanish in reading, language, and mathematics (Grades K–8) as well as science and social studies (Grades 1–8): www.riversideinsights.com/solutions/logramos-tercera-edicion?tab=0

Aprenda 3 offers assessment of reading, mathematics, language, spelling, listening comprehension, science, and social science: www.pearsonassessments.com (enter "Aprenda 3" in the search bar)

Minority-language assessments for students

CAL provides *Early Language Assessments*: www.cal.org/resource-center/publications-products/early-language-assessments

CAL is developing a specialized, web-based, teacher-training course for assessing children's Chinese-language development using the SOPA: www.cal.org/what-we-do/projects/wopa

ACTFL offers information on the *AAPPL assessment*: www.actfl.org/assessment-professional-development/assessments-the-actfl-testing-office/aappl

PART II

What is counterbalanced instruction?

The purpose of Part II is to provide an empirically based rationale for integrating a stronger language focus across the immersion and dual language (ImDL) curriculum and to outline the key features of a counterbalanced approach to doing so. Chapter 3 begins with research-based explanations for students' shortcomings in the minority language, which in turn supports the call for ImDL classrooms that are discourse rich and language rich. Counterbalanced instruction is introduced as a means to improve students' proficiency by shifting their attention between content and language, while skill acquisition theory is invoked to support instructional interventions integrating a focus on morphosyntax to help students move from effortful use of the minority language to more automatic use. Chapter 4 then outlines and illustrates the CAPA (contextualization, awareness, practice, and autonomy) model, which serves as a blueprint for designing instructional sequences that enable students to link form with meaning in contexts related to content, while honing their metalinguistic awareness and engaging in purposeful use of the target language, ranging from contextualized practice to more autonomous use.

3

COUNTERBALANCED INSTRUCTION

Its rationale and key characteristics

The preceding chapters laid the groundwork for understanding the defining characteristics of different immersion and dual language (ImDL) program models, their foundational principles, and key ingredients for their successful implementation. The purpose of this chapter is to provide an empirically based rationale for integrating a stronger language focus across the ImDL curriculum and to outline the key features of a counterbalanced approach to doing so. Specifically, the chapter addresses the following questions:

- Why are there shortcomings in minority-language development?
- What is counterbalanced instruction?
- What theories of learning can be drawn on to support instruction designed to improve minority-language development?
- What aspects of language should ImDL teachers focus on through counterbalanced instruction?

The chapter begins by explaining some of the reasons for shortcomings in ImDL students' minority-language development, which were described in Chapter 1. It then proposes a reconceptualization of ImDL pedagogy that more systematically integrates language and content as a means to scaffold development in the minority language.

Why are there shortcomings in minority-language development?

In Chapter 1, we established the need to improve students' skills in using the minority language. We will expound upon various ways of scaffolding minority-language development throughout the rest of this book. To provide students with the support they need to develop even higher levels of proficiency in the minority language, however, one needs first to understand the reasons underlying some of their linguistic shortcomings. In this section, we present research evidence concerning well-known limitations of ImDL education (identified in Harley et al., 1990 and Swain, 1985, 1988) that are believed to constrain students' continued development in the minority language unless counterbalanced by the kinds of compensatory instructional techniques outlined throughout this book.

 RESEARCH REPORT

Semantic processing at the expense of syntactic processing

- Having to process language for meaning does not always require precise syntactic and morphological knowledge. In such cases, students are able to skip over grammatical information, as they focus mainly on key vocabulary items and draw on their contextual knowledge to understand the meaning.
- This means that grammatical features of the minority language that are not crucial for comprehension or for getting meaning across can be bypassed as students engage in semantic rather than syntactic processing. Over time, however, students may miss nuances in meaning encoded by morphosyntax, such as tense and aspect, that can be crucial in understanding subject matter.

(Cameron, 2001; Harley, 1993; Skehan, 1998;
Swain, 1985, 1988)

 RESEARCH REPORT

Functionally restricted input

- Content teaching on its own is not necessarily good language teaching because of the limited range of language forms and functions to which it exposes students.
- Some examples of functionally restricted language used by French immersion teachers and thought to influence students' productive repertoire in French include:
  - verb tenses, of which 74–75% occur in the present-tense or imperative forms, 14–15% in the past tense, 6–8% in the future tense, and 3% in the conditional mood;
  - absence of formal *vous* and presence of *tu* to indicate indefinite reference and also plural reference (*vous* and *tu* are second-person pronouns in French, both equivalent to *you* in English);

- lexical clues for grammatical gender (i.e., whether nouns are masculine or feminine): only half of all determiners and adjectives and fewer than a third of all direct object third-person pronouns are clearly marked for grammatical gender.

(Lyster & Rebuffot, 2002; Poirier & Lyster, 2014; Swain, 1985, 1988)

 RESEARCH REPORT

Language and content kept separate

- Early classroom observations (Allen, Swain, Harley, & Cummins, 1990) revealed that it was relatively rare for French immersion teachers to:
  - refer during content-based lessons to what had been presented in a grammar lesson;
  - set up content-based activities specifically to focus on form related to meaning.
- More recent research has confirmed that ImDL teachers, most of whom have been trained as generalists and/or content teachers, have difficulty identifying specific linguistic features to focus on because they lack training in how language works and how to focus on it in meaningful ways while teaching content (Cammarata & Tedick, 2012). Moreover, students in ImDL programs tend to be held more accountable for content learning than for L2 development.
- Separating content and language, however, is now thought to "deprive students of opportunities to focus on specific features of language at the very moment when their motivation to learn them may be at its highest" (Lightbown, 2014, p. 30).

 RESEARCH REPORT

Comprehension emphasized at the expense of production

- Early classroom observations (e.g., Swain, 1985) revealed that subject-matter instruction did not necessarily invite much student production and that French immersion teachers tended to provide learners with inconsistent feedback (see Chapter 6).
- These and other instructional practices can be traced to the initial conceptualizations of ImDL, which were strongly influenced by Krashen's (1985) claim that L2 learning is driven primarily by *comprehensible input*

and best proceeds implicitly without any attention drawn intentionally to language form.

- There is now considerable theoretical support and empirical evidence—much of it from ImDL settings—that exposure to comprehensible input alone is insufficient for continued L2 growth.

To sum up, the shortcomings in students' productive abilities in the minority language are considered to result from having underestimated the extent to which students need to attend to and engage with the minority language during subject-matter and theme-based instruction. Indeed, since the early 1990s, L2 education theorists have stressed the importance of integrating form-oriented and meaning-oriented approaches to ensure continued development in the target language (e.g., Long, 1991; Stern, 1990).

Making ImDL classrooms language rich and discourse rich

Researchers now agree that ImDL and other content-based programs need to be carefully planned from a language perspective. As Lightbown (2014) summed it up: "After decades of research on language acquisition in CBLT [content-based language teaching] in a variety of educational and social contexts, it is clear that language acquisition does not 'take care of itself'" (p. 129). Contrary to initial conceptualizations of ImDL education, substantial exposure to the minority language via subject-matter instruction does not obfuscate the need to focus on language and instead creates many meaningful contexts into which a focus on language can be effectively integrated. But what are the best ways to focus on language in ImDL classrooms? A wide range of practices have certainly been observed.

For example, Day and Shapson (1996) observed marked differences in instructional strategies employed by ImDL teachers during science lessons. In one language-rich science classroom, students were seen "as a community of learners engaged in discourse about science" (p. 80). In another science class, the limitations of traditional pedagogy were more evident as the teacher "repeated or rephrased what [students] said, wrote the answers on the board, and had students take notes" (p. 56). In both cases, a focus on language was evident but was operationalized in very different ways. Based on many classroom observations, Day and Shapson concluded that instructional practices that emphasize discourse and the use of language as an instrument for learning have more to contribute to scaffolding language development than less interactive practices.

Considerable differences among teachers were also observed in a large-scale study of 23 ImDL classrooms ranging from Grades 1 to 3 in Newfoundland, leading to the following conclusion: "Despite a common curriculum, teachers organize and instruct their classes differently, and these differences are significant with respect to the learning outcomes for pupils" (Netten & Spain, 1989, p. 499). An intriguing result of this study is that a low-ability class actually excelled in their achievement in the minority language compared with a higher-ability class. The success of these students was attributed to their teacher's instructional practices, which included the following:

- teacher-student interaction using a question/answer technique rather than a lecture format;
- opportunities for meaningful interaction among peers rather than only listening to the teacher;
- use of language rather than non-verbal clues to convey meaning;
- explicit rather than implicit correction.

Netten and Spain argued strongly in favor of more language-oriented ImDL classrooms (see also Netten, 1991) that "encourage active and purposeful communication on the part of as many pupils as possible" (p. 500). Teachers who orchestrate opportunities for students to engage with language in these ways are more apt than others to succeed in moving their students' development in the minority language forward.

But what instructional approaches enable teachers to systematically engage their students in this way? The core principle advocated throughout this book is that of a counterbalanced approach that integrates language across content areas. In other words, the most promising conditions for both continued language growth and conceptual development of content knowledge is an integrated curriculum that has a dual focus on language and content.

A counterbalanced approach intentionally draws attention to language in discourse contexts related to subject matter or literacy themes so that students engage with the forms and functions of the minority language in contextualized and meaningful ways. This involves shifting students' attention between language and content, as illustrated by the following vignettes of ImDL teachers who were observed successfully integrating a focus on language during their content lessons.

 ## RESEARCH REPORTS

Teacher vignettes

1. Mme Legault, a Grade 1 immersion teacher, combines language and content instruction as she negotiates both form and meaning with students during science lessons. As she interacts with students, she provides rich and varied input and then helps students to improve the form and content of their own utterances by providing feedback that includes questions, paraphrases, comments, translation, elaboration, and requests for translation or elaboration. Her interactional strategies

have a pedagogical function that aims to encourage and facilitate language production on the part of the students and also, to a lesser degree, to allow students to negotiate the unfolding of certain activities (Laplante, 1993).

2. Rachelle, a Grade 4 immersion teacher, draws attention to relevant language features as she interacts with students during science and language arts lessons about well-adapted mammals and meteorology. During these lively discussions, she maintains a central focus on meaning yet succeeds in eliciting synonyms, antonyms, homophones, more precise terms, and words with similar structural properties, as well as correct grammatical gender, spelling, and pronunciation. By drawing attention to language in this way during meaningful interaction, Rachelle provides her students with opportunities to notice, in unambiguous ways, relevant form-function links in the minority language (Lyster, 1998d).

3. Leonard, a Grade 8 immersion teacher, presents a combined science and language arts lesson on the greenhouse effect in the form of a discussion. The lesson is planned yet presented as a "spontaneous" discussion to begin two consecutive school days. Leonard adopts a multifaceted approach to teaching vocabulary, which draws attention to the phonological, grammatical, syntactic, and sociolinguistic properties of words, in addition to meaning. His strategies include repetition, use of multiple synonyms, and revisiting words in a variety of contexts and in different parts of the lesson (Lapkin & Swain, 1996).

4. Concha, a Grade 5 immersion teacher, engages her students in a collaborative writing activity to enhance their understandings of the purpose and structure of the US Bill of Rights. Before engaging in three back-to-back experiences with writing a bill of rights, students are introduced to various language structures they will need to do so, including complex sentences with subordinate clauses containing the subjunctive mood. While the content focus remains on basic individual rights and liberties, Concha articulates clear language objectives, provides models of the types of sentences students will need, reviews how the subjunctive is formed, and reminds students to check their writing for gender and number agreement with articles and nouns as well as subject-verb agreement. She uses a rubric to assess their writing that addresses both their content understandings and their linguistic accuracy (Fortune & Fernández del Rey, 2003).

5. A Grade 1 immersion teacher, Mary Carmen, plans a unit about water. She uses a graphic organizer to serve as a scaffold for both content learning and language development. In one of the lessons, she directs her students to complete a graphic organizer comparing examples and non-examples of the three states of water (i.e., solid, liquid, and gas).

> She includes an additional language task for students to practice the
> linguistic structures (e.g., conjunctions, and verbs in both affirmative
> and negative forms) that they need to compare and contrast examples
> of the three states. For example: "Water in a swimming pool is an exam-
> ple of a liquid. In liquid water, we can swim, but we can't ice-skate"
> (Cammarata, 2005).

What is counterbalanced instruction?

Apparent in the foregoing vignettes is a counterbalanced approach that shifts
the instructional focus between language and content. This interplay between
language and content is achieved by attributing complementary status to both
language and content objectives in the ImDL curriculum. Counterbalanced
instruction does not mean, however, that there is an equal or balanced focus on
language and content. Counterbalance entails an ongoing shift in emphasis to
prevent either language or content from taking on a disproportionate role in the
ImDL curriculum that eclipses the importance of the other (see Figure 3.1).

The notion of counterbalance thus aims to diffuse dichotomous views of
instruction as being only about language or only about content. In contrast to
such a rigid separation, language and content can be conceptualized as complementary options in a dynamic relation that optimizes L2 learning. In this
view, growth in the minority language is expected to result from counterbalanced instruction that incites learners to vary their attentional focus between
the content to which they usually attend in classroom discourse and language
features that are not otherwise attended to. The effort expended to shift attention
between form and meaning in this way increases depth of processing and develops students' metalinguistic awareness. Metalinguistic awareness helps students
to detect linguistic patterns in meaningful input and communicative exchanges,
and is thus essential for supporting their continued language growth.

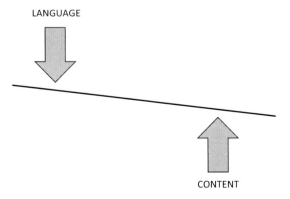

FIGURE 3.1 Counterbalanced instruction

KEY CONCEPT

Depth of processing refers to the extent to which a learner reflects on new information and links it to other relevant information. The greater the depth of processing, the greater the likelihood that information will be stored in long-term memory and become more readily accessible.

 KEY CONCEPT

Metalinguistic awareness is the ability to objectify language as an analyzable code and is thus prerequisite to early literacy development. It also strengthens learners' ability to detect language patterns in content-based input in ways that can contribute to their developing language system.

Young ImDL students in early-start programs who have been primed by their instructional setting to be meaning oriented can understand content without precise syntactic and morphological knowledge of the target language (Swain, 1988), as they draw instead on "vastly greater stores of schematic and contextual knowledge" (Skehan, 1998, p. 26). As they do so, "learners are driven to look for the message in the input before they look at how the message is encoded linguistically" (Benati, 2013). Most ImDL teachers would agree that their students focus more on meaning than on form, and, in fact, ImDL teachers often encourage their students to "go for meaning" given the content-driven nature of ImDL programs. The purpose of counterbalanced instruction is to shift students' attention to language in the context of content instruction, when they wouldn't otherwise be attending to language, in order to strengthen their ability to more effectively engage with the minority language.

In ImDL classrooms, counterbalanced instruction entails reactive and proactive approaches to integrating language and content. A *reactive approach* includes oral scaffolding techniques, such as questions and feedback in response to students' language production, that serve to support student participation while ensuring that classroom interaction is a key source of learning. A reactive approach includes in-the-moment strategies for drawing students' attention to language or getting them to produce more extended discourse. A *proactive approach* involves pre-planned instruction designed intentionally to highlight connections between subject-matter content and the language needed to engage with that content. Although often defined as distinct approaches, reactive and proactive approaches are best implemented in tandem. The implementation of reactive and proactive approaches as complementary is in line with Day and Shapson's (1996) case studies of ImDL teachers, which led to the conclusion that both planned language instruction and the many unplanned opportunities teachers can seize on to enhance language learning are of equal importance.

Counterbalanced instruction creates opportunities for students, in the context of content-based or meaning-oriented tasks, to notice and use various features of the minority language that might otherwise be misused, unused, or unnoticed in classroom discourse. It thus differs from the kind of traditional language instruction that isolates language from any content other than the mechanical workings of the language itself. Yet, integrating a focus on language in contextualized ways across the curriculum requires systematic planning, which may at first seem challenging to many teachers, whose professional training may have led them to believe that they need to focus mainly on content and can expect language to emerge incidentally. The purpose of this book is to help teachers overcome this challenge.

Theoretical underpinnings of counterbalanced instruction

This section addresses some of the theoretical underpinnings of a counterbalanced approach designed to strengthen ImDL students' proficiency in the minority language. We draw on *skill acquisition theory* to explain the cognitive processing involved in developing students' metalinguistic awareness in a way that ultimately affects their language production. DeKeyser (2007) sums up skill acquisition theory and related research as follows:

> Skill acquisition theory accounts for how people progress in learning a variety of skills, from initial learning to advanced proficiency. Skills studied include both cognitive and psychomotor skills, in domains that range from classroom learning to applications in sports and industry. (p. 97)

Our own interest in skill acquisition theory and how it relates to ImDL education stems from the pivotal role it attributes to both practice and feedback in leading learners from effortful to more automatic use of the minority language (Lyster & Sato, 2013; Ranta & Lyster, 2007).

What is skill acquisition theory?

Skill acquisition is best described as the inter-related development of *mental representations* stored in memory and the *processing mechanisms* that access those representations. In this view, acquiring a complex skill entails the development of *declarative knowledge*, which plays a causal role in the development of *procedural knowledge* (Anderson, 1996). Declarative knowledge is "knowing about" concepts, propositions, and schemata, including static information such as historical or geographical facts encoded in memory. Procedural knowledge is "knowing how" to do things. This involves the ability to apply rule-based knowledge to cognitive operations, such as solving problems or following steps toward an end goal, and to motor operations. Proponents of skill acquisition theory propose that L2 development entails a gradual transition from effortful use that relies on declarative knowledge to more automatic use of the target language that relies on procedural knowledge, brought about through practice and feedback in meaningful contexts.

Common examples of transitioning from slowly accessing declarative knowledge to effortlessly accessing procedural knowledge in our daily lives include learning how to shift gears in order to drive a car with manual transmission or learning the position of characters on a computer's keyboard or a smartphone's touchscreen keypad in order to type or text quickly. A simple yet powerful example involves opening a combination lock using three numbers: two turns to the right to the first number followed by one turn to the left passing the first number then arriving at the second number; finally, a quick turn to the right to the third number will open the lock. At first, one needs to concentrate on these simple steps while keeping the numbers in working memory, until eventually one can open the lock with considerable speed without having to recall the procedure and numbers each time. Once the procedure has become automatized to the point of being executed effortlessly, we can say that the declarative knowledge (of the three steps and three numbers) has become proceduralized.

With respect to language, as seen in Figure 3.2, declarative knowledge refers to knowledge about language items and sub-systems, such as word definitions, rules, and paradigms. Procedural knowledge involves language processing, including comprehension and production through quick access to mental representations stored in memory. For example, many learners of English L2 might have declarative knowledge of the inflections required to form present-tense verbs in English (i.e., add *s* to third-person singular verbs: *he or she eats*, but *I, you,*

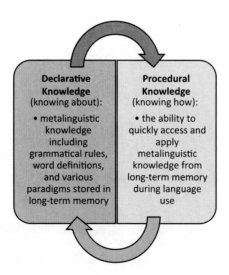

FIGURE 3.2 Interplay between declarative and procedural knowledge

we, they eat). In spontaneous production, however, learners might overgeneralize verb forms and continue producing *he eat* or *she eat*, in which case their declarative knowledge has not yet been proceduralized. Declarative knowledge is often equated with explicit knowledge of language, whereas procedural knowledge is considered implicit and can thus be employed automatically without much conscious effort.

As seen in the preceding examples, skill acquisition involves a transition from controlled processing to automatic processing (Shiffrin & Schneider, 1977). Controlled processing requires a great deal of attention and use of short-term memory, whereas automatic processing operates on routinized procedures available in long-term memory. The transition from controlled to more automatic processing results from multiple opportunities in contexts clearly linking form with meaning to access rule-based declarative representations so that they become easier to access and thus proceduralized (DeKeyser, 1998). In this view, new tasks can initially only be handled using controlled processing. Practice plays an important role in improving performance so that it gradually becomes more rapid and stable. This occurs when components of a skill become automatized, which then frees up attentional resources for use in higher-level processing.

Applying the theory to explain language development in ImDL classrooms

The distinction between declarative and procedural knowledge is useful for understanding ImDL students' interlanguage development and apparent *plateau effects* characterized by ostensibly "fossilized" forms. Johnson (1996) pointed out that naturalistic approaches to language learning such as ImDL are designed to bypass the initial development of declarative knowledge and serve instead to directly develop procedural encodings of the target language. The emphasis on early language use in ImDL classrooms encourages the deployment of procedures that operate on linguistic knowledge which has not yet been acquired in the target language, thus necessitating recourse to other mental representations such as knowledge of L1 structures. As Johnson (1996) argued, interlanguage representations that are proceduralized early on "quickly become highly automatized and impermeable to change" (p. 99; see also McLaughlin, 1987).

⚗ KEY CONCEPT

Interlanguage is a dynamic and evolving version of the target language that contains both target-like and non-target-like forms. Interlanguage is a term that refers to the language used by L2 learners as they progress through different stages of development (Selinker, 1972).

> **SPECIAL NOTE**
>
> Fossilized language by definition is incapable of change or development and so is not a very promising way to characterize the language used by young ImDL students who are still learning. The premise of this book is that interlanguage forms can be restructured as a result of well-planned instructional support.

The good news is that the resultant interlanguage forms may develop into more appropriate forms through a *restructuring* of knowledge representations (McLaughlin, 1987, 1990). The restructuring of a learner's interlanguage can be activated by instructional activities that first promote the perception of language functions and their appropriate forms in various contexts, followed by their use in written and oral production activities. The challenge for teachers is to push students to develop new target-like representations that compete with more easily accessible interlanguage forms (Ranta & Lyster, 2007). Leading ImDL students to reanalyze some of the non-target-like representations that they acquired implicitly is, in a way, like trying to "defossilize" these interlanguage forms.

Thus, whereas declarative knowledge is generally thought to play a causal role in the development of procedural knowledge, the interplay between declarative and procedural knowledge is more realistically seen as bidirectional (Lyster & Sato, 2013). That is, ImDL students whose exposure to the minority language was early enough to activate primarily implicit learning processes will benefit from practice and feedback opportunities designed to make the implicit knowledge that they had acquired in relatively naturalistic ways more explicit through analysis and thus available for restructuring. Students may have internalized interlanguage variations of these features and now need to step back and reanalyze them by drawing on their growing metalinguistic awareness while engaging in various opportunities for language practice.

Young learners in ImDL classrooms are indeed known to make good use of their implicit knowledge of the minority language in the form of formulaic "chunks" or prefabricated routines (e.g., Björklund, Mård-Miettinen, & Savijärvi, 2014; Weber & Tardif, 1991). Formulaic language is "stored and retrieved whole from memory at the time of use, rather than being subject to generation or analysis by the language grammar" (Wray, 2002, p. 9). For example, young French immersion students are likely to understand and even produce inverted questions such as *Quelle heure est-il? (What time is it?), Quel âge as-tu? (How old are you?)*, or *Quel temps fait-il? (What's the weather like?)* without yet having developed explicit knowledge of rules governing the formation of inverted questions and, thus, without the ability to generate other inverted questions on their own. Instead, they have been able to memorize these questions as unanalyzed chunks. It can be said that the success of early ImDL programs lies in young learners' predisposition for internalizing a great deal of the language to which they are exposed without having to stop and analyze it.

KEY CONCEPT

Chunks are groups of words that learners have been able to acquire without knowing any rules for their formation. They are very useful in communication because they can be retrieved quickly and are also useful as stepping stones to further learning, but they do not necessarily help learners generate similar forms governed by the same rules without some analysis. "How *are you* doing?" can be considered a memorized chunk in English if the learner isn't yet able to generate inverted question forms in other contexts where the learner might ask "What *you are* doing?" without subject-auxiliary inversion.

Because of their students' capacity for implicit learning and for internalizing formulaic chunks of language, ImDL teachers do not need to be too concerned about exposing their students to language whose mechanical workings they have yet to understand. For example, teachers do not need to avoid using seemingly difficult verb forms such as conditional or subjunctive forms, based on the premise that students will not understand them because they have not yet studied them. Nor do teachers need to expect students to avoid such forms and to opt instead for simpler and non-idiomatic indicative forms, again because they have not studied them. This is because students can use such forms without explicit knowledge by drawing on unanalyzed chunks stored in memory.

As students progress though the program, formulaic language chunks can eventually become the target of counterbalanced instruction. In this way, as previously mentioned, the learning does not proceed from explicit representations of declarative knowledge but, rather, from increasingly explicit representations of implicitly acquired and unanalyzed knowledge. Drawing on the previous example of inverted question formation in French, when the time is right to draw French immersion students' attention to various ways of forming questions in French, including inverted forms, a good starting point would be to use as models the unanalyzed chunks they've already been using, such as *Quel temps fait-il?* and *Quel âge as-tu?* Because their knowledge of the minority language is initially largely implicit and composed of unanalyzed chunks, teachers can engage them increasingly over time in analyses of formulaic language as a means of developing a more generative rule-based system. According to Bialystok (1994), this will increase students' ability to access their linguistic knowledge and thereby support the development of literacy skills.

The importance of meaningful practice in skill acquisition

According to skill acquisition theory, practice plays a pivotal role in learning any kind of complex skill. Admittedly, however, the idea of "practicing language" has a bit of a tarnished reputation, which DeKeyser (2010) attributes to the mechanical drills and meaningless repetition associated with audio-lingual methods. He makes a strong case for types of practice that go beyond "drill and kill" and that fit instead within a "broader definition of systematic practice and fulfill specific functions in the learning process that mere communicative input and interaction cannot" (2010, p. 159). There is thus a renewed consensus that practice is necessary and can be effective if it is meaningful rather than mechanical, especially in the light of DeKeyser's (1998) convincing argument that practice is simply "engaging in an activity with the goal of becoming better at it" (p. 50). Accordingly, whether the instructional goal is to develop new declarative knowledge followed by opportunities for its proceduralization, or to restructure existing declarative knowledge that has already been proceduralized as interlanguage representations, the transition requires practice over many trials in contexts clearly linking form with meaning (DeKeyser, 1998).

Unfortunately, however, in much typical second- or foreign-language teaching, there is a tendency to consider instruction sufficient even if it aims only to develop declarative knowledge, without proceeding to the next step of providing sufficient opportunities for students to proceduralize their declarative knowledge (Bange, 2005). As a result, foreign-language teachers often lament, for example, that their students can conjugate verbs on a test but are incapable of producing them spontaneously in oral interaction. This is why counterbalanced instruction is designed to hone both declarative and procedural knowledge by enhancing students' metalinguistic awareness in the form of declarative knowledge and providing opportunities for practice to support the development of procedural knowledge.

Bange (2005) identified a challenge for teachers in developing students' procedural knowledge in classroom settings: Procedural knowledge is acquired through action (i.e., learning by doing: we learn language by using language), so learners are expected, paradoxically, to use the language they are still in the process of learning. He argued that the solution to the paradox lies in social interaction and, more specifically, in the scaffolding provided by teachers to students so they can perform actively until they are able to function independently (see Part III).

From this perspective, Bange (2005) brings together Anderson's work on skill acquisition and Bruner's work on scaffolded interaction in a coherent fashion that underscores the complementarity of cognitive and social perspectives. Together, these complementary perspectives underpin a counterbalanced approach that creates optimal conditions for learning both language and content in classroom settings. Incorporating Bruner's (1971) argument that "growth of mind is always growth assisted from the outside" (p. 52) and the corollary view that "mental processes are as social as they are individual and as external as they are internal" (Block, 2003, p. 93), we will interweave throughout this book both cognitive and social views of learning. Such a perspective applies aptly to school settings, where "learning is a social as well as a cognitive process, one influenced by the relationships between student and teacher and among students" (August & Hakuta, 1997, p. 85).

Skill acquisition theory posits that practice is essential to skill development in the target language because it provides learners with opportunities to proceduralize their declarative knowledge. Because skill acquisition theory attributes an important role to both practice and feedback, it resonates well with Swain's (1993) output hypothesis. The output hypothesis, in fact, stems from observations of ImDL classrooms, which brought to light the need for more student production and teacher feedback in these contexts.

 RESEARCH REPORT

The output hypothesis

The output hypothesis states that "through producing language, either spoken or written, language acquisition/learning may occur" (Swain, 1993, p. 159). Swain (1993, 1995) identified four functions of output:

1. Output helps to develop fluency.
2. Output pushes learners to move from semantic processing to syntactic processing and thus to notice what they do not know or know only partially. As a result, learners might pay more attention to relevant input or search their own linguistic resources to help close the gap.
3. Output has a metalinguistic function that enables learners to use language in order to reflect on language. Such "meta-talk" can arise, for example, during collaborative writing tasks requiring students to engage in dialogue about their writing.
4. As learners stretch their interlanguage to meet communicative needs, they use output as a way of testing hypotheses about new language forms, which in turn may lead to feedback from teachers or peers.

See Swain (2005) for a summary of research related to the output hypothesis.

The emphasis in counterbalanced instruction on shifting attention between language and content during contextualized and purposeful language use is also in line with *transfer-appropriate processing* (Lightbown, 2008a; Segalowitz, 2000). According to transfer-appropriate processing, memories are best recalled in conditions similar to those in which they were encoded. Therefore, the context in which learning occurs should resemble the context in which the learning will be put to use. This means that aspects of the minority language that are attended to during interaction with a communicative purpose—rather than during decontextualized grammar lessons—are more likely to be retrieved in similar contexts of real communication. Returning to the foreign-language teaching example above, the reason that students are able to conjugate verbs on tests is because that is what they are taught to do. Expecting students to be able to accurately transfer their knowledge of verb conjugation to contexts of spontaneous oral interaction, if they have not yet been provided with sufficient opportunities to do so, is not in line with the notion of transfer-appropriate processing. Given the potential of ImDL classrooms to bring to the fore various forms and functions of the minority language in the context of authentic communication and learning activities with a purpose, they lend themselves well to transfer-appropriate processing.

 **KEY CONCEPT**

Transfer-appropriate processing is a notion from cognitive psychology that posits that the context in which learning occurs should resemble the context in which the learning will be put to use. Accordingly, language features learned in isolated grammar lessons are remembered in similar contexts but hard to retrieve in the context of communicative interaction, whereas language features attended to during content-driven interaction are more easily retrieved in similar contexts of interaction with a communicative purpose (Lightbown, 2008a; Segalowitz, 2000).

A challenge in designing practice activities is that they need to engage students in a certain degree of repetitiveness. That's what practice is: By definition, it necessarily involves some repetition. For example, *The Compact Oxford English Dictionary* defines practice as "doing something repeatedly so as to become more skilful in it" (Soanes & Hawker, 2008, p. 798). Repetition, however, does not mean being void of meaning. On the contrary, Segalowitz (2000) explained that effective practice is not only extensive and repetitive, but also genuinely communicative in nature and therefore transfer-appropriate. At the same time, the practice needs to be *deliberate*, meaning that students must engage in activities "with the purpose of attaining and improving skills" and not only in "everyday activities in which learning may be an indirect result" (Ericsson, Krampe, & Tesch-Römer, 1993, p. 367).

An illustration of a repetitive yet communicative practice activity is the "Find Someone Who" activity, which turns students into interviewers equipped with checklists to complete as they circulate among their classmates conducting a survey. For example, let's say the main content objective pertains to how certain mammals have adapted to their environment in ways that help them to find or store food and to hide or flee from predators, while one of the language objectives targets the use in English of the present perfect tense-aspect form and its use in inverted questions (i.e., *Have you ...?*). To activate students' prior knowledge of various mammals before they explore evolutionary adaptations, students can conduct a survey among their classmates to find out who has already seen in real life certain mammals: *Have you ever seen a camel? Have you ever seen a giraffe? Have you ever seen a polar bear, a porcupine, a skunk, a fox, a kangaroo?* etc. While the results can then be tabulated and used as a springboard for zooming in on the adaptations of certain mammals, students will have had many opportunities to process the target forms by means of repetitive yet meaningful practice related to the subject matter. The two examples below show ways that teachers have creatively embedded meaningful repetition into their instruction.

 TEACHER SPOTLIGHT

Amanda Woods, a Grade 1 English immersion teacher at Katoh Gakuen in Numazu, Japan, designed a unit to help her novice students to use the language chunk *I would like to …* as a means to express their preferences on a variety of topics. The unit was contextualized around a non-fiction text called "Ways People Live" by Emile Neye, which shows how different climates (hot, cold, dry, and wet) influence peoples' homes and clothing. Following lots of teacher modeling of *What would you like to …?* and *I would like to …* concerning food, clothing, games, and homes, students engaged in extensive and repetitive practice over several lessons as they surveyed their classmates to find out who would like to: eat X, Y, or Z for dinner; play X, Y, or Z; wear X, Y, or Z, etc. During the various surveys, exchanges such as the following occurred repeatedly on a range of topics and with many different interlocutors:

S1: Where would you like to live?
S2: I would like to live where it is cold. What about you?
S1: I would like to live where it is dry, because I don't like rain.

After the interviews, students returned to the whole group for sharing their results, which again provided opportunities for repetitive yet meaningful practice as they reported, in full sentences, the students who would like to live where it is hot, where it is cold, etc.

 TEACHER SPOTLIGHT

Monique Paulson taught at Waadookodaading Ojibwe Language Institute, a K–5 indigenous language revitalization immersion charter school in Hayward, Wisconsin. She developed a series of activities to teach young, preliterate learners how to accurately use *"ina"*, a question marker for yes/no questions. Children learning Ojibwe often tack *ina* onto statements; for example, instead of saying the intended "I want to drink," students add the *ina* marker and say "Do I want to drink?" Monique decided to contextualize the focus on *ina* within the curricular topic of classroom routines and rules, because embedded within that focus is an emphasis on helping students learn to make requests. The goal was to engage students in repetitive yet meaningful practice to provide ample opportunities for input exposure as well as student output.

Monique began the instructional sequence with a modeling activity. Together with the elder assigned to her classroom, Monique used puppets and modeled several dialogues like the following:

- Makwa (Bear): *Giwii-minikwen ina nibi?* (Do you want to drink water?)
- Animosh (Dog): *Eya', niwii-minikwen.* (Yes, I want to drink water.) [Makwa hands Animosh a glass of water.]
- Makwa: *Ahaw. Minikwen.* (Okay. Drink.)

In addition to modeling the language with the puppet dialogue, they stressed *ina* verbally and paused right after the word to draw students' attention to it. They also painted question marks on children's hands and instructed them to raise their marked hand every time they heard *ina* used throughout the day. In addition, they had students practice making requests with *ina* before "free choice" time.

Later they engaged children in a game based on "Mother May I?" to bring in many opportunities for meaningful repetition. Students were placed in a line and had to make requests to move forward. They were only able to move forward if they used *ina* accurately (and the abbreviated *na* after verbs ending in vowels). The student assigned to the head position responded with statements (such as: *Eya' gidaa-bimoode.* [Yes, you can crawl.]). The simple questions they practiced included the following:

- *Nindaa-bimoode na?* (Can I crawl?)
- *Nindaa-niim ina?* (Can I dance?)
- *Nindaa-bimibaatoo na?* (Can I run?)
- *Nindaa-gwaashkwan ina?* (Can I jump?)
- *Nindaa-bimose na?* (Can I walk?)

During this activity Monique provided corrective feedback as needed. The game was ideal for young children in that it integrated meaningful language repetition, gross motor development, and counting skills (as children needed to ask for a specific number of paces to move forward and then count them).

What language features require counterbalanced instruction?

Language is a multifaceted phenomenon ranging from discrete elements, such as phonemes and morphemes, to its indispensable role in all communication and its intrinsic links with human cognition. In this book, we try to cover all bases by proposing instructional approaches targeting discrete aspects of the minority language in Chapter 4 and, in Chapter 8, instructional approaches focusing more on discourse and the academic language functions that students need to develop in order to use the minority language as a means to fully engage with subject matter. Underlying both orientations is the notion of counterbalance, in the sense that both are driven by content *and* language learning objectives. Also common to both orientations is the need for teachers to ask themselves what language their students need in order to accomplish academic tasks in age-appropriate ways. Language undoubtedly permeates all aspects of learning, as expressed by Cameron Barnard, an English immersion science teacher at Katoh Gakuen elementary school in Numazu, Japan: "The science curriculum requires a huge focus on language. Without language, there is no learning" (personal communication, March 2019).

One way to answer the question of what language students need in order to engage with content is to identify *content-obligatory language* (Snow, Met, & Genesee, 1989), which will be further expounded upon in Chapter 8. Content-obligatory language includes technical vocabulary and other domain-specific expressions, as well as language functions that predominate in a particular content area, such as informing, defining, analyzing, classifying, predicting, inferring, explaining, justifying, and inquiring. This involves making students explicitly aware of the following:

1. the academic language functions they need to understand and communicate in a specific content area (Dalton-Puffer, 2013, calls these *cognitive discourse functions*);
2. the conventional text structures or genres that are characteristic of particular disciplines, such as science reports, historical accounts, math problems, and essays (e.g., Llinares, Morton, & Whittaker, 2012).

Implementing a functional approach to emphasize the ways in which discipline-specific language conveys particular kinds of meanings is key to ImDL pedagogy and critical to effective pedagogy in any instructional context. We return to academic language functions and discourse types in Chapter 8. In the remainder of this chapter, we suggest ways for teachers to identify grammatical features to focus on, which sets the scene for Chapter 4 and its focus on integrating a grammatical focus into theme-based and subject-matter instruction.

Learners in ImDL classrooms pick up a great deal of language through meaningful input and purposeful interaction, without explicit attention; this is why ImDL education has been so successful. As explained in Chapter 1, language features that seem to be easily acquired through exposure to content-based instruction include structural patterns that are similar to students' L1, high-frequency vocabulary, and items that are phonologically salient (i.e., easy to notice in the stream of speech because of intonational stress). This type of learning without explicit instruction fits well with young learners' predisposition for implicit learning.

However, as previously mentioned, there are many key features of the minority language that are not easily "picked up" via implicit learning, thus begging the question of what language features and patterns teachers need to draw explicit attention to. Answers to this question, although not as straightforward as one would hope for, are crucial, given that one of the greatest challenges experienced by ImDL teachers is the selection of target-language features on which to focus (Cammarata & Tedick, 2012).

What is morphosyntax and why focus on it?

There are many features of the minority language that students do not learn accurately from mere exposure. The resultant inaccuracies stem from a complex interaction of these features' structural properties, their occurrence (or non-occurrence) in typical classroom discourse, and the learner's own cognitive predisposition (Long, 1996). In this regard, Harley (1993) identified the following features as those worthy of special attention:

1. those that differ in non-obvious or unexpected ways from the student's L1;
2. those that are irregular, infrequent, or lacking in perceptual salience;
3. those that do not carry a heavy communicative load with respect to meaning.

Other features that warrant attention are:

4. those involving a misleading similarity between the two target languages, because such features are those that learners "are most likely to have long-term difficulty acquiring through communicative interaction" (Spada, Lightbown, & White, 2005, p. 201);
5. those involving a single form in one language but two forms in the other language (Ellis, 1986), because learners, for the sake of economy, may adopt one form at the expense of the other (e.g., informal and formal second-person pronouns in Romance languages versus the single form *you* in English).

Many prime candidates for counterbalanced instruction thus fall within the realm of what linguists call *morphosyntax*. Morphosyntax is another word for grammar, bringing together both morphology (i.e., the study of words and their formation) and syntax (i.e., the study of sentences and their formation). *Inflections*, for example, are morphosyntactic categories. Inflections refer to changes in the form of a word to express a grammatical function such as tense, number, or person. When an inflectional change affects not only a single word but necessitates changes to surrounding words, this entails morphosyntax. For instance, simply changing the word *boy* to *boys* leads to other changes in the following sentence: *The boy is playing by himself.* ⇒ *The boys are playing by themselves.* In this simple example, some of the morphosyntactic features can be considered redundant in the sense that plurality is marked three times rather than only once (*boy* ⇒ *boys*; *is* ⇒ *are*; *himself* ⇒ *themselves*). Given their redundancy and the fact that they do not convey any *additional* meaning, many morphosyntactic features are prone to slipping under the radar in classrooms whose primary focus is on meaning. Indeed, many features of morphosyntax have long been recognized as the most difficult for L2 learners, especially features with low salience and those with a lack of communicative value (Goldschneider & DeKeyser, 2001; Han, 2004; Mackey, 2006).

Accordingly, many features of Romance languages such as Spanish, French, Portuguese, and Italian are likely to need special attention for learners whose primary language is English. For example, grammatical gender is challenging for these learners, because it does not exist in English in the same way: *casa* and *maison* mean *house*, and the fact that they are feminine nouns is unrelated to the fact that they denote buildings for human habitation. Yet, using a noun with a given gender has multiple effects at the sentence level without contributing anything to meaning. Consider the following two sentences in French, in which meaning is held constant:

Son nouveau vélo blanc est beau. ["His new white bicycle is beautiful."]
Sa nouvelle bicyclette blanche est belle. ["His new white bicycle is beautiful."]

Bicyclette and *vélo* both mean *bicycle*, but the former is feminine and the latter is masculine. Given rules of noun-adjective agreement, the choice of one noun over the other entails a total of four other changes in the sentence!

Similarly, verbal inflections in Romance languages are challenging for learners whose primary language is English, because they are different from verbal inflections in English, often irregular, and not always salient unless attention is intentionally drawn to them. Examples from Japanese of morphosyntactic features that differ greatly from English are past forms of adjectives and post-verbal particles denoting the direction and the agent of an action. A good example from Mandarin and Hmong is the use of classifiers, also known as measure words. Taken together, the list of challenging yet crucial morphosyntactic features of the non-English languages targeted by ImDL programs seems endless.

In cases where English-language development is of prime concern, as in much of the research on content and language integrated learning (CLIL) and research on English-language learners in the US, there is less emphasis placed on morphosyntactic development than in our treatment of scaffolding non-English languages throughout this book. This is because, as Swan (2018) argues, "English happens to be a morphologically light language" (p. 256). He refers to an "English bias" in theories of second language acquisition (SLA) that have developed from studying the acquisition of English, and argues that languages with more inflectional grammars than that of English "cannot easily be picked up from simple exposure to the limited input available to most students" (p. 256). He concludes as follows:

> It is not at all certain that the act of faith whereby forms are taken to be learnable largely through classroom interaction would be possible if an inflecting language were the focus of language teaching theory to the extent that English is. (p. 256)

This is why we emphasize, in this chapter and the next, a counterbalanced approach that systematically draws attention to the minority language, including its grammatical structures (viz., morphosyntactic features), in discourse contexts related to subject matter or literacy themes. The purpose is to support students' developing knowledge and subsequent use of the target features in meaningful contexts. For this to happen, content and language objectives need to be given complementary status so that students' attention shifts between language and content in contextualized and seemingly seamless ways.

Selecting language features

Although ImDL teachers can benefit from the identification of a scope and sequence regarding language features to target across grade levels, it remains imperative for teachers to understand that this is a guide for them and does not necessarily reflect an agreed-upon order of acquisition from a language learning perspective. Learning an additional language does not follow a clear linear path and instead is much more cyclical in nature. This means that, if teachers agree that a given target structure should be explicitly addressed in Grade 4, students will need already to have had multiple exposures to that feature well before Grade 4 and then will need multiple opportunities during and after Grade 4 to revisit and recycle their developing knowledge of that feature in a wide range of contexts.

A linear sequence of language features to follow across grade levels is usually designed on the basis of a progression from simple language to more complex language. Although such a progression may serve the purpose of helping to structure the ImDL curriculum, it is again imperative for teachers to understand that there is little agreement, first, on what distinguishes simple and complex language, and second, on whether complex language actually requires more explicit intervention than simple language (see Research Report: Simple versus complex structures).

 RESEARCH REPORT

Simple versus complex structures

One way to distinguish simple structures from complex structures is by taking into account the number of transformations required to produce the structure. In this view, simple structures are those consisting of only one transformation (e.g., past tense in English: *Tom lives in Tokyo* ⇒ *Tom lived in Tokyo*), whereas complex structures consist of two or more transformations (e.g., question formation in English: *Tom lives in Tokyo* ⇒ *Does Tom live in Tokyo?*). However, the results of empirical studies investigating the learning of complex versus simple grammatical structures are inconsistent, arguably due in part to the lack of consensus in how to conceptualize complexity.

This line of research reflects two dominant and contradictory points of view. One proposal is that explicit instruction is more effective for complex structures than for simpler structures because complex structures are considered more salient and thus more likely to be noticed and learned than simple structures. Another proposal, however, is that more complex structures are less likely to be learned than simpler ones because complex structures demand more attention in sentence processing, thus creating a cognitive overload, and these attentional constraints are predicted to have a negative impact on L2 learning.

(DeKeyser, 2005; Housen, Pierrard, & Van Daele, 2005;
Hulstijn & de Graaff, 1994; McLaughlin & Heredia, 1996;
Schmidt, 1990, 2001; Spada & Tomita, 2010)

In the absence of definitive criteria for designing a clear progression from simple to complex language, and especially without any guidelines on how to differentially teach simple versus complex language, teachers need to rely on the resources most readily available at their fingertips: their own students! That is, to identify language features to focus on, ImDL teachers need to listen carefully to their students and to read their written work attentively with a view to identifying language difficulties that their students are experiencing. As Han and Selinker (1999) proposed, what merits instructional attention is an empirical question, and so teachers need to practice "empirical pedagogy" (p. 248). That is, they need to engage in interlanguage analysis to guide their decisions regarding what language to focus on. In so doing, teachers must give priority to language features that (a) entail recurring errors made by most students and (b) are necessary for the successful completion of tasks in specific content areas. In science, for example, can students conduct an experiment using only the present tense, or will they need the future tense to make predictions and the past tense to describe their experiment and its outcomes? In geography or social studies, what prepositions and other spatial expressions will students need to specify locations on a map?

 SPECIAL NOTE

In addition to consulting reference books and research on L2 development, a good way for teachers to determine the language on which to focus in their teaching is to listen carefully to their students and to read their written work attentively with a view to identifying the language difficulties that their students are experiencing.

Summary

This chapter has provided a rationale for a counterbalanced approach that fosters optimal conditions for continued growth in the minority language by systematically shifting ImDL students' attention between language and content. The rationale drew on skill acquisition theory to emphasize the key roles of repetitive yet meaningful practice in conjunction with feedback in helping students to proceduralize their declarative knowledge, which moves them forward from effortful use of the minority language to more automatic use. This chapter also characterized language as a multifaceted phenomenon and then focused on the acquisition of grammar to pave the way for the next chapter. Language as discourse and as a tool for learning will be addressed in Part IV.

 Application activity 1

In this chapter, it was suggested that ImDL teachers need to focus on features of the minority language that:

1. differ in non-obvious or unexpected ways from English;
2. are irregular or infrequent, or lack perceptual salience;
3. do not carry a heavy communicative load;
4. seem similar to English but in a misleading way;
5. entail only one form whereas English has two (or vice versa).

Identify one or more language features (or grammatical sub-systems) in the language in which you teach and that correspond to each of the five criteria.

 Application activity 2

In this chapter, we presented five vignettes of ImDL teachers to illustrate good examples of counterbalanced instruction, as all teachers showcased in the vignettes showed evidence of shifting their students' attention between language and content.

Below are five more vignettes of ImDL teachers, adapted from either Salomone (1992a) or Day and Shapson (1996). First, read the vignettes and decide which teacher strategies fit more with a counterbalanced approach than others.

Then discuss with your colleagues or classmates the pros and cons of the various instructional techniques used by these five ImDL teachers. During your discussion, identify the strategies that you tend to use and those that you do not use, trying to explain why or why not.

Finally, if you are currently a teacher, write a vignette following the examples in this chapter to describe succinctly the strategies that best characterize your own approach, highlighting those that are focused more on language or more on content, or on both. If you are not yet a teacher, write a succinct vignette that describes yourself ideally applying a counterbalanced approach in a prospective ImDL classroom.

1. For Marie, a Grade 1 ImDL teacher, ensuring that her instructional techniques are suitable for her students' developmental level is of prime importance. She involves students physically and intellectually and then challenges them with more advanced activities when they are ready. She perceives herself as a subject-matter teacher and not as a language teacher. Believing that children learn to speak by hearing, she exposes her students to rich input, including her own carefully enunciated and grammatical use of the immersion language, as well as through songs, games, rhymes, and all subject-matter and classroom management activities. Discipline is of considerable importance to Marie, and so she espouses positive reinforcement strategies with the goal of developing responsible behavior among her students (Salomone, 1992a).

2. In her Grade 2 ImDL classroom, Nadine believes in teaching not only subject matter but also the immersion language. Verb conjugation posters decorate the classroom walls along with posters illustrating grammatical points. Nadine frequently provides corrective feedback, especially as students read aloud. Her teaching is artistic and creative: for example, story problems are illustrated with drawings, and her students are asked to imagine a frog jumping from number to number in order to tell time. Nadine shows a deep affection for her students, and does not see her role as that of a disciplinarian (Salomone, 1992a).

3. In her Grade 3 ImDL classroom, Patrice uses instructional strategies that emphasize clear routines and child-to-child instruction. She frequently uses comprehension checks to elicit visual, physical, or verbal responses. She routinely reads to her students, and writing activities are frequent. She uses modeling for error correction and never tells students explicitly about their errors. Her classroom control is excellent and often involves preventive discipline. Improving each child's self-image is a top priority for Patrice, who shows genuine concern for her students' likes, dislikes, and general mood (Salomone, 1992a).

4. Patience, a sense of humor, clarity, reliability, and intensity are characteristic of Estelle's behavior with her Grade 5 ImDL students. She clearly articulates classroom routines and integrates language lessons with subject-matter instruction. For example, a geography lesson about continents includes a discussion of map scale and mathematical calculations of distance; a lesson about time is organized around the theme of the Olympic Games and involves social studies, science, math, and language arts. Language teaching techniques include teacher repetition and requests for students to use the immersion language. Child-cued instruction designed to accommodate individual developmental stages is apparent in her students' involvement with peer teaching and experience-based activities (Salomone, 1992a).

5. Michel, a Grade 7 ImDL teacher, often begins his science lessons by drawing on his students' knowledge to introduce the textbook material, but without encouraging much discussion or exploration of students' answers. Instead, he tends to expect their responses to conform to pre-determined categories. He speaks clearly and provides a good model of the immersion language, but he elaborates very little and does not encourage students to expand their answers. Students rarely give more than one-word or one-phrase answers, and there is little interaction among them. Language is used for communication mainly between the teacher and the students (Day & Shapson, 1996).

4

CONTEXTUALIZATION, AWARENESS, PRACTICE, AND AUTONOMY

The CAPA model

As explained in the previous chapter, counterbalanced instruction creates opportunities for students, in the context of content-based or meaning-oriented tasks, to notice and use various features of the minority language that might otherwise be misused, unused, or unnoticed in classroom discourse. It thus differs from traditional approaches to language instruction whose primary focus is on language that has been decontextualized to facilitate analysis of its mechanical workings.

Integrating a focus on language in contextualized ways across the curriculum requires systematic planning that may at first seem challenging to many teachers whose professional training may have led them to believe that they need to focus mainly on content and can expect language to emerge incidentally. The purpose of this chapter is to help teachers overcome this challenge by outlining an instructional sequence comprising four phases—contextualization, awareness, practice, and autonomy—and thus called the CAPA model.

First, a detailed account of each of the four phases of the CAPA model is presented. Three instructional sequences whose design was guided by the CAPA model are then illustrated as a means to guide immersion and dual language (ImDL) teachers in designing and implementing content-driven instruction that targets specific language features. The goal of the instructional sequence is to scaffold students so they can reach higher levels of proficiency in the minority language.

The CAPA model and its four phases

As presented in Figure 4.1, the CAPA model comprises four main phases: contextualization, awareness, practice, and autonomy. Each phase entails at least one instructional activity or task but can, and often must, entail more than one

Contextualization establishes a meaningful context related to content usually by means of a text that has been adapted to make specific target features appear salient and frequent.

Awareness encourages students to notice and to reflect on the target features in a way that helps them to discover the patterns governing their use in the text.

Practice provides opportunities for students to use the target features in a meaningful yet controlled context and to receive corrective feedback.

Autonomy enables students to use the features in more open-ended and autonomous ways in order to develop fluency, motivation, and confidence in using the target language.

FIGURE 4.1 The CAPA model

activity, depending on the scope of the sequence. In other words, the CAPA model is flexible, and its use in instructional design can range from planning a couple of lessons to planning lengthy instructional units. In this way, the CAPA model can be used not as a rigid recipe to follow but, rather, as a blueprint to guide the design and implementation of instruction that integrates language and content.

The four phases are ideally implemented sequentially but, as in all teaching, can be implemented in a way that involves returning to a previous phase before moving forward. Although the model is illustrated as four distinct phases, they are inter-related by the focus on both content and language, and thus overlap. Such overlap is not a shortcoming but instead helps to support the cyclical or spiral nature of language learning by providing opportunities for students to revisit and recycle incipient knowledge in both new and familiar contexts.

The remainder of this section outlines in more detail the general orientation of each phase. In addition to a description and rationale for each phase, an activity is presented in the form of a Teacher Spotlight to illustrate each phase. The activities are extracted from an instructional sequence based on the CAPA model and designed by three Grade 4 teachers at Lennoxville Elementary School in Lennoxville, Quebec: Caroline Côté, Isabelle Desbiens, and Nancy Richard. They chose to integrate a focus on the *passé composé* in French within their history unit on Jacques Cartier and his three voyages to the New World.

For readers unfamiliar with French, we provide forthwith a brief description of the *passé composé*. The *passé composé* is a past tense in French generally used to refer to actions completed in the past, similar to the preterit in Spanish or the simple past in English. The *passé composé* has two parts: an auxiliary verb and a past participle. The auxiliary derives from either the verb *avoir* (*to have*) or the verb *être* (*to be*) and functions in tandem with the past participle to complete a compound verb phrase such as *Je suis tombé* (*I fell*) or *J'ai mangé* (*I ate*). For the most part, auxiliary forms derive from the verb *avoir*, but a small set of high-frequency verbs use *être*. Understandably, L2 learners of French overgeneralize the use of *avoir* as an auxiliary, resulting in frequent errors such as *j'ai allé* instead of *je suis allé* for *I went*.

In the spirit of counterbalanced instruction and before embarking on the design of instructional sequences based on the CAPA model, it's imperative that both content and language objectives be clearly identified. In the case of the instructional sequence designed by the three Grade 4 teachers, there were two main content objectives:

- Students will be able to describe some of the causes and effects of Jacques Cartier's three exploratory voyages to what became Canada.
- Students will become familiar with the sequence of events that made Jacques Cartier a key figure in the history of Quebec.

At the same time, the sequence targets two inter-related language objectives:

- Students will use the *passé composé* to describe past events with verbs such as *grandir* (to grow up), *donner* (to give), *rencontrer* (to meet), *naître* (to be born), *partir* (to leave), *arriver* (to arrive), etc.
- Students will accurately use either *avoir* (to have) or *être* (to be) as the auxiliary verb in the *passé composé* to describe completed events in the past.

Contextualization

The contextualization phase in the CAPA model serves to establish a meaningful context related to content, usually by means of a written or spoken text in which target features have been (or will be) enhanced to appear more salient or more frequent. In the case of a written text, having the target features highlighted in the initial stages is optional, because some teachers find that highlighted language features in a written text distract their students in a way that prevents them from focusing on the subject-matter content, while other teachers do not. One option is for the teachers to use the text without highlights during the contextualization phase in order to maintain a focus on meaning and then to use it with highlights during the awareness phase.

Although a written text often serves as the springboard to launch an instructional sequence based on the CAPA model, spoken texts work just as well, such as the teacher-made video in the next Teacher Spotlight. Other possibilities include dialogues with puppets or various audio files such as podcasts, in addition to photos and other types of visual stimuli.

A good way to envision the initial text or texts that are central to the contextualization phase is by drawing on the concept of backward design, which is a key component of instruction designed to integrate language and content (see Chapter 7). That is, teachers need to begin by selecting texts containing the language that students will be expected to produce during the final autonomy phase. They may need to modify the text to ensure that the target forms appear frequently enough to be noticed later during the awareness phase and to serve as models throughout the sequence.

TEACHER SPOTLIGHT

Contextualization

During the contextualization phase, the Grade 4 students watched a video about the life of Jacques Cartier called *"La course vers le nouveau monde"* ("The Race to the New World"), which had been prepared by the teachers. The video literally mapped out the key exploits in the life of the explorer using a time-lapsed procedure to create an animated feature. The voice-over narration, also prepared by the teachers, was filled with many instances of the *passé composé* using both *être* and *avoir* as auxiliary verbs.

After watching the video, the content focus stayed in the foreground as students discussed the main points surrounding Jacques Cartier's three voyages. Students took note of the dates of his travels and their effects on the subsequent influx of White Settlers to what came to be known as New France. The teacher asked many questions about the text that used and elicited instances of the *passé composé*, but did not at this point make any metalinguistic comments about its use.

The contextualization phase is a pivotal one, because it sets the stage for the whole sequence by introducing the subject-matter topic—a topic that remains constant throughout the sequence, at times in the foreground and at times in the background. Students during this initial phase need to be focused on the subject-matter content, because having a good grasp of the content will free up their cognitive resources during the next phases when they zoom in on specific language features appearing in the text. Selecting the right written or spoken text to adapt is thus important and requires some extra work, as teachers may need to modify the text to make the target features sufficiently frequent.

We cannot stress enough the imperative to have a language-rich point of departure, whether this entails a written and/or oral text (or several language-rich texts) or other types of media—as long as they expose students to multiple examples of the target features in context. Later in the sequence, students will engage in pattern detection and also in opportunities for practice, but in order for those tasks to help students refine their declarative knowledge and develop procedural knowledge, they need first to be exposed to "input for acquisition," which is defined by VanPatten (2017) as "language that learners hear or see in a communicative context that they process for meaning" (p. 167). VanPatten continues:

> This definition [of input for acquisition] excludes what many instructors believe to be key ingredients for acquisition such as explicit information and practice aimed at a particular feature. That is, explicit information about, say, how past tense works is not linguistic input for past tense. Only samples of past tense used in communicative contexts can serve as input for the acquisition of past tense. (p. 167)

The input provided during the contextualization phase, therefore, is critical, given that "it provides the crucial evidence from which learners can form linguistic hypotheses" (Gass & Mackey, 2007, p. 177). For this reason, opportunities for language analysis and language practice come later in the sequence rather than at the beginning. To engage with the content of the text during the contextualization phase, students can benefit from pre-reading tasks or other types of scaffolding that teachers generally employ to facilitate comprehension (see Chapter 5). To understand the content, however, students do not yet need to have an explicit understanding of how the selected language features function in the text—these will be brought into the foreground later. At this stage, students need to engage with a meaningful context that has been established through linguistically rich input presented in the form of written or oral texts or other types of audio-visual stimuli. The subsequent awareness and practice activities then serve, respectively, to consolidate the target forms in students' consciousness and to foster easy access during use (see DeKeyser, 1998).

Awareness

A crucial step in L2 learning is for learners to process target features in the input as intake, and, in order for input to become intake, some degree of noticing must occur (Schmidt, 1990). Whereas *input* refers simply to the language data to which learners are exposed, *intake* refers to the language data that have begun to enter the learner's cognitive system. Therefore, exposure to rich input, although "an essential component for learning" (Gass & Mackey, 2007, p. 177), is only the tip of the iceberg in ImDL classrooms. Students need to engage much more with the target language than only through exposure to input if they are to move forward in their language development. They need to notice aspects of the target language in the input and to develop relevant metalinguistic awareness in ways that support their continued language growth. The awareness phase enables students to do just that.

The awareness phase first promotes noticing by drawing learners' attention to problematic target features (such as various morphosyntactic features identified in Chapter 3) that have been enhanced to appear more salient and/or frequent in oral and written input. Various ways of making target forms more salient in the input and, therefore, more readily noticed by learners were proposed by Sharwood Smith (1993) as *input enhancement*. In the case of written input, input enhancement includes typographical enhancement such as color coding or bold-facing. In the case of oral input, intonational stress and gestures can be utilized.

The awareness phase then invites learners to do more than merely notice enhanced features in the input and instead to engage in some degree of analysis or reflection by means of rule-discovery tasks, metalinguistic exercises, or opportunities to compare and contrast language patterns. In some cases, the contrasted patterns may entail differences between the minority language and English. Also known in the literature as *consciousness-raising tasks*, awareness activities engage learners either receptively or productively, or both, and serve to consolidate the cognitive restructuring of rule-based declarative representations (see Chapter 3).

 TEACHER SPOTLIGHT

Awareness

During the awareness phase, the text of the video's narration was projected on an interactive whiteboard, with instances of the *passé composé* in bold. A short extract of the text concerning the explorer's first voyage (along with an English translation for the reader) is provided below as an example. This is a good example of a teacher-made text showing that repetitiveness can be meaningful. After all, Jacques Cartier made a total of three voyages to what became known as New France, so there were multiple opportunities for using the target forms.

Premier voyage de Jacques Cartier

Jacques Cartier **est né** en France à St-Malo en 1491. Il **a grandi** dans une famille de pêcheurs de morue. Donc, il **a appris** très jeune à naviguer sur un bateau. En 1532, le roi François 1ᵉʳ l'**a choisi** pour explorer le Nouveau-Monde. En avril 1534, Jacques Cartier **a levé** l'ancre et il **est parti** avec deux navires.

Cartier **est arrivé** dans la baie des Chaleurs et **a rencontré** des Micmac (des Amérindiens) pour la première fois. Les Français **ont donné** des petits couteaux et des miroirs et, en retour, les Micmacs leur **ont donné** les fourrures qu'ils portaient. En juillet, Cartier **est arrivé** à Gaspé. Il y **a planté** une croix et il **a déclaré** que les terres appartenaient au roi de la France.

Jacques Cartier's First Voyage

Jacques Cartier **was born** in France in St-Malo in 1491. He **grew up** in a family of cod fishermen. So, he **learned** very young how to travel by boat. In 1532, King Francis I **chose** him to explore the New World. In April 1534, Jacques Cartier **raised** anchor and **left** with two ships.

Cartier **arrived** in Chaleur Bay and **met** with the Mi'kmaq (Native Americans) for the first time. The French **gave** small knives and mirrors, and in return the Mi'kmaq **gave** them the furs they were wearing. In July, Cartier **arrived** in Gaspé. He **planted** a cross and **declared** that the land belonged to the King of France.

The teacher led students to first identify the verbs in the *passé composé* and then together to create a list of verbs that use the auxiliary *avoir*, such as *grandir (to grow up)*, *donner (to give)*, and *rencontrer (to meet)*, and those that use the auxiliary *être*, such as *naître (to be born)*, *partir (to leave)*, and *arriver (to arrive)*. As necessary and appropriate, a mini-lesson or metalinguistic discussion ensued regarding the formation of the *passé composé*, not only with respect to the choice of auxiliary but also concerning the past participle. The teachers implementing this sequence used various classroom resources as scaffolds throughout the sequence, including different posters in the classroom depicting patterns relating to (a) past participles in French, (b) regular "er" verbs conjugated in the *passé composé*, and (c) verbs that use *être* as an auxiliary.

Awareness in the CAPA model refers to *metalinguistic awareness* (see Chapter 3) and can be subdivided into two types (Ellis, 2002):

1. awareness in the sense of **consciously noticing formal properties** of the target language (e.g., the ending of that French verb is -*ent*; the gender of that Spanish noun is feminine);
2. awareness in the sense of **developing an analyzable representation** of the target form (e.g., the ending of that French verb is -*ent* because it's third-person plural; the gender of that Spanish noun is feminine because the noun ends in -*a* and is preceded by "*la*").

The awareness phase in the CAPA model addresses both types of awareness: first, getting students to notice specific target forms appearing in the text(s) presented in the contextualization phase and then scaffolding students in ways that help them to detect the patterns governing the use of the target forms. Depending on the age of the learners, development of this latter type of explicit awareness may involve having students induce the "rules" (so they can actually state them) or simply having students detect the patterns with the expectation (given sufficient exposure) that they will internalize them for subsequent use. In either case, getting students to detect patterns may be more effective than simply giving them a rule explanation to start with. As Julie Meilleur found in her Grade 6 ImDL class at Lennoxville Elementary School, "having students themselves detect the target language features proved to be more effective than giving them the information" (personal communication, May 2017).

Research has not always shown a direct relationship between metalinguistic awareness and its influence during spontaneous production. In other words, as teachers know from observing their own students and as explained in Chapter 3, knowing a rule in the sense of being able to formulate it (i.e., declarative knowledge) does not necessarily ensure that the rule will be applied during actual language use (i.e., procedural knowledge). This is why we stress that metalinguistic awareness is not an end in itself but, rather, a means to an end—an end that will be pursued subsequently in the practice and autonomy phases of the instructional sequence. In other words, metalinguistic awareness is only useful if it ultimately feeds into how one actually uses the target language—and this takes time along with opportunities for practice and feedback.

Practice

Following the awareness phase, the practice phase continues to engage learners' metalinguistic awareness with the objective of internalizing metalinguistic knowledge through comprehension and production processing. Traditional grammar practice consisting of written exercises such as fill-in-the gap exercises and sentence transformation practice are unlikely to serve this internalization process. Such types of practice can be useful for consolidating new declarative knowledge but are not typically experienced by students as opportunities for meaningful use (Ranta & Lyster, 2018).

The practice phase needs to provide opportunities for students to use the target features in meaningful ways, but in contexts that are structured enough so that teachers can provide corrective feedback that is clear, relevant, and related to the language objectives. The purpose is to push students beyond their usual interlanguage production and to expect greater accuracy in their use of the minority language, specifically with respect to the target features. This push is necessary to help destabilize interlanguage forms and to facilitate the restructuring of declarative knowledge while initiating the proceduralization process, as described in the previous chapter.

There are many types of practice from which to choose, ranging from controlled or guided practice to more open-ended or "free" communicative practice. This distinction parallels Loschky and Bley-Vroman's (1993) distinction between *task-essentialness*, which prevents the successful completion of a task unless the elicited structure is used, and *task-naturalness*, whereby the elicited structure may arise naturally but the task can easily be completed without it. We describe both types of practice forthwith, but hasten to add that the practice phase of the CAPA model should ideally emphasize task-essentialness and thus be relatively controlled or guided, which means not only necessitating the use of the target forms but also ensuring that teachers will have opportunities to provide corrective feedback. Students will have opportunities during the autonomy phase to use the target language in less constrained ways, and, before then, they need opportunities to begin the proceduralization process with the support of teacher scaffolding and a focus on accuracy.

An example of task-essentialness can be found in the activities used by Doughty and Varela (1998) in their study of content-based English as a second language (ESL) science classes, targeting the simple past and the conditional past. A group of 11–14-year-old students conducted a set of experiments in accordance with their regular science curriculum. They had to make oral predictions before conducting each experiment; then, after each experiment, as they reported their results, they needed to include what they had predicted prior to the experiment. So, if their prediction prior to the experiment was, for example, "I *think* the rubber ball *will bounce* higher than the soccer ball and the basketball," then they would subsequently need to report the following: "I *thought* the rubber ball *would bounce* higher than the soccer ball and the basketball." The post-experiment reporting thus created an obligatory context for use of the simple past (*thought*) and the conditional past (*would bounce*), making their use essential to task completion.

In contrast, here is an example of task-naturalness. Suppose you ask your students to bring in copies of photos of themselves engaged in some of their favorite activities when they were much younger, with the objective of having them describe the photos as a means to encourage the use of past tenses (as in Harley's, 1989, study conducted in Grade 6 French immersion). A student might say, "In this photo, I *was* only four years old and I *was learning* how to skate." That would be a natural way to describe the photo, but the student could just as easily (and appropriately) use the present tense: "In this photo, I *am* only four years old and I *am learning* how to skate." Use of the past tense is not essential to the completion of this task.

🏴 TEACHER SPOTLIGHT

Practice

During the practice phase, each student received one of five images illustrating an important event or place related to Jacques Cartier. The teacher wrote on the board a list of verbs in the infinitive to be used to describe one of the events. Each student selected at least one verb from the list and wrote a description of the event using the verb in the *passé composé*.

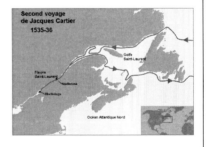

Then, students mingled with other students to find those with the same image and, together as a group, they synthesized their descriptions to create a historical account based on the image, which they then read orally to the whole class, giving the teacher an opportunity to provide corrective feedback as necessary. This activity required teacher guidance to ensure the use of the *passé composé*, because, as previously mentioned, it is feasible for students to use the present tense to refer to images. Use of the *passé composé* in this practice activity was thus task-natural but not task-essential.

To scaffold minority-language development, practice activities need to involve the processing of language for communicative purposes. However, designing practice activities that are both controlled (in the sense of requiring the use of specific target forms) and communicative in purpose is no small undertaking. To do so, teachers need to put a lot of thought into whether the tasks actually do elicit sufficient use of the target forms, and whether the tasks seem purposeful and connected to the content area. As we saw in Chapter 3, student-led surveys or interviews work well for communicative language practice with a content focus. As we will see later in this chapter, well-planned games, picture-description tasks, and question-and-answer sessions also provide opportunities for practice that is repetitive in design but communicative in purpose.

Autonomy

Instructional sequences guided by the CAPA model come full circle during the autonomy phase by bringing back into the foreground the subject-matter topic or theme that served as the starting point. Similarly to the preceding practice phase, the autonomy phase is designed to elicit the use of the target language features, but now even more closely linked to the subject-matter topic with fewer constraints and slightly less teacher scaffolding. This is to enable students to use the features to the best of their ability in more open-ended and autonomous ways to develop fluency, motivation, and confidence in using the target language. Even though students should feel that the autonomy phase provides them with a safe playing field for taking risks and testing hypotheses related to the language features that were foregrounded during the awareness and practice phases, this phase still needs to be designed in ways that foster accuracy and provide opportunities for corrective feedback.

Ideas for appropriate activities in the autonomy phase can be adapted from the students' regular subject-matter curricula. That is, as they focus on content objectives, teachers can identify tasks that students are expected to accomplish in the relevant content area. Examples of such tasks include the following:

- conducting and reporting on an experiment in science class;
- creating and presenting a timeline in social studies;
- explaining the steps required to solve a math problem;
- engaging in a debate over a past or current issue;
- interviewing a historical character;
- conducting research on a person to write and orally present his or her biography;
- explaining how the geographical features of a real or invented country influence its climatic conditions.

Teachers need to be creative in imagining how to adapt these tasks to elicit the use of language features targeted during the awareness and practice phases. At the same time, the autonomy phase lends itself well to the inclusion of language objectives that target not only language forms but also academic language functions (e.g., explaining, comparing, and evaluating; see Chapter 8).

 TEACHER SPOTLIGHT

Autonomy

In the autonomy phase, students in small groups of two or three needed to draw on both the linguistic and content knowledge that they gained in the previous activities to produce a timeline depicting some of the landmark events that punctuated Jacques Cartier's career. They illustrated the timeline with the images already used and/or drawings of their own and prepared a legend for each key event on the timeline using the *passé composé* to portray a trajectory of Jacques Cartier's experiences as an explorer. The following example illustrates how this task created obligatory contexts for having to choose between *avoir* and *être* as the correct auxiliaries:

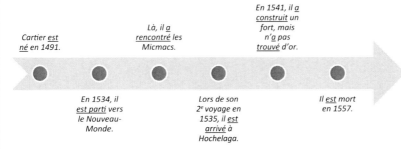

[Cartier was born in 1491 → In 1534, he left for the New World → There he met the Mi'kmaq. → During his second voyage in 1535, he arrived at Hochelaga → In 1541, he built a fort but did not find gold → He died in 1557.]

This final task may not appear as open-ended in terms of language production as one might normally expect from students during a phase devoted to learner autonomy. However, one can consider the degree of autonomy to be adequate insofar as each group needed to discuss and then select what it considered to be the most important among the many events in Cartier's life. Consequently, each group's timeline was different. As each group presented its timeline to the class, the teacher had the opportunity to provide feedback on both language and content. After the presentations, the timelines were put up for display on the classroom walls.

The autonomy phase is planned so that the target structures will arise naturally, but it may be the case that, without constant teacher guidance, students will continue to misuse the target features or even avoid them while completing the tasks. It remains imperative, however, that neither the teacher nor the students lose sight of the language objectives during this phase. To help students and also the teacher to stay tuned in to both content and language objectives, the autonomy phase lends itself well to an assessment component, such as a rubric designed to assess students' performance. See Chapter 10 on the use of rubrics for student performance assessment.

Applying the CAPA model

The CAPA model allows variable emphases to be placed on content and language, as illustrated in Figure 4.2. That is, an instructional sequence designed in accordance with the CAPA model begins with a primary focus on content during the contextualization phase and then zooms in on language during the awareness and practice phases. Language is thus in the foreground during the awareness and practice phases, while the content topic continues to provide context, even though it may temporarily slip into the background. During the autonomy phase, the primary instructional focus is again on the content that served as the starting point. The subject-matter topic should remain constant throughout the sequence, at times in the foreground and at times in the background.

Figure 4.2 illustrates which phases focus more on content and which focus more on language but does not represent this proportionally in terms of time or importance. That is, the spaces allocated to awareness and practice are smaller than the spaces allocated to contextualization and autonomy, but this is for the purpose of depicting the notion of "zooming in" on language. We might

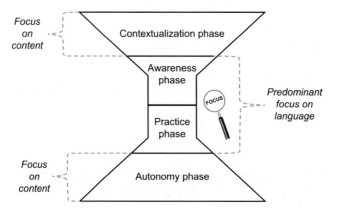

FIGURE 4.2 Variable emphases on content and language in the CAPA model

consider this to be a "narrow" focus relative to the focus on content, because it zooms in on linguistic details, but it does not require less time or imply less importance.

One way for ImDL teachers to focus more on language in some contexts than in others is to distribute these activities across the language class and different content areas. Whereas the focus on language in the awareness and practice phases might lend itself well to language arts classes, the greater focus on content during the contextualization and autonomy phases might be better suited to subject-matter classes. Although not necessary and proposed here only as an option, this is fairly easy for ImDL teachers to do if they teach both language arts and subject-matter classes. If they share these responsibilities with other teachers, this is where teacher collaboration plays a key role (see Chapter 2).

To further illustrate the application of the CAPA model in the design and implementation of instructional sequences in ImDL classrooms, two examples are featured next in Teacher Spotlight capsules. Both were designed by teachers. The first sequence was designed for young learners in Grades 1 and 2, integrating the theme of pirates and hidden treasure with a language focus on prepositions of location in French. The second sequence was designed for a Grade 5 two-way immersion classroom, integrating a focus on the forms and functions of preterit and imperfect verbs in Spanish into the study of biographical accounts.

As you read through the examples, keep in mind that they are relatively brief summaries intended to illustrate the four phases in the sequence. Consequently, they do not convey the full extent of either teacher scaffolding or the planning process underpinning successful implementation. A fuller account of teacher scaffolding appears in Part III, and more detailed accounts of both instructional design and assessment appear in Part IV.

Both sequences target difficult features of the minority language, namely, prepositions and past tense, both of which require an ongoing focus if they are to be internalized. Accordingly, neither sequence should be seen as a "one-shot deal." The context of ImDL classrooms is conducive to an ongoing focus insofar as typical ImDL programs extend over several years of elementary school. In this regard, because these are ImDL classrooms, it is most probable that the students are not being exposed for the very first time to the target features, which gives ImDL teachers the added advantage of aiming high in their expectations because they are not starting from scratch and can embed the language focus in lessons with a communicative purpose.

Finally, our goal is to provide guidance to teachers in designing their own instructional sequences that are part of their curriculum and that meet the needs of their students. The goal is not necessarily for teachers to implement these same sequences but, rather, to be inspired to create their own sequences appropriate for their specific ImDL setting.

⚓ TEACHER SPOTLIGHT

Pirates, treasure, and prepositions

Céline Carbonneau of Pope Memorial Elementary School in Bury, Quebec, used the CAPA model to design a learning module for her split Grade 1–2 class as part of its social studies curriculum. The overall theme of the module is pirates and treasure, and the language objective targets prepositions of place and direction in addition to the four cardinal points and vocabulary related to the theme of pirates.

The specific content objectives were formulated as follows:

- Students will situate certain elements in relation to other elements on a simple map.
- Students will be able to use the four cardinal points to express directions on a simple map.

The language objectives were also twofold:

- Students will accurately use prepositions of place and direction to describe location: e.g., *devant* (*in front of*), *à côté* (*beside*), and *dans* (*in*).
- Students will describe the location of items on a map using the four cardinal points and key vocabulary terms related to pirates: e.g., *le coffre* (*chest*), *le trésor* (*treasure*), *l'île* (*island*), and *les pirates* (*pirates*).

Contextualization

To begin, the teacher introduces "pirates" as the theme for the upcoming weeks and, together with students, creates a chart indicating what they already know about pirates and what they would like to learn more about. She reads to them parts of an illustrated children's encyclopedia about pirates (de Guibert & Delafon, 2010), which serves as a reference book throughout the sequence, and students comment on various images relative to what they know about pirates. Then, taking on the role of a pirate and choosing a pirate name, each student makes a painting of an aerial view of their very own treasure island to be used as a treasure map in subsequent activities. As a final step, the teacher provides each student with a compass rose to paste in the corner.

In a seemingly unrelated activity, the outcomes of which resurface later, the teacher divides the class into groups of four and then photographs each group as they follow the teacher's directions, which include the target prepositions of location (e.g., "hide under the big table"; "stand in front of the whiteboard"; and "stand on your chairs"). The teacher uses gestures as scaffolding when students don't understand.

Awareness

The first awareness activity introduces the children to a colorful plastic parrot named Jello—purported to be a pirate's parrot. The teacher has prepared 12 different photos of Jello in various situations clearly depicting the 12 target prepositions. She also has the prepositions written on flash cards, and so, as a group, students are asked to match the right preposition with the right picture of Jello (who is in a cage, on the sofa, under the sofa, beside the dog, etc.).

This is followed by a game called *"Où est Jello?"* ("Where is Jello?") in which the teacher places Jello in various positions around a stool (of course, it's a pirate's stool) and asks students to answer in full sentences to describe where Jello is in response to her question, *"Où est Jello maintenant?"* ("Where is Jello now?") (e.g., "Jello is to the left or the right of the stool, between the stool and Mme Carbonneau, or close to or far from the stool."). Their various answers are then written on poster paper, which is put on display to provide models for subsequent activities.

To initiate the second awareness activity, the teacher reads a letter to the class that she claims to have received from Jean Barque, a pirate who invites the students to follow his clues in order to find a hidden treasure chest. He provides the first clue by naming a particular student to look on the teacher's desk, under the bookshelf, etc. There the student will find the next clue, which identifies a different student to also look in a specific place. All these clues have been strategically hidden by the teacher and use prepositions to help individual (or groups of) students to find them: e.g., *"Jayden, saute jusqu'à la porte et regarde **dans** la boite de recyclage"* ("Jayden, jump over to the classroom door and look inside the recycling bin"). The last of many clues leads students to a map of their school.

Showing the map to students, the teacher helps the class to identify it as a map of the school and then follows up with questions to elicit the use of prepositions as students describe various locations such as the gym, the bathroom, the Kindergarten classroom, etc. (e.g., the bathroom is beside the office, the Grade 1 classroom is across from the Grade 2 classroom, etc.). An X indicates where Jean Barque has hidden the treasure: in the kitchen beside the cafeteria. Teacher and students head off to find the treasure chest hidden in the school kitchen.

Back in the classroom, the contents of the treasure chest are revealed, which include—in addition to some imitation gold coins for each student— realia to be used in subsequent activities: namely, the photos of students taken during the first phase as well as the maps they each made.

Practice

For the first practice activity, students reassemble in the groups they were initially photographed with, and the teacher gives each group their 12 photos. The students orally describe each of the 12 photos using prepositions, and then write a sentence to annotate each photo: for example, "We are standing behind the sofa;" "The girls are on the table;" "The boys are under the table."

For the second practice activity, the teacher displays the map of her treasure island for all to see. It includes a compass rose, which students are guided to explain in terms of the four cardinal points: north, south, east, and west. She has various cutout images such as a pirate, a parrot, a treasure chest, a boat, a shark, a volcano, and a palm tree. Individual students are asked to place an image on the map and to describe its location: for example, "The palm tree is in the north;" "The pirate is beside the palm tree;" "The volcano is in the south;" "The treasure is under the volcano;" "The shark is in the water to the east of the island." Then, students each work with their own treasure island they had previously painted. Now it's their turn to place various images in or around their island following the teacher's directions: for example, "Place the boat to the west of the island and the volcano in the south of the island."

Autonomy

Students each prepare their treasure island by affixing the various images relative to the location where they've hidden the treasure. Then, students each present their treasure island orally to the others, answering questions about the treasure's location by using prepositions in full sentences: for example, "*Il est à l'ouest du palmier; il est sous le volcan*" ("It's west of the palm tree; it's under the volcano").

Students are then asked to write a secret message to Jean Barque the pirate explaining how to find the hidden treasure. Grade 1 students write three sentences and Grade 2 students write five. For example: "*Tu arrives à l'ouest de la plage. Ensuite, tu te diriges près du volcan. Enfin, tu tournes vers le nord et tu avances jusqu'à un palmier géant. Le coffre au trésor est caché sous le palmier.*" ("You arrive to the west of the beach. Then you head close to the volcano. Finally, you turn to the north and head to a giant palm tree. The treasure chest is hidden under the palm tree.")

TEACHER SPOTLIGHT

Biographies and the preterit and imperfect

Katie Perron, a Grade 5 two-way immersion classroom teacher in the Saint Paul Public Schools in Minnesota, used the CAPA model to design and implement an entire unit. Amy Young, a PhD student at the time, aided in the development of the unit. There was a wide range of proficiency in Spanish among pupils in the class; some students had very low proficiency and others were recent arrivals from Mexico with native proficiency. Katie had noticed that some of her English L1 students were not able to use the preterit and imperfect past tenses accurately. Moreover, some of her Spanish L1 students avoided using past tenses, preferring the use of the present tense whenever possible. When these students did use past tenses, they were not always able to produce them accurately. Therefore, Katie and Amy decided to focus on these two past tenses in Spanish within the context of a unit on Biography.

There were two primary content objectives:

- Students will demonstrate an understanding of the biography genre and biographies of well-known people.
- Students will select a person to research, collect information, write a biographical report, and give an oral presentation of the biography.

The instructional sequence also targeted two language objectives:

- Students will accurately use the preterit and imperfect past tenses to write and orally present a biography of a selected figure.
- Students will increase their metalinguistic awareness of when (in which contexts) to use the preterit and imperfect past tenses.

Contextualization

During the contextualization phase, Katie introduces students to the genre of biography, using a biographical text about Pelé, the famous Brazilian soccer player. The text contains many examples of preterit and imperfect verb forms. Together, the class read the text aloud and discuss what they learned about Pelé's life, keeping the content focus at center stage. Katie asks many questions about the text, using both preterit and imperfect verb forms, but at this point does not present any information about their use. Also during this phase, Katie creates two sets of student groups. She first divides the class into three groups based on her assessment of their Spanish proficiency: high (A), intermediate (B), and low (C). She then forms both homogeneous (dark grey circles below) and heterogeneous groups (by proficiency), and she uses these group formations for different activities throughout the unit.

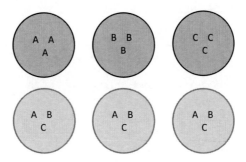

Awareness

Katie begins the awareness phase by engaging the students in a directed highlighting activity to encourage them to notice the verb forms. She gives a copy of the text to each student along with a yellow and a green highlighter. She solicits two volunteer students to come to the front of the room. Julio is given a copy of the text with all preterit verb forms highlighted in yellow, and Juliana is given a copy with all imperfect verb forms highlighted in green. Katie places a yellow Post-it on Julio's forehead and a green one on Juliana's to help students remember which color they should use as the volunteer students read the verbs. Then she begins to read the text aloud, instructing students to follow along at their desks. When she comes to a preterit verb form, she stops, and Julio reads it while students highlight that verb in yellow on their copies. When Katie comes to an imperfect verb form, Juliana reads it, and students highlight it in green.

After this noticing activity, students get into their homogeneous groups. Katie distributes a T-chart to each student and instructs them to write all the verbs highlighted in yellow in the left column and all the verbs highlighted in green in the right. Then she asks them to look for and discuss any patterns they see in the verb endings. They share their observations with the whole class. This is an appropriate time for a mini-lesson on verb stems and verb endings for both preterit and imperfect forms.

The next day, students meet in their assigned heterogeneous groups and return to the Pelé text and their individual T-charts. Katie instructs them to start looking for patterns in the text to see if they can figure out in which contexts preterit versus imperfect verbs are used. She asks them to look for "clue" words or phrases such as *un día* (*one day*), *de repente* (*suddenly*), or *en ese momento* (*at that moment*), which typically signal use of the preterit, or *durante su niñez* (*during his childhood*), *siempre* (*always*), or *todos los días* (*every day*), which often signal use of the imperfect. As a whole class, and with Katie's input and feedback, students collaboratively construct rules for the different uses of each tense. Katie writes these rules on poster paper (one sheet for each tense), which she posts in the classroom. She also includes clue phrases. She adds to the posters over the next few days as students continue to engage in activities and further develop their metalinguistic awareness of how the tenses work.

A final awareness activity takes place again in students' homogeneous groups, where they read photocopied pages from a biography of Frida Kahlo that has been written in the present tense. Each group is given different pages of the text. They are instructed to change each verb (as appropriate) to the past tense and are encouraged to explain their reasoning to each other (to continue to activate their metalinguistic awareness). Katie circulates among groups to provide feedback.

Practice

The first practice activity takes place the next day with homogeneous groups working as teams for a competitive whole-class game. Each team is given an individual white board and a marker. They rotate turns. Katie projects a website showing a modified cloze activity with a text about Superman (http://personal.colby.edu/~bknelson/SLC/superhombre.html). A short excerpt is provided below. Katie reads aloud a phrase, and when she comes to a pair of verbs in parentheses (one preterit, one imperfect), she reads both verbs, and the member of each team who has the white board writes the verb he or she thinks is correct as quickly as possible. They get a point for their team for selecting the correct verb and another point if they're able to explain why it should be preterit or imperfect. The explanation part harkens back to awareness, showing how the phases of the CAPA model can overlap.

Cuando Kal-El (fue, era) joven él (vivió, vivía) en el planeta Krypton. Pero un día sus padres se (despidieron, despedían) de él y lo (pusieron, ponían) en una nave espacial para salvarlo de la explosión de Krypton. Después de un viaje largo, él (llegó, llegaba) a un pueblo en Kansas donde Jonathan y Martha Kent lo (encontraron, encontraban).

[When Kal-El *was* young, he *lived* on the planet Krypton. But one day his parents *said* goodbye to him and they *put* him in a space ship to save him from an explosion of Krypton. After a long trip, he *arrived* in a small town in Kansas where Jonathan and Martha Kent *found* him.]

The second practice activity helps students prepare for the Autonomy phase. Students write five or six sentences in the past tense about their selected figure using a graphic organizer that Katie developed. They read and practice their sentences orally with a partner. They then share their sentences orally (without using the written scaffold) in an "inside/outside" circle activity (slide and share). The students in the inside circle first share their sentences with the students opposite them in the outside circle. Katie gives a signal, and the students in the outside circle share their sentences. Katie then gives a signal, and the inside circle members move one student to the right. The cycle repeats. The activity proceeds in much the same way until all students in the inside circle have had a chance to share their sentences with all students in the outside circle and vice versa. Katie circulates and provides feedback as needed.

Autonomy

For the autonomy phase, students create a "wax museum" of historical or present-day figures. Katie asks each student to select a figure of his or her choice. Students use a variety of resources to write a biography about that person. They also create a set of PowerPoint slides to use during oral presentations. The Autonomy phase takes weeks, with students writing drafts and Katie providing feedback on both the content of their biographies and PowerPoint slides as well as their use of the preterit and imperfect tenses.

When students' PowerPoint presentations are ready, they rehearse their oral presentations with each other, and they bring clothing and props from home (with Katie supplementing as needed) to create costumes. Meanwhile, Katie collects multiple data projectors and sets up the school gymnasium with tables and projectors around the periphery. The entire school community (including parents) are invited to visit the "wax museum" on a specific day. Student presenters appear in costume, and they strike a pose, which they hold until someone asks to hear their presentation. Katie brings a collection of South American and Spanish percussion instruments (maracas, bells, güiros, and castanets) and places one at each student's table. As visitors come by, they shake or play the instrument to indicate their interest in hearing the presentation. The "wax museum" figure comes to life and displays the PowerPoint slides while giving the presentation.

But does it work?

Research evidence

Research has demonstrated positive effects of instruction that integrates a language focus into the ImDL curriculum. Specifically, in the Canadian context, a set of seven quasi-experimental studies undertaken in French immersion classrooms between 1989 and 2013 yielded overall positive effects for the integration of form-focused instruction on a range of challenging target features in French. Like the CAPA model, form-focused instruction is designed to draw learners' attention to target features "as they are experiencing a communicative need" (Loewen, 2011, p. 582) and thus differs considerably from decontextualized language instruction.

The instructional interventions in these studies all strove to enhance students' metalinguistic awareness of the target features while providing opportunities for their use in meaningful contexts with a content or thematic focus. The target features in these studies included grammatical gender (Harley, 1998; Lyster, 2004), second-person pronouns (Lyster, 1994), conditional verb forms (Day & Shapson, 1991), functional distinctions between perfect and imperfect past tenses (Harley, 1989), verbs of motion (Wright, 1996), and word formation (Lyster, Quiroga, & Ballinger, 2013). Taken together, the results of these studies showed that, in more than 75% of the 40 tests given either as immediate or delayed posttests to assess both knowledge and productive use of the target features, students participating in the language-focused interventions improved more than students left to their own devices to "pick up" the target forms from the regular curriculum (Lyster, 2016).

Teacher testimonials

The teachers we have worked with and referred to in Part II were quick to embrace the need for content and language integration in ImDL pedagogy. Despite the challenges initially associated with the additional time required to plan for content and language integration, most concurred that it's well worth the extra time. Céline Carbonneau of Pope Memorial Elementary School expressed her view of integrating content and language integration as follows: "This approach allows me to target specific language difficulties that my students are having and to address them in a structured way that is also concrete and motivating for my students." Describing the effects of her unit on pirates and prepositions designed in accordance with the CAPA model, she elaborated:

> Seeing their interest—how they were all so eager about what we were doing—I thought, OK, I'm really captivating them. I liked having to structure my thoughts about teaching language—to take something small and really push it, then verify whether it's really working.

Similarly, Nancy Richard, one of the teachers who co-designed the unit on Jacques Cartier and the *passé composé* in French, summed up the effects of using the CAPA model as follows:

> I realized it was a success at the end when my students presented their timelines. Some students who have a lot of difficulty in French were nonetheless very successful in terms of both French grammar and Jacques Cartier's life. I think it was from often having repeated and always manipulating the same information while sometimes focusing on French and sometimes on history—that really helped a lot.

Amanda Woods of Katoh Gakuen Elementary School said of her unit targeting the language chunk *I would like to* ... that she "personally enjoyed planning and executing the CAPA sequence." She added that her "focus on language felt very discrete before; the CAPA sequence helped make it more connected" and summed up her Grade 1 students' reactions as follows:

- Students really enjoyed the tasks and activities.
- There was so much language happening in the classroom.
- Many opportunities for feedback and for "noticing."

Katie Perron shared the following perspectives about implementing her unit on biographies and past tenses in Spanish:

> During large and small group work, students were eager to participate and commented on the different uses of imperfect and preterit while still focusing on the overall content objectives of the lessons. Advanced Spanish L1 students were initially confused as to why we're using each particular verb form. I think with the progression of lessons, though, they got better at it. Then the English L1 speakers ... really latched onto the form of it and liked having a formula for being able to speak and write it. The advanced Spanish L1 speakers were able to use a wide range of complex verbs accurately, which could be attributed to a deeper intuitive understanding and their overall very strong proficiency in Spanish.

Katie's comments highlight the challenge of focusing on form in a two-way context where English L1 students need significant explanations and scaffolding to be able to understand and produce complex grammatical forms while many Spanish L1 students produce accurate forms intuitively and effortlessly.

 RESEARCH REPORT

With respect to Katie Perron's unit in her Grade 5 two-way immersion classroom, Tedick and Young (2016) conducted a study on its implementation. The study focused on eight focal students (four English L1 and four Spanish L1) whose proficiency in Spanish was lower than that of the remaining Spanish L1 students in the class. Based on an analysis of recorded observations of classroom interaction directly before and two months after the implementation of the unit, all eight focal students increased their accuracy in the use of preterit and imperfect verb forms. However, because the study was observational in nature (and not quasi-experimental), it is not possible to claim definitively that the form-focused instruction led to increased accuracy. Qualitative analysis of the data showed that the very low-proficient English L1 speakers ($n = 3$) continued to produce inaccurate forms in the post-sequence lessons, although they repeatedly produced a few forms accurately: namely, *entendí* (*I under-stood*) and *inventó* (*he or she invented*). Nevertheless, the five students who were at low-intermediate levels of Spanish (one English L1 and four Spanish L1) did produce more accurate preterit and imperfect verb forms after the instructional sequence with a range of different verbs. This finding led Tedick and Young to suggest that there may be a threshold level of proficiency neces-sary for form-focused instruction to have an impact. Moreover, given the com-plexity of preterit and imperfect past tenses and the fact that this was the first time that students had been exposed to form-focused instruction, the three very low-proficient English L1 speakers were unable to benefit as much as if the language focus had been on a less complex grammatical form.

Similarly, in a classroom study targeting the same past-tense distinction in French (*passé composé* versus *imparfait*), Harley (1989) concluded that the amount of time devoted to this aspect of French grammar was likely not enough to allow a more sustained advantage. Indeed, the verb system is con sidered to be "a major hurdle for learners of any age" (Harley, 1986, p. 59). This does not mean, however, that teachers should avoid using the CAPA model to design instruction targeting complex grammatical features (see Chapter 3). On the contrary, ongoing attention to complex forms such as functional dis-tinctions in tense and aspect is required across grade levels, because students need more exposure to these features in meaningful contexts rather than less. Such an approach fits well with the view that language development is more cyclical than linear in nature (Cameron, 2001; Skehan, 1998; Stern, 1992) and that, consequently, students will benefit from multiple opportunities to revisit and recycle their developing knowledge in a wide range of contexts.

Summary

This chapter introduced the CAPA model as a blueprint for designing an instruc-tional sequence comprising four phases: contextualization, awareness, practice, and autonomy. The four phases are inter-related by their dual focus on the same subject-matter content and target language features, although the contextualiza-tion and autonomy phases place primary emphasis on content whereas the aware-ness and practice phases zoom in on language. The rationale for the four phases was drawn from research on instructed SLA, which predicts the following:

The acquisition of specific target language features occurs when students have opportunities to

1. encounter the target features in the context of written or spoken texts related to content;
2. develop their awareness of the target features in contexts associated with content;

3. practice using the target features in contexts concerning content and conducive to feedback;
4. use the target language features autonomously as they engage purposefully with the content.

Concrete examples of sequences designed in accordance with the CAPA model were outlined to guide teachers in designing their own instructional sequences. The CAPA model will resurface in Chapter 8, which outlines a more detailed account of lesson-level instructional design in ImDL classrooms.

Application activity

Identify a topic in a content area or a language arts theme that you teach. Then, identify a language feature related to this topic or theme that your ImDL students find challenging. Drawing on the CAPA model illustrated throughout this chapter, design an instructional sequence that integrates a focus on your selected target feature(s). The instructional sequence should include four inter-related phases with a minimum of one activity per phase:

1. a contextualization phase that establishes a meaningful context by means of a text that has been adapted to make the target features appear salient and frequent;
2. an awareness phase that encourages students to notice and to reflect on the target features in a way that helps them to discover the patterns governing their use in the text;
3. a practice phase that provides opportunities for students to use the target features in a meaningful yet controlled context and to receive corrective feedback;
4. an autonomy phase that enables students to use the features in open-ended and autonomous ways in order to develop fluency, motivation, and confidence in using the target language.

Online resources for readers

Online instructional sequences in French based on the CAPA model

There is a French-language website at www.mcgill.ca/etsb/that is home to eight teacher-designed instructional sequences based on the CAPA model and intended for social studies. In addition to full versions of two of the sequences described in this chapter (i.e., "Jacques Cartier and the *passé composé*" and "Pirates, treasure, and prepositions," examples of other sequences are "Iroquoian villages and grammatical gender," "Indigenous cultures and 3rd-person plural verbs," and "Montreal's first streetcars and the *imparfait*." These are available for any teacher to use or to adapt, or as models for developing similar sequences.

La course vers le nouveau monde ("The Race to the New World")

The video used in the Grade 4 social studies unit about the life of Jacques Cartier (see page 104) is available in French on YouTube at www.youtube.com/watch?v=_vsqzjD_oe8&feature=youtu.be with the compliments of the three teachers who designed and implemented this instructional sequence: Caroline Côté, Isabelle Desbiens, and Nancy Richard.

PART III
What is scaffolding?

Part III addresses the instrumental role of scaffolding in ImDL pedagogy as a means to help students understand and engage with language and content at levels higher than they would be able to reach on their own. In Chapter 5, we first outline verbal, procedural, and instructional scaffolding as strategic ways to support students in their comprehension and production of a language they are still learning. Then, through examples from actual classroom interactions, we explore questioning techniques and follow-up strategies that encourage student language production while consolidating their content knowledge. Chapter 6 is concerned with how to provide clear and meaningful corrective feedback so that it engages students as active participants and benefits their continued growth in the minority language.

5

EFFECTIVE SCAFFOLDING AND QUESTIONING TECHNIQUES

This chapter first identifies a range of scaffolding strategies that support student comprehension and student production. The chapter then explores a range of questioning techniques with an emphasis on those that push students to use quantitatively more language and qualitatively more complex language. The chapter aims to answer the following questions:

- What is scaffolding and how can it be employed effectively in ImDL classrooms?
- What types of teacher questions more than others serve to increase both the quantity and the quality of student output while also helping students to deepen their understanding?

Scaffolding

Oral interaction plays a key role in driving L2 development forward because learners rely on semantically contingent speech (i.e., speech that is directly related and in response to their own) as a primary source of language data (Long, 1996). For communication to be successful during oral interaction, learners need to play active roles in both comprehension and production.

With respect to comprehension, oral interaction provides learners with opportunities to control the input to some extent, as they can ask their interlocutors to modify their speech in ways that make the input more accessible and thus more likely to be processed as intake (see Chapter 4). Because not all input becomes intake, one of the teacher's roles is to create an environment where as much input as possible will become intake. Because some degree of noticing must occur in order for input to become intake (e.g., Schmidt , 1990), teachers can draw on the scaffolding techniques outlined in this and the next chapter to help students notice features of the minority language that they would otherwise not attend to.

In terms of production, oral interaction affords opportunities for learners to produce the minority language in meaningful ways that also contribute to language development. But in immersion and dual language (ImDL) classrooms, how can learners fully participate in oral interaction, as a means to engage with both language and content while developing their production abilities, if the language of communication is one that they are still learning and thus know only partially? This is where teacher scaffolding plays a pivotal role.

 **KEY CONCEPT**

Scaffolding refers to different types of support and assistance provided by teachers to help students understand and engage with content at levels higher than they would be able to reach on their own.

Scaffolding was initially invoked as a means to characterize parent–child interaction and was qualified as that which "enables a child or novice to solve a problem, carry out a task or achieve a goal which would be beyond his unassisted efforts" (Wood, Bruner, & Ross, 1976, p. 90). It is often associated with Vygotsky's (1978) "zone of proximal development" or ZPD, which is the difference between what children can achieve on their own and what they might achieve when assisted by another. The notion of scaffolding has since been aptly applied to teacher–student interaction and considered to encapsulate effective teaching.

As a metaphor borrowed from the construction industry, scaffolding has often been considered a temporary support (e.g., Cazden, 1983). However, in ImDL classrooms, teacher scaffolding is a key instructional strategy throughout the entire program from beginning to end. Although the nature of the scaffolding changes as students progress and become more autonomous, the need to provide support for student learning is no less apparent in higher grades, where academic language and content become increasingly more complex.

Specifically regarding ImDL pedagogy, scaffolding is at its core and requisite for students' academic success. The fact that learners need to engage with both language and content just ahead of their current level of ability—rather than only with language and content they already know—is a reality of ImDL education and arguably one of the reasons for its success. That is, the dual focus on language and content in ImDL requires deeper levels of processing, as students need to engage with new subject matter in a language they are still learning. The cognitive effort necessitated by this dual focus has the potential to strengthen (rather than weaken) both content and language learning. For this to happen, though, teachers need to engage in scaffolding that enhances and structures oral classroom discourse in ways that facilitate both student comprehension and production. Thanks to the scaffolding provided by teachers and also peers, students are better equipped to deal with the challenge of engaging with content in a language they know only partially, as they draw on the contextual clues provided in the scaffolding and also on prior knowledge.

 KEY CONCEPT

Classroom discourse refers to the means used by teachers and students to engage in verbal exchanges (through use of questions, answers, directives, confirmations, feedback, etc.) whose purpose is didactic or conversational (or both).

One type of scaffolding assists students in understanding content presented through the minority language, and another type supports them in productively using the minority language to engage with the content. In the hurly-burly of actual classroom discourse, however, there is a dynamic relationship between strategies for scaffolding student comprehension and those for scaffolding student production, but we outline them separately forthwith for the sake of clarity. In both cases, we will classify the scaffolding techniques as verbal, procedural, or instructional (Echevarría, Vogt, & Short, 2008).

Scaffolding for student comprehension

To ensure comprehension, ImDL teachers have at their disposal a wide range of strategies that facilitate the learning of curricular content through the minority language. Together, these scaffolding techniques give students many chances to understand the target language and curricular content.

1. *Verbal scaffolding for comprehension* involves linguistic redundancy, whereby teachers express more or less the same message but in different ways by using self-repetition, paraphrases, synonyms, and multiple examples. In addition, to further enhance this type of teacher talk and to make their speech comprehensible as well as salient so that it becomes a rich source of language input for their students, teachers can modify their rate of speech, articulation, and intonation in ways that are appropriate for their students' ages and abilities. For example, teachers can include natural pauses between phrases to give students time to process the language, in addition to using body language and facial expressions to accompany their speech and thereby support comprehension.

> ### 🖐 KEY CONCEPT
>
> *Teacher talk* is the speech used by teachers to enhance and structure classroom discourse in ways that facilitate both content and language learning.

2. *Procedural scaffolding for comprehension* refers to the activity frames and routines that teachers employ to ensure predictability and thus to facilitate comprehension. Teachers can ensure predictability in instructional routines by using clear boundary markers between activities to orchestrate daily routines in a way that facilitates classroom management and maximizes opportunities for learning. They need also to draw extensively on their students' background knowledge to aid comprehension, using instructional routines such as think-pair-share and role plays to activate prior knowledge. By pairing or grouping in this way, teachers can draw on the students themselves to help one another understand content lessons and support each other's language use and development.

3. *Instructional scaffolding for comprehension* refers to the various devices embedded in instructional activities to facilitate students' comprehension of both language and content, as well as understanding of the activity itself. For example, teachers can provide students with graphic organizers to facilitate comparisons or to illustrate a text structure in order to support comprehension of both content and language. In addition to graphic organizers, instructional scaffolding entails a range of instructional tools such as age-appropriate books and other print resources, props, graphs, maps, word walls, manipulatives, imagery, and various visual and multi-media resources such as film, video, interactive whiteboards, and other computerized projections.

Scaffolding for comprehension is at the core of ImDL pedagogy. Because of these strategies, ImDL teachers do not need to resort to using English to facilitate comprehension of the content presented in the minority language. Instead, they can engage in teacher talk that serves a didactic function to highlight both language and content by building linguistic and non-linguistic redundancy into their use of the minority language. This is important because the overuse of English for explanatory purposes decreases the students' need and motivation to process content through the minority language and thus reduces opportunities for their cognitive engagement with the minority language. Reference to English, however, can play an important metalinguistic role to highlight cross-linguistic similarities and differences, a topic addressed in Chapter 9.

The nature of scaffolding for comprehension needs to evolve as students progress through the ImDL program. Over time, the scaffolding needs to be adjusted in age-appropriate ways that enable students to engage with the minority language with increasingly greater autonomy. Scaffolding that relies too much on linguistic redundancy, gestures, and other visual and non-linguistic support to facilitate comprehension is unlikely over time to make the kinds of increasing demands on the learners' language system that are necessary for continued language development. This means that ImDL teachers need to engage in a delicate balancing act of providing, on the one hand, just the right amount of support to make the minority language comprehensible, while being demanding enough, on the other hand, to ensure that learners engage in higher-order cognitive skills and increasingly gain the ability to process content with less direct teacher support.

Scaffolding for student production

Teachers need also to provide support for their students to engage in extended use of the minority language. The use of verbal, procedural, and instructional scaffolding to support student production enables teachers to structure classroom interaction in ways that push students to elaborate their ideas as much as possible while also providing them with regular opportunities for independent use of the minority language.

1. *Verbal scaffolding for production* aims to promote learning and to facilitate student language production during teacher-student interaction. It includes a variety of corrective feedback types (see next chapter) as well as a balance of display questions (to which the teacher knows the answer) and referential questions (to which the teacher does not know the answer). Verbal scaffolding also includes strategically planned follow-up questions that avoid evaluative comments and instead push students to clarify and elaborate their ideas in ways that require higher-order thinking and thus more complex language (more on this in the next section). At the same time, teachers need to give students sufficient "wait time" to interpret questions and formulate their responses.

2. *Procedural scaffolding for production* involves the creation of multiple opportunities for students to use the minority language in independent ways. Accordingly, teachers need to orchestrate a variety of interactive configurations, such as dyads, think-pair-share, cooperative learning groups, and learning centers, all designed to promote learning from and with peers (e.g., peer editing, peer tutoring, and peer feedback) while also fostering interpersonal communication. More presentational modes of communication can be achieved through role plays, simulations, debates, and presentations. Although the goal is autonomous use of the minority language, such groupings need to be well structured and scaffolded by teachers to elicit sustained use of academic oral and written language. For example, to ensure that students are able to and motivated to use the minority language when working together, teachers need to spend time going over the language they will need to use to accomplish the tasks.

TEACHER SPOTLIGHT

Amy Egenberger, a former Spanish immersion teacher in Minnesota, encouraged her students to seek help from each other by reminding them with this verbal cue: "Primero tres, a mí después." [First three, then me.]

3. *Instructional scaffolding for production* is similar to instructional scaffolding for comprehension in that both include various print and multi-media resources to support learning. To lead to student production during the aforementioned interactive groups, for example, instructional scaffolding includes (a) explicit training in the interpersonal strategies required for successful collaboration and (b) the teacher's modeling, which prepares students to make use of the relevant resources at their disposal. Just as tools are critical to scaffolding for comprehension, they can also be used as scaffolds for production. For example, teachers can offer sentence starters or sentence frames displayed in the classroom to aid student production. Similarly, instructional scaffolding includes teaching familiar "chunks" of language: for example, "May I go to the bathroom?"; "How do you say…?"; or "I have a question." Some teachers create posters of language chunks with corresponding pictures and post them in the classroom as reminders to students to use these phrases on a regular basis. In addition to facilitating oral production in this way, teachers need regularly to create written tasks and assignments that are well scaffolded and invite extended student discourse. They can use graphic organizers as a scaffold not only for understanding subject-matter content but also for producing specific academic language discourse patterns such as compare/contrast. For example, a simple T-chart can be a useful graphic organizer for students to identify and then compare pros and cons, causes and effects, or facts and opinions.

 KEY CONCEPT

Graphic organizers are visual displays that help students to see relationships between ideas or concepts. See *Resources for Readers* at the end of this chapter for access to customizable graphic organizers that scaffold for comprehension and production. Below is an example of a graphic organizer called the Frayer Model that can be used for building student vocabulary (retrieved from www.teacherspayteachers.com/FreeDownload/Spanish-Frayer-Model-Vocabulary-Graphic-Organizer-739409):

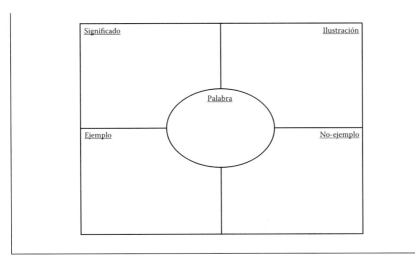

By providing just the right amount of assistance that students need in order to process the minority language for both comprehension and production, ImDL teachers can promote both language development and the acquisition of content knowledge. The image of a teacher scaffolding learners so that they can process language at a level that they would be unable to manage on their own provides a helpful metaphor for appreciating the strategic role played by teacher questions, addressed in the next section.

Teacher questions

In their seminal study of classroom discourse, Sinclair and Coulthard (1975) found that the most typical teaching exchange consists of three moves: an initiating (I) move by the teacher; a responding (R) move by the student; and an evaluative (E) move by the teacher.

The IRE sequence has been disparaged as the quintessence of transmission models of teaching and typical of teacher-centered classrooms. It has been criticized for engaging students only minimally and for maintaining unequal power relationships between teachers and students.

Notwithstanding the criticism, the IRE sequence continues to permeate classroom discourse, due arguably to its potential for providing structure and predictability while helping teachers to monitor students' knowledge and understanding. That is, it equips teachers with a means to assess their students in an ongoing manner in the course of interaction and thus a means to also plan and evaluate their teaching. Nassaji and Wells (2000) noted that, in classroom discourse, "it is necessary for somebody to ensure that the discussion proceeds in an orderly manner and that, as far as possible, all participants contribute to, and benefit from the co-construction of knowledge" (p. 378). In their analysis of literature and science classes from Grades 1 to 6, they found a prevalence of IRE exchanges. They concluded that IRE exchanges played an important role in initiating discussion and that the teacher's initiating move enabled both students and teachers alike to contribute substantively to understanding an issue for which there was no single correct answer and in which the goal was to consider a variety of alternatives.

Teachers' initiating moves in the IRE exchange are often classified as either display or referential questions. Referential questions are further categorized as *closed* (having only one possible answer, such as "Which book did you read?") or *open* (having many possible answers and requiring a higher level of thinking, such as "Why do you think the character responded that way?"). Display questions are often criticized for limiting the students' possibilities to try out their own ideas, but teachers have been observed using both display and referential questions with equal effectiveness (Haneda, 2005). In ImDL classrooms, display questions have proven to be an important part of content learning, because they help teachers to verify content mastery and thus are not limited to inciting students only to display linguistic knowledge (Salomone, 1992b). Similarly, in Italian content-based classes, display questions served effectively to verify comprehension of subject matter delivered in the L2 and were just as effective as referential questions for eliciting extensive responses from students (Musumeci, 1996).

More important than the teacher's initial question in the IRE exchange, however, is the teacher's choice of evaluative move and the extent to which it allows the teacher to work with the student's response in a variety of ways. Nassaji and Wells (2000) found that IRE exchanges beginning with a display question can develop into more equal dialogue if, in the third turn, the teacher actually avoids evaluation and instead poses follow-up questions to request justifications or counter-arguments. In this regard, the IRE sequence is likely to be more effective as an IRF sequence (Initiation-Response-Follow-up) in which the evaluative move is replaced by a follow-up move that aims to: (a) elaborate on the student's response or provide clarification; (b) request further elaboration, justification, explanation, or exemplification; or (c) challenge students' views (Haneda, 2005). This is because evaluative comments such as "very good" may inhibit learning opportunities insofar as they serve a "finale" function that precludes further attempts by others to articulate their (mis)understanding or explore alternative answers (Wong & Waring, 2009).

At the same time, however, it remains both improbable and undesirable for teachers to ask a preponderance of questions to which they do not know the answers. As they work dialogically with students, teachers need to provide scaffolding that includes a variety of initiating moves ranging from display to referential questions as well as a variety of follow-up moves. Well-planned follow-up questions help students to deepen their understanding and provide opportunities for students to use language that is more complex than that found in the shorter answers that are so typical of classroom discourse. In a similar vein, to create more opportunities for extended student responses specifically in content and language integrated learning (CLIL) classrooms, Dalton-Puffer (2006) recommended that teachers use fewer questions eliciting facts, which tend to result in minimal responses, and more questions about students' beliefs and opinions that require them to explain, define, or give reasons.

To illustrate a range of follow-up questions, Echevarría and Graves (1998) drew on Tharpe and Gallimore's (1988) proposal for "instructional conversations," a reactive approach used with small groups of children to provide assistance and instruction that are contingent on student production. Specifically in the context of content-based instruction, Echevarría and Graves (1998) classified three types of helpful questioning techniques designed to enrich instructional conversations and to facilitate students' understanding of ideas and concepts that they would otherwise be unable to express on their own:

1. Promotion of more complex language and expression
   - *"Tell me more about …"*
   - *"What do you mean by …"*
   - *"In other words, …"*
   - *"Why do you think that?"*
2. Elicitation of bases for statements or positions
   - *"How do you know?"*
   - *"What makes you think that?"*
3. Fewer known-answer questions
   - *"Look at the page and tell me what you think the chapter will be about."*
   - *"What can you learn from reading this label?"*
   - *"How are these plants different?"*
   - *"Why would the colonists do that?"*
   - *"Tell me more about that."*
   - *"On what basis would you group these objects?"*

- *"Why might that be?"*
- *"What makes you think this might be different?"*

These types of follow-up question fit well with a social-constructivist approach to education, which addresses "issues, concepts, and tasks in the form of problems to be explored in dialogue rather than as information to be ingested and reproduced" (Williams & Burden, 1997). According to this view, the essence of learning and teaching is found in dialogue where "the most valuable talk occurs in the context of exploration of events and ideas in which alternative accounts and explanations are considered and evaluated" (Wells, 2001, p. 3). This kind of dialogue has been referred to as *dialogic teaching* (Alexander, 2003), which guides learning by drawing on students' curiosity while promoting the co-construction of meaning and the development of critical thinking skills. In this view, meaning is thought to be co-constructed in the sense that knowledge is socially constructed through dialogue because much of it is tentative or relative rather than absolute. For example, scientific knowledge is different today from what it was 50 years ago and still continues to evolve. Similarly, historical knowledge entails a great deal of interpretation of multiple and changing perspectives rather than unitary and static accounts. In this approach, students are as involved in developing answers as they are in formulating new questions. For this to happen, teachers need to plan their interventions in such a way as to arouse students' curiosity while pushing them forward in their thinking.

Putting questions into question

In 1988, one of the authors (Roy Lyster) participated with his Grade 8 French immersion students in a video produced by the Ontario Institute for Studies in Education in Toronto (Argue, Lapkin, Swain, Howard, & Lévy, 1990). In addition to the final product (a professional video about 75 minutes long used for ImDL teacher education), he was given a video recording with hours of unused footage. It is from this source that he transcribed the following exchanges for the purpose of analyzing his own questioning techniques in terms of their effectiveness. We highly recommend that teachers everywhere either video-record or audio-record themselves while teaching and interacting with students. This is perhaps the best way for a teacher to gain insight into the interactional patterns that characterize the classroom and the ways in which we scaffold the interaction.

Let's look at the questioning and scaffolding techniques Roy used with his students during a discussion about the novel *Max* by Monique Corriveau (1966). First, read the exchange, taking note of the questions he poses and the scaffolding he attempts to use to support students in answering questions. Think about these questions in terms of their success (or lack of success) in getting students to reflect on and to use language.

1.	T:	*Et quel est le titre de ce chapitre, du deuxième chapitre? Sima?*	T: And what's the title of this chapter, of the second chapter? Sima?
2.	S:	*« Le refuge »*	S: "The Refuge."
3.	T:	*OK, « Le refuge ». Et je vous avais demandé de trouver la signification de ce titre. Qu'est-ce que ça veut dire « un refuge »? Pourquoi est-ce que ce chapitre s'appelle « Le refuge », Tim?*	T: OK, "The Refuge." And I had asked you to find the meaning of this title. What does "refuge" mean? Why is this chapter called "The Refuge"? Tim?
4.	S:	*[?] la protection [?]*	S: [?] protection [?]
5.	T:	*Oui tu es sur la bonne voie, oui. Soyons un peu plus précis que « la protection ». Oui?*	T: Yes, you're on the right track, yes. Let's be a little more specific than protection. Yes?
6.	S:	*Une cachette.*	S: A hiding place.
7.	T:	*Oui, c'est bien, une cachette. Et essayez de relier les deux définitions maintenant. Karen?*	T: Yes, that's good, a hiding place. And now try to connect the two definitions. Karen?
8.	S:	*Une place pour cacher, pour te sauver danger.*	S: A place to hide, to save from danger.
9.	T:	*C'est bien. OK, un endroit, un lieu où tu peux te cacher, pour te mettre à l'abri d'un danger, oui. Et donc pourquoi est-ce que ce chapitre s'appelle « Le refuge »? Liz?*	T: That's good. OK, a place where you can hide, seek shelter from danger, yes. And so why is this chapter called "The Refuge"? Liz?
10.	S:	*Parce que Max va cacher, prendre le refuge pour la nuit.*	S: Because Max is going to hide to take the refuge for the night.
11.	T:	*Et où est-ce qu'il se cache? Quel est son refuge? Jason?*	T: And where does he hide? What's his refuge? Jason?
12.	S:	*L'Aquarium.*	S: The Aquarium.
13.	T:	*Oui, à l'aquarium. Maintenant, quel autre mot, quels sont les autres mots qui viennent du mot « refuge »? Les mots qu'on entend souvent maintenant, dans les nouvelles par exemple. D'autres, un mot qui vient du mot « refuge ». Oui?*	T: Yes, at the Aquarium. Now, what other word, what other words come from the word *refuge*? Words that we often hear now, in the news for example. Other, a word that comes from the word *refuge*. Yes?
14.	S:	*Réfugié.*	S: Refugee.
15.	T:	*Réfugié, oui. Et qu'est-ce que c'est un réfugié? Lucy?*	T: Refugee, yes. And what is a refugee? Lucy?
16.	S:	*C'est quelqu'un qui, qui se cache.*	S: It's someone who, who hides.
17.	T:	*OK, se cache peut-être, mais c'est surtout, c'est pas forcément qui se cache, mais, soyons un peu plus précis. Oui? Sima?*	T: OK, hides maybe, but it's more, it's not really who hides, but, let's be a little more specific. Yes? Sima?
18.	S:	*Quelqu'un qui part.*	S: Someone who leaves.
19.	T:	*Pourquoi? Pourquoi « qui part »?*	T: Why? Why "who leaves"?
20.	S:	*Uh, beaucoup de prisons, uh*	S: Uh, many prisons, uh
21.	T:	*Oui, mais essaie de penser à la définition de Tim du mot « refuge ». Qu'est-ce qu'un réfugié cherche? Il se cache, mais … Oui? Liz?*	T: Yes, but try to think of Tim's definition of the word *refuge*. What is a refugee searching for? He's hiding, but … Yes? Liz?
22.	S:	*La protection.*	S: Protection.
23.	T:	*OK, il veut se protéger de quelque chose, OK. Peut-être de quelque chose qui va pas dans son pays, donc il cherche à fuir, à échapper à un danger, par exemple, OK …*	T: OK, he wants to protect himself from something. Maybe something that's not right in his country, so he's trying to flee, to escape from danger, for example, OK …

Roy asks questions to get students to explain what a refuge is and why the chapter is called *"Le refuge."* At the same time, he scaffolds the interaction in a way that encourages students (Turn 5, "You're on the right track") while pushing them to make connections (Turn 7, "Try to connect the two definitions") and to be more specific (Turn 17, "Let's be a little more specific"). He gets students to generate words from the same family (Turn 13, "What other words come from the word *refuge*?") while making links to current events: "Words that we often hear now, in the news" (in 1988, thousands of Somali refugees began arriving in Canada, fleeing civil war in their country).

We can tease apart the questions and the scaffolds as follows, to illustrate that the scaffolds serve to guide the students' participation in the dialogue.

Questions	Scaffolding
Quel est le titre de ce chapitre? [What's the title of this chapter?]	*Tu es sur la bonne voie.* [You're on the right track.]
↓	↓
Qu'est-ce que ça veut dire « un refuge »? [What does *refuge* mean?]	*Soyons un peu plus précis.* [Let's be a little more specific.]
↓	↓
Pourquoi est-ce que ce chapitre s'appelle « Le refuge »? [Why is this chapter called "The Refuge"?]	*Essayez de relier les deux définitions.* [Try to connect the two definitions.]
↓	↓
Où est-ce qu'il se cache? [Where does he hide?]	*Les mots qu'on entend souvent maintenant, dans les nouvelles* [Words that we often hear now, in the news.]
↓	
Quel est son refuge? [What is his refuge?]	
↓	↓
Quels sont les autres mots qui viennent du mot « refuge »? [What other words come from the word *refuge*?]	*Soyons un peu plus précis.* [Let's be a little more specific.]
↓	↓
Pourquoi « qui part »? [Why "who leaves"?]	*Essaie de penser à la définition de Tim …* [Try to think of Tim's definition …]
↓	
Qu'est-ce qu'un refugié cherche? [What is a refugee searching for?]	

Roy tries to lead students to identify *refugié* as a derivative of *refuge* as they seek definitions for both nouns. In response, the students are able collectively to convey that a refuge is a hiding place where one seeks protection from danger, and that a refugee is someone who leaves his home country in search of protection. At the same time, Roy provides various ways of expressing similar notions through a range of verbal clauses that share similar patterns:

- *se mettre à l'abri d'un danger* [seek shelter from danger]
- *se protéger de quelque chose* [protect himself from something]
- *chercher à fuir* [try to flee]
- *échapper à un danger* [escape from danger]

However, although he incorporates the above clauses into his own speech, he does nothing to draw attention to them and does nothing to encourage the students to use them. As a result, the students' utterances are usually short noun phrases (e.g., "*la protection*," "*une cachette*," and "*danger*"), sentence fragments ("*quelqu'un qui part*"), and non-idiomatic phrases ("*une place pour cacher, pour te sauver danger*"). Even though Roy asks them to be more specific, they are not really pushed to elaborate or given the support they would need to produce more sophisticated language that would be useful for discussing refuges and refugees, such as the verb clauses above as well as others that express the idea of running away or fleeing (e.g., *se sauver de; s'enfuir de*).

Continuing the discussion of the plight of the eponymous character of *Max* in Chapter 2, Roy asks students to put themselves in Max's shoes and to imagine how he must have felt as he took refuge overnight in a small projection room in the Aquarium du Québec:

1.	T:	*Maintenant, faites semblant que vous êtes Max et que vous êtes entré en cachette dans l'aquarium. Vous allez dans cette salle de cinéma qui est toute vide parce qu'il y a personne, y a pas de réunions en ce moment et vous devez passer la nuit là et vous êtes tout seul sauf les poissons. À quoi est-ce que vous penseriez si vous étiez Max? À quoi est-ce que vous penseriez? Tim?*	T: Now, pretend that you are Max and you've sneaked into the Aquarium. You go into the theatre and it's empty because there's nobody, there are no meetings going on, and you have to spend the night all alone, except for the fish. What would you think about if you were Max? What would you think about? Tim?
2.	S:	*Euh, après la nuit, où est-ce que tu vas passer.*	S: Um, after the night, where you're going to pass.
3.	T:	*Oui, oui. Liz ?*	T: Yes, yes. Liz?
4.	S:	*Hum, dans le matin, comme si tu, hum, allais dehors et si, comme si quelqu'un va te voir.*	S: Um, inside the morning, like if you, um, went outside and if, like if someone is going to see you.
5.	T:	*Oui, peut-être. Quelles seraient peut-être les émotions de Max à ce moment-là? Oui?*	T: Yes, maybe. What would Max's emotions maybe be then? ... Yes?
6.	S:	*La peur.*	S: S: Fear.
7.	T:	*OK, peut-être la peur. Autre chose? Dan?*	T: OK, maybe fear. What else? Dan?
8.	S:	*Peut-être la tristesse.*	S: Maybe sadness.
9.	T:	*Peut-être, oui, parce qu'il est tout seul. Oui?*	T: Maybe, yes, because he's all alone. Yes?

10.	S:	*Con… euh, confusé, c'est, euh…*	S:	Con… um, confuse.
11.	T:	*Qu'il est confus.*	T:	He's confused.
12.	S:	*Oui, confus.*	S:	Yes, confused.
13.	T:	*Oui, oui, c'est bien, oui.*	T:	Yes, that's good. Yes?
14.	S:	*Fâché.*	S:	Angry.
15.	T:	*Oui, très fâché.*	T:	Yes, very angry.
16.	S:	*Mais ça ne fait rien si, euh, le public le voit, n'est-ce pas, parce que le policier n'a pas, euh, dit à le … comme le public ne sait pas que Max est probablement coupable.*	S:	But it doesn't matter if the public sees him, right, because the police didn't say, like the public doesn't know that Max is probably guilty.
17.	T:	*Oui, c'est bien, sauf que … qu'est-ce qu'on avait écrit dans le journal ? Est-ce qu'on avait publié son nom ? On n'a pas publié sa photo, mais est-ce qu'on a publié son nom ? Oui ou non ? Jason ?*	T:	Yes, that's good, except that, what had been written in the newspaper? His picture hadn't been published, but was his name published? Yes or no, Jason?
18.	S:	*Oui.*	S:	Yes.
19.	T:	*Oui, tout à fait. Dans l'article de Lebrun, il a dit qu'on soupçonne Max. Oui ?*	T:	Yes, exactly. In Lebrun's article, he said that Max was a suspect. Yes?
20.	S:	*Il serait très soucieux.*	S:	He would be very concerned.
21.	T:	*Oui, très soucieux, c'est un très bon mot. OK. Très inquiet.*	T:	Yes, very concerned. That's a really good word. OK. Very worried.

Roy is trying hard to get students to think about the emotions that might be felt by someone hiding out and being sought after. He seems to have planned his initiating questions, but not any follow-up questions. Consequently, the students were not pushed much as they produced words that were on target but in very short utterances: "fear," "sadness," "confused," and "angry." At the very least, Roy could have expected slightly longer utterances with subject pronouns and verb phrases more consistent with those in the questions, that is, either first- or third-person subject pronouns and verbs in the conditional to identify probable yet uncertain feelings:

- *J'aurais peur.* [I would be afraid.]
- *Il serait triste.* [He would be sad.]
- *Il serait confus.* [He would be confused.]
- *Il serait fâché.* [He would be angry.]

While expecting richer language such as this, a good opportunity would have arisen to stress the use of *avoir* in *j'aurais peur* in contrast to the use of *être* in *il serait confus, fâché,* or *soucieux*. The distinctions between "be" and "have" equivalents in Romance languages lead to recalcitrant errors by learners wrongly assuming similar patterns to those in English. These learners can benefit from attending to these differences in meaningful contexts, such as this one, where they are explaining the feelings of the novel's main character.

Above all, what is missing here are good follow-up questions asking students to explain why they or Max would be afraid, confused, sad, angry, or worried. For example, to respond to his students, instead of saying "OK" or "Yes, that's good," Roy should have asked them to elaborate on what Max would be afraid of or whom he would be angry with and why he would be sad or confused. Such follow-up questions are important to plan in advance and to ask in order to get students using quantitatively more language and qualitatively more complex language. If it's worth the time, in the context of this novel study, to ask questions about feelings, then it must be worth the time to expect more than fragmented answers of only one or two words. Also missing in this exchange is any corrective feedback following student errors—the topic of the next chapter.

In both discussions about *Max*, it remains unclear what Roy's language objectives are, and one is left wondering exactly what the learning objectives are. As has often been observed in ImDL classrooms, the primary objective seems to be for students to demonstrate their comprehension of a text, but without the kind of scaffolding that would enable them to use age-appropriate language to do so. This type of teacher-centered interaction is reminiscent of Harley's (1993) observation of ImDL classrooms:

> A substantial portion of the effort in the communicative enterprise may be off-loaded onto the teacher. This is doubtlessly appropriate and necessary in the early stages but in the long run may not encourage an independent approach to SLA [second language acquisition] that is seen as a prerequisite for expertise in any domain. (p. 248)

Even in the context of college-level content-based instruction, Musumeci (1996) found that teachers "appear to understand absolutely everything the students say" (p. 314). The teachers strove to derive meaning from students' speech and, to do so, "supplied key lexical items and provided rich interpretations of student responses, rather than engage in the kind of negotiation which would have required learners to modify their own output" (p. 314). Musumeci further noted:

> While this kind of "filling in the spaces" by the teacher may have helped to create coherent conversational texts, it also made the teachers responsible for carrying the linguistic burden of the exchange, and it reduced the students' role to one of supplying linguistic "hints" to the teacher, rather than functioning as full partners in the exchange. (p. 315)

Similarly, in her observations of ImDL classrooms in Louisiana, Haj-Broussard (1993) found that what would have been considered scaffolding in earlier grades became a "crutch" at the Grade 4 level, or what she called the French "language safety net":

> Teachers would infer the students' French answers and then finish their statements. Although this demonstrated to the students that the teachers understood what they were saying, it also resulted in the students only producing very simple utterances or no utterances at all. Further, it did not allow them the chance to engage in extended discourse. (p. 143)

One could thus say that, in Roy's discussions with his students about *Max*, despite his good intentions of providing students with a "language safety net," the communicative enterprise was "offloaded onto the teacher," who was "carrying the linguistic burden of the exchange," while students were not engaged "as full partners in the exchange."

At the time, however, Roy was under the impression that he was asking good questions and scaffolding the interaction in ways that might even be considered exemplary. Yet, a critical and enlightened look at the roles imputed to students in the interaction leads us now to suggest that he could have done much more. For example, he could have guided students to produce more language and directed their attention more systematically to particular language structures that are indispensable for addressing the themes in question. Accordingly, we would like to conclude this section by making the point that, even if we think we have planned good questions, we cannot really assess their effectiveness until we examine the students' engagement in the interaction in terms of the quantity and quality of their contributions. And this is best done by audio- or video-recording oneself and, ideally, transcribing the interaction to examine it more closely. This leads us to propose such an undertaking as an Application Activity at the end of the chapter.

Questions leading to pushed output

The output hypothesis was presented in Chapter 3 along with the benefits of "pushed output." According to Swain (1995), when learners are pushed in their output during interaction, they are able to "reprocess" their output in ways that reveal the "leading edge" of their interlanguage (p. 131). Accordingly, we would be remiss if we didn't conclude this chapter with some better examples of teachers pushing students to produce more than short answers and asking effective follow-up questions. We present two short examples from different ends of the school-age spectrum, the first being with Grade 9 students and the second with Grade 1 students, to illustrate the possibilities for pushing students with good follow-up questions at any grade level. Both examples below show teachers asking questions that push students to explain, define, or give reasons.

The first example is from an English immersion Grade 9 science class at Gyoshu Junior & Senior High School in Numazu, Japan. The topic of the lesson is the causes and effects of pollution. To pique students' interest, the teacher, Gay-Ann

Bagotchay, is about to show a video clip titled "Dear Future Generations: I'm Sorry" (www.youtube.com/watch?v=eRLJscAlk1M) featuring Prince Ea, an American spoken word artist and filmmaker. She first shows students a still image from the beginning of the clip of Prince Ea standing in a desert-like environment beside a dead tree, and asks students to predict what the video is about and, in particular, what Prince Ea is sorry for.

1. T: OK, what I'd like you to start off with your group is to think about what you think he is sorry for. By looking at the picture, what do you think he is sorry for?
    [Students discuss in groups]
    [...]
2. T: OK?
3. S1: For using the earth's resources ...
4. T: Can you say that again.
5. S1: Using the earth's resources ...
6. T: What is he sorry for?
7. S1: He is sorry for using all the earth's resources.
8. T: OK. Can you give an example of an earth resource?
9. S1: Rare metals.
10. T: Rare metals. OK, so why are we thinking about metals? Aside from metals, what do you think that he is sorry for, that we are overusing or that we are using too much of? Yes?
11. S1: Forest.
12. T: OK. Can you say that in a sentence? He's sorry for ...
13. S1: He's sorry for using all the natural resources such as water ...
14. T: Such as water
15. S1: ... and trees.
16. T: And trees. And why do you think trees?
17. S1: Because when he uses, that generation, that generation uses all the trees, the life cycle will be ...
18. T: Why are you thinking of trees? What does the picture tell you? We are overusing trees? [silence] You only have this picture, right? So why aren't you thinking of raw materials, why are you only thinking of trees?
19. S2: Because there's no trees.
20. T: In a sentence.
21. S2: Ah, I think that man is sorry for trees because, um, there's no trees in that picture, and there's like a dead tree near the guy.
22. T: OK, so we'll watch the video and then what I'd like to you do is think of what is the purpose of the video, OK?

Gay-Ann persists in eliciting complete sentences, sometimes directly ("Can you say that in a sentence?") and sometimes indirectly ("Can you say that again?";

"What is he sorry for?"). In so doing, Gay-Ann is able to push one student from a sentence fragment, "Because there's no trees," to a much more detailed explanation: "I think that man is sorry for trees because, um, there's no trees in that picture, and there's like a dead tree near the guy." In addition, Gay-Ann is adept at asking good follow-up questions:

> "Can you give an example of an earth resource?"
> "Why do you think trees?"
> "Why are you only thinking of trees?"
> "Aside from metals, what do you think that he is sorry for?"

In comparison with Roy's interaction with his students, Gay-Ann's exchanges unfold more as instructional conversations because they aim to provide assistance and instruction that are contingent on the students' oral production.

To end on a somewhat lighter note than deforestation, the final extract is from France Bourassa's Grade 1 French immersion class at Cedar Park Elementary School in Pointe-Claire, Quebec. She is about to introduce students to the Canadian landscape artists known as the Group of Seven, and begins by asking students about what other artists they've studied, one of whom was Pablo Picasso.

1.	T:	*Elles étaient comment les images de Picasso?*	T:	What were Picasso's paintings like?
2.	S1:	*Drôles.*	S1:	Funny.
3.	T:	*Elles étaient drôles, très bien.*	T:	They were funny, very good.
4.	S2:	*Vraiment drôles.*	S2:	Really funny.
5.	T:	*Mais pourquoi elles étaient vraiment drôles?*	T:	But why were they really funny?
6.	S3:	*Parce que…*	S3:	Because …
7.	S1:	*Parce qu'il a une moustache comme ça!* [student makes a gesture to depict a curly moustache]	S1:	Because he has a moustache like this! [student makes a gesture to depict a curly moustache]
8.	T:	*Ah, ce n'était pas Picasso, ça c'était Dali. Salvador Dali et sa très grande moustache. Très bien. Vivian?*	T:	Oh, that wasn't Picasso, that was Dali. Salvador Dali and his huge moustache. Vivian?
9.	S4:	*Parce que c'était drôle.*	S4:	Because they were funny.
10.	T:	*Oui mais pourquoi est-ce que les tableaux de Picasso étaient drôles? Qui peut m'expliquer pourquoi c'était drôle? Veux-tu essayer, Holly?*	T:	Yes, but why were Picasso's paintings funny? Who can explain why they were funny. Do you want try, Holly?
11.	S5:	*C'est, comme, parce que, c'est pas des, comment tu dis «real»?*	S5:	It's, like, because, it isn't, how do you say "real"?
12.	T:	*des vraies*	T:	real
13.	S5:	*des vraies personnes.*	S5:	real people.

In this discussion, several students share the opinion that Picasso's paintings are funny. Not satisfied with this simple answer, France pushes her students to explain their point of view by asking one of the most powerful follow-up questions: "Why?" The merit of asking questions eliciting opinions followed by requests for elaboration is the prospect of piquing students' interest and thus their participation while providing a safe playing field for taking risks and testing hypotheses about the target language. In this case, with France's support, Holly is able to explain that Picasso's paintings are funny because they do not depict real people.

Summary

This chapter addressed the roles of teacher scaffolding and teacher questions in counterbalanced instruction. Scaffolding was presented as a core component of ImDL pedagogy that supports students' active engagement with respect to both comprehension and production in a language they are still learning. Teacher questions were presented as one type of scaffolding that, if used effectively as follow-up requests for elaboration, can serve to increase both the quantity and the quality of student output while also helping students to deepen their understanding. The next chapter continues with scaffolding techniques by focusing on teachers' use of corrective feedback and students' engagement with this key component of counterbalanced instruction.

Application activity

Video-record yourself teaching in a whole-class context (20–30 minutes), being sure that the episode involves student-teacher exchanges and interaction. Select a 3–5-minute excerpt to transcribe for a deeper reflection. Engage in a reflective analysis of your interaction with students, taking into consideration the following questions.

First, engage in a "macro-analysis" of the entire recording.

1. What is the primary interactional pattern you observe (e.g., IRE? IRF? Other?)?
2. In general, how much of the language did you produce and how much did students produce?
3. Which students tended to participate and which didn't? (Consider a range of factors related to student diversity such as gender, ethnicity, language background, etc.)
4. How did you attempt to foster student participation and engage all learners?
5. What kinds of questions did you ask? What was the nature of student responses to those questions?
6. What types of follow-up moves did you use to extend student production? How did students respond to those follow-up moves?

7. Did you respond to student errors, and if so, how?
8. Based on what students did/did not produce, what kinds of linguistic structures might you have been able to bring a focus to had you planned in advance?
9. What has been especially eye-opening in your review of the recording?

Then, engage in a "micro-analysis" of the transcribed excerpt.

1. How much of the language did you produce and how much did students produce? Calculate the average number of words you produced per turn versus the average number of words students produced.
2. Identify the types of questions you asked (i.e., display or referential) and describe the nature of student responses to those questions. Describe the patterns you detect.
3. Identify the types of follow-up moves/questions you asked to extend student production (e.g., asking for clarification or justification). How did students respond to those follow-up moves?
4. Describe the ways in which you responded to student errors or identify missed opportunities—errors that you didn't respond to in any way.

Next, devise a plan for improvement based on what you've read in this chapter. Consider these questions:

1. How can you modify your questions and follow-up moves to elicit more student language?
2. How can you promote more equitable discourse patterns in your class and ensure that more students participate in whole-class discussion?
3. What corrective feedback techniques (see Chapter 6) should you practice and begin to utilize to respond to student errors?

Practice a range of strategies—new questioning techniques, incorporation of follow-up moves, and corrective feedback—to elicit more language and more accurate language from students, bring attention to a specific linguistic feature, and so on.

Once you feel more confident in using these strategies, video-record yourself again and go through the same process as before. What differences do you see between the first and second recordings? What do you notice about how students respond to your questions and follow-up moves? How have your teaching practices improved, and what areas do you still need to focus on? What has been challenging about incorporating these new strategies into your teaching?

Online resources for readers

Customizable graphic organizers that serve as scaffolds for both comprehension and language production are available at the Center for Advanced Research on Language Acquisition (CARLA) website: http://carla.umn.edu/cobaltt/modules/strategies/go rganizers/index.html

6

CORRECTIVE FEEDBACK

This chapter further expounds on the role of scaffolding in counterbalanced instruction by focusing on different types of corrective feedback and their potential effectiveness. The chapter addresses many questions that teachers ask about corrective feedback, giving special attention to the following:

- What is the purpose of corrective feedback?
- What are the different types of corrective feedback?
- Is it important for students to repair their errors following corrective feedback?
- What does research tell us about the effectiveness of corrective feedback?
- How does corrective feedback help teachers to scaffold student production?
- What about written corrective feedback?

Overview of corrective feedback (CF) and its purpose

At first glance, CF—defined as a teacher's response to a learner's error—seems simple enough. However, providing CF in the context of immersion and dual language (ImDL) classrooms is not always straightforward, because of the dual focus on language and content. Notwithstanding its complexity from a classroom discourse perspective, CF plays an important scaffolding role in counterbalanced instruction, because it provides teachers with a means to integrate a language focus during subject-matter instruction. It also plays a key role in the CAPA (contextualization, awareness, practice, and autonomy) model that was introduced in Chapter 4.

CF is also known as *error correction*, a term that we avoid in this book in order to emphasize that teachers can provide CF but they do not actually correct students' errors: it's up to the students themselves to correct their errors. In this regard, the purpose of CF can be explained in terms of *linguistic evidence*, which is either positive or negative. Positive evidence is information about what is possible in the language, provided through exposure to target exemplars in the input, whereas negative evidence is information about what is not possible in the language, usually provided through explanations or feedback (Gass, 1997). L2 learners need exposure to both positive and negative evidence. Positive evidence includes all types of exposure to the minority language in both written and oral modes, which need to be instructionally enhanced through the verbal scaffolding and teacher talk presented in the previous chapter, as well as through more proactive approaches that involve deliberate planning for language objectives in the curriculum (see Part IV) and that draw attention to selected features of the minority language by means of increased frequency and salience (see Chapter 4). To complement the positive evidence and strengthen its effectiveness, negative evidence in the form of CF serves to scaffold language development, especially when students exhibit ongoing difficulties with particular forms and structures in the minority language.

Given the potential for language development to occur as a result of CF that is well planned and strategically implemented, it is important to engage in discussions with students about errors as an intrinsic part of the learning process and about the benefits of CF in this process. Discussion with students is all the more important because, according to research, students express a willingness to receive CF, whereas teachers express being reluctant to provide CF, believing that students prefer not to be corrected (e.g., Brown, 2009; Cathcart & Olsen, 1976: Jean & Simard, 2011; Roothooft & Breeze, 2016; Schultz, 2001). There is thus a mismatch between teachers' practices and students' expectations. To avoid the potentially negative effects of such mismatches on learning, teachers are encouraged to explain their objectives as explicitly as possible to students and, in cases of mismatches between teacher and learner expectations, to resolve them through consultation and negotiation (Nunan, 1989). If you have any doubts about the extent to which your students like to receive CF, just ask them—and also discuss with them the different CF techniques you will learn about in this chapter.

The purpose of CF is *not* to ensure that errors do not occur. Indeed, students can learn from their errors, because errors mean that they are testing their hypotheses about the language. However, to learn from their errors, students need to have their wrong hypotheses disconfirmed by negative evidence. Thus, whereas errors can be seen as signs of learning, this is only the case if they are transitional and temporary. If they become a recurring part of the students' productive repertoire, without moving closer toward target language norms, they are considered fossilized, and this can happen in the absence of sufficient linguistic evidence—both positive and negative.

 SPECIAL NOTE

Errors can be good! If students only produce what they know how to say or write accurately, their language proficiency will not improve. Students need to take risks with language in order to push their language development forward. At the same time, it's critical that they receive feedback on those errors if they are to learn from them.

Written CF and oral CF are equally important. In this chapter, however, we conclude with a section on written CF but otherwise focus mainly on oral CF for three reasons. First, there is a substantial body of research on oral CF, much of which has been conducted specifically in the context of ImDL classrooms. Second, many teachers already do provide written CF, and have developed ways of doing so, but may be less sure about how to provide oral CF without interrupting students and raising their *affective filter*: hence our focus on oral CF to convince teachers of not only its effectiveness but also its feasibility. Third, the extensive research on oral CF has been more conclusive than research on written CF with respect to effectiveness. That is, the positive effects of oral CF have been confirmed by research (see Li, 2010, and Lyster & Saito, 2010, for meta-analytic reviews), which indicates that CF plays a pivotal role in the kind of scaffolding that teachers need to provide to learners to promote continuing growth in the L2. In contrast, the findings regarding written CF have been inconsistent and have thus led to ongoing debates about its effectiveness (e.g., Bitchener, 2008; Bruton, 2009; Chandler, 2004, 2009; Ferris, 2004; Truscott, 2009).

 KEY CONCEPT

The *affective filter* is what determines a learner's internal emotional state. According to Krashen (1982), when the filter is high, learners will feel anxious and unmotivated, preventing language acquisition from occurring. When the filter is low, learners feel positive, and this opens the channels for acquisition.

RESEARCH REPORT

The power of feedback

A review of research on feedback in the education literature, aptly titled "The power of feedback," stresses the pivotal role played by feedback in *all* learning. The review concludes that feedback, in comparison to other instructional variables, has one of the highest influences on learner achievement, and also that some types of feedback are more powerful than others. The authors explain that feedback and instruction are intrinsically linked:

- "Feedback and instruction are intertwined in ways that transform the process into new instruction rather than informing the learner only about correctness" (p. 82).

Accordingly, the authors put forth that students benefit more from CF that is connected with prior or concurrent instruction than from CF provided only randomly:

- "Feedback can only build on something; it is of little use when there is no initial learning or surface information" (p. 104).

(Hattie & Timperley, 2007)

Types of CF

Several researchers suggest that CF is most likely to be effective when provided "within the context of meaningful and sustained communicative interaction" (Spada & Lightbown, 1993, p. 218; see also Doughty, 2001; Lightbown, 1991, 1998, 2014; Long, 1996, 2007). In this view, CF is considered most effective during oral interaction when students have something meaningful to say, arguably due to its immediacy and its capacity for strengthening the connections learners need to make between form and meaning. If the feedback is delayed, it might still serve to increase students' metalinguistic awareness and contribute to their declarative knowledge, but it is less likely to affect their procedural knowledge and thus be incorporated into their spontaneous language production. Immediate oral CF thus has a powerful role to play in consolidating oral skills during contextualized language use, as opposed to the decontextualized reflection afforded by delayed CF. Notwithstanding these arguments in favor of immediate CF, research comparing the effectiveness of immediate and delayed CF has so far been inconclusive. The timing of CF is thus worthy of further exploration in the context of "isolated form-focused instruction," which is provided "after an activity in which students have experienced difficulty with a particular language feature" (Spada & Lightbown, 2008, p. 186; see also Quinn & Nakata, 2017).

Providing oral CF "in the heat of the moment" can be challenging for teachers whose focus is on content and who are reluctant to appear interruptive as their students are using the minority language to the best of their ability. To find out how Canadian French immersion teachers manage this challenge, Lyster and Ranta (1997) analyzed in detail the transcribed data of 18.3 hours of classroom interaction, which had been audio-recorded in four immersion classrooms at the Grade 4–5 level. They analyzed 14 subject-matter lessons and 13 French-language arts lessons with a thematic focus, avoiding lessons where language form was the primary objective, because they wanted to document how teachers and students engage in error treatment during communicative interaction.

Their analysis identified six specific types of CF, which can be classified into two main families: *reformulations*, which provide learners with correct forms, and *prompts*, which do not provide learners with correct forms and instead provide clues to help them to self-repair. These feedback types are defined in Table 6.1 along with examples; the teachers' CF moves in each example are followed by "→ **CF**".

Can you think of some other types of CF not included in Table 6.1? One type of CF that is missing is *non-verbal feedback*, also known as *paralinguistic signals* (Sheen & Ellis, 2011). The six types of CF in Table 6.1 are all verbal types of feedback, because the Lyster and Ranta study from 1997 was based on audio-recordings, without video. So, it's important to add to this typology the non-verbal paralinguistic signals that teachers are known to use. A good example of non-verbal CF is found in Lightbown and Spada's (1990) study of a teacher who responded to specific errors mainly with explicit hand signals, a funny face, and dramatically raised eyebrows. Her students outperformed other students not exposed to such feedback (for more about non-verbal feedback, see Nakatsukasa & Loewen, 2017).

Another way that teachers have been known to use prompts creatively is by combining repetition of error with other types of CF. Lyster and Ranta found that repeating the student's error as in the example in Table 6.1 ("You *hear* people screaming?") did not occur frequently in isolation but instead occurred often with other types of CF, as in the metalinguistic clue in Table 6.1 ("Kiss? You need past tense.") and also in the elicitation example ("They went in their *cabane*. What's another word for *cabane*?"). Repetition of error can be useful, because learners are not always aware of what was wrong with their utterance, so they might benefit from someone repeating what they just said. They can also benefit from hearing what they said in juxtaposition with what they should have said. This is a type of CF that Södergård (2008) observed in her study of a Swedish immersion kindergarten classroom, calling it *choice of language*. In Spanish, for example, if a learner gets the grammatical gender marking wrong in the noun phrase *the doll*, saying "*El muñeca*," the teacher might ask, "*¿Es el muñeca o la muñeca?*"

TABLE 6.1 Definitions and examples of six different types of CF

<table>
<tr><td rowspan="2">REFORMULATIONS</td><td>

1. Explicit correction

The teacher supplies the correct form and clearly indicates that what the student had said was incorrect.

T: Yes, fish need water, so in our fish tank we've got fish; we've also got some plants … What are the plants for?

S: For eat the fish.

T: No. For the fish to eat. Not to eat the fish, but the fish to eat. → **CF**

(Fleta Guillén, 2007)

2. Recasts

The teacher implicitly reformulates the student's utterance, minus the error.

T: Mariano, what did you do?

S: I don't go to the party.

T: I didn't go to the party. → **CF**

S: I didn't go to the party.

(Fleta Guillén, 2007)
</td></tr>
<tr><td>

3. Clarification requests

By using phrases such as "*Pardon me*" and "*I don't understand,*" the teacher conveys an apparent failure to understand the student's message.

S: Who has fin?

T: Sorry, I beg your pardon? → **CF**

(Oliver & Mackey, 2003)

4. Metalinguistic clues

Without supplying the correct form, the teacher provides comments, information, or questions related to the form of the student's utterance.

S: He kiss her.

T: Kiss? You need past tense. → **CF**

S: He kissed.

(Ellis, Loewen, & Erlam, 2006)
</td></tr>
</table>

PROMPTS

5. Elicitation

The teacher directly elicits correct forms from students in one of three ways: by asking questions (e.g., *How do we say that in English?*), by pausing to allow students to complete the teacher's utterance (*It's called a …?*), or by asking students to reformulate their utterance.

S: They went … they went in the *cabane.*

T: They went in their *cabane.* What's another word for *cabane*? → **CF**

Ss: Treehouse.

(Blanc, Carol, Griggs, & Lyster, 2012)

6. Repetition of error

The teacher repeats the student's erroneous utterance, adjusting the intonation to highlight the error.

T: What did you hear when your eyes were shut?

S: I hear people screaming.

T: You *hear* people screaming? → **CF**

S: I heard people screaming.

(Lyster, 2017)

Yet another creative way that ImDL teachers have been observed prompting students is to respond to the *literal meaning* of their non-target utterances, as seen in the following exchange during a math game in Spanish:

T: *¿Cuántas fichas tienes?* [How many tokens do you have?]
S: *Tienes 4 fichas.* [You have 4 tokens.]
T: *¿Yo? No tengo ninguna ficha.* [Me? I don't have any tokens.]

A recurring error made by learners of Spanish is in the verbal inflections that distinguish first- and second-person reference. Spanish is a *pro-drop language* (i.e., a pronoun-dropping language), meaning that it's not necessary to use a subject pronoun such as *you* or *I*, because these notions are already encoded in the verb endings. Consequently, learners of Spanish who are more used to relying on pronouns than verb endings to garner this information have a tendency to reply using the same verb form that their interlocutor used to address them: in this case, "*tienes …*" ("*you have …*") instead of "*tengo …*" ("*I have …*"). The difference clearly affects meaning, and so a teacher's prompt responding literally to what students have said has the potential to make them more aware of this important form-meaning mapping in Spanish.

 TEACHER SPOTLIGHT

Carrie Hartinger-Broughton, an English immersion teacher at Katoh Gakuen Elementary School in Numazu, Japan, summed up her experience in using a variety of corrective feedback types as follows: "Reflecting on the type of corrective feedback used most often motivated me especially to try out other forms of corrective feedback with students. Varying my corrective feedback has led to greater student uptake, noticing, and more overall language gain."

Céline Carbonneau, a French immersion teacher at Pope Memorial Elementary School in Bury, Quebec, had this to say about corrective feedback: "Corrective feedback is important but it's also highly valued by students and the results from its use are obvious."

Frequency of CF and distribution of different types of CF

Early classroom observation studies suggested that the use of CF was not a priority for ImDL teachers. For example, a study by Allen et al. (1990) revealed that error treatment was dealt with in "a confusing and unsystematic way" (p. 67). Only 19% of the grammatical errors were followed by CF, and when teachers did provide CF it generally appeared to be motivated by an "irritation" factor. The researchers cautioned that such "unsystematic, possibly random feedback to learners about their language errors" (p. 76) could have a "detrimental effect on learning" (p. 67).

Since Allen et al.'s (1990) seminal research, ImDL teachers have been observed using CF more frequently. For example, subsequent studies have shown that immersion teachers provide CF after an average of 62% of their students' errors in French immersion classrooms in Canada (Lyster & Ranta, 1997), 61% in Japanese immersion classrooms in the US (Lyster & Mori, 2006), and 64% in English immersion classrooms in South Korea (Lee, 2006). Together, these figures indicate that it might be feasible for teachers to provide CF on roughly half or even more of their students' errors.

The goal is definitely not to provide CF on *all* oral errors! In making decisions about which errors to target, teachers need to give priority to recurring and shared errors (made by not just one but many students), while taking into account their current language objectives and especially those driving their proactive instructional interventions, which will be addressed in Part IV of this book. The intuition that some teachers might have for providing CF only on errors that impede communication simply does not work very well in ImDL classrooms, where students quickly become skilled at getting their meaning across in spite of linguistic gaps—which is indeed a useful skill and one to be encouraged. However, most teachers come to easily understand their students' interlanguage, so waiting for communication to actually break down might entail a long wait and a loss of many teachable moments!

 RESEARCH REPORT

Is more feedback better than less feedback?

Lightbown (2008a) argued that if students constantly receive CF they might develop the expectation that the teacher will always provide a corrected version and thus either cease to notice the CF or lose their motivation for self-monitoring and effortful generation of the target language. Arguing in favor of actually reducing the amount of CF in classrooms, Lightbown (2008a) stated that, "When feedback is focused on a limited number of objects or available in some classroom activities but not others, learners can take greater responsibility for creating and monitoring their own output" (p. 41).

Three studies of teacher-student interaction specifically conducted in ImDL classrooms compared the frequency distribution of recasts, prompts, and explicit correction, as defined in the previous section. The three classroom contexts, all at the Grade 4–5 level, included CLIL classrooms in Spain with English as the target language (Llinares & Lyster, 2014), French immersion classrooms in Quebec (Lyster & Ranta, 1997), and Japanese immersion classrooms in the US (Lyster & Mori, 2006). The findings revealed that teachers in all three settings

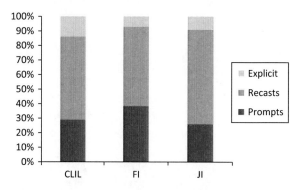

FIGURE 6.1 Percentage distribution of CF types across contexts (FI, French immersion; JI, Japanese immersion)

used recasts, prompts, and explicit correction in similar proportions, with recasts being the most frequent, followed by prompts, then explicit correction, as seen in Figure 6.1. In all cases, recasts accounted for the majority of all CF moves: 54% in French immersion, 57% in CLIL, and 65% in Japanese immersion. This begs the question as to why recasts occur so frequently in ImDL classrooms, which is addressed later in this chapter.

Types of learner repair

While it's crucial for teachers to be aware of the different types of CF at their disposal, it is equally important for them to be aware of the range of possible student responses following CF. This is because the purpose of CF is to provide students with not only *information* about the well-formedness of their utterances but also the *means* for them to move toward more advanced levels of performance (Lantolf & Poehner, 2008; Leung, 2007; Purpura, 2004). In this sense, the teacher's CF move provides information (i.e., linguistic evidence: positive or negative, or both), while the student's response to the CF has the potential to serve as an indication of the student's current level of performance. This is especially relevant in contexts of *assessment for learning*, where teachers aim to monitor their students' current levels and to push to the next level.

✍ KEY CONCEPT

Assessment for learning is defined as "the process of seeking and interpreting evidence for use by learners and their teachers to decide where learners are in their learning, where they need to go and how best to get there" (Broadfoot et al., 2002, pp. 2–3). It is also known as formative assessment or learner-oriented assessment (see Chapter 10).

To refer to the range of possible student responses to CF, Lyster and Ranta (1997) used the term *uptake*. Learner uptake includes either (a) learner repair or (b) utterances still in need of repair. Learner repair entails the student's correct reformulation of an error, whereas learner responses still in need of repair include simple acknowledgements such as "yes," hesitations, off-target responses, partial repair, and occurrences of either the same or a different error. When considering the potential effects of different types of CF, learner responses with repair are of greater importance than responses still in need of repair.

 KEY CONCEPT

Uptake is defined as "a student's utterance that immediately follows the teacher's feedback and that constitutes a reaction in some way to the teacher's intention to draw attention to some aspect of the student's initial utterance" (Lyster & Ranta, 1997, p. 49).

There are two distinct types of learner repair: repetition and self-repair. Recasts and explicit correction can lead only to a student's repetition of the correct form provided by the teacher, whereas prompts can lead, not to repetition, but to self-repair. Self-repair following a prompt requires a deeper level of processing than repetition of a teacher's recast, because, to self-repair, students need to reanalyze their output and to attend to the retrieval of alternative forms. As explained in Chapter 3, depth of processing refers to the extent to which students reflect on new information and relate it to other relevant information. The greater the depth of processing, the greater the probability that information will be stored in long-term memory and become more readily accessible.

It is important to acknowledge that one instance of learner repair immediately following CF does not mean that the learner has internalized the new form: L2 learning is a developmental process that is not reflected in one instance of repair. Nonetheless, a prediction that has arisen from descriptive studies of different types of CF and learner repair is that different types of repair are likely to affect L2 development differentially over time, because different types of repair (i.e., either repetition or retrieval and production) entail different types of cognitive processing.

 RESEARCH REPORT

But doesn't CF break the flow of communication in classroom interaction?

"It is likely the case that teachers are reluctant to encourage self-repair more consistently lest the flow of communication be broken. However, our classroom observations as well as the data analysis revealed that none of the

feedback types stopped the flow of classroom interaction and that uptake—
that is, the student's turn in the error treatment sequence—clearly does not
break the communicative flow either; on the contrary, uptake means that the
student has the floor again. The classrooms we observed and analyzed were
not considered to be traditional classrooms and yet the discourse was structured in ways that allowed teachers to intervene regularly; they were able to
do so by interacting with students without causing frustration because students appeared to expect such interventions."

(Lyster & Ranta, 1997, pp. 57–58)

Another type of learner repair following teacher CF is called *peer-repair*, which
occurs when the correct form is provided by a student other than the one who made
the error. Peer-repair occurs in Turn 10 of the following Grade 3 discussion about
The Day of the Dragon King by Mary Pope Osborne (Lyster et al., 2009, p. 374):

1) S1: I have something to add to that. When they fire the books …
2) T: Go ahead.
3) S1: When they fire the books, um.
4) T: When they what?
5) S1: When they fire the books.
6) T: What do you mean, when they fire the books?
   [Students talk among themselves]
7) T: No. Let her say it in another way. Explain it to me in another way.
8) S1: [Silence]
9) T: When they put fire on the books. What's that, when we put fire, to
   make a fire? What do we do, when we put things in the fire?
10) Ss: Burn.
11) S1: Burn.
12) T: Burn things, good. Continue.
13) S1: But, when they burned it, the guy just burned the books that he didn't
   write. He kept the books that he write, that he wrote.

In Chapter 3, we explained why the most effective ImDL classrooms are those
that are language rich and discourse rich. The preceding exchange is both language and discourse rich for the following reasons:

1. The student herself initiated the exchange in Turn 1 ("I have something to
   add to that").
2. Her non-target output ("fire the books") resulted in considerable negotiation in Turns 4–12 between herself, the teacher, and other students.
3. This focus on language over several turns did not deter her from clearly
   making her point about the story in Turn 13.

4. In Turn 13 she not only incorporated the target form into her statement; she also self-corrected, quickly changing "the books that he write" to "that he wrote."

When students are pushed by their teacher to be more accurate while being supported by their peers in this endeavor, they become more aware of their speech and more likely to self-correct, which can be seen as the ultimate goal of CF.

The peer feedback provided in the preceding exchange was straightforward and salient, involving a single vocabulary item whose misuse can impede comprehension. Not all peer feedback is as effective, as can be seen in the following exchange, which targets verbal morphology rather than a lexical item. The exchange took place in a Grade 5 two-way immersion (TWI) classroom observed by Tedick and Young (2016, p. 797). The teacher was checking on the progress of a small group. She first offered two prompts (a clarification request in Turn 3 followed by a repetition of error in Turn 5) as signals for Student 1 to produce her verb in a finite rather than an infinitive form. A third prompt in Turn 9 then served as a literal response to the student's use of a second-person finite form. Interestingly, Student 2, a native Spanish-speaking peer, intervened twice with the correct form (Turns 6 and 8), but Student 1 appeared to ignore her peer's CF.

1) T: *¿Ya leyeron todo?* [Did you read everything?]
2) S1: *Sí. Esto de aquí. Pero no a leer esta parte aquí.* [Yes. This here. But no to read this part here.]
3) T: *¿No qué?* [No what?]
4) S1: *No leer este parte.* [No to read this part.]
5) T: *¿No leer este parte?* [No to read this part?]
6) S2: *No leímos.* [We didn't read.]
7) S1: *No leíste.* [You didn't read.]
8) S2: *No leímos.* [We didn't read.]
9) T: *Yo ya lo leí.* [I already read it.]
10) S1: *¿No leamos?* [We don't read.]

Some research with young adult learners has shown that they may intentionally disregard their classmates' CF due to mistrust of each other's linguistic abilities (Philp, Walter, & Basturkmen, 2010; Yoshida, 2008). However, the peer CF provider in the preceding example was a young native speaker of Spanish, so perhaps the CF receiver wasn't wary of the provider's linguistic abilities but instead was more focused on the teacher's CF, which to some students may appear more socially and pedagogically appropriate (Lyster, Saito, & Sato, 2013). In such cases, however, teachers can design instruction to "shape patterns of interaction in an attempt to maximize the creation and exploitation of learning opportunities" (Naughton, 2006, p. 179) and can do so through *strategy training* designed to encourage students to focus on language together.

In a French-English ImDL setting similar to TWI, Ballinger (2013, 2015) investigated the effects of strategy training on the extent to which young learners engaged with a peer in collaborative tasks. For the purpose of increasing students' awareness of each other's language production, Ballinger provided instruction that modeled collaborative strategies and included provision of peer CF. The instruction proved effective, but the quality of the peer interaction and the extent to which students engaged in "reciprocal learning strategies" were tempered by pair dynamics. Research to date on peer CF suggests that peer CF has the potential to positively affect L2 development but, for this to happen, the classroom needs first to be established as a collaborative learning environment (Sato, 2017). How to instill a collaborative mindset among students is a ripe area for further exploration and research.

 RESEARCH REPORT

How important is immediate learner repair after CF?

- Some studies suggest that whether or not learners repeat a recast does not affect L2 development, while other studies have suggested that repeating a recast at the very least indicates that the recast was noticed.
- However, these studies have been done with adult learners, so we still do not know for sure whether it is important or not for young learners to repeat the teacher's recast.
- What we do know from research is that, for prompts to be effective, they need to be followed by student-generated repair (i.e., either self-repair or peer-repair). There is no point in a teacher saying "Sorry, I don't understand" or "Is there a better way of saying that?" without expecting some sort of response from students.

(Egi, 2010; Loewen & Philp, 2006; Lyster & Izquierdo, 2009)

 RESEARCH REPORT

CF types in relation to error types and learner repair

Research has shown that teachers and interlocutors tend to provide more CF on grammatical errors than on other types of errors (e.g., Carpenter, Jeon, MacGregor, & Mackey, 2006; Kim & Han, 2007; Lyster, 1998b; Mackey, Gass, & McDonough, 2000). These same studies, however, have also shown that learners generate more successful repair and accurate perceptions of CF on vocabulary and pronunciation errors.

In a study conducted in ImDL classrooms, Lyster (1998b) found the following patterns regarding the types of errors made by students in relation to the types of CF used by the teachers and whether the CF was followed by learner repair or not:

1. Teachers used more recasts than prompts to correct *pronunciation* ...
   ... and, students repaired more pronunciation errors after recasts than after prompts.
2. Teachers used more prompts than recasts to correct *vocabulary* ...
   ... and, students repaired more vocabulary errors after prompts than after recasts.
3. Teachers used more recasts than prompts to correct *grammar* ...
   ... **but**, students repaired more grammar errors after prompts than after recasts.

These patterns were interpreted to mean that the teachers were on the right track in their decisions to provide recasts after pronunciation errors and prompts after vocabulary errors but that they could use prompts more frequently in response to grammatical errors.

Recasts

Recasts are the most frequent type of CF used across a range of instructional settings (Brown, 2016), and this includes ImDL settings. Specifically in the context of ImDL classrooms, research suggests that recasts can be used effectively to maintain the flow of communication and to keep students' attention focused on content, thereby providing scaffolding that enables learners to participate in interaction that requires linguistic abilities exceeding their current developmental level. Notwithstanding these benefits, there is no evidence that recasts are the most effective way for ImDL teachers to draw attention to students' errors.

The extent to which students repeat recasts depends on the instructional setting, with frequent repair following recasts in Japanese immersion and CLIL classrooms at the Grade 4–5 level but not much repair following recasts in French immersion classrooms at the same level (Llinares & Lyster, 2014). What we don't know, however, is whether these differences across instructional settings differentially affect target language development. This is an important avenue to explore further in classroom-based research, because teachers want and need to know the value of pushing students to repeat recasts, especially in contexts of assessment for learning, where teachers aim to monitor their students' current levels and to push to the next level.

Llinares and Lyster (2014) attributed the greater effectiveness of recasts for eliciting repetitions from students in CLIL and Japanese immersion to differences in the types of recasts used by the teachers: namely, *didactic recasts* in CLIL and Japanese immersion, and *conversational recasts* in French immersion. Didactic recasts are explicit in terms of their salience and intention to elicit learner repair;

they are short and delivered with intonational stress to highlight the modification. In contrast, conversational recasts are more implicit and less intentional in getting students to correct their errors (Sheen & Ellis, 2011). What follows is an example of a conversational recast that occurred in a Grade 4 French immersion classroom (Lyster & Mori, 2006, pp. 291–292).

1)	S:	*Nous sommes allés au Biodôme parce que ma grand-mère elle a jamais allé à là-bas.*	S:	We went to the Biodome because my grandmother never goed to there.
2)	T:	*Elle était jamais allée.*	T:	She had never gone.
3)	S:	*Puis on a allé à /Jungle Adventure/ et on a gagné des prix.*	S:	Then we goed to Jungle Adventure and we won prizes.
4)	T:	*C'est quoi ça?*	T:	What is that?

The student's error in choice of auxiliary and tense in Turn 1 is recast by the teacher in Turn 2, but there is no repair as the student simply continues recounting his March Break activities in Turn 3 without repeating the recast. Not only does the student not repeat the teacher's recast: As he proceeds, he makes a similar error in Turn 3, which the teacher ignores in Turn 4 and instead asks the student to elaborate on the content of his message, thus reinforcing the conversational nature of this exchange.

By way of contrast, the next example illustrates didactic recasts provided in the context of a Grade 4 English-medium CLIL classroom in Spain during a similar type of personal account in which the teacher is much more consistent in recasting the student's errors (from Llinares & Lyster, 2014, p. 9).

1) S: On Sunday I go to a
2) T: I went to
3) S: I go to a
4) T: I went
5) S: I went to a … How do you say *exposición* [exhibition]?
6) T: Exposition, exhibition.
7) S: Exhibition and I find and I found a … a … person that that that is making with two, … with two … *dos palos* [two sticks]
8) T: She was making
9) S: She was making glass

The teacher's initial recast in Turn 2 is followed by the same error in Turn 3, so the teacher provides a similar recast in Turn 4 but, this time, she makes it more salient by placing the correct verb in final position ("I went"). This more explicit recast is followed by the student's repair in Turn 5 but then two turns later by yet another use of the present tense in Turn 7, which the teacher again recasts in Turn 8 and which is repeated by the student in Turn 9. Notice in Turn 7 how the student self-corrects ("and I find and I found …"), which may well be the desired effect of the teacher's continued recasting of present tense into past tense.

In contrast to such an intentional and explicit use of didactic recasts, conversational recasts risk becoming sources of linguistic ambiguity, which may even contribute to ImDL students' continued use of non-target forms in the minority language. The ambiguity in ImDL classrooms derives in part from the frequent use of recasts to confirm or disconfirm the veracity (i.e., truth value) of the student's message, as in the following example in which the student says *"le assistante"* rather than the obligatory contracted form, *"l'assistante."*

S: *Oui, c'est le assistante.*   S: Yes, it's the assistant.
T: *C'est l'assistante. Ensuite, c'est …?*   T: It's the assistant. Next, it's …?

These very same confirming functions motivate the even more frequent use of *non-corrective repetition* by ImDL teachers, an example of which follows:

T: *Ça c'est à-peu-près quelle grandeur, mes amis?*   T: That's about what size, my friends?
S: *La grandeur de ta règle.*   S: The size of your ruler.
T: *La grandeur de ta règle? Excellent, à-peu-près*   T: The size of your ruler? Excellent, just about.

** KEY CONCEPT**

A **non-corrective repetition** is a teacher's verbatim repetition of a student's utterance to acknowledge and rebroadcast the student's contribution.

Students must figure out whether the teacher's follow-up move is confirming the meaning of their utterance or correcting its form, or perhaps both. This becomes even more difficult when many non-corrective repetitions are not verbatim repetitions and thus further resemble recasts, as in the following example:

S: *Des congés. On prend des congés.*   S: Holidays. We take holidays.
T: *On va prendre des congés, oui!*   T: We're going to take holidays, yes!

Lyster (1998a) found that non-corrective repetition occurred even more frequently than recasts in French immersion classrooms and that, together, recasts and non-corrective repetition followed almost one-third of all student utterances. From a student's perspective, it must seem that there is a lot of teacher echoing going on in these classrooms, as recasts and non-corrective repetition are both used to provide or seek confirmation or additional information related to the student's message. Whether ImDL teachers recast ill-formed utterances or repeated well-formed utterances, their intentions appeared to coincide with the functions attributed to repetition in classroom discourse by Weiner and Goodenough (1977): (a) to acknowledge the content of the student's utterance and (b) to "rebroadcast" the student's message in order to ensure that the whole class has heard.

To add to the ambiguity from the learners' perspective, ImDL teachers regularly use signs of approval to encourage their students' use of the minority language, but they do so equally often with recasts, non-corrective repetition, and even topic-continuation moves immediately following errors (Lyster, 1998b). The indiscriminate use of signs of approval with both recasts and non-corrective repetition alike suggests again that ImDL teachers use recasts and non-corrective repetition to fulfill similar discourse functions (i.e., to confirm the veracity of learners' messages) and do not consistently use recasts to provide negative evidence (i.e., information about ungrammaticality).

 KEY CONCEPT

Signs of approval include affirmations such as *yes, that's it,* and *OK,* and praise markers such as *Very good, Bravo,* and *Excellent.* In both parent-child interaction (e.g., Penner, 1987) and teacher-student interaction in ImDL classrooms (e.g., Lyster, 1998a), there is a tendency for signs of approval to be used to affirm truth value rather than linguistic accuracy.

This is illustrated in the following example extracted from a class discussion in social studies about the manufacturing of chocolate-covered marshmallow cookies, well known in Quebec, called Whippets, formerly known as Empire cookies (from Lyster, 1998c, p. 62):

T: *Alors, qu'est-ce que les gens ont dit quand ils ont goûté? Ils ont dit ...*
S: *Ils adorent ...*
T: *Qu'ils adoraient ce fameux biscuit l'Empire. Excellent!*

T: So, what did the people say when they tasted the cookies? They said ...
S: They love ...
T: That they loved these famous Empire cookies. Excellent!

This Grade 4 teacher sets up an obligatory context for the past tense with "*Ils ont dit ...*" ("They said...") and so in response to the student's use of the present tense "*Ils adorent*" ("They love"), she uses the past tense "*Qu'ils adoraient*" ("That they loved") in a recast that concludes with a sign of approval ("*Excellent!*"). From the students' perspective, the approval marker *Excellent* is likely to stand out in a way that overrides the corrective potential of the teacher's recast. It may be the case that such signs of approval are inevitable in ImDL classrooms, where teachers and students alike are more focused on content than on language. In these contexts, signs of approval serve to say "yes" to content while the recasts serve to say "no" to form, but with the inevitable result that learners are more likely to notice the positive feedback ("yes" to content) than the morphological modification in a recast ("no" to form).

This type of exchange is complex for teachers to manage on the fly. We, of course, do not suggest that they refrain from praising their students but, rather, that they be aware of sending mixed messages about language. For example, they need to find ways of supporting the content of students' utterances while pushing them forward in their use of language, as in "That's an excellent idea, but is there a better way of saying it?"

A closer look at interaction in a Grade 4 science lesson illustrates the ambiguity of recasts from a learner's perspective and their lack of salience in content-based lessons. The science lesson is about the water cycle and is taught by Marie to her Grade 4 middle-immersion students (Lyster, 2007, 99–102). Because Student 2's error entails grammatical gender, M and F in the English translation denote masculine and feminine forms, respectively.

1)	T:	*Qu'est-ce que c'est un ruisseau encore?*	T:	What's a stream again? …
2)	S1:	*C'est comme un petit lac.*	S1:	It's like a small lake.
3)	T:	*Un petit lac qu'on a dit?*	T:	Did we say a small lake?
4)	S2:	*C'est un petit rivière.*	S2:	It's a-M small-M river.
5)	T:	*C'est ça. C'est plus une petite rivière, OK? Parce qu'un lac c'est comme un endroit où il y a de l'eau mais c'est un…?*	T:	That's it. It's more like a-F little-F river, OK? Because a lake it's like a place where there's water but it's a …?
6)	Ss:	*Comme un cercle.*	Ss:	Like a circle.
7)	T:	*C'est comme un cercle … Puis là elle se retrouve près d'une forêt. Et qu'est-ce qu'ils font dans la forêt? William?*	T:	It's like a circle … And then she finds herself near a forest. And what is it that they do in the forest? William?
8)	S3:	*Ils coupent des arbres.*	S3:	They cut down trees.
9)	T:	*Ils coupent des arbres.*	T:	They cut down trees.

Marie begins in Turn 1 by asking students to define a stream. The student's response in Turn 2 is wrong in terms of content but linguistically accurate and is repeated by Marie in Turn 3 as a confirmation check. The next student's answer in Turn 4 is correct in terms of content, but the grammatical gender in French is incorrect. In Turn 5, Marie confirms the correct meaning with "*c'est ça*" ("that's it") and then unobtrusively supplies the correct grammatical form in a recast. In Turns 7 and 9, Marie repeats verbatim the students' responses, which are accurate in both content and form.

The focus of the exchange then turns to the adventures of Perlette, a personified drop of water whose adventures are being followed through the water cycle.

1)	T:	*Alors là, elle décide de demander au soleil de venir la réchauffer. Pourquoi pensez-vous qu'elle veut se faire réchauffer? Oui?*	T:	And then she decides to ask the sun to come and warm her up. Why do you think she wants to warm herself up? Yes?
2)	S1:	*Parce qu'elle est trop froid pour aller dans toute les [?]*	S1:	Because she has too cold to go into all the [?]
3)	T:	*Parce qu'elle a froid, OK. Oui?*	T:	Because she is cold, OK. Yes?
4)	S2:	*Elle est trop peur.*	S2:	She has too scared.
5)	T:	*Parce qu'elle a peur, oui.*	T:	Because she is scared, yes.

Marie's initiating question about Perlette elicits two student responses, both containing well-known errors made by L2 learners of French in the use of *avoir* (*to have*) and *être* (*to be*). The first response in Turn 2 is followed by a recast and the sign of approval *OK* in Turn 3. Yet, because the phonological difference between the morphemes *a* and *est* (i.e., /a/ and /ɛ/) is not salient unless stressed with exaggerated intonation, young learners are unlikely to perceive the difference and instead will interpret the recast as a confirmation of their message. In this sense, the recast serves to reinforce an already well-established error. Moreover, the next non-target utterance in Turn 4 contains the same error but is again followed by a recast in Turn 5 along with a sign of approval ("*Oui*").

The distinctions between the equivalents of *be* and *have* in Romance languages are a source of confusion for students whose dominant language is English, when used, for example, as auxiliaries in French compound verb forms or as lexical verbs in Spanish and French in expressions such as "I am hungry" ("*J'ai faim;*" "*Tengo hambre*") and "He is six years old" ("*Il a six ans;*" "*Él tiene seis años*"). Recasts in response to errors caused by the wrong choice of one of two forms comprising a binary distinction (e.g., *be/have, être/avoir, estar/tener, ser/estar, le/la, el/la, savoir/connaître,* or *saber/conocer*) are potentially ambiguous. That is, if there is nothing overtly disapproving in the recast, it may appear to confirm that the two forms are either the same or different but interchangeable. Thus, even if students do notice the reformulation, they could infer that the recast is an alternative way of saying the same thing.

The students are thus left to their own devices to figure out whether the teacher's various follow-up moves are confirming the meaning or the form of their utterances (or both). For example, the non-corrective repetition "*un petit lac*" serves to disconfirm the veracity of the student's response (because a river is not like a lake), while also confirming its form. At the same time, the non-corrective repetitions "*comme un cercle*" and "*Ils coupent des arbres*" serve to confirm both the form and the veracity of student responses. In the case of recasts, "*une petite rivière*" and "*elle a peur*" serve to confirm the veracity of the students' responses while disconfirming the erroneous forms, although in the hurly-burly of classroom interaction about subject matter, the students are more likely to interpret the recasts as saying "yes" to content without noticing the minor changes in the recasts. These examples encapsulate a dilemma for ImDL teachers, whose mandate is to teach both language and content: that is, how can teachers reinforce the content of student utterances while providing clear messages about language form?

Recasts can effectively serve to move lessons forward when the forms in question are beyond the students' current abilities, as we see in the next example from the same science lesson about the water cycle. At this point, Perlette is in a forest, and students are asked how trees are transported during the logging process.

1)	T:	*Qu'est-ce qu'on fait pour transporter*	T:	What do they do to transport the
		le bois?		wood?
2)	S:	*Euh, tu mets le bois dans l'eau et*	S:	Um, you put the wood in the water
		les euh, [...] emporte le arbre au un		and the um, [...] carries tree to an
		place puis un autre personne qui met		place and another person who puts the
		le bois.		wood.
3)	T:	*C'est ça. Alors, on met le bois dans*	T:	That's it. So, they put the wood in the
		la rivière pour qu'il soit transporté		river so it gets transported from one
		d'un endroit à l'autre.		place to another.

To respond to Marie's question, the student tries his best in Turn 2 to explain how the wood is transported down the river but is lacking the morphosyntactic means to do so accurately and clearly. Fortunately, Marie understands and is able to provide a recast that nicely summarizes what the student meant but without focusing on any one particular error, likely because there are several. We consider this a good example of a useful recast—not useful for providing negative evidence but useful for providing positive evidence. That is, the student is not provided with the means to repair the ill-formed utterance, but the recast is nonetheless useful for scaffolding the interaction. The focus stays on content, the lesson moves forward, and the class is exposed to a good target model that some students may notice right away while others might benefit more from the cumulative effect of such good models over time.

 RESEARCH REPORT

Recasts: Why and when to use them

- Recasts move lessons ahead when target forms are beyond students' abilities and/or entail complex structures.
- Recasts provide support on the spur of the moment to help learners complete learning tasks and/or express their understandings of content.
- Recasts can promote a shift toward a more academic register by enabling the teacher to "relexicalize" a student's everyday words into more technical ones.
- When the context is sufficiently unambiguous to allow young students to focus on language, recasts can draw attention to errors if they are invested with a didactic purpose that increases their salience in at least one of the following ways: The recast is (a) kept short to isolate the target form, (b) focused on only one error, (c) delivered with intonational stress to highlight the modification, and/or (d) accompanied by relevant gestures.

(Gibbons, 1998, 2003; Loewen & Philp, 2006;
Lyster, 1998a, 2007; Mohan & Beckett, 2001;
Nakatsukasa, 2016; Sharpe, 2006)

Prompts

In favor of more direct and overt CF than recasts, Seedhouse (1997) argued that teachers' preferences for using implicit types of CF such as recasts mark linguistic errors as embarrassing and problematic, which in turn contradicts the pedagogical message that "it's OK to make linguistic errors" (p. 567). This section explores the utility of prompts, which do not co-occur with signs of approval and are especially compatible with content teaching, as they resemble the "clueing" procedure or "withholding phenomenon" identified by McHoul (1990) in his study of feedback in subject-matter classrooms.

Prompts can be used to help students to improve control over already internalized forms and can thus be used only to push students to retrieve knowledge that already exists in some form (e.g., declarative form). This is feasible in ImDL classrooms where learners have been exposed to lots of input through subject-matter instruction, resulting in the encoding of ample target-language knowledge that continues to be accessible for comprehension but that requires further activation before becoming part of a learner's productive repertoire. Prompts are an effective way to revisit target features and grammatical sub-systems so that they become increasingly accessible for learners during communicative interaction.

Rachelle, a Grade 4 early immersion teacher, illustrates the use of prompts in the following exchange (from Lyster, 2007, pp. 110–111). The exchange is extracted from a science lesson about mammals and their natural defenses against predators.

1)	T:	*Le lièvre. Joseph pourrais-tu nous dire quels sont les moyens que tu vois, toi, d'après l'illustration là?*	T:	The jackrabbit. Joseph could you tell us what are the means of defense that you see from this picture?
2)	S1:	*Il court vite, puis il saute.*	S1:	It runs fast and it hops.
3)	T:	*Il court vite.*	T:	It runs fast.
4)	S2:	*Il bond.*	S2:	It jump.
5)	T:	*Il bond?*	T:	It jump?
6)	Ss:	*Il bondit.*	Ss:	It jumps.
7)	T:	*Il bondit, c'est le verbe …?*	T:	It jumps, from the verb …?
8)	Ss:	*Bondir.*	Ss:	To jump.
9)	T:	*Bondir. Il fait des bonds. Hein, il bondit. Ensuite. […] Le porc-épic? Sara?*	T:	To jump. It jumps about. Right, it jumps. Next. […] The porcupine? Sara?
10)	S3:	*C'est les piques* sur le dos. C'est…*	S3:	It's the pines* on its back. It's …
11)	T:	*Les piques. Est-ce qu'on dit «les piques»?*	T:	The pines. Do we say "the pines"?
12)	S4:	*Les épiques*.*	S4:	The upines*.
13)	T:	*Les …?*	T:	The …?
14)	S5:	*Les piquants.*	S5:	The quills.
15)	T:	*Les piquants, très bien. Les piquants.*	T:	The quills, very good. The quills.

In Turn 3, Rachelle repeats the first student's well-formed response to confirm its meaning and then, in Turn 5, recasts the next student's ill-formed response. Other students immediately provide the target form in Turn 6, which Rachelle confirms by repeating in Turn 7, and then asks for its infinitive form. Several students propose the verb *bondir,* which Rachelle confirms in Turn 9 by repeating and providing a synonymous phrase (*"Il fait des bonds"*) along with a final repetition of *"Il bondit"* before calling on Joseph to continue. The lesson continues, uninterrupted by Rachelle's prompts.

The topic then switches to porcupines and the precise word in French for *quills.* In response to Sara's creative but non-target suggestion in Turn 10, Rachelle's prompt in Turn 11 combines a metalinguistic clue with repetition of the error. In Turn 12, a different student proposes yet another invented term, which incites Rachelle to use a prompt that not only aims to elicit the target form but also serves as a rejection of the non-target form and, thus, as negative evidence. This simple move succeeds in eliciting the correct term in Turn 14, which is approved and repeated by Rachelle in Turn 15.

Noteworthy in this exchange and others like it (see Lyster, 2007, pp. 113–114) is the students' creativity and linguistic prowess as they play with the component parts of the word *porcupine* to suggest "pines" and "upines" (i.e., "*piques*" and "*épiques*") as possibilities. This short sequence integrated into a spirited discussion about porcupines and other mammals is not only playful but also valuable for consolidating emergent metalinguistic awareness. Early classroom research revealed that immersion teachers tended not to focus on structural information about vocabulary (Allen et al., 1990) and that, as would be expected in the absence of instruction on lexical derivation, immersion students were limited in their productive use of derivational morphology (Harley, 1992; Harley & King, 1989). The opportunity for students in Rachelle's class to propose component parts of words as meaningful units during a content lesson can thus be seen as a useful endeavor with potential for honing the students' word formation skills.

The examples of prompting in the preceding excerpts do not support the now dated claims made by Krashen (1994) and Truscott (1999) that oral CF on accuracy causes anxiety and breaks the communicative flow, or claims by Long (2007) that prompts interfere with the delivery of curricular content. Because the educational objectives of this science lesson are, first, to familiarize students with a range of defense mechanisms used by specific mammals against their predators and, second, to enable students to express their understanding of these natural defense systems, it is fitting that they be pushed to use accurately the verb *bondir* (*jump*) as they discuss jackrabbits and the noun *piquants* (*quills*) to discuss porcupines. This lively discussion about jackrabbits and porcupines enables both teacher and students to engage in collective scaffolding and allows students to test their creative hypotheses. If we remove

Rachelle's prompts and associated responses, students contribute much less to the remaining exchange:

1)	T:	*Le lièvre. Joseph pourrais-tu nous dire quels sont les moyens que tu vois, toi, d'après l'illustration là?*	T:	The jackrabbit. Joseph could you tell us what are the means of defense that you see from this picture?
2)	S1:	*Il court vite, puis il saute.*	S1:	It runs fast and it hops.
3)	T:	*Il court vite.*	T:	It runs fast.
4)	S2:	*Il bond.*	S2:	It jump.
5)	T:	*... Hein, il bondit. Ensuite... [...] Le porc-épic? Sara?*	T:	... Right, it jumps. Next ... [...] The porcupine? Sara?
6)	S3:	*C'est les piques sur le dos. C'est ...*	S3:	It's the pines on its back. It's ...
7)	T:	*Les piquants, très bien. Les piquants.*	T:	The quills, very good. The quills.

Without Rachelle's prompts, the students are left with only recasts, and the resulting interaction lacks the pedagogical richness and creative experimentation that enlivened the interaction with prompts. Of both theoretical and practical interest here is the potential for prompts to draw students' attention to form while maintaining a central focus on meaning.

Prompts, however, are not always more effective than recasts because, if not well formulated, they too can also suffer from a lack of clarity and directness. And some prompts are more effective than others. This was evident in the low rates of repair following clarification requests in French immersion classrooms (Lyster & Ranta, 1997) and by Koike and Pearson's (2005) observation that, in response to clarification requests, the learners would say the same response much louder a second time!

 RESEARCH REPORT

Prompts: Why and when to use them

L2 learners benefit more from being pushed to retrieve target-language forms than from merely hearing the forms in recasts (and then possibly repeating them) for the following reasons:

- Retrieval from existing knowledge strengthens associations in memory so that subsequent retrieval is easier and quicker.
- Learners remember information better when they take an active part in producing it rather than having it provided by an external source.

Teachers are encouraged to use prompts in the following situations:

- When students have control over the content, such as during a Monday morning discussion of their weekend or holiday break, and during content lessons when they already have some familiarity with the topic (e.g., content is being reviewed rather than presented for the first time).

- When students are already familiar with the form but need to be pushed (i.e., reminded) to use it accurately.
- When the error occurs frequently and appears to have fossilized.
- When the error entails a simple structure and is thus reparable on the spur of the moment.
- When the error results from a binary distinction (e.g., *be/have*, *être/avoir*, *estar/tener*, *le/la*, or *el/la*), thus making recasts too ambiguous.

(Clark, 1995; de Bot, 1996; Lyster, 2016; Lyster & Sato, 2013)

Using both recasts and prompts as scaffolding

Given the focus on meaningful subject-matter content or language arts themes in ImDL classrooms, continued recasting of students' errors will not ensure continued development of accuracy in the minority language. When students' attention is focused on meaning and the teacher provides a recast, they are likely to remain focused on meaning, not form, as they expect the teacher's immediate response to confirm or disconfirm the veracity of their utterances. In ImDL settings, prompts—as interactional moves aiming overtly to draw learners' attention to their non-target output—enable teachers to draw students' attention to form and momentarily away from meaning. This is important in ImDL classrooms, where learners have many opportunities to communicate but have a tendency to do so with a classroom code easily understood by both teacher and peers. At the same time, however, continued prompting of learners to draw on what they have not yet begun to acquire will be as ineffective as continued recasting of what students have already acquired to some extent but fail to produce accurately. For this reason, it is recommended that teachers use a variety of CF types. This means that ImDL teachers need to be cognizant of their use of CF to avoid overusing recasts at the expense of other types of CF. This would be in keeping with Lyster and Ranta's (1997) simple conclusion from years ago regarding ImDL classrooms: "Teachers might want to consider the whole range of techniques they have at their disposal rather than relying so extensively on recasts" (p. 56). In doing so, teachers need to orchestrate, in accordance with their students' language abilities and content familiarity, a wide range of CF types befitting the instructional context.

 SPECIAL NOTE

Frequent recasting of forms with which students are already familiar is not an effective strategy for continued L2 development. Similarly, prompting learners to draw on what they have not yet acquired will be equally ineffective. Therefore, teachers need to be adept at orchestrating both types of CF.

We now look at a teacher who uses a range of CF types with her L2 learners of English in an Australian mainstream Grade 5 science classroom. Gibbons (1998, 2003) observed these science lessons as the teacher implemented a three-step instructional sequence, consisting of:

1) small-group work during which students experimented with magnets;
2) oral reporting by the students of their experiments;
3) journal writing in which they reported on the experiment.

In the oral reporting stage guided by the teacher, the teacher used explicit comments such as: "We're trying to talk like scientists," "Your language has got to be really precise," and "The language you choose is very important" (Gibbons, 1998, p. 105). The teacher interacted with individual students in ways that scaffolded their contributions, "allowing for communication to proceed while giving the learner access to new linguistic data" (Gibbons, 1998, p. 110). Gibbons (2003) identified three main techniques that the teacher used during the stage of teacher-guided reporting to help the children reconstruct their experiences:

1) recasting;
2) signaling how to reformulate (i.e., prompting followed by a recast);
3) indicating a need for reformulation (i.e., prompting followed by self-repair).

Recasting was used by the teacher primarily to promote a shift toward a more scientific register. This is in line with broader definitions in the field of education that consider recasts not only as a type of CF but also as a scaffolding strategy that entails "the teacher's relexicalising a student's everyday word or words into more technical ones" (Sharpe, 2006, p. 218). This type of relexicalizing is seen in the following exchange (from Gibbons, 2003, p. 260):

1) T: OK, can you then tell me what you had to do next?
2) S: When we had, em the things the first one, like if you put it up in the air like that ... the magnets you can feel, feel the em, that they're not pushing?
3) T: When you turn the magnet around? You felt that
4) S: Pushing and if we use the other side we can't feel pushing
5) T: OK so when, they were facing one way, they/ you felt the magnets *attract* and *stick together*/ when you turn one of the magnets around you felt it, *repelling*, or *pushing away*. OK, thank you, well done Charbel.

In this example, the teacher reformulates the student's use of "pushing" and "not pushing" into the stylistically more appropriate forms that are at the heart of this lesson on magnetism: "attract" and "repel." Gibbons (2003) invested such recasts with a style-shifting function and described their use as "an ongoing process of recapping by the teacher, who re-represents or recontextualizes learners' experiences and the events they are talking about in a way that fits the broader pedagogic objectives of the curriculum" (p. 257).

Gibbons also showed how the teacher finally moved beyond recasting and instead pushed learners to stretch their language resources. For example, in the following teacher-student exchange from Gibbons (2003, p. 261), the teacher initially signals to the student that a reformulation is necessary, and then finally supplies a reformulated version of the student's meaning, "only after the learner has had opportunities for self-correction" (p. 261):

1) T: What did you find out?
2) S: If you put a nail onto the piece of foil, and then pick it, pick it up, the magnet will … That if you put a nail under a piece of foil, and then pick, pick the foil up with the magnet, still, still with the nail, under it … it won't
3) T: It what?
4) S: It won't/ it won't come out
5) T: What won't come out?
6) S: It'll go up
7) T: Wait just a minute. Can you explain that a bit more Julianna?
8) S: Like if you put a nail and then foil over it and then put the nail on top of the foil, the nail underneath the foil/ Miss I can't say it
9) T: No, you're doing fine I/ I can see
10) S: Miss forget about the magnet/ em the magnet holds it with the foil up the top and the nail's underneath and the foil's on top and put the magnet in it and you lift it up, and the nail will em, hold it/ stick with the magnet and the foil's in between
11) T: Oh/ so even with the foil in between, the magnet will *still* pick up the nail alright does the magnet pick up the foil?
12) S: No

This exchange illustrates how the teacher's requests for clarification in Turn 5 and for elaboration in Turn 7 along with encouragement (Turn 9) push the learner to stretch her language resources: "Julianna is at the outer limits of what she can do alone. Yet, because of the precise and contingent nature of the teacher's scaffolding, the text is characterized by the student's, rather than the teacher's, reformulations" (Gibbons, 2003, p. 262).

In the next exchange, the teacher uses an elicitation move to signal that a reformulation is necessary, "but, knowing that the learner can achieve it alone, she hands the responsibility over to the student" (Gibbons, 2003, p. 263). Notice the excellent open-ended request that initiates the exchange:

1) T: Tell us what you found out.
2) S: We found out that the south and the south don't like to stick together.
3) T: Now let's/ let's start using our scientific language, Michelle.
4) S: The north and the north repelled each other and the south and the south also, repelled each other but when we put the/ when we put the two magnets in a different way they/ they attracted each other.

This example illustrates how the teacher's elicitation of more appropriate language ("let's start using our scientific language") results in longer and more complete learner discourse than does a recast, an important outcome for teachers to consider when selecting CF to encourage students to increase and to refine their use of the target language.

Decisions about whether to provide recasts or prompts need to take into account the students' familiarity with the content of the lesson. That is, interaction about content with which students are unfamiliar lends itself well to the use of recasts, whereas interaction about content familiar to students provides ideal opportunities for the use of prompts. Teachers might be reluctant to draw attention to language during informal conversations with students (e.g., about their weekend or spring break), seeing them as good opportunities for students to express themselves freely without the constraints of formal feedback. However, these moments are ideal for providing helpful feedback precisely because students are in complete control of the content, which helps to free up their attentional resources to focus on language.

 RESEARCH REPORT

The case for variety in CF use

Classroom research comparing different types of CF has shown overall positive effects for all types of CF as well as some advantages for prompts and explicit correction over recasts (for detailed summaries, see Ellis, 2012; Lyster et al., 2013; Sheen, 2011). For example, a meta-analysis of 15 classroom studies of CF, which all told included 827 student participants (Lyster & Saito, 2010), showed that all types of CF—whether recasts, prompts, or explicit correction—had significant effects, meaning that they were all more effective than no CF. The between-group comparisons yielded medium effects for recasts and large effects for both prompts and for explicit correction, while the within-group comparisons also yielded medium effects for recasts and large effects for both prompts and explicit correction. Research at this point, therefore, supports the use of a variety of CF types with some advantages for prompts over recasts. Although recasts are useful for scaffolding interaction when target forms are beyond a learner's current abilities, as Nicholas, Lightbown, and Spada (2001) concluded, "there is a point beyond which recasts are ineffective in changing stabilized interlanguages" (p. 752). Beyond such a point, learners benefit more from being pushed to self-repair by means of prompting, especially in cases where recasts could be perceived ambiguously as approving their use of non-target forms and where learners have reached a developmental plateau in their use of the non-target forms.

Finally, because recasts are useful scaffolds that enable learners to participate in interaction even when they lack sufficient knowledge of the forms at stake, and because prompts can be used only to push learners to retrieve knowledge that already exists, some may interpret this to mean that teachers should use recasts with younger learners and prompts with older learners. However, this is not necessarily the case. Lyster and Saito's (2010) meta-analysis suggested that younger learners (under 18) benefit more from prompts than recasts, whereas older learners (18+) are able to benefit equally from recasts and prompts. They concluded that "teachers might consider enhancing the pedagogical potential of CF not only by reformulating child learners' non-target-like forms (i.e., recasting) but also by providing a variety of unambiguous signals and metalinguistic clues through various other types of CF" (p. 295). Otherwise, young learners are likely to have difficulty in detecting linguistic information in classroom input without guided support (see Lightbown, 2008b; Muñoz, 2008). In contrast, older learners, with their greater analytical abilities, might be able to make the most of different CF types to notice linguistic information in an autonomous manner, resulting in similar gains irrespective of CF types.

As for whether teachers should even bother providing any type of CF to very young learners, the answer is a resounding "yes!" as long as the CF is selective and tailored to their needs and abilities. This is because research suggests that younger learners are especially sensitive to the impact of CF (Mackey & Oliver, 2002; Oliver, 2000), because it engages implicit learning mechanisms that are more characteristic of younger than of older learners. This line of research has actually shown that CF "leads to development more quickly for child learners than for adults" (Mackey & Oliver, 2002, p. 473).

⃝! SPECIAL NOTE

As long as teachers tailor their CF to be age appropriate, there is no reason for them to believe that CF is not suitable for children. On the contrary, CF can be delivered in ways that match children's natural tendency for learning through scaffolded interaction.

Written corrective feedback

As mentioned at the beginning of this chapter, the effectiveness of oral CF has been easier to demonstrate than that of written CF. This may have to do with the immediacy of oral CF, which pushes learners to process the CF in real time during meaningful interaction. In contrast, students generally receive CF on their writing much later, possibly days after the time of writing. Nonetheless, a recent meta-analysis of 21 studies exploring the effectiveness of written CF confirmed that it does indeed lead to greater grammatical accuracy in L2 writing (with moderate effects; see Kang & Han, 2015), which is in sharp contrast with the more pessimistic view (e.g., Truscott, 1996) that written CF is ineffective and should be abandoned! A particularly important finding from the research on the effectiveness of written CF is that intermediate and advanced learners appeared to benefit much more than beginners (Kang & Han, 2015).

Regarding immediacy, there is now much potential to provide written CF more immediately thanks to various synchronous communication tools increasingly available through online learning platforms. In any case, however, it's not entirely clear that, for CF to be effective, it needs to be immediate. For example, based on their review of the literature, Manchón and Vasylets (2019) proposed various characteristics of written CF that contribute to language learning, one of which is the greater availability of time in writing than in speaking as well as the more visible and permanent nature of written CF, which in turn has the potential to engage learners in problem solving that requires greater depth of processing than spontaneous oral CF.

With respect to different types of written CF, the strategy whereby teachers actually provide the correct form is referred to as *direct correction*, whereas the CF strategy used to indicate that an error has been made without providing the correct form is referred to as *indirect correction* (Ellis, 2009).

Direct corrections almost always provide the correct form, either by means of a reformulation or explicitly accompanied by a signal that something is wrong (e.g., a word is crossed out or the correct word is inserted above the wrong word). Sometimes, direct corrections are accompanied by comments, questions, or metalinguistic explanations that contain the correct form (e.g., "You use *would* when […] I think you wanted to use *will*") (Guénette & Lyster, 2013).

In contrast, indirect corrections are delivered with either a code or a comment that serve to draw attention to the error without providing the correct form. Indirect coded corrections flag the error by means of an error code (e.g., "sp" for spelling or "p" for punctuation) or a clear indication of the type of error. Indirect corrections with comments flag the error by means of metalinguistic comments, suggestions, or questions without providing the correct form (Guénette & Lyster, 2013).

Distinctions between direct and indirect correction in written CF are thus similar to the distinction in oral CF between recasts and prompts, respectively. Also similar is the observation that L2 teachers tend to give far more direct corrections than indirect corrections when providing CF on writing to their students (Ferris, 2006; Furneaux, Paran, & Fairfax, 2007; Guénette & Lyster, 2013; Lee, 2004). This is probably because recourse to direct corrections equips teachers with a means to ensure that their CF is as clear as possible by virtue of an actual model of what is accurate in the target language. Indirect corrections, whether accompanied by a code or a comment, need to compensate for the lack of a model by providing codes or comments with extreme clarity in order for them to be useful to students for subsequent self-correction.

In spite of a preponderance of direct corrections, some argue that indirect corrections are probably more effective than direct corrections insofar as they place greater processing demands on learners as they endeavor to correct their errors. In this view, learning involves moving away from other-repair (i.e., direct correction) toward more reliance on self-repair (i.e., indirect correction) (e.g., Aljaafreh & Lantolf, 1994). However, Kang and Han's (2015) meta-analysis failed to detect any significant differences between direct and indirect corrections. They argued that the effects of either direct and indirect corrections are probably tempered by other factors such as learners' proficiency level, with beginners benefiting more from direct corrections and more advanced learners from indirect corrections. Given the inconclusive results of research comparing the effects of direct and indirect corrections, we recommend that teachers use a variety of written CF techniques, similar to our recommendation that teachers use a variety of oral CF types.

One final choice teachers need to consider when providing written CF is whether to provide CF selectively or comprehensively. *Comprehensive correction* entails correcting all errors in a written text, whereas *selective correction* entails targeting preselected types of errors, usually pertaining to the linguistic objectives of the current unit of study. Selective correction is thus feasible in a counterbalanced approach to ImDL instruction, which requires identification of both content and language objectives in the ImDL curriculum. However, Kang and Han's (2015) meta-analysis found no significant differences between comprehensive and selective correction, again leaving the door open for teachers to use both types in accordance with their specific language learning objectives.

Notwithstanding its many potential benefits, written CF can be effective only if it is integrated into a recursive process of writing that requires students to use the CF as they engage in editing and revising stages. This is known as *process writing*, which was documented specifically in the context of ImDL classrooms by Hall (1993). Process writing is an instructional approach that views writing as a set of at least three dynamically inter-related stages characterized by negotiation with peers and teachers alike:

1. The prewriting stage involves planning and collective brainstorming so that, ideally, students write about something they have already discussed orally. Hall (1993) suggested that French immersion students needed three times longer to plan than their peers writing in their L1.
2. The writing stage entails drafting, revising, and editing, during which time feedback is provided either orally (during a writing "workshop" or "conference") or in writing by the teacher and/or peers. An essential premise of process writing is that feedback is more useful between drafts rather than on the final product submitted for evaluation.
3. The publishing stage of process writing is critical and ideally involves authentic audiences (e.g., students can share their work with either younger or older students at other grade levels).

Thus, whereas written CF is provided about students' writing, it can be provided not only in writing but also orally during collaborative conversations and even offline via audio files. The purpose in all cases is to encourage students during the writing process to reflect on what they want to say and to help them make appropriate choices about language form and stylistic conventions.

As mentioned earlier regarding the potential of peer CF, teachers are not the only CF providers in the classroom: ImDL students can engage collaboratively in the writing process, especially during the revision stage. In their study of the effects of peer revision on the written texts of Grade 5 French immersion students, Blain and Painchaud (1999) found that students incorporated more than half of their peers' CF into their revisions, with greater effects on spelling than on grammar. As suggested earlier with respect to oral CF, students need the guidance of teacher scaffolding in the form of strategy training in order to develop their skills as both CF providers and receivers during the writing process.

Summary

This chapter has addressed the multifaceted roles of CF in ImDL classrooms in terms of its various types, functions, and effects. Even though the provision of CF has been shown by research to be more effective than its absence, there are still many variables that interact to moderate its effectiveness. This chapter has aimed to increase teacher awareness of the different types of CF so they can move away from overusing one type of CF (i.e., recasts) at the expense of others. The purpose has been to support teachers in making informed decisions about how to use CF selectively and effectively as a means to scaffold classroom interaction. They can do so by using CF in ways that are clear and meaningful so that it benefits their students' continued growth in the minority language. Although the emphasis was placed on oral CF in this chapter, written CF is also of importance in ImDL classrooms and evokes some of the same practical and theoretical issues that were raised regarding oral CF. In both cases, teachers are encouraged to use a variety of CF types in ways that optimize clarity and that engage students as active participants.

Application activity 1: Oral feedback coding exercise

Identify the type of oral corrective feedback used by the teacher (followed by: ⇒). See Appendix E for answer key.

Example 1

S: They also said that the volcano was starting at 12:00, was starting to get out.
T: Oh, the volcano was going to erupt at 12:00. ⇒

Example 2

S: I live Japan.
T: Oh, can we fix that? There's one little word we need. ⇒

Example 3

S: In the beginning, it have a like a farmer that wanted to give a favor.
T: Yes, there was a farmer, a young boy who gave a note to Jack and Annie. ⇒

Example 4

S: Mrs. Jones travel a lot last year.
T: Mrs. Jones travel a lot last year? ⇒

Example 5

T: Why do you think it was good advice to go home?
S: So they don't get dead.
T: They won't die. Is something bad going to happen? ⇒

Example 6

T: What did you find out about the Vikings?
S: They live in Europe.
T: They lived in Europe. ⇒

Example 7

T: What's the emperor of China?
S: It's like the boss of all of China.
T: Yes, but what's a better word than boss? ⇒

Example 8

S1: Her name was Maya, and she died when my parent was in the /salon/ eating and me in the /cuisine/ and she was on two feet and she fell down and she dead like that.

T: Who was in the /salon/? What is that in English? ⇒

S2: Living room.

T: Living room. Who was in the living room?

S1: My parent.

T: And who was in the kitchen? ⇒

S1: Me.

T: You were in the kitchen. Where was your dog?

S1: In the kitchen, with me.

Example 9

S: Why does he fly to Korea last year?

T: Pardon? ⇒

Example 10

T: *Qu'est-ce que vous voyez en haut du tableau? On lève la main si on peut me répondre. ... Keisha?* [What do you see at the top of the board? Raise your hand if you can answer. ... Keisha?]

S: *Un ligne du temps.* [A timeline-M.]

T: *Je vois...* [I see ...] ⇒

S: *Une ligne du temps.* [A timeline-F.]

Example 11

S: I would like to wear shirt, because ...

T: Can you say it one more time? ⇒

Example 12

S: He don't like books.

T: He doesn't like books. ⇒

Example 13

S: And so, we can use the Pythagorean theorem. So, we need this and this to find this one.

T: Ah, this and this and this. OK. We have a word for "this." ⇒

Example 14

S1: What would you like to eat food?

T: Eat. You can just say, "What would you like to eat?" ⇒

S1: What would you like to eat?

S2: I like to eat …

T: Oh no, you missed something. ⇒

S2: I would like to eat corn, because it is yummy. How about you?

S1: I would like to eat pumpkin, because it is delicious.

Example 15

T: We need one more thing. Without this thing, you cannot use an alcohol burner.

S: We need match.

T: Match? Just one? ⇒

Example 16

S: Can we, you know when it was the volcano, can we do like, /*on devine**/ the title?

T: You'd like to guess the title? Oh, we can do that. ⇒

---

*on devine *means we guess in English.*

Application activity 2: What's wrong with this prompt?

As mentioned in this chapter, prompts are not always more effective than recasts because, if not well formulated, they too can suffer from a lack of clarity and directness. Read the following exchange between a teacher and a student in a Grade 4 social studies lesson about homes in New France and the fact that most were made of wood. The teacher asks students in this multicultural classroom what the homes in their countries of origin are built of. A student answers by describing his grandparent's house in Greece.

After reading the exchange, identify the different types of CF used by the teacher and then explain why they do not seem successful. See Appendix E for answer key.

1)	S:	*Oui mais la maison que mes grands-parents vivent en dedans, c'est avec les briques.*	S:	Yeah, but the house that my grandparents live inside of, it's with bricks.
2)	T:	*OK. La maison que mes grands-parents vivent en dedans, ça ne se dit pas comme ça en français. Comment tu vas dire ça?*	T:	OK. The house that my grandparents live inside of, we don't say it like that. How are you going to say it?
3)	S:	*Euh …*	S:	Uh …
4)	T:	*S'ils y vivent, est-ce qu'ils sont en dedans?*	T:	If they live there, are they inside of it?
5)	S:	*Oui.*	S:	Yes.
6)	T:	*Alors, c'est pas nécessaire de dire «en dedans». La maison où mes grands-parents vivent. Hein? Dans laquelle mes grands-parents vivent. Très bien.*	T:	So, you don't have to say "inside of it." The house where my grandparents live. In which my grandparents live. Very good.
7)	S:	*Ben, ils vivent pas là, ils vivent aux États-Unis maintenant.*	S:	Well, they don't live there; they live in the US now.

PART IV

Curriculum planning and assessment

Part IV addresses immersion and dual language (ImDL) teachers' need to be adept at designing instruction and assessment that integrates subject-matter content and the language needed to engage with that content. Drawing upon the principles of "backward design," Chapter 7 introduces a template for unit-level instructional design and walks readers through the process of developing curriculum unit plans that are linked to standards or outcomes and that integrate content, language, and culture. Chapter 8 continues the curriculum planning process with a focus on module and lesson instructional design. It presents a second planning template and describes in detail how ImDL teachers should go about planning lessons that incorporate a focus on both content and language. It also introduces a process for developing detailed learning objectives, with special emphasis on developing focused language objectives. Chapter 9 further conceptualizes integrated language learning as an effective means for supporting students' biliteracy development. It focuses specifically on bilingual read-aloud projects as a meaningful approach to forge cross-linguistic connections while maintaining separate spaces for instruction in each program language. Finally, Chapter 10 brings attention to performance assessment. It emphasizes an approach to classroom-based assessment that integrates three modes of communication as well as language and content. The chapter ends with a brief description of teacher performance assessment and the introduction of a self-assessment tool that teachers can use to reflect on their ability to apply the pedagogical practices that are described throughout the book.

7

UNIT-LEVEL INSTRUCTIONAL DESIGN

The preceding section discussed instructional scaffolding with an emphasis on strategies to extend students' language production and to provide corrective feedback. In this chapter, we begin our discussion of integrated curriculum planning and assessment. We present a unit-level instructional design process that integrates content, language, and culture. This chapter and the next are intended to be used in immersion and dual language (ImDL) teacher preparation or professional development programs so that teachers can move through the curriculum planning process with guidance and feedback. The process described involves planning with considerable attention to detail. ImDL teachers typically go through this detailed planning process as part of a team in a course or series of workshops. Once they experience this approach to instructional design, they develop a much greater awareness of what planning for integrated content and language instruction entails and use parts of the templates introduced to plan independently or collaboratively with partner teachers or grade-level team members.

The purpose of this chapter is to address the following questions:

- What is backward design?
- What is the difference between unit, module, and lesson planning?
- What goes into planning units, modules, and lessons that integrate content, language, and culture?
- What are facts, concepts, and generalizations, and how do they inform curricular design?
- What is the difference between state- or provincial-level standards/outcomes and unit-level goals?

Introduction

Teachers are fundamentally instructional designers. They craft curriculum, learning experiences, and assessments based on school district or board content requirements, which align with state-level learning standards or provincial-level outcomes, as well as on learner needs and gaps in their understandings. In the US, content *standards* exist at both national and state levels. These are roughly equivalent in Canada to the general and specific learning *outcomes* outlined at provincial levels, although there is some terminological variation across provinces (e.g., expectations and competencies). Throughout this chapter we use the terms *standards* and *outcomes* interchangeably to refer to government-level requirements. Classroom curriculum is comprised of lessons, assignments, and materials used to organize and teach particular subject-matter content.

Public ImDL programs are responsible for meeting the same standards that other English-medium schools in the school district meet. The published curricular materials purchased by school districts (reading series, mathematics or science programs, social studies textbooks, etc.) are sometimes in English, but even if they are available in the minority language, they typically need to be modified, and additional planning must occur on the part of teachers to ensure that the curriculum is appropriate for L2 learners and that it attends to language in meaningful ways. The bottom line is that ImDL teachers need to be experienced at designing instruction that focuses on both subject-matter content and the language needed to engage with that content.

Backward design

Well known for their planning framework called "*Understanding by Design*," Wiggins and McTighe (2005) define "backward design" as a results-based approach to instructional design that emphasizes "begin[ning] with the end in mind" (Covey, 1989, p. 98, cited in Wiggins & McTighe, 2005, p. 1). We made reference to backward design in Chapter 4 regarding the CAPA (contextualization, awareness, practice, and autonomy) model. When it comes to curricular planning, before teachers identify materials and develop learning experiences, they need to identify precisely what they want students to learn as a result of a particular curriculum unit and what evidence they need to determine whether students have learned what they wanted them to learn. We borrow some aspects of the backward design approach in our instructional design process and planning templates.

Units, modules, and lessons

In this and the next chapter, we discuss instructional design according to three inter-related components: units, modules, and lessons. Units are comprised of modules, which are made up of daily lessons. Beginning with unit planning allows teachers to conceptualize the entire unit before they begin the detailed work of

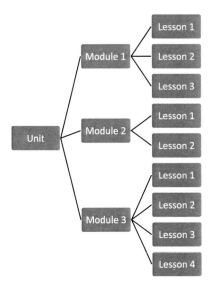

FIGURE 7.1 Relationship between units, modules, and lessons

module and individual lesson design. Figure 7.1 shows the hierarchical relationship between the unit and its modules and lessons. A thematic curriculum unit (discussed further below) is typically broken down into various topics. Each topic is addressed in a sequence of linked lessons that we call a module. In this chapter, we introduce and exemplify a template for unit-level design, and in Chapter 8 we present a template for module and lesson design. In keeping with the counterbalanced approach introduced in Chapter 3, our instructional design templates are intended to aid teachers in thinking through the content and language possibilities for a curricular unit and the modules and lessons that comprise it. We begin by discussing some ways that ImDL teachers need to set the stage for instructional design.

Setting the stage for instructional design

A critical aspect of instructional design is knowing one's students. It is important for teachers to be aware of the gender make-up of their classrooms (including students who identify as gender non-conforming), in addition to the ethnic/cultural, linguistic, and socioeconomic backgrounds of their students. This awareness helps teachers to select appropriate materials and design activities using a culturally responsive lens (Gay, 2018; see Chapter 2). Knowing students' linguistic backgrounds is key because of the instructional design implications, especially in two-way immersion (TWI) and developmental bilingual education (DBE) programs. Escamilla and colleagues (2014) aptly point out that simultaneous bilinguals (children exposed to two or more languages between the ages of 0 and 5) and sequential bilinguals (those exposed to an L2 after age 5) are likely to have different strengths and challenges as well as different learning trajectories. This linguistic information can inform a variety of instructional decisions, including grouping arrangements. Teachers should also acknowledge students with special needs, as this information is critical in planning for instructional differentiation.

Equally important is having a clear idea of students' minority-language proficiency levels. Some ImDL programs assess students' proficiency in the minority language and thus provide teachers with reliable information about their students' language competencies. However, many programs do not provide such assessment data, and teachers must therefore estimate their students' language proficiency in the four modalities or skills—listening, speaking, reading, and writing—to inform their instructional design. ImDL teachers might find proficiency descriptors we mentioned in Chapter 2—the ACTFL Proficiency Guidelines and Common European Framework of Reference for Languages (CEFR)—to be helpful sources for estimating students' proficiency levels. Also, language development descriptors established by the WIDA Consortium could be useful, and resources provided by the Canadian Association of Immersion Professionals (ACPI) for French immersion are valuable (see *Resources for Readers* at the end of this chapter). The WIDA levels are well conceptualized and can be useful for describing proficiency levels of L2 learners of other languages.

Students who are learning content through an L2 need meaningful and comprehensible input while also being challenged to produce language in developmentally appropriate ways (see Chapter 3). Inevitably, ImDL classrooms serve students with a wide range of proficiency levels in the program's languages, and it is important for teachers to understand the range represented in their classrooms. In TWI contexts, teachers must, on the one hand, design instruction that makes accommodations for L2 learners of the program languages, while, on the other hand, providing enough challenge for students who are already proficient in the language of instruction to continue to push their language development forward. Having a sense of students' language proficiency levels will aid teachers in differentiating language objectives, learning activities, and assessments (concepts explored in detail in Chapter 8).

Unit-level instructional design

Once the stage is set in teachers' minds, unit-level instructional design can begin. ImDL classroom instructional design may be interdisciplinary (integrating two or more subject areas) and should be organized around a central theme, with instruction and learning experiences as well as assessments being structured to fit that theme. In this section, we introduce a template for ImDL unit-level instructional design (Figure 7.2), which is intended to serve as a guide to facilitate the systematic planning of a curricular unit to be taught in the minority language (although the same template could be modified for English instruction). The template provides a general overview of the unit, with a description of the context and a summary of the unit's goals, associated state or provincial competencies, key subject-matter

ImDL Unit Design Template	
Unit Particulars	
Unit Theme/Big Idea:	Time Frame:
Key Generalization:	Subject Matters Targeted:
Students' Background Knowledge and Skills	
Knowledge/Understandings:	Essential Skills:
Key Concepts (by subject) and Module Topics	
Standards/Outcomes	
Content (by subject):	Language and Culture:
Unit-Level Goals	
Knowledge/Understandings: Students will understand that…	Skills: Students will be able to…
Unit-Level Summative Performance Assessment and Other Assessment Activities	
Unit References and Resources	

The left margin labels are: **Context** (top), **Desired Results** (middle), **Evidence** (lower).

FIGURE 7.2 ImDL Unit Design Template

concepts and topics to be targeted in modules and lessons, as well as a brief description of the evidence to be gathered to assess students' learning and language use. A detailed module/lesson planning template, which is to be used in conjunction with the unit-level instructional design template, is presented in Chapter 8. The unit-level template serves as an overview or brief summary of the goals and content the unit will target. As we describe each part of the template, we ask readers to refer to a sample unit overview on *Adaptations* that appears in Appendix A. Note that in this example we include key information described above under *Setting the stage for instructional design* so that the specific context for which the unit was designed is clear to the reader.

 TEACHER SPOTLIGHT

The unit on *Adaptations* that we use to exemplify unit, module, lesson, and performance assessment design (Chapters 7, 8, and 10) was crafted by a team of teachers who took a class on ImDL curriculum development and assessment with Tedick. The team included: Verena Burkart, Megon Coon, Kirsten Rue, Rachel Stiling, Sarah Vander Laan, Lisa Zuñiga, and Amanda Zwiefelhofer. Although all the teachers collaborated on the creation of the unit and completion of the instructional design templates, Burkart, Stiling, Vander Laan, and Zuñiga were primarily responsible for designing lessons, whereas Coon, Rue, and Zwiefelhofer took the lead on developing the summative performance assessment (Chapter 10).

The teachers designed the unit originally for a one-way, early total Spanish immersion Grade 3 classroom, but the unit overview and sample module shared in this book have been adapted for a 90:10 TWI context in order to illustrate the differentiation that needs to occur in planning for two-way classrooms. Other modifications have also been made to more clearly illustrate the concepts described in the chapters in Part IV.

Although the instructional design template is presented in linear form, it is not completed in a linear fashion. Instructional design is more cyclical in nature. For example, although specific standards may be identified early on in the planning process, as unit planning unfolds, it is quite likely that additional competencies may be added or others deleted. Similarly, the topics for the unit's modules will initially be determined, but they, too, will likely undergo changes during the planning process, as will assessment activities.

Context

The first part of the template establishes the context for the unit. In this section, the teacher summarizes the overall theme of the unit and the subject area(s) it targets and also identifies the background knowledge and skills that students already have that are relevant for this particular unit.

Unit particulars

To begin planning, ImDL teachers specify the overall theme or "big idea" of the unit and its estimated time frame. They also clarify the key "generalization" or "take-away" as well as the subject matters that the unit targets. Thematic instructional design is critical for ImDL classrooms, as it allows teachers to address content standards from a range of subject areas within the context of one unit. Thematic teaching also interrupts the "segmentation and isolation" that has come to define school curriculum (Kucer, Silva, & Delgado-Larocco, 1995, pp. 1–3). Today's schools often emphasize the teaching of isolated facts, and literacy instruction, in particular, is typically segmented by dividing written language into separate parts that are too often divorced from meaning. In many ImDL settings, there is so much time devoted to mathematics and literacy/language arts instruction in elementary schools that other subject areas such as science and social studies receive much less attention. In the US in particular, what is assessed on standardized measures drives the content of the curriculum, especially in elementary settings. Kucer et al. argue that segmentation and isolation have had debilitating consequences: "Teachers feel disempowered by a curriculum that dictates what is to be taught when, and students experience confusion as they jump from skill to skill, from fact to fact, and from room to room" (p. 3).

In our conceptualization, themes are parallel to what Wiggins and McTighe (2005) call *big ideas*. They define a big idea as "a concept, theme, or issue that gives meaning and connection to discrete facts and skills" (p. 5). Big ideas and themes are by definition abstract and transferable. Examples include adaptation, continuity and change, environment, friendships and community, survival, heroes and heroines, and the distributive property (in mathematics) (Kucer et al., 1995; Wiggins & McTighe, 2005).

Developing curriculum from a thematic perspective emphasizes "generalizable and conceptual knowledge" rather than mere acquisition of facts and figures (Kucer et al., 1995, p. 6). To guide teachers in their planning, Kucer et al. propose three knowledge levels—facts, concepts, and generalizations (see Figure 7.3). These levels vary in degree of abstraction and are related to one another, as illustrated through examples from the *Adaptations* unit found in Appendix A. Facts represent specific information at a low level of abstraction (e.g., Frogs are amphibians), whereas concepts signify categories of information comprising many facts (e.g., classification). Generalizations, which are at the highest level of abstraction, show the relationship between two or more concepts (e.g., Location and climate affect adaptation). Kucer et al.'s definition of generalizations is similar to Wiggins and McTighe's (2005) concept of "enduring understandings," which they define as generalizations formulated to describe what the teacher wants the students to understand about the big idea. Generalizations or enduring understandings are the principal take-aways—the key conceptual understandings that students walk away with at the end of a unit. Curriculum units inevitably include more than one generalization or enduring understanding, but in

Generalizations
Statements describing relationships between two or more concepts that summarize many facts; key take-aways or enduring understandings. *Examples*: All living things adapt to their environment. Key characteristics are used to classify living things. Location and climate affect adaptation.

Concepts
Words or phrases that symbolize categories of information comprised of many facts; an abstract idea of something that we create. *Examples*: adaptation, classification, climate, culture, environment, habitat, heredity, human impact, survival.

Facts
Statements of specific information at the lowest level of abstraction. *Examples*: Frogs are amphibians. Reptiles have dry and scaly skin. Desert animals get water from the food they eat and/or store it in their bodies. Some animals like seals and whales have thick layers of fat under their skin to be able to survive in cold climates.

FIGURE 7.3 Relationship between knowledge levels

this part of the instructional design framework, teachers need to identify the key generalization—the one that stands out as most important to the theme and unit.

It is important to note that the knowledge levels reflected in Figure 7.3 are not necessarily linear—learning does not always begin with facts, transfer to concepts, and then conclude with generalizations (Kucer et al., 1995). Generalizations may develop first, and facts might then be identified to support those generalizations. As the facts are considered and organized, the concepts may naturally emerge.

Importantly, language is the primary tool through which students develop and express their understandings of facts, concepts, and generalizations. Thus, teachers must develop learning experiences that require students to *use* language to show their understandings. Moreover, assessment of learning should emphasize language use as a means to determine whether and how well students have learned the conceptual and generalizable knowledge.

 SPECIAL NOTE

Language is the primary tool through which students and teachers develop and express their knowledge. Thus, attention to language throughout all facets of instructional design is critical.

Thematic curriculum design also involves ensuring that materials align with the generalizations and concepts being emphasized, are selected for varying levels of difficulty, and present different perspectives. It also involves designing activities that help students to seek out common issues and ideas and that promote a deeper understanding of the generalizable and conceptual knowledge that is the focus of the unit (Kucer et al., 1995). Thus, for both unit-level and module-level design, it is important for teachers to emphasize generalizable and conceptual knowledge. Although facts are certainly important, they should not be the sole level of knowledge that a unit (or module or lesson) emphasizes. Thematic instructional design also may integrate several subject areas. Our sample unit (see Appendix A) integrates science, literacy and language arts, and social studies.

 KEY CONCEPTS

Thematic instructional design

- emphasizes generalizable and conceptual knowledge;
- includes materials that clarify and explore the generalizations and concepts and present different perspectives;
- incorporates activities that promote deeper understanding of the generalizations and concepts; and
- may integrate several subject areas.

Students' background knowledge and skills

Also included in the "context" portion of the template is a space for teachers to identify students' background knowledge and skills. In designing instruction, teachers need to be aware of what students already know (knowledge and understandings) in relation to the unit theme as well as what they can already do (skills). For instance, in the example shown in Appendix A, students have knowledge of the life cycles of living things and are able to ask and answer questions (skill). Taking the time to reflect on students' background knowledge and skills makes clear to teachers how they can use this information as a bridge to building new concepts and skills.

Desired results

The first stage of the backward design approach entails identifying "desired results" (Wiggins & McTighe, 2005). This stage of planning involves pinpointing what teachers want students to know/understand and be able to do by the end of the unit. In this stage, teachers must be clear about the overall aim of the unit, by referring to selected content standards prescribed at the state or provincial level and developing associated unit-level goals. They also need to identify the key subject-matter concepts that the unit will address. In addition, teachers specify the topics that will shape the modules comprising the unit. These topics may be conceptualized in the form of questions or enduring understandings. A unit-level theme is typically very broad (e.g., *Adaptations*); therefore, it is necessary to make choices about the content that can be included in the unit given the time frame allotted. As Wiggins and McTighe remind us, "[this] stage in the design process calls for clarity about priorities" (p. 18).

Key concepts and module topics

In this section of the template, teachers name the key concepts the unit will include (by subject matter). For example, the *Adaptations* unit involves key science concepts, such as adaptation, classification, habitat, and survival. The topics that will comprise the unit modules are also identified in this section. In our example, these are framed as questions, such as "Why do living things adapt?"

State or provincial standards/outcomes and unit-level goals

Desired results also include content and language (and culture) competencies as well as unit-level goals, which indicate what teachers want students to know/understand and be able to do at the end of the unit. State or provincial standards tend to be very broad and represent what the department or ministry of education believes is important in K–12 learning, instruction, and assessment. Unit-level planning typically draws upon these competencies, as they specify what students should know and be able to do at each grade level.

In the US, most states have adopted the Common Core State Standards (CCSS), a set of standards for Grades K–12 in English language arts/literacy and mathematics that are intended to prepare students for college and careers (National Governors Association Center for Best Practices, Council of Chief State School Officers, 2010). They were developed by state education leaders and governors in 48 states. Examples can be seen in the *Adaptations* unit overview (Appendix A). States have also identified grade-level content standards for other subject areas.

Most US states base their foreign-language standards on the American Council on the Teaching of Foreign Languages (ACTFL)'s *World-Readiness Standards for Learning Languages* (The National Standards Collaborative Board, 2015). The 11 standards are organized in 5 areas:

- Communication: using language (a) to interact with others (interpersonal communication); (b) to interpret and analyze information that is heard, read, or viewed (interpretive communication); and (c) to present information and ideas to others orally or in writing (presentational communication);
- Culture: using language to explore, explain, and reflect on the relationship among cultural practices (patterns of behavior and social interaction), products

(tangible and intangible creations such as dance and literature), and perspectives (meanings, attitudes, values, and beliefs that underlie practices and products);

- Connections: using language to expand knowledge of other disciplines, to think critically and solve problems, and to access information and diverse perspectives that are available through the language studied and its cultures;
- Comparisons: developing insight into the nature of language and culture through comparisons between students' own language(s) and culture(s) and the ones studied;
- Communities: using language with cultural competence to participate in multilingual communities within and beyond the classroom, and to engage in life-long learning of language for enjoyment, enrichment, and advancement.

These standards align well with the overarching goals of ImDL education, and we encourage teachers to use them to identify desired results with respect to language and culture.

Once competencies are identified for the unit, teachers must take another step and identify unit-level goals that align with those competencies. These articulate what students should know/understand and be able to do by the end of the unit. In other words, goals specify what can be achieved in one curriculum unit in relation to the broader standards.

🔑 KEY CONCEPTS

Unit-level goals correspond to state or provincial content and language standards but are described in ways that show what students are expected to know/ understand and do *within the context of a unit*. Both a state (US) standard and provincial (Canada) competency are shown to illustrate their similarity.

State-level standard:

CCSS.ELA-Literacy.W.3.2—[Students will] write informative/explanatory texts to examine a topic and convey ideas and information clearly.

Provincial competency:

[Students will] write self-expressive, narrative and information-based texts. (Government of Québec, 2001)

Unit-level goals associated with this standard/competency:

- summarize information from a variety of sources;
- compare and contrast the adaptations of different living things;
- explain how adaptations help living things survive in their environments.

Evidence

In this final planning section of the instructional design template, teachers briefly describe the ways in which student performance will be assessed at both the summative (end-of-unit) and formative (during individual lessons) levels. This section corresponds to Stage 2 of the backward design approach, which requires teachers to identify acceptable evidence to help them determine whether students have achieved the desired results (Wiggins & McTighe, 2005).

Unit-level summative performance assessment

Although traditional paper and pencil tests are still very much a part of assessment practices in ImDL classrooms, they tend to focus exclusively on content understandings, and all too often ask students only to demonstrate their recall of facts. If we want to know how students can *use* language to express their content learnings, performance assessments become essential. Performance assessments involve tasks that are meaningful and worthwhile; they get at what students can actually do with language to demonstrate what they have learned about the content. Performance assessments are not only designed differently from traditional tests; they are also graded or evaluated differently. Student performance is assessed on the basis of clearly defined performance indicators or criteria (typically in the form of rubrics) that emphasize how well and how accurately students can use language to communicate and what understandings about the content they can demonstrate through language. We explore these issues in more depth in Chapter 10.

Students in ImDL classrooms should be held accountable for their content learning *and* their language learning, and, when possible, their cultural understandings (whenever these are a significant part of the curriculum unit). They should be actively engaged while using language in meaningful ways to show their content understandings. We find ACTFL's Integrated Performance Assessment (IPA) (Adair-Hauck et al., 2013) to be a powerful classroom-based assessment tool and recommend that teachers use a modified version of this framework as a summative assessment at least once during the school year. Originally developed for traditional foreign-language teaching, the IPA involves three integrated performance tasks that correspond to the three communication standards (interpretive, interpersonal, and presentational communication). We have modified the IPA for the ImDL context by bringing in more focus on academic content and adapting the recommended rubrics. The IPA framework allows teachers to assess how well students are able to (a) comprehend what they read or hear/view (interpretive communication), (b) use language in spontaneous interaction (interpersonal communication), and (c) use language to communicate to an audience orally and/or in writing (presentational communication). The example we provide in the *Adaptations* unit overview (Appendix A) provides a brief description of IPA tasks. A detailed description of the IPA can be found in Chapter 10, and a full IPA for the *Adaptations* unit appears in Appendix C.

Even if a full IPA is not developed for a unit, performance tasks should still be the main approach to summative-level assessment in ImDL classrooms. ImDL teachers tend to be adept at creating communicative tasks that can be used as performance assessments. These serve as autonomous activities wherein students are using language independently and in open-ended ways to communicate their content understandings (see Chapter 4 and further description in Chapter 8 under module-level instructional design). Below is a slightly modified example of a performance assessment developed by an ImDL teacher. Even though it does not include all the elements of an IPA, it provides an excellent example of performance assessment that attends to both content and language. Students' creation and presentation of posters for the audience of kindergarteners were *autonomous* activities that served as the final performance assessment of the unit.

 TEACHER SPOTLIGHT

Moslais Xiong, a Grade 1 TWI teacher (Hmong/English) in St. Paul, Minnesota, developed a science/language arts unit on animals and their habitats. The culminating performance assessment involved students' creation of a zoo exhibit for kindergarteners in the program. Students selected an animal that they wanted to learn more about and did research using books and other sources provided by the teacher to create a poster in Hmong to describe interesting facts about the animal (physical characteristics, diet, predators/prey, habitat, etc.). They also illustrated the poster with pictures found on the Internet or in books. The task was heavily scaffolded with detailed guidelines for how to create the posters and with a completed one used as a model. Moslais offered feedback to students as they prepared their posters. The posters were displayed in the school gymnasium, and students presented information about their animals orally to kindergarteners. Moslais developed a rubric to assess the content of the posters as well as students' written and oral presentational language. She paid special attention to students' use of two classifiers—*tus* (required when identifying the animal) and *lub* (required when describing the habitat), as these had been a key linguistic focus of the unit.

Other assessment activities

In addition to identifying the summative performance assessments, the instructional design template asks teachers to briefly describe other assessment activities that are planned for the various modules and lessons comprising the unit. These are formative assessments that check students' achievement of the desired results on a daily, ongoing basis throughout the unit. They may be in the form of interactive activities that the teacher observes during the awareness, practice, or autonomous phases of the module, homework assignments, collection of "quick writes" or "exit tickets," review of completed graphic organizers, quizzes, and so on. These are described in more detail in the section titled *Evidence: Lesson-level formative assessment procedures* in Chapter 8 and are also mentioned in Chapter 10.

Unit references and resources

The last part of the instructional design template provides a space for teachers to list the references and resources they have consulted to develop the unit. These will include books, websites, articles, and so on. In the *Adaptations* example (Appendix A), we have shared a few of the references and resources that were identified by the team of teachers who developed the unit. These are especially important if the unit is to be shared with other teachers. This section also helps teachers keep track of useful sources for future instructional design.

Summary

With its focus on unit-level instructional design, this chapter has introduced a planning template for designing instruction at the unit level. Unit-level planning requires teachers to develop clarity around exactly what they want students to know and be able to do by the end of the unit by identifying content and language standards and outcomes, developing unit-level goals related to content and language, and specifying the end-of-unit summative assessment activities that students will complete to demonstrate their learning. We outline in the following chapter, by means of a template for developing modules and lessons as well as a detailed discussion on learning objectives, how to focus on language in the context of planning for content instruction.

 Application activity: *Using the template to design instruction*

Use the unit-level instructional design template introduced in this chapter to develop an overall plan unit for your classroom. Reflect on what you find to be helpful and challenging about designing instruction according to this template.

Online resources for readers
Proficiency descriptors
ACPI resources

ACPI has a speaking rubric that has videos of immersion students at the various CEFR levels. They also have some useful writing rubrics. They are an excellent resource, and most of their written works are available in English and French.

For video clips: www.acpi.ca/ressources/referentiel-de-competences-orales/clips-video
For writing: www.acpi.ca/ressources/referentiel-ecrit
For oral production: www.acpi.ca/ressources/referentiel-de-competences-orales

The WIDA Consortium

https://wida.wisc.edu/
The WIDA Consortium is a member-based organization comprised of US states, territories, and federal agencies that are committed to the research, design, and implementation of a high-quality, standards-based system for PreK–12 English learners. WIDA includes an Early Years program to support multilingual children as well as a Spanish division. WIDA has expanded globally with WIDA International Consortium (having over 400 member schools).

Resources for curriculum development

CoBaLTT Project

http://carla.umn.edu/cobaltt/lessonplans/search.php
There is a wealth of resources for content-based curriculum development at the Center for Advanced Research on Language Acquisition (CARLA) website (CoBaLTT project), including fully developed content-based units (some designed for ImDL contexts).

CARLA immersion resource websites

http://carla.umn.edu/immersion/resources.html
The CARLA Immersion Project has developed lists of resources for Spanish, Mandarin Chinese, French, and Ojibwe and Yup'ik ImDL programs.

Multi-media presentations

BrainPOP®: www.brainpop.com
BrainPOP Español®: https://esp.brainpop.com

International Children's Literature Library

http://en.childrenslibrary.org/
Books in many of the world's languages are available for free. Each book's pages can be displayed on a screen or whiteboard.

Colorín Colorado

www.colorincolorado.org/
Under "Books and Authors" at the site there are links to many books that are available for purchase (some bilingual, although most in English), including those representing cultural diversity (American Indian/Alaska Native and more).

Language Lizard® LLC

www.languagelizard.com/
Provides access to bilingual children's products in over 50 languages.

8

MODULE AND LESSON INSTRUCTIONAL DESIGN

As with the previous chapter, which focused on unit-level instructional design, we envision immersion and dual language (ImDL) teachers reading and working through the concepts in this chapter in the context of structured teacher preparation or professional development courses or workshops. The concepts introduced are best understood through application paired with the provision of guidance and feedback. In this chapter, we continue our discussion of instructional design that integrates language, content, and culture with a focus on module and lesson development. We address these questions:

- What is the difference between social and academic language?
- What kinds of objectives are required for ImDL module and lesson planning?
- What is the difference between standards/outcomes, unit-level goals, and lesson-level objectives?
- What are content-obligatory and content-compatible language objectives, and why are they both important?
- What goes into writing focused language objectives?
- How can lesson objectives and activities be differentiated for different learner groups?
- How can the CAPA (contextualization, awareness, practice, and autonomy) model be used to sequence lesson activities?

Introduction

After the overall unit design has been conceptualized (as illustrated in Chapter 7), the teacher needs to develop modules made up of individual lessons that will comprise the unit. Our approach to module/lesson design emphasizes planning for language instruction in relationship to content objectives and lesson activities, because it is through language that students come to grasp concepts and express their understandings. The sample module and lessons showcased in Appendix B have detailed language objectives as well as paying explicit attention to language expectations and language instruction throughout lesson activities. Because of this emphasis on language in our approach to instructional design, we begin this chapter by describing the nature of social (communicative) and academic language, as ImDL students and teachers use both in the classroom.

Social and academic language

Social language tends to be interactional in nature (involving interaction between interlocutors and negotiation of meaning). Cummins (1979) referred to it as *basic interpersonal communication skills* (BICS). In contrast, "academic language is the set of words, grammar, and organizational strategies used to describe complex ideas, higher order thinking processes, and abstract concepts" (Zwiers, 2008, p. 20). Cummins called this kind of language *cognitive academic language proficiency* (CALP). ImDL students develop and express their understandings of the content they are learning by means of academic language. Their ability to use academic language proficiently is absolutely indispensable to content-area learning and success in school and beyond. Table 8.1 presents characteristics of social and academic language.

TABLE 8.1 Characteristics of social and academic language

Social language	Academic language
• is interactional in nature and focuses on maintaining social relationships	• is transactional in nature and focuses on transference of information
• is listener oriented	• is message oriented (often explicit for a "distant audience")
• typically contains shorter turns, one-word or short phrase utterances, and incomplete sentences	• typically contains longer turns, more sustained discourse, and complete sentences
• is typically cognitively undemanding (more concrete)	• is typically cognitively demanding (more abstract)
• is less structured or organized; tends to be circuitous and less grammatically complex	• is typically structured, organized, and grammatically complex
• is wordy and circumlocutory	• is concise and lexically dense
	• contains complex use of reference
	• makes frequent use of the passive voice
	• uses figurative expressions (*read between the lines; shed light on*)

(Adapted from Brown & Yule, 1983, Gibbons, 2009, and Zwiers, 2008)

This side-by-side description is helpful, but it is also important to note that social and academic language should be seen as lying on a continuum rather than as a dichotomy, as depicted in Figure 8.1 (adapted from S. Ranney, personal communication, March 2017).

Academic language also involves frequent nominalization (Gibbons, 2009; Zwiers, 2008), that is, changing certain parts of speech (e.g., verbs, conjunctions, or adjectives) or even whole clauses and sentences into nouns: *adapt* becomes *adaptation, survive* becomes *survival, lose their homes* becomes *loss of habitat*. Gibbons (2009, p. 52) shows how a whole sentence can be nominalized: "The drought was very long and so many people starved" becomes "The length of the drought caused mass starvation." Additionally, academic language contains nominal groups, that is, long strings of words (multiple adjectives and descriptive prepositional phrases) and clauses that provide detail and information to represent a single thing. For example:

> On Sunday, February 17, 2019 an expedition team spotted *an adult female tortoise,* Chelonoidis phantasticus, *more commonly known as the Fernandina Giant Tortoise and believed to be extinct for over 100 years*, on a remote island of the Galápagos.

Academic language supports points with evidence. It conveys nuances of meaning with modals (*could, would, shall, might, ought to*, etc.) and uses qualifiers such as *relatively* and *mostly* to soften the message (Zwiers, 2008). ImDL teachers must teach academic language overtly in order to ensure that students produce age-appropriate academic discourse. For this to happen, they must also provide the necessary scaffolds. Being clear about the language ImDL teachers want students to produce is a first step, and language objectives serve as important mechanisms for developing this clarity.

ImDL module/lesson instructional design

In order to scaffold the module and lesson planning process for ImDL teachers, we have developed an instructional design template (Figure 8.2). At the very top of the template, the teacher identifies the number of the module (within the series of modules that comprise the unit) and its topic as well as the overall time frame for the

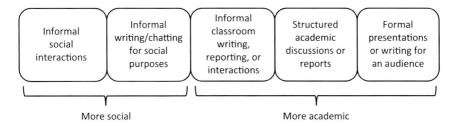

FIGURE 8.1   Social and academic language on a continuum

ImDL Module/Lesson Design Template		
Module Number: **Module Topic:** **Time Frame:**		

<table>
<tr><td rowspan="14">Desired Results</td><td colspan="3">Primary Learning Objectives</td></tr>
<tr><td colspan="3">Content:

</td></tr>
<tr><td colspan="3">Language (discourse type/functions/grammatical features/vocabulary):</td></tr>
<tr><td colspan="3">Content-obligatory:</td></tr>
<tr><td>All students</td><td>Students learning through L2</td><td>Bilinguals/Students learning through L1</td></tr>
<tr><td colspan="3">Content-compatible:</td></tr>
<tr><td>All students</td><td>Students learning through L2</td><td>Bilinguals/Students learning through L1</td></tr>
<tr><td colspan="3">Secondary Learning Objectives</td></tr>
<tr><td colspan="2">Cultural/Cross-Cultural:</td><td>Cross-Linguistic:</td></tr>
<tr><td colspan="2">Learning Strategies:</td><td>Social/Affective:</td></tr>
</table>

FIGURE 8.2   ImDL Module and Lesson Design Template

Materials and Technology Resources

Learning Activities (with pair/grouping and differentiation strategies)
Contextualization Phase – Lesson(s)/Duration:
Awareness Phase – Lesson(s)/Duration
Practice Phase – Lesson(s)/Duration
Autonomy Phase – Lesson(s)/Duration

Learning Experiences/Instruction

Formative Assessment Procedures

Evidence

FIGURE 8.2 Continued

module. Modules typically involve 30–60-minute lessons over several days, although this varies depending upon the grade level and module content and expectations. The example we provide from the *Adaptations* unit is a five-day module on how geographic location and climate affect animal adaptations (see Appendix B). This example is used to illustrate the sections of the template, our focus for the remainder of this chapter.

 KEY CONCEPTS

In our approach to instructional design, a **module** generally involves 30–60-minute **lessons** over several days, even up to a week, although the time frame can vary widely.

Desired results

Just as with unit-level instructional design, module-level planning begins with desired results (Wiggins & McTighe, 2005). In this section of the template, the teacher identifies learning objectives that are achievable in the individual lessons—precisely what the students are expected to know/understand and be able to do in the lessons that make up this module. Objectives are aligned with unit-level standards and goals (see Chapter 7) but written at a micro level to zoom in on the expectations for the lessons that comprise the module. Below we show the relationship between a content standard, a unit-level goal, and a lesson-level objective.

 KEY CONCEPTS

Lesson-level objectives correspond to unit-level goals and are described in ways to show what students are expected to know/understand and do *within the context of a single lesson.*

State-level standard:

CCSS.ELA-Literacy.W.3.2—[Students will] write informative/explanatory texts to examine a topic and convey ideas and information clearly.

Unit-level content goals:

Students will:

- summarize information from a variety of sources;

- compare and contrast the adaptations of different living things;
- explain how adaptations help living things survive in their environments.

Lesson-level content objective:

- Students will write an informative paragraph comparing two animals from different climates to report on how adaptations help living things survive.

Lesson objectives are always written in terms of what students will do, not what the teacher will do. They should be achievable within the lesson and measurable. Objectives should be specific and focused; they should not include multiple embedded objectives.

KEY CONCEPTS

Lesson-level instructional objectives are:

- written with respect to what students will do;
- aligned with unit-level goals;
- written at the micro/lesson level—they reflect what students are expected to know/understand and do within the lesson;
- achievable within the lesson;
- measurable;
- specific (not vague);
- focused—they do not embed multiple objectives into one.

There are both primary and secondary learning objectives. Primary objectives include content and language objectives, and secondary objectives include cultural/cross-cultural, cross-linguistic, learning strategies, and social/affective aims (Hamayan et al., 2013).

Desired results—primary learning objectives

Primary objectives, focused on content and language, should be shared with learners in student-friendly language so that students are clear about the content and language foci of the lesson. In keeping with the counterbalanced approach, our module and lesson instructional design template assign complementary status to content and language objectives.

Content objectives

Content objectives specify what students should know/understand and be able to do when it comes to academic content areas. They should be categorized by subject area (literacy/language arts, science, social studies, etc.). Aligned with unit goals, these objectives need to be cognitively challenging and age appropriate. Content objectives should be the same for all students in the classroom (with instructional modifications as needed to differentiate for particular learners). Content objectives should get at the *what* (i.e., the content learning) that underlies the *how* (i.e., the activities students engage in to show their content learning). Example A in the box below is not a well-written objective because it simply describes an activity that students will do. Example B is well written because it specifies precisely what understandings students will demonstrate by engaging in that activity.

Example A	Example B
Students will complete a graphic organizer.	Students will identify similarities and differences between frogs and tadpoles.

Language objectives

The next section of the template includes space for developing specific language objectives. During the instructional design process, teachers need to make decisions about what language to focus on in a particular lesson. Because it's not possible to attend to all the vocabulary and all aspects of the language students will be expected to use in one lesson, teachers must make thoughtful choices as they plan. In Chapter 3 we described the language features that need attention through counterbalanced instruction. That description will be helpful to teachers in making decisions about the language to emphasize in a lesson. In addition, in making such decisions, the teacher needs to take into account students' declarative language knowledge (what they know about language) and procedural language knowledge (what they can do with language) (see Chapter 3).

Language objectives are different from literacy/language arts objectives. Literacy/language arts objectives are in the content realm and identify general literacy/language arts learning aims such as "students will write an informative paragraph" or "students will demonstrate comprehension of text." In contrast, language objectives are more specific and address the various components of language that students need to carry out lesson activities and achieve content and other learning objectives. These components include discourse type; communicative and academic language functions; grammatical features; and words, phrases, or useful chunks of language (vocabulary). ImDL teachers should specify clear language objectives in the module for every lesson (note that the same objective often applies to more than one lesson within the module, as is evident in Appendix B). In the following sections, we describe two types of language objectives, introduce a scaffold for writing language objectives, and discuss the importance of differentiating language objectives, particularly in TWI contexts, which serve both minority-language and majority-language students.

🖐 KEY CONCEPTS

Literacy/language arts objectives fall under the category of content objectives. They identify general literacy/language arts learning outcomes, for example:

- Students will write an informative paragraph to compare and contrast two animals.

Language objectives are specific and identify the components of language needed to carry out lesson activities and achieve learning objectives. They encompass:

- discourse type (e.g., report, dialogue, or argument)
- communicative or academic language functions (e.g., compare and contrast; describe)
- grammatical features (e.g., gender, verb tenses, connectives, and prepositions)
- vocabulary (e.g., words and formulaic chunks)

For example:

- Classify: Students will compare and contrast frogs and tadpoles using determiners such as *both* and conjunctions such as *but*; for example, tadpoles have gills for breathing, but frogs don't.

Content-obligatory and content-compatible language objectives

Two types of language objectives correspond to the kinds of language introduced by Snow, Met, and Genesee (1989): content obligatory and content compatible. **Content-obligatory language** was described in Chapter 3 as the language students need to know and use to engage with subject-matter content. It represents the language that is *essential* for communicating about and accessing the content of the lesson. This language primarily includes content-specific, often technical vocabulary, or what Dutro and Moran (2003) call "bricks." Brick words represent vocabulary specific to the concepts and content of the lesson. Brick words for the *Adaptations* lessons showcased in this chapter include, for example, *adaptations, habitat, survival, predator, prey*, and *climate*. Content-obligatory language also contains academic language functions and the grammatical features or patterns that are needed to discuss different subject areas. It may also reflect genres or discourse patterns associated with particular subject areas (reports, narratives, persuasive text, etc.).

Content-compatible language, in contrast, is not essential to the content of the lesson, but constitutes other language that is well suited to the lesson and serves to expand students' vocabulary, grammar, and discourse skills. It is language that *supplements* the content-obligatory language or can be emphasized in conjunction with the content focus of the lesson. The vocabulary that is typically emphasized in these objectives is what Dutro and Moran (2003) call "mortar" vocabulary. Mortar words hold together the brick words. They are the general-utility words and phrases needed for constructing sentences, and they determine the relationships between and among words. Examples of mortar vocabulary are connecting words (*because, whereas*), prepositions and prepositional phrases (*under, in front of*), basic verbs (*is, uses, lives*), pronouns (*they, it*), and general academic vocabulary that is typically transferable across subject domains (*analyze, characteristics, compare*) (Dutro & Moran, 2003). Content-obligatory language objectives may also contain this latter type of mortar vocabulary, that is, general academic vocabulary.

Both types of language objectives should be written in detail and should include the four inter-related components defined below: discourse type, language function, grammatical feature, and related vocabulary.

Language objective components

Discourse type describes the genre or text type of the oral or written language that students are expected to produce. Students need experience "doing different kinds of things with language in order to develop the range of registers and genres they are expected to comprehend and produce and that are the basis of evaluation of their learning" (Schleppegrell, 2012, p. 413). Therefore, activities should expose students to and prompt them to produce a wide range of discourse types. Table 8.2 presents a list of different oral and written discourse types (adapted from Cook, 1989). Identifying the discourse type helps teachers to think through the expected scope of students' language production; that is, whether students are expected to produce words or phrases, sentences, connected sentences, paragraphs, or more, and with what kind of organization. For example, if students are assigned a written report, they are expected to produce paragraph-level discourse or more. If they are engaged in a dialogue or conversation, their utterances will comprise sentences, possibly connected sentences, and most likely words and phrases.

Language functions refer to language that is used to actually *do* something. Savignon (1997) described a language function as "the use to which language is put, the purpose of an utterance rather than the particular grammatical form an utterance takes" (p. 19). In the classroom, students use language to express both communicative/social and academic functions. Communicative language functions reflect the social purposes of language and have been organized into categories by a number of scholars. Finocchiaro and Brumfit (1983), for example, identified five functional categories:

TABLE 8.2 Examples of oral and written discourse types

Oral discourse	Written discourse	Oral and/or written
Announcement	Argumentative essay	Advertisement
Argument	Article	Eulogy
Audio file	Biography/Autobiography	Explanation
Chant	Booklet	Instructions
Consultation	Brochure	Invitation
Conversation	Catalogue	Message
Debate	Comic strip	Report
Dialogue	Email	Play
Discussion	Essay	Poem
Interview	Exposé	Riddle
Jingle	Flyer	Song
Joke	Graphic organizer	Story
Lecture	Greeting card	Summary
Narration	Journal	Survey
Presentation	Label	Synopsis
Puppet show	Letter	
Rap	List	
Recount	Magazine	
Role play	Manga	
Seminar	Manual	
Sermon	Map	
Skit	Math problem	
Speech	Menu	
Video clip	Newspaper	
Voicemail	Note	
Voice-over	Novel	
	Obituary	
	Pamphlet	
	Poster	
	Recipe	
	Script	
	Sign	
	Tweet	

1. *personal*: to clarify one's ideas, to express thoughts and feelings (love, joy, fear, or anxiety), to express moral or social concerns and everyday feelings of hunger, warmth, and so on;
2. *interpersonal*: to enable individuals to establish and maintain personal and working relationships (e.g., greeting, apologizing, (dis)agreeing, complimenting, inviting, etc.);
3. *directive*: to influence the actions of others and accept/refuse direction from others (e.g., requesting, suggesting, instructing, persuading, commanding, etc.);
4. *referential*: to report/talk about things, actions, events, and people in the present, past, and future (e.g., identifying, asking, defining, describing, evaluating, etc.);

5. *imaginative*: to discuss elements of creativity or artistic expression (e.g., discussing a movie, book, or TV show; creating stories, plays, or poems; solving problems or mysteries, etc.).

Academic language functions involve language use about academic content or the language used in professional, formal contexts. The same categories listed above can apply to academic functions (especially the latter three), but the nature of the language will change (see social versus academic language discussion above). We can see in the following examples how a function such as *persuading* can be either more social or more academic depending on the context and the interlocutor's intention:

- social/communicative: persuading someone to go to a movie they're not interested in;
- academic: persuading others to take a particular side in an academic debate.

Dalton-Puffer (2013) identified seven academic language functions (i.e., "cognitive discourse functions") relevant for school-based learning: *classify, define, describe, evaluate, explain, explore,* and *report*. We have added an eighth: *inquire*. These appear in Table 8.3 along with similar functions in the same category.

Language functions are expressed through the use of **vocabulary** words, phrases, or formulaic chunks and **grammatical features,** such as grammatical gender, verb tenses, prepositional phrases, and participles. The same function can be expressed in many different ways using different grammatical features and different vocabulary.

Scaffold for writing language objectives

The scaffold presented in Figure 8.3 asks that teachers identify the four linguistic components described above to establish clarity about the language they want students to produce. The scaffold also provides space for showing examples of the

TABLE 8.3 Academic language functions

Main function	*Related functions*
Classify	compare, contrast, match, structure, categorize, subsume
Define	identify, characterize
Describe	label, identify, name, specify
Evaluate	judge, argue, justify, take a stance, critique, recommend, comment, reflect, appreciate
Explain	reason, express cause/effect, draw conclusions, deduce
Explore	hypothesize, speculate, predict, guess, estimate, simulate, take other perspectives
Report	inform, recount, narrate, present, summarize, relate
Inquire	ask, examine, request, solicit, query, question, quiz

(Adapted from Dalton-Puffer, 2013, p. 235)

1. Discourse type:

2. Communicative or academic functions:

3. Examples of the language students need to produce:

4. Grammatical features:

5. Vocabulary:

6. Written language objectives: content-obligatory and content-compatible

FIGURE 8.3 Scaffold for writing language objectives (adapted from http://carla.umn.edu/cobaltt/modules/curriculum/formula.html)

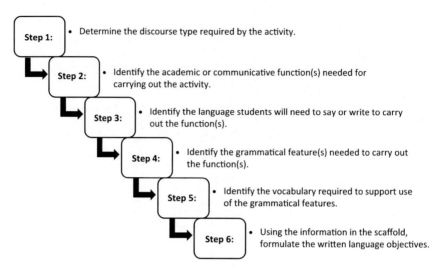

FIGURE 8.4 Steps for writing detailed language objectives

language students will need to produce and for writing the language objectives (both content obligatory and content compatible). It corresponds to the six steps for writing language objectives, which are summarized in Figure 8.4. Figure 8.5 provides an example of a completed scaffold.

Teachers can use the scaffold and follow the steps outlined in Figure 8.4 to write detailed, focused language objectives. Before writing language objectives, it is important to consider students' language capabilities and needs and, based on these, to determine what language to focus on in relation to the lesson's content objectives as well as secondary objectives (cross-linguistic, social/affective, etc.). To begin, teachers should focus on a task or activity in the lesson they have developed and attend first to the content-obligatory language needed to carry out that activity. Teachers then follow the steps described in Figure 8.4.

In **Step 1**, teachers determine the expected discourse type for either oral or written production. Will students be expected to engage in a debate, or write a poem? After writing the discourse type in the scaffold, teachers move on to **Step 2**, which entails identifying the function(s) needed for carrying out the activity—will students be describing, comparing and contrasting, explaining, reporting, or doing something else with language? It's not uncommon for an activity to require more than one language function. After the function(s) are added to the scaffold, teachers consider **Step 3**. This step is important, as it requires teachers to identify and write down the language students will actually need to produce to carry out the function. Then, in **Step 4**, teachers examine the sample language identified in Step 3 to ascertain the grammatical feature(s) students need to use to perform the function(s). Again, these are added to the scaffold. **Step 5** involves pinpointing the vocabulary (words, phrases, and formulaic chunks) needed to perform the function with the specified grammatical features. For example, if one of the grammatical features is the present tense, teachers identify specific verbs that students will need to produce in the present tense. For languages that have grammatical gender (Arabic, French, Spanish, German, Russian, and others), it is important to introduce new nouns with their articles both within the language objectives and during classroom instruction (see also Chapter 9). Finally, in ***Step 6***, teachers use the information in the scaffold to formulate written objectives that include all four components (emphasizing just one function per objective). If the objective is to be shared with students (as we recommend), it may need to be rewritten in more student-friendly language. The process can then be repeated for other activities and for identifying content-compatible objectives. The process is illustrated below and in Figure 8.5. Additional examples of well-written language objectives can be found in Appendix B.

The steps outlined above are illustrated in the activity below, which comes from a teacher-developed lesson about frogs and tadpoles. Imagine that the following activity has been assigned to Grade 2 students.

> After completing a Venn diagram in pairs, students are given an additional language task that appears at the bottom of the Venn diagram handout. They are asked to describe similarities and differences between tadpoles and frogs.

Step 1: Identify the discourse type. In this example, students are expected to report factual information. This information is added to the scaffold (Figure 8.5).

   Discourse type: Report

Step 2: Identify the function(s). In our example, the function is clearly stated in the description of the activity. Once identified, the function is added to the scaffold.

   Function: describe similarities and differences between tadpoles and frogs

Step 3: Identify the language students will need to produce. Teachers need to write down the kind of language they expect students to produce in this activity. Some examples are:

1. Both frogs and tadpoles can swim.
2. Frogs have legs, but tadpoles don't. They have tails.
3. Frogs can jump, but tadpoles can't.
4. Tadpoles have gills to breathe, but frogs don't. They breathe with lungs when on land and through their skin when in water.

Step 4: Identify grammatical features. When we look at the kinds of sentences students will be producing (Step 3), we can identify the forms they need to write such sentences. These are then added to the scaffold (Figure 8.5).

   Grammatical features: nouns, present tense of key verbs, auxiliary and modal verbs, contractions, and conjunctions

Step 5: Identify the vocabulary corresponding to the function and features. We can see that students need vocabulary corresponding to the grammatical features listed. This vocabulary is also added to the scaffold (Figure 8.5).

Vocabulary: frogs, tadpoles, legs, lungs; have, swim, jump; can/can't, do/don't; both; and, but

Step 6: Formulate the written objectives. Finally, we take into account all four elements included in the scaffold to write the objectives shown in Figure 8.5. Note in Step 6 that we identify the four elements to illustrate how the four work together in the objectives.

---

1. Discourse type: Report

2. Communicative or academic functions: describe similarities and differences between tadpoles and frogs

3. Examples of language students need to produce:
1. Both frogs and tadpoles can swim.
2. Frogs have legs, but tadpoles don't. They have tails.
3. Frogs can jump, but tadpoles can't.
4. Tadpoles have gills to breathe, but frogs don't. They breathe with lungs when on land and through their skin when in water.

4. Grammatical features:	**5. Vocabulary:**
• singular/plural nouns	• frogs, tadpoles, gills, legs, tails, lungs, etc.
• present tense	• have, swim, jump, breathe
• auxiliary and modal verbs & contractions	• can, do, can't, don't
• determiner & conjunctions	• both & and, but

6. Written language objectives: content-obligatory
Report (discourse type): Students will describe similarities and differences between tadpoles and frogs (function):

—with singular and plural nouns (feature) like *frogs, tadpoles, gills, legs, tail, lungs,* etc. (vocabulary)

—with verbs in the present tense (feature) like *have, swim, jump, breathe* (vocabulary).

—using auxiliary and modal verbs (feature) like *can* and *do* (vocabulary) and their contracted negative forms (feature) like *can't, don't* (vocabulary).

—with conjunctions (feature) like *and, but* (vocabulary) and determiners (feature) like *both* (vocabulary).

FIGURE 8.5 Completed scaffold for writing language objectives

Because students should be aware of the language they're expected to produce, the teacher should rewrite and then share the objective(s) in student-friendly language. For example,

Report: I can describe how tadpoles and frogs are the same and different:

- with nouns such as *frogs, tadpoles, tail, legs, gills*;
- with verbs such as *have, swim*, and *jump*;
- using *can/can't* and *do/don't*;
- with *both* and connecting words such as *and, but*.

The steps are then repeated for other content-obligatory and content-compatible language objectives. To illustrate some content-compatible language for this sample activity, we can consider the functions students will need to produce to manage the activity and the language they need to carry out those functions (Steps 2 and 3). Students need to:

- share knowledge statements: *I know how they are the same*;
- express opinions and ideas: *I believe that…*; *I think that…*;
- agree and disagree: *I agree/don't agree. I think you're right*;
- ask questions to seek clarification and take turns: *Can you repeat, please? Do you know another difference? Do you have another idea? Anything else? Can you think of anything else?*

Based on this information, a content-compatible language objective might be written as follows:

> Dialogue (discourse type): During the Venn diagram activity, students will ask questions to seek clarification and take turns (function) in the present tense (feature) with auxiliary verbs such as *do* and *can* (vocabulary) and lexical verbs such as *repeat, know*, and *think* (vocabulary).

This content-compatible language should be reviewed and modeled by the teacher immediately before the activity to remind students of the language they need to take turns, seek clarification, and otherwise negotiate meaning and manage the task. Doing so will help students to remain in the minority language throughout the activity.

Differentiating language objectives

It is inevitable that all classrooms will have a range of proficiency levels, and it is important for ImDL teachers to differentiate language objectives accordingly. This is especially the case in two-way immersion (TWI) contexts where there are students who are simultaneous bilinguals and/or speak the minority language in the home along with students who are just learning the minority language. TWI teachers always have to plan for these different groups of learners. They must ensure that they are scaffolding instruction and making accommodations as needed for students who are learning the language as an L2, while at the same time providing enough challenge for students who already know the minority language. This practice of providing that extra linguistic challenge can be described as "upping the language ante." The module/lesson design template provides space for teachers to differentiate some language objectives for each linguistic group: (a) bilinguals or students learning through L1 and (b) students learning through L2. Some of the language objectives will be the same for both groups, but others need to be differentiated to increase linguistic expectations for the students who are already bilingual or learning through their home language. Drawing upon one content-obligatory and one content-compatible language objective of those presented above, we suggest in Table 8.4 some ways to increase linguistic expectations for bilinguals or students learning through L1. This kind of differentiation can be equally effective in one-way immersion (IMM), developmental bilingual education (DBE), and indigenous-language revitalization immersion (IRI) programs for students who seem to acquire the L2 more easily or quickly than other students and who would benefit from the additional challenge.

It can be complicated to identify language "dominance" in learners, and some students learning through L1 or L2 may have language delays that necessitate additional differentiation and support. Nevertheless, ImDL teachers need to come up with ways to constantly challenge students to produce more complex

TABLE 8.4 Examples of "upping the language ante" for bilinguals or students learning through L1

Students learning through L2	Bilinguals or students learning through L1
• describe similarities and differences with conjunctions such as *and* or *but* and determiners such as *both*; e.g., Both frogs and tadpoles can swim.	• describe differences with conjunctions such as *whereas* or *however*; e.g., Frogs have legs, whereas tadpoles have tails. • describe similarities with present-tense expressions such as *are similar in that* … or *have in common* or *share* …; e.g., Frogs and tadpoles have the ability to swim in common, or Frogs and tadpoles have in common the ability to swim.
• express opinions and ideas with the present tense of verbs such as *believe* and *think*; e.g., I think that both frogs and tadpoles can breathe.	• express opinions and ideas with present tense of verbs such as *find, suppose, propose, suggest,* or *guess*; e.g., I suppose that both frogs and tadpoles can breathe. • express opinions and ideas with statements beginning with present-tense expressions such as *My idea/ perspective/opinion/thought/belief is that* …; e.g., My thought is that both tadpoles and frogs can breathe.

language according to both students' proficiency levels and grade levels. Young (2016) conducted a study to explore a functional approach to differentiation in a Grade 3 TWI classroom, which is briefly described below.

 RESEARCH REPORT

Of 24 students in a Grade 3 TWI classroom, Young (2016) selected five focal students: one Spanish home language, three English home language, and one who spoke both languages at home. They represented a range of proficiencies in Spanish. Following a "design-based research" approach, Young worked with the classroom teacher to design instructional language supports to promote more complex Spanish-language production during small-group math and reading activities. They identified functions to emphasize during math activities (encouraging, comparing, and reporting) and reading activities (questioning, making connections, and summarizing). Next, they developed target statements and questions and organized them according to complexity, ranging from one word (*¿Conexiones? Connections?*) to more syntactically complex options (*¿Cuál sería una conexión que tengas con la lectura? What would be a connection that you have to the reading?*). These differentiated language options were then integrated into classroom scaffolds that were posted in the classroom and distributed (as handouts) to students. The teacher also modeled the target phrases each day before the reading and math sessions. Students could select which statements to use based on their ability to produce them. Over time, they were encouraged to use increasingly complex language during the math and reading activities and to discuss their language use choices during large-group interaction after the activities.

Prior to the instructional intervention, students' oral language was assessed using an oral proficiency assessment developed by the Center for Applied Linguistics. Data were collected for 15 weeks, and then students' oral language was assessed again using the same tool. A series of linguistic complexity measures (such as length of utterances) were used to examine differences in students' oral language production between the initial and final assessments. Students' oral language improved on several of the linguistic complexity measures. All the focal students used longer utterances and more complex structures. However, the English home language students appeared to benefit more than the Spanish home language students, leading Young to conclude that more academic options were necessary for Spanish home language students. Qualitative analysis showed that the less proficient students responded especially well to the intervention. They participated more in the small-group activities and appeared to take more risks with language.

As evidenced in this section, writing language objectives is a detailed process, which can be challenging and time-consuming. Nonetheless, when teachers are clear about the language they want students to produce, they are much more likely to follow through with an emphasis on that language in their instruction, and students are much more likely to produce that language.

 SPECIAL NOTES

When teachers have clarity around the language they want their students to produce, students are more likely to produce that language.

The examples of language objectives appearing in the sample module/lesson plan (Appendix B) are quite comprehensive, but not every module or lesson requires so many language objectives. They are provided as good models for teachers to review in order to comprehend and be able to apply the scaffold for writing language objectives introduced in this chapter. If ImDL teachers are able to write *at least one* language objective per lesson that includes the four linked components—discourse type, function, feature, and vocabulary—they are on the right track. With practice, it becomes easier to write detailed language objectives, and, over time, it will begin to feel quite natural to plan lessons with such attention to language.

We conclude this section with a quote from one of the teachers who participated in the creation of the *Adaptations* unit, Verena Burkart. The quote is from her final written reflection on the process of engaging in curriculum planning following our model:

> Clearly articulating language and content objectives has reinforced my conviction that "upping the language ante" is not only manageable, but priority. I can contribute sophisticated language and communication tasks that … students can be realistically prepared to achieve and feel empowered doing.

Desired results—secondary learning objectives

As mentioned above, secondary language objectives include those in the following categories: cultural/cross-cultural, cross-linguistic, learning strategies, and social/affective. Students' attention can be brought to the secondary objectives as their focus emerges in lesson activities. For example, as teachers are explaining a pair or small-group activity, they can remind students that they are expected to work collaboratively by listening and responding to each other's ideas and thoughts respectfully (social/affective objectives). In this section, we discuss learning objectives in each of these categories in turn.

Cultural/cross-cultural objectives

Cultural objectives identify content or concepts related to culture in general, or a particular culture (whether representative of the program's languages or of other cultures), and cross-cultural objectives involve cross-cultural comparison. These objectives "promote an understanding of other cultures and the ability to function effectively in them" (Hamayan et al., 2013, p. 88). For example, in a Grade 4 unit on climate and geography, a cultural objective may be written as follows:

- Students will develop an initial understanding that the climatic conditions of distinct regions of Ecuador influence cultural practices (e.g., jobs and household chores) and products (e.g., clothing and cuisine).

In a bioengineering unit developed for Grade 3 Mandarin immersion on designing model membranes, cultural and cross-cultural objectives pertaining to the country of El Salvador were included because the unit was built around a storybook that was set in El Salvador (Minnesota Mandarin Immersion Collaborative, n.d.). For example:

- Students will recall what they know and identify what they want to know about the country of El Salvador in the following categories: geography, climate, food, and sports.
- Students will identify cultural symbols, practices, and perspectives of luck in El Salvador, China, and the US.

Importantly, curriculum units should affirm cultural diversity by reflecting the cultures represented by the program's languages as well as students' home cultures by drawing on family and community "funds of knowledge" (Moll, Amanti, Neff, & González, 1992). These are the "historically accumulated and culturally developed bodies of knowledge and skills essential for household or individual functioning and well-being" (p. 133). These essential cultural practices and understandings are reflected in families' daily routines and practices in relationship to household management (cooking, finances, and childcare), religion, contemporary and folk medicine, agriculture, and so on. For example, many Hmong families are talented vegetable farmers. Imagine how much richer a unit on growth and plants would be for a Hmong TWI program (or any program with Hmong heritage learners) if the teacher were to tap into Hmong families' funds of knowledge. Adults could be invited to classrooms or even audio- or video-recorded, or the students could take a field trip to a family farm.

It is possible that not all curricular unit themes will lend themselves easily to the inclusion of cultural or cross-cultural objectives, but we encourage ImDL teachers to consider ways to bring in some attention to these issues, particularly given that one of the three main goals of ImDL education is cultural understanding or competence. As explained in Chapter 1, majority-language students need to acquire an understanding of and appreciation for the culture(s) of the target-language group associated with the program as well as their home culture(s). Minority-language students must cultivate a positive identity with their home culture(s) and that of the majority-language community. In IRI programs, reclaiming one's indigenous cultural identity and coming to understand traditional indigenous cultural values and practices are critical for students. Addressing these various aspects through the curriculum is important, and establishing clear cultural/cross-cultural/intercultural objectives helps teachers to do so in a systematic way.

Cross-linguistic objectives

Students benefit as language learners from making comparisons between and among the languages they know and are learning (see Chapters 2 and 9). Cross-linguistic objectives align with activities that are designed to encourage students to draw upon their knowledge of both (or more) languages when reading, writing, and solving problems or to use their knowledge of one language to learn about the other language. They are also designed to bring students' attention to similarities and differences between and among their languages to enhance their metalinguistic awareness (Hamayan et al., 2013) or metalanguage (Escamilla et al., 2014). Cross-linguistic objectives can focus on vocabulary (e.g., identifying cognates), grammar, syntax (sentence structure and word order), morphology (how words are formed), genre (how texts are organized), punctuation, spelling patterns, sociolinguistic appropriateness, and idioms—essentially any part of language. Some examples of cross-linguistic objectives are:

- Students will determine the meaning of the prefixes *mal-* (French) and *un-* (English) using words such as *malheureux* or *malsain* (*unhappy, unhealthy*).
- Students will identify cognates and discuss spelling patterns in Spanish and English (e.g., *-ción* = *-tion*, *-mente* = *-ly*).
- Students will compare and contrast salutations (greetings) and complimentary closings of letters written in Mandarin and English or in Yup'ik and English.

These objectives and their accompanying classroom activities can help students to understand that one language can serve as a resource for learning another.

When engaging in activities involving cross-lingual connections, we recommend that ImDL teachers and students stay in the language of instruction as much as possible, without resorting to concurrent translation or significant use of English during instructional time in the minority language (see Chapter 2). We provide some concrete examples of how this can be done effectively in Chapter 9 (see also Ballinger et al., 2017).

Learning strategies objectives

Learning strategies are defined as thoughts and/or actions that students use to read or complete a learning activity. There is substantial research supporting the use of learning strategies in content-based instruction (e.g., Grabe & Stoller, 1997; O'Malley & Chamot, 1990). A number of different categories of learning strategies have been proposed, and among them are metacognitive and cognitive strategies. "Metacognitive strategies involve thinking about the learning process, planning for learning, monitoring the learning task, and evaluating how well one has learned" (O'Malley & Chamot, 1990, p. 138). Examples include selective attention (deciding in advance to pay attention to specific aspects or details), self-management, and self-evaluation. In contrast, cognitive strategies have less to do with planning and monitoring and are more directly related to task performance as students interact with the material to be learned, manipulating it mentally or physically and applying specific techniques to the learning task. Note-taking, summarizing, and grouping (ordering and classifying material) are examples of cognitive strategies.

ImDL teachers need to teach learning strategies because students should know how to monitor their own learning, take notes, or utilize resources. Teachers cannot assume that students can learn such skills without explicit instruction. Objectives targeting learning strategies should be considered for each lesson. Below are a few examples.

- Students will utilize classroom resources independently to create posters.
- Students will visualize characters and events during shared reading.
- Students will make predictions about the ending of the story.
- Students will evaluate their work after completing math story problems (e.g., ask themselves if they followed the steps correctly, if their answer makes sense, or if they could approach the problem differently).

By explicitly teaching learning strategies, ImDL teachers fulfill an overarching goal of education; namely, supporting students so they are *learning how to learn*, based on the premise that the best curriculum is "one which focuses on the process of learning rather than its product" (Stern, 1990, p. 258).

Social/affective objectives

The affective domain of learning focuses on growth pertaining to attitudes, motivation, emotions, and values. Social development is about learning how to interact in appropriate ways with other children and adults. Social/affective objectives, then, target these areas. Children need to be taught how to work collaboratively with one another and how to listen, give feedback, and respond to peers in respectful ways. Examples of social/affective objectives are:

- Students will work collaboratively in pairs and small groups, contributing actively (not dominating or remaining passive).
- Students will practice listening and responding to others' ideas and thoughts respectfully.

- Students will carry out assigned cooperative group learning roles actively to ensure timely completion of the task.

Coupled with primary objectives, these secondary objectives help teachers to consider all aspects of student learning that will take place in the lessons. The next section of the template asks teachers to describe the approach to instruction.

Learning experiences/instruction

According to Wiggins and McTighe (2005), learning experiences and instructional activities are only designed once the desired results and evidence of learning have been planned. This is appropriate, with the understanding that the planning process is not linear but, rather, cyclical and dynamic. As teachers plan the experiences and activities for lessons, it is possible, if not likely, that some of the unit-level goals and ideas for assessment will evolve. Indeed, module and lesson planning also proceed in a more cyclical than linear manner. At the lesson level, determining learning experiences and activities and identifying evidence of learning go hand in hand. For this reason, we place evidence of learning at the end of the module/lesson design template, after learning experiences, with the assumption that these will likely be planned concurrently.

This section of the template provides spaces for teachers to list the materials and technology resources they will need for the lessons and to plan in detail the learning experiences and activities that will lead students to achieve the desired results. Ideally (and depending upon grade level), learning experiences and activities within one module should engage students in using language across all four modalities—listening, speaking, reading, and writing. Learning activities may involve structured pair interaction, whole-class instruction, cooperative group work, and so on. The possibilities are endless. Classroom learning experiences should be differentiated for different learner groups and needs, and teachers also need to consider the grouping strategies they will follow to maximize learning and equitable interaction. Appendix B provides detailed descriptions of learning activities and identifies ways in which learning experiences may be differentiated for different learner groups.

Materials and technology resources

To the degree possible, a wide range of materials—realia, pictures, diagrams, graphs, models, demonstrations, videos, audio files, magazines, websites, computer software, etc.—should be identified and/or developed to support learning (see Chapter 4). The materials must support the unit's concepts and generalizations or enduring understandings. When possible, materials should integrate content areas (science, literature, and social studies) and represent various perspectives and genres (narratives, reports, and poems). Text-based materials should be at different readability levels to support differentiation. Identifying a wide range of materials representing different levels is more challenging for certain ImDL program languages, especially indigenous languages such as Ojibwe or Cree, and others, such as Hmong. It can even be difficult to identify materials in French or Spanish, let alone in languages that are not as prevalent in Canada and the US.

Materials should also draw upon family and community funds of knowledge (Moll et al., 1992), as discussed above. Teachers must select materials with these aspects in mind to ensure that materials are culturally relevant. Some programs have sought grant funding or have taken it upon themselves to engage ImDL teachers in developing culturally relevant materials. We described one such project with the Yup'ik community of Alaska in Chapter 1 (Siekmann et al., 2017). Several Minnesota teachers are publishing books that represent diverse cultures, including Hmong ImDL teachers (Rao, 2019). Teachers can also engage students in writing materials; for example, books they develop for their own classroom, for younger learners in the program, or for the library. These need to be of high quality and published only after the students have produced multiple drafts, have received feedback, and have revised and edited their work.

It is typically a good idea to enlist the assistance of media center personnel to help locate materials for units, as they are an invaluable resource. We recommend that ImDL teachers identify linguistically, culturally, and content-rich books and other materials that lend themselves for use with multiple themes. A rich text can be revisited with different foci or purposes. See a variety of resources for identifying materials at the end of Chapter 7.

Differentiation

Differentiated instruction refers to tailoring instruction to individual student needs in mixed-ability classrooms. In ImDL contexts, differentiation is also important for addressing linguistic diversity in the classroom (Young, 2016). Differentiation can occur through curricular elements (content, process, or product) and student characteristics (readiness, interests, learning profiles [i.e., learning styles], abilities, physical and emotional needs, etc.) (e.g., Tomlinson, 2003). Table 8.5 describes differentiation by type (adapted from Santamaria, 2009). Student characteristics should be taken into account when differentiating through content, process, and products. Also important is student affect—their emotions, attitudes, and motivation—in the differentiation process.

It is essential to vary differentiation strategies over time and take stock of what seems to work well with the range of learners in the classroom. Blaz (2006, p. 5) describes differentiation as being:

- for *all* students (not primarily for students with learning challenges);
- student centered, flexible, and varied;
- grounded in assessment and progress monitoring.

TABLE 8.5 Description of differentiation types

Differentiation through	*Description*
content	• adjusting input level (complexity and type of materials) • creating different tasks requiring different levels of ability and/or language proficiency • clarifying key concepts and generalizations for all learners
process	• flexible grouping • pairing/grouping students based on ability, proficiency level, and personality (both homogeneously and heterogeneously) • balancing teacher-assigned and student-initiated activities
product	• administering initial and ongoing assessments of student readiness, interests, and goals • setting clear expectations and offering a variety of options for final projects • using assessment as a teaching tool

Blaz further characterizes differentiation as involving:

- heterogeneous groups (not ability tracking);
- a variety of whole-class, group, and independent learning;
- multiple approaches or options for content, process, and product (rather than individualized instruction);
- proactive planning that goes beyond modifying instruction up or down in difficulty;
- continual reflection and adjustments to help all students learn to their potential;
- a change in philosophy about how learning should occur;
- a belief system whereby "all learners come to the classroom with potential ready to be accessed."

Some examples of differentiated language objectives, lesson activities, and groupings appear in Appendix B.

Grouping strategies and cooperative learning

As explained above, an important part of differentiated instruction is flexible grouping and pairing strategies. We also briefly discussed grouping and pairing strategies in Chapter 5 as a means of scaffolding for both student comprehension and language production. Effective grouping arrangements are critical in ImDL classrooms because they influence the quality of interaction that students will have and because they serve as forums for students to learn important collaborative and communication skills. Kucer et al. (1995) aptly describe some characteristics of peer collaboration as follows:

> To develop a sense of collaboration, the learner must recognize that the knowledge created by the group surpasses the immediate abilities of an individual member. ... Collaboration requires that the learning community understand and value diversity; members need to view differences in perspective as natural, important, and necessary to the learning process. ... Collaboration also supports risk-taking. The group shares the vulnerability that results from mistakes. (p. 13)

Peer collaboration in the classroom is often fostered through cooperative learning activities. Cooperative learning supports content and language development as well as cross-cultural understanding (Kagan, 1992). Three fundamental principles guide effective cooperative learning: simultaneous interaction, positive interdependence, and individual accountability. Cooperative structures afford more opportunities for students to produce language because they involve numerous groups interacting at the same time. Successful cooperative groups are planned so that each group member has a specific role to play or portion of the task to complete. This setup promotes positive interdependence because the group's work cannot be done successfully unless all members contribute in some meaningful way. This principle also relates to individual accountability, in that each group member's required contribution is made clear to all members of the cooperative group so that each person is accountable for the group's success.

Garmston and Wellman (2016) offer seven "norms of collaboration" to enhance the quality and productivity of group interactions. These appear in Table 8.6. We have added the descriptions to explain how we see these norms playing out in classrooms.

These norms of collaboration represent somewhat complex interactive behaviors and should be introduced gradually, with teacher modeling. For example, to teach paraphrasing, teachers can rely upon the "Paraphrase Passport" strategy (Kagan, 2001), which can be done with the whole class or in small groups or pairs. This strategy is based on one simple rule: Before sharing his or her idea or contribution, a student must paraphrase what the person who spoke immediately before said. Sentence frames, such as "I think I heard you say ...." or "Do you mean to say ...?", may be used to aid students in engaging in this activity. The previous speaker must perceive that his or her idea was accurately paraphrased before he or she gives the other student the "passport" to speak. Similar types of strategies could be used to model and teach the other norms over time. Students should have ample opportunities to practice these behaviors.

How are cooperative groups and pairs best organized to maximize collaboration? Flexible grouping and pairing are key, and teachers need to take into account students' language proficiencies, personalities, and, at times, abilities.

TABLE 8.6 Norms of collaboration

Norms of collaboration	Descriptions
1. pausing	taking the time to think before speaking and to make sure you understand what another has said before responding
2. paraphrasing	rephrasing what another has said to ensure you've understood correctly or to express agreement/disagreement with the idea; ("I think I heard you say …")
3. posing questions	asking group members questions to advance the conversation and to check your understanding
4. putting ideas on the table	being willing to share your ideas and offer your perspectives
5. providing data	sharing evidence (from readings, class discussions, etc.) to support your ideas and statements
6. paying attention to self and others	attending carefully to your peers' ideas and to your own to ensure that you are explaining clearly and responding with kindness; making sure you are not dominating the conversation or being too passive
7. presuming positive intentions	assuming that your peers are taking the group work seriously and sharing ideas to the best of their ability; being kind to your peers even when there are misunderstandings; avoiding put-downs

Sometimes students will benefit from working with more capable peers (with respect to both language and content understandings). Doing so allows them to learn within the "zone of proximal development" or the ZPD (Vygotsky, 1978), as explained in Chapter 5. This concept comes to mind when we consider that many scholars have recommended that students be paired or grouped heterogeneously in two-way contexts, that is, pairing a Spanish home language student with an L2 learner of Spanish. For example, Howard, Sugarman, Perdomo, and Temple Adger (2005) state that heterogeneous grouping will "help ensure that all groups will be able to complete the task successfully, and that all individuals within each group will participate and understand what they have done" (p. 142). A study by Young and Tedick (2016) brought this recommended and oft-observed practice into question.

 RESEARCH REPORT

Young and Tedick (2016) used data collected for a form-focused study (Tedick & Young, 2016) for this analysis. They analyzed the small-group interactions of four focal students in a Grade 5 TWI classroom: an English home language (EHL) student with low Spanish proficiency and another with intermediate-low proficiency, and two Spanish home language (SHL) students, one with inter-mediate-low and one with advanced proficiency in Spanish. Students had been assigned to both heterogeneous and homogeneous (by proficiency) groups in the original study, and Young and Tedick did a micro discourse analysis to identify how students positioned themselves in small groups and how their positioning patterns seemed to either scaffold or constrain student learning.

They found that when the students with lower levels of proficiency (two EHL and one SHL) worked in heterogeneous groups they were marginalized, silenced, or "bullied linguistically" (ridiculed, over-corrected, and made fun of) by their more Spanish proficient peers. In contrast, when they worked with peers who had similar levels of proficiency, they participated actively and equally and scaffolded each other's learning through their interaction.

The pattern was notably different for the SHL student with advanced Spanish. She was always eager to participate and take on the role of teacher or expert. In homogeneous groups her peers pushed back on her attempts to take over, and their resistance allowed them to also take on the role of expert in their interactions, facilitating the focal student's linguistic "respect" for her peers. When working in the heterogeneous group, she took on the expert role, dominating the interaction and imposing her own ideas. She also engaged in "excessive languaging" (using language to mediate her own thinking), and in so doing often confused her peers.

The results of the Young and Tedick study showed that the teacher's idea of assigning the more proficient speakers "facilitator" roles in heterogeneous groups often backfired. Instead, these assignments exacerbated unequal status in the small groups. This, of course, was not the teacher's intention. She assigned these roles because the text was challenging, and she believed that the more proficient speakers would help the less proficient ones in comprehending it. Young and Tedick suggested that "this assumption—that heterogeneous groups will naturally lead to peer assistance—may reflect a 'false promise' of heterogeneous grouping unless teachers carefully prepare students for and carefully structure the activity" (p. 156).

Students benefit from working with a range of different groups, sometimes being assigned to groups/pairs with peers at similar levels and other times to groups/pairs with mixed levels. Students also benefit from whole-class instruc-tion, especially when it is structured to extend student language production (Chapter 5) and to provide corrective feedback (Chapter 6). When it comes to small-group or pair interaction, what is key is *preparing* students for the group/pair work and making sure that they know what successful collaboration looks like and sounds like (as in the norms described above).

As mentioned earlier, students can be taught collaborative behaviors through modeling and role play. For example, as reported in Chapter 6, Ballinger (2013,

2015) investigated the effects of strategy training on the quality of peer collaboration as English-dominant and French-dominant students worked in pairs. The strategy instruction proved effective, but the quality of the peer interaction and the extent to which students helped one another varied considerably according to pair dynamics, leading to the conclusion that, for peer collaboration to be effective, the ImDL classroom needs first to be established as a collaborative learning environment.

Teachers should give students feedback not only on their content understandings and language production, but also on how they interact and collaborate with others. One way to do this is to write encouraging or constructive feedback on Post-it notes and give them to students *while* they are interacting in pairs or small groups (so as not to interrupt the flow of the group work with teacher comments). Students' ability to collaborate and resolve conflicts respectfully can also be assessed both formatively and summatively.

Learning phases: The CAPA model

As explained in Chapter 4, the CAPA model serves as a blueprint to guide instructional design that integrates language and content. In our approach to instructional design, the CAPA model is used to sequence the activities that comprise the lessons in a module. The CAPA phases are learning phases that connect the lessons of a module together. Taken together, these phases highlight that every lesson in an ImDL classroom needs to provide an opportunity for language and content integration.

The initial ***contextualization*** phase orients students to the main topic of the module. It focuses on meaning, that is, on the academic content that is emphasized in the module. This phase activates students' prior knowledge, including making links to previous modules or lessons in the unit. Activities in this phase assume that students have already had some exposure to the language they need to carry out the activities, even though teachers are likely to expose students to new forms or vocabulary that they will be expected to produce in subsequent phases. The contextualization phase also includes activities that pique students' interest. In the sample module shown in Appendix B, in the contextualization phase students review the learnings of previous lessons and engage in a modified think–pair–share to draw upon their prior knowledge and elicit their thoughts about the topic of the module.

The ***awareness*** phase begins to draw students' attention to the language they will need to use during the practice and autonomy phases. It provides an opportunity for teachers to make overt connections to the lessons' language objectives. This phase involves extensive modeling on teachers' part. Learning experiences in this phase are both receptive and productive. As explained in Chapter 4, students need to notice the language being used in the input and to develop metalinguistic awareness to promote further language growth. As the target-language features and functions are highlighted by their increased frequency in the teachers' modeling, the students' attention is drawn to the language they'll need to engage with the content in subsequent phases. As illustrated in Appendix B, the teacher, along with a student volunteer, models the steps students will need to take to describe assigned animals with respect to their structural and behavioral adaptations. Each step of the process emphasizes the language they will need to successfully complete that step. Finally, the awareness phase also offers opportunities to draw students' attention to cross-lingual connections (see Appendix B).

In the *practice* phase, students are given the opportunity to use the language that was modeled for them in the awareness phase while they engage in content learning. The learning experiences are structured in a way that allows teachers to monitor student performance and provide corrective feedback related to the language and content objectives. Activities are designed to shift students' attention between content and language and to involve ample repetition of the language they are expected to use. In our example (Appendix B), pairs of students create animal adaptation cards by engaging in the steps that were modeled during the awareness phase. The teacher circulates around the classroom to provide assistance, respond to questions, and give corrective feedback.

Finally, the *autonomy* phase engages learners in applying the concepts they have learned during the previous phases in new situations. The goal is to extend students' content understandings and language growth by providing a somewhat new context for them to demonstrate their learning and use the target language of the module. This phase involves learners in open-ended, autonomous activities that are designed so that the target language reflected in the objectives will arise naturally. Learning experiences get students interacting about the subject-matter content while at the same time promoting accuracy and eliciting corrective feedback from teachers. These autonomous activities serve as opportunities for assessing students' content understandings and ability to use the language emphasized in the module. Our example in Appendix B shows that students work with new partners to complete a graphic organizer to compare and contrast the adaptations of two different animals. Later, each student independently writes a paragraph in his or her science journal to compare and contrast the two animals. Students' completion of both activities is then assessed.

Evidence: Lesson-level formative assessment procedures

The final section of the module and lesson design template provides a space for teachers to briefly describe their formative assessment procedures. When teachers engage in assessment, they collect information that helps them make decisions that further promote student learning. At the lesson level, formative assessment assists teachers in determining whether learning objectives were achieved. ImDL teachers need to continuously monitor how students' content understandings and abilities to express themselves through language are developing. Doing so gives teachers an indication of how effective their instruction is and what they may need to do differently to achieve better outcomes. Formative assessment also represents an opportunity for providing students with feedback on their learning and language development.

A lesson's learning experiences and activities can often be designed in a way that embeds an opportunity for assessment. The goal is for teachers to gather information so as to be able to reflect on and adjust their instruction and to give students feedback on their learning. Both formative and summative assessment are discussed in more detail in Chapter 10.

Summary

This chapter has introduced a planning template for designing the modules and lessons that comprise the unit. Throughout this chapter, we have emphasized how to bring in a focus on language in the context of planning for content instruction; for example, through the development of detailed language objectives. We have also described how the phases of the CAPA model can be used to organize and sequence lessons and integrate language and content. In the next chapter, we continue our focus on instructional design as we address the topic of biliteracy development.

Application activity 1: What's wrong with this objective?

Review the instructional objectives below and identify those that meet the criteria for well-written lesson objectives. The objective category is listed after the objective. For those that are not well written, explain what they may be lacking or why they are not well written (adapted from http://carla.umn.edu/cobaltt/m odules/curriculum/problem_areas.html). See answers in Appendix E.

Examples of "good" and "bad" objectives

---

1. Students will identify the literary characteristics of a fairy tale. [content]
2. Students will listen to a community member talk about animals that are native to her home country of Ecuador. [culture]
3. Students will be able to recognize and identify numbers (1–20) and be able to trace or write these numbers in printed form. [content]
4. Students will make predictions. [learning strategy]
5. Teach the names of shapes. [content]
6. Students will give oral presentations. [language]
7. Students will demonstrate knowledge of the numbers 1–10 by writing them in relationship to the number of objects they represent. [content]
8. Students will develop an initial awareness that the distinct regions of Ecuador and their climatic conditions influence cultural practices (e.g., jobs and household chores) and products (e.g., clothing and cuisine). [culture]
9. Students will learn the alphabet. [content]
10. Students will demonstrate their understanding of a letter's major components by writing a short personal letter based on a model. [content]
11. Students will work in pairs. [social/affective]
12. Students will use context clues to predict the meanings of unfamiliar words in a text. [learning strategy]

Application activity 2: Writing language objectives

Three classroom activities are described below. Following the six-step scaffold introduced in this chapter, write at least one content-obligatory and one content–compatible language objective for each activity. The format you should use for developing each of the objectives appears below. For TWI contexts, consider how the language objectives may be differentiated for the different linguistic groups. After you write the objectives, write them again in student-friendly language.

1. Discourse type:

2. Communicative or academic functions:

3. Examples of the language students need to produce:

4. Grammatical features:

5. Vocabulary:

6. Written language objectives: content-obligatory and content-compatible

1. In groups of four, Grade 1 TWI students will orally present a poster with labeled drawings of one of the four main stages of a butterfly's life cycle from egg to butterfly. During the presentation, each student will describe how the butterfly-to-be looks at one of the four stages and what happens as it transitions from one stage to the next. Students will use adverbs of time to accurately sequence the four stages within the life cycle.

2. After reading a story, Grade 4 TWI students are assigned to pairs (one minority-language student and one majority-language student in each pair). They are tasked with completing a graphic organizer to summarize the five story elements (setting, characters, plot, conflict, and resolution) and then to write a summary paragraph.

3. Grade 7 IMM students are engaged in a jigsaw cooperative group activity. There are five students per "expert" group. In the initial "expert" group,

they are to read an excerpt of an article about human impact on the Amazon rain forest. They have been instructed to work together to come up with the main idea(s) and key details to summarize the excerpt and to come to consensus about how to teach this content to other students who haven't read the excerpt (students in the "home" groups).

 Application activity 3: Using the template to design instruction

Use the module/lesson design template introduced in this chapter to develop lessons for a curricular unit (linked to a unit plan you developed at the end of Chapter 7). Reflect on what you find to be helpful and challenging about designing instruction according to this template.

 Online resources for readers

Content-based curriculum development

There is a wealth of resources for content-based curriculum development at the Center for Advanced Research on Language Acquisition (CARLA) website (CoBaLTT project). For example:

> *Formula for creating language objectives and practice activities:*
> http://carla.umn.edu/cobaltt/modules/curriculum/formula.html
>
> *List of communicative and academic functions:*
> http://carla.umn.edu/cobaltt/lessonplans/chart-comfunctions.html
>
> *Customizable graphic organizers that scaffold for both content and language:*
> http://carla.umn.edu/cobaltt/modules/strategies/gorganizers/index.html
>
> *Description of instructional strategies to support content-based instruction:*
> http://carla.umn.edu/cobaltt/modules/strategies/index.html
>
> *Elementary Immersion Learning Strategies Resource Guide*:
> https://carla.umn.edu/immersion/documents/eils-guide.pdf

This guide is interactive, allowing users to skip to topics of interest or printable resources such as lesson plans, charts, and worksheets. Topics include (1) definitions, descriptions, and examples of learning strategies, (2) how to teach strategies, and (3) selecting strategies by subject area. The appendices provide additional resources, including the learning strategies lists and definitions translated into several languages.

9

SCAFFOLDING BILITERACY DEVELOPMENT

Part IV has so far encouraged teachers to integrate a more systematic focus on the minority language by attending to language when planning content-based curricular units, modules, and lessons. This chapter proposes a slightly different perspective on integration by outlining *integrated language learning* as an effective means for strengthening students' biliteracy development. Ways of making connections between the minority and majority languages will be explored in this chapter with a view to creating greater coherence across the immersion and dual language (ImDL) curriculum. We focus on the following questions:

- What is biliteracy?
- How is biliteracy instruction different from literacy instruction in one language?
- What instructional strategies can be used to foster development of students' oracy, reading, writing, and metalanguage?
- What is cross-lingual transfer?
- How can teachers collaborate to foster cross-lingual connections through bilingual read-aloud projects?

What is biliteracy?

The term *biliteracy* is often defined simply as the ability to read and write in two languages. We prefer the more comprehensive conceptualization of biliteracy offered by Escamilla et al. (2014). They describe biliteracy as a holistic and complete system of bilingual learning (including oracy, reading, writing, and metalanguage [or metalinguistic] development) that develops in an integrated way across two languages. These four components—oracy, reading, writing, and metalinguistic development—work in tandem to promote the acquisition of literacy skills and thus need attention in both languages in an integrated way.

When ImDL teachers approach instruction from a biliteracy perspective, it means that they understand that students' literacy development is occurring across both program languages and that they must take advantage of opportunities to make cross-linguistic connections explicit. This does not mean that separate literacy instruction in each program language ceases to occur. On the contrary, ImDL teachers will need to engage in practices to develop students' literacy in each of the program languages (whether one teacher is responsible for both or two teachers work in partnership). As we discuss in this chapter, literacy approaches need to be language specific, but there are also important ways to connect literacy instruction in each language that converge into what is called biliteracy instruction.

Oracy

Escamilla et al. (2014) explain that "oracy is an aspect of oral language, but it includes a more specific subset of skills and strategies within oral language that more closely relates to literacy objectives in academic settings" (p. 21). In this sense, oracy includes dialogue (meaningful student participation in discussions around literacy), language structures (expansion of the grammatical and syntactic complexity of students' speech), and vocabulary (expansion of students' word and concept range). The importance of oracy in the development of biliteracy cannot be overstated; research has documented that oral language is the foundation for developing written vocabulary and reading comprehension in both literacy (one language) and biliteracy (see review in Escamilla et al., 2014). A great deal of the content of this book has focused on developing oracy in ImDL students, particularly how to plan for and teach specific language structures and academic language functions while expanding students' oral language production during classroom interaction and providing targeted corrective feedback. Other recommended approaches to foster oracy development include:

- Reading aloud for fluency development: After reading a text for meaning, students (with teacher support) read the same text aloud repeatedly (echo reading, choral reading, reading to partners, etc.).
- Readers' theater: Students read from a script to dramatize a written work; emphasis is on oral expression and facial expressions to communicate the feelings and emotions of characters they play.
- Oracy centers: Learning centers in the classroom provide opportunities for independent or small-group/pair oracy practice (e.g., fluency centers where students listen to and read along with a recording of a text, pairs or small groups can engage in echo or choral reading, etc.).

Vocabulary development is a key predictor not only of reading comprehension but also of fluency for both L1 and L2 learners (e.g., August & Shanahan, 2006). Research on ImDL students' language development has emphasized the need for an intentional focus on vocabulary development with recommendations for explicit, systematic attention to building students' vocabulary and word knowledge (e.g., Allen et al., 1990; Fortune & Ju, 2017; Fortune & Tedick, 2015). Internalizing new words and using them appropriately requires multiple encounters in meaningful contexts. Although a thorough discussion of vocabulary teaching is beyond the scope of this chapter, we offer a few research-based recommendations.

ImDL teachers who approach instruction from a biliteracy frame of mind (i.e., taking into account that students are developing biliteracy rather than literacy in just one language) understand that similarities between languages should be emphasized in vocabulary instruction across languages (as in drawing attention to cognates). They understand that linguistic differences need to inform vocabulary instruction as well. For example, when teaching languages with grammatical gender (Arabic, French, German, Spanish, etc.) to students whose L1 does not have this feature, it is imperative to introduce new nouns with their articles. Carroll (1989) argued that native speakers of languages with grammatical gender learn new words as unanalyzed chunks composed of a determiner (article) + noun. For example, in Spanish *la puerta* means *door*. Native-speaking children learn this word as a chunk: *lapuerta*. They "process determiners and nouns, at least initially, as coindexed chunks; when these chunks are later analyzed as separate constituents, the noun still retains its inherent gender specification" (Lyster, 2004, p. 408). In contrast, English-speaking learners of these languages do not learn determiners as parts of nouns but rather "as distinct syntactic words and independent phonological units" (p. 408). This different kind of processing for L2 learners helps to explain why grammatical gender can be so difficult to acquire and why introducing nouns with their articles—as a chunk—is so important.

ⓘ SPECIAL NOTES

When working with a language having grammatical gender, ImDL teachers should *always* use nouns with their articles. Although grammatical gender is acquired early and rather easily in a child's L1, it can be very difficult to acquire in a new language, especially if the learner's L1 does not have grammatical gender (as in English).

ImDL teachers can also expand students' vocabulary knowledge by attending to structural and generative properties of words to increase students' morphological awareness. This can occur, for example, by teaching word bases and families (e.g., *direct* ⇒ *directive, director, direction, directly*). It is important to make cross-lingual connections by focusing on similar patterns during instructional time in each language, whether the same teacher (responsible for instruction in both languages) makes such connections or whether two teachers collaborate to make connections between languages (see examples below). Another recommendation is to take time to explicitly teach phrasal verbs in English and their equivalent renderings in the minority language. English can be challenging for L2 learners in that the meaning of one verb changes with the addition of what are called *particles* (either prepositions or adverbs)—go *out*, go *in*, go *up*, and go *down*—whereas in minority languages such as French and Spanish (among many others), there are different verbs for each of these. English speakers learning Spanish have a tendency to translate literally from English to the minority language—*go out* ⇒ *ir* (go) *afuera* (out)—rather than using the correct equivalent, *salir*.

For languages that are not cognate with English (i.e., that do not have words related in origin to words in English), such as Mandarin Chinese and Japanese, there are still connections to be made. For example, both phonological and morphological awareness are predictors of learning to read in Chinese, although morphological awareness is more important (Perfetti & Dunlap, 2008). Morphological awareness transfers not only between alphabetic languages but also between logographic and alphabetic languages (Pasquarella, Chen, Lam, & Luo, 2011; Perfetti & Dunlap, 2008). In addition, Mandarin has a large number of compound words, and students' compound awareness in English has been shown to correlate with Mandarin vocabulary development and reading comprehension (Pasquarella et al., 2011).

In sum, spending time teaching vocabulary in contextualized ways is time well spent. Making connections between instructional languages will help students build their vocabulary and word knowledge more efficiently.

Reading

Reading instruction in ImDL programs needs to emphasize foundational skills (concepts of print, decoding, and fluency), comprehension skills and strategies, as well as skills for reading different genres or text types throughout the grade levels (Escamilla et al., 2014). Students need opportunities to develop and apply such skills and strategies both within and across program languages and to come to understand how the languages are similar and different. Even with languages having different writing systems, such as Mandarin and English, connections can and should be made across languages. Current research shows that Grade 4 students in a Mandarin ImDL program use the same types of reading strategies to decode unknown words and make sense of text in both Mandarin and English (T. Fortune, personal communication, May 2019). Also important to the teaching of reading is that instruction in each language be as specific to each language as possible. Escamilla et al. (2014) argue that "methods and strategies should … consider how the internal structure of each language is different" (p. 7). They offer the following examples related to Spanish and English (p. 7):

- The role of syllabification in English is not as strong as in Spanish. In Spanish, syllable awareness emerges before phoneme awareness and is a stronger predictor of reading success.
- The building blocks of English are the names and sounds of each letter, whereas in Spanish literacy development, vowels are the first building blocks, followed by consonants.
- In English, children begin by learning consonants, but in Spanish they begin by learning vowels. Learning letter names in Spanish is less important than matching vowels to consonants to form syllables.

These differences have enormous implications for early literacy and biliteracy instruction in Spanish/English ImDL programs.

Because logographic languages are so different from alphabetic languages, it should be relatively easy for teachers in Mandarin and Japanese programs to adopt strategies that are specific to their respective languages. For example, Mandarin ImDL students need to be able to recognize the phonetic and semantic graphic components (radicals) of characters. They need to be taught to notice and look for semantic radicals in characters. For example, the semantic radical meaning *female* appears in characters for *mother*, *girl*, *sister*, *aunt*, and *grandmother*. Moreover, writing characters in Mandarin is fundamental to learning to read (Perfetti & Dunlap, 2008) and, thus, needs to be an important component of reading instruction in Mandarin.

Reading instruction in both languages in an ImDL program should be driven by approaches that are recommended in the literature (see Table 9.1). These types of reading activities can and should be coordinated across instructional languages. For example, students can be taught a specific comprehension strategy in one language and then be reminded to use it during instruction in the other language. Student knowledge of the strategy will transfer from one language to the next, so explicit instruction of a strategy need not be repeated in each language. Bilingual read–aloud projects are another way to connect reading experiences across languages.

Reading instruction continues to be necessary as students advance in grade level. As the cognitive level of academic content increases, so too does the linguistic level, and reading material becomes increasingly challenging. Students will benefit from a continued focus on reading skills through explicit teaching of comprehension strategies (pre-, during-, and post-reading) as well as text structures (titles, section subheadings, figures, etc., and their purposes), text patterns (e.g., compare/contrast), and text types or genres (e.g., different literature genres, reports, editorials, etc.).

TABLE 9.1 Recommended approaches to reading instruction (e.g., Escamilla et al., 2014; Gibbons, 2015; Lyster et al., 2009, 2013; McLaughlin, 2012)

Approach	Description
Interactive read-alouds	Teacher reads text aloud to students with frequent interaction and structured pre-reading, during-reading, and post-reading activities
Guided reading	Teacher works with small groups having similar reading levels
Shared reading	Teacher reads for and with students in a whole-class format with more active student involvement in reading the text
Collaborative reading	Teacher-structured opportunities for students to read with peers
Independent reading	Students read independently with teacher provision of different texts and genres
Bilingual read-alouds	Reading and biliteracy tasks that begin in one language during instructional time in that language and continue in the other language (described in more detail later in this chapter)
Explicit teaching of comprehension strategies	Teacher directly models and teaches students to use comprehension strategies (e.g., making connections, self-questioning, determining importance, visualizing, etc.)
Reading centers	Learning centers in the classroom for independent or small-group/pair reading (decoding, comprehension) activities

Writing

The writing of students being schooled bilingually develops differently from that of students being schooled only in English. For example, phenomena such as the use of strategic code-switching (alternating languages), spontaneous literacy (development of literacy occurs in a language even though literacy instruction is only happening in another language), and interliteracy (linguistic elements from one language are applied to the other language while writing) have been observed (Gort, 2006). These phenomena occur in a bidirectional fashion (i.e., L1 ⇔ L2). Research has also revealed that bilingual students' writing skills in each language develop at different rates (Gort, 2006).

L2 learners and students learning through two languages will benefit initially from more direct, whole-class instructional approaches to writing rather than approaches that advocate for much more independent writing (e.g., Gibbons, 2015). Yet, as students advance in age and develop their abilities, more independent methods can be effective. Table 9.2 displays a number of approaches that can support students' writing development. These, of course, should occur in both

TABLE 9.2 Recommended approaches to teaching writing (e.g., Escamilla et al., 2014; Gibbons, 2009, 2015; McLaughlin, 2012)

Approach	Description
Language experience	Teacher engages students in a shared experience, such as a field trip or a classroom experiment; afterwards, teacher leads whole-class discussion about the experience and records students' thoughts and ideas; teacher then uses shared writing to construct a text about the experience
Modeled writing	Teacher demonstrates the process of writing a text and engages young learners in discussion about concepts of print, different writing functions, early literacy skills such as spelling high-frequency words and basic punctuation; teacher can help more advanced learners refine skills, develop cohesive elements, or tackle a new genre
Shared writing	Teacher and students plan and construct a text together, including setting the purpose for writing, co-constructing text, revising and editing, and extending learning by illustrating the text, creating a book, making copies for students to take home, and so on.
Interactive writing	Teacher leads the writing but children write the texts themselves, sometimes copying and sometimes writing known letters/words on their own—best done in small groups
Guided writing	Like guided reading, teacher works in small groups with students on a focused task; students construct texts individually with teacher support and interaction among peers
Collaborative writing	Students write with peers while teacher monitors and supports their work; after working in small groups or with a partner, students share their work with the whole class
Independent writing	Students write independently following a process approach whereby they write drafts and receive feedback from teacher and/or peers in the process and engage with the teacher in writing conferences
Teaching-learning cycle	Teacher scaffolds the academic writing process for students through four phases: building the field (building content knowledge of the topic), modeling the genre (teaching about the language of the text type), joint construction of text (shared writing), and independent construction of text (independent writing)
Writing centers	Learning centers in the classroom for independent or small-group/pair writing activities

instructional languages and across a variety of genres. Writing becomes increasingly important as students advance in grade and requires significant attention at the secondary level. Many of the recommended approaches shown in the table can be adapted for use at the secondary level.

At times, writing instruction should also be approached from a biliteracy mindset. For example, students could develop bilingual books after writing about similar topics in each of the program languages (see example described and illustrated later in this chapter). It is important for ImDL teachers to be aware that, just as with oracy and reading, writing development occurs across languages, and teachers can make overt connections between program languages to foster students' writing development. For example, when students are writing in the minority language, ImDL teachers can bring students' attention to sentence structure and show how sentences are structured differently than they are in English. This is important in all languages, but especially so in Mandarin and Hmong, for example, which tend not to have complex grammatical systems but which differ significantly when it comes to how sentences and discourse are structured. Also, issues related to punctuation differences and spelling can be addressed, as well as vocabulary, such as teaching students how to identify cognates and false cognates.

Metalinguistic development

Escamilla et al. (2014) use the term *metalanguage* to refer to thinking and talking about language. In essence, it is the articulation of metalinguistic awareness, which needs to be developed within and across both program languages. As explained in Chapter 3, metalinguistic awareness is the ability to objectify language as an analyzable code and is thus prerequisite to early literacy development. Escamilla et al. (2014) specify that it includes "the ability to identify, analyze, and manipulate language forms, and to analyze sounds, symbols, grammar, vocabulary, and language structures between and across languages" (p. 67). Developing metalinguistic awareness can help students forge cross-linguistic connections and vice versa. Although Escamilla et al. and others (e.g., Beeman & Urow, 2013) promote the purposeful use of instructional languages side by side, we advocate approaches that largely maintain separate spaces for instructional languages while making cross-lingual comparisons explicit. We return to this topic below and provide examples of how such connections can be made while respecting the "linguistic and contextual integrity for each language on its own" (Lyster et al., 2013, p. 171).

Teaching for biliteracy

An ImDL program that emphasizes biliteracy development does not teach two unrelated literacy classes based on approaches used with monolingual children. Rather, it ensures that there are systematic connections between the two literacy blocks. If one teacher is responsible for literacy instruction in both languages, making such connections can be quite straightforward but still requires focused attention and planning. If there are two partner teachers, each responsible for literacy instruction in one of the program languages, collaborative planning and instruction are needed. We describe an approach to such collaboration later in this chapter. Although connections need to be planned for and made across the literacy instruction in the two languages, it is imperative that teachers do *not* teach the exact same literacy lesson in both languages—what's taught in the minority language should not be repeated later the same day in English and vice versa (although it *is* acceptable to share the same book or text in both languages, as described below). Moreover, when teaching for biliteracy, it is not necessary to mix languages extensively (if at all) in order to make connections across languages. Cross-language connections can be created with creative planning and collaboration, because students transfer knowledge and literacy skills from one language to the other.

Teaching for transfer

As explained above, biliteracy instruction targets two languages rather than only one. It is backed by research advocating cross-lingual connections that intentionally activate the L1 as a cognitive resource to support L2 learning (e.g., Cook, 2001; Swain & Lapkin, 2013). Jim Cummins (2007) has been instrumental in promoting L1-L2 connections to support biliteracy development:

> It seems reasonable to teach for two-way cross-lingual transfer (L1 to L2, L2 to L1) in order to render the process as effective as possible. … Learning efficiencies can be achieved if teachers explicitly draw students' attention to similarities and differences between their languages and reinforce effective learning strategies in a coordinated way across languages. (pp. 231–233)

The logic of teaching for two-way transfer is based on what Cummins (1989, 2000) identifies as a *common underlying proficiency* (see Figure 9.1) that allows cognitive/academic and literacy skills learned in one language to be transferred to another.

He explains the model as follows, using a Spanish-English ImDL program as an example:

> Spanish instruction that develops Spanish reading and writing skills (for either Spanish L1 or L2 speakers) is not just developing *Spanish* skills, it is also developing a deeper conceptual and linguistic proficiency that is strongly related to the development of literacy in the majority language (English). In other words, although the surface aspects (e.g., pronunciation, fluency, etc.) of the different languages are clearly separate, there is an underlying cognitive/academic proficiency which is common across languages. (Cummins, 1989, p. 45)

Cummins (2007) argued that cross-lingual instructional strategies serve to subvert "the two solitudes assumption" (p. 229) that typically keeps the two languages of instruction separate in ImDL programs, even though the goal is

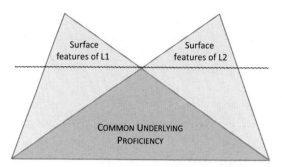

FIGURE 9.1 The linguistic interdependence model (from Cummins, 1989, p. 45, and reproduced with the author's permission)

literacy in both languages (see Chapter 2 for discussion). But how can ImDL teachers effectively encourage their students to draw on their knowledge of both languages of instruction for metalinguistic purposes while at the same time encouraging them to use the minority language as a primary means of communication? ImDL teachers need answers to this question, because competition between the minority language and English for time and status in Canadian and US schools usually ends up favoring the more dominant language—English.

Much of Cummins's work has been done with minority-language students whose home language is not English. As explained in Chapters 1 and 2, it is of vital importance that minority-language students are able to draw on their home language to help them perform well at school and to develop a sense of pride about their home language. If English is the student's dominant language, however, too much reliance on it will inevitably lead to its overuse at the expense of the minority language, due simply to its majority status and omnipresence in the US and Canada. It is thus crucial that the minority language has its own space, but this creates a dilemma for teachers keen on developing strong connections between both languages of instruction and committed to encouraging students to draw on all their available resources to maximize learning. The solution to the dilemma lies in *collaboration between partner teachers* who teach different languages to the same group of students. Through collaboration, they can facilitate connections between languages while maintaining communication in each language in its respective context. Even a teacher who is responsible for literacy instruction in both languages can make such connections with careful planning and while remaining in one language during instructional time in that language.

The purpose of collaboration between partner teachers is to create coherence across the ImDL curriculum while scaffolding biliteracy development in efficient ways. The co-designed interventions enable students to develop connections between languages and to draw on all available resources in ways that support integrated language learning. This type of collaboration thus fits well with *professional learning communities*, which involve collaborative efforts to ensure student success (DuFour, Dufour, & Eaker, 2008).

Bilingual read-aloud projects

Partner teachers can collaborate to implement an integrated approach that scaffolds biliteracy development by drawing on age-appropriate children's literature. To illustrate such an approach, we will report on two bilingual read-aloud projects undertaken in ImDL classrooms in the Montreal area (Lyster et al., 2009; Lyster et al., 2013). The partner teachers participating in these published studies co-designed and implemented biliteracy tasks that began in one language during its allotted class time and continued in the other language during its class time. In this way, borders between languages and classrooms were crossed as students engaged in the tasks, even though communication in each language continued as usual in separate spaces. Although we have often considered "content" throughout this book as stemming from subject areas such as social studies and science, children's literature is also a rich source of content that stimulates student motivation and language growth.

The Magic Tree House Project

Lyster et al. (2009) undertook a bilingual read-aloud project in partnership with three pairs of partner teachers in Grades 1, 2, and 3. The partner teachers read aloud to their students from the same three chapter books over four months, alternating the reading of one chapter from the French edition and another from the English edition. Prior to each read-aloud session, teachers asked their students to summarize the content of the previous reading, which had taken place in the other language of instruction, and after each reading they asked their students to make predictions about the next chapter, thereby generating a great deal of student interaction.

Written by Mary Pope Osborne, the books were part of the Magic Tree House series, published in English by Random House and in French as the *Cabane Magique* series by Bayard Jeunesse. This well-known series offers a wide selection, and many of its books have been translated into other languages, thereby making it a useful resource for biliteracy projects. Its highly educational focus lends itself well to an integrated approach that begins in language arts and continues in content areas such as social studies or science. Many of the stories share a common theme of "books" and how writing has changed over time. The two main characters travel back in time in a magic tree house to recover books in danger of being lost or destroyed.

The following highlights the content of the three books used in what came to be known as the Magic Tree House Project:

- In *Vacation Under the Volcano*, the characters travel back to 79 AD to retrieve the legend of Hercules. In Roman times, the readers are informed, books were scrolls made of papyrus and written in Latin with pens made of reeds and octopus ink.
- In *Day of the Dragon King*, the duo is sent to ancient China to retrieve the Chinese legend of the silk weaver and the cowherd. Readers become aware

that in ancient China, before the invention of paper, books were made of bamboo strips displaying Chinese calligraphy.

- In *Viking Ships at Sunrise*, the characters travel to Ireland to retrieve an ancient Irish tale about a sea serpent. Readers learn that in Ireland during the Middle Ages, books were handwritten in Latin and decorated by monks in monasteries using sheepskin and pens made of goose quills.

These stories provided content that was addressed across the students' curriculum in both French and English, while enabling them to learn a new concept along with two new words. *Vacation Under the Volcano* allowed students to learn about ancient Roman cities, including the story of Pompeii and its infamous volcano, which teachers related to the study of natural disasters. They also learned about sundials, a new concept for them, which they learned in both languages (*cadran solaire/sundial*). *The Dragon King* allowed teachers to focus on content related to silk production as well as well-known landmarks such as the Great Wall and the Terracotta Army. *Viking Ships at Sunrise* focused on Viking invasions and related seafaring notions, as well as on medieval monasteries and the role monks played in book-making, thus introducing students to *monasteries* and *monastères*, to *invaders* and *envahisseurs*. Whereas two new words for a new concept might be considered an additional learning challenge for students, all participating teachers believed that the dual focus helped to reinforce the concepts for the children.

Students participated enthusiastically during the reading of the stories in both languages. Moreover, their interest in continuing to read stories on their own from the same book series was striking: 22 of the 23 participating Grade 3 students and 14 of the 23 participating Grade 2 students stated that they continued to read other books in the Magic Tree House series on their own. The two schools that did not already have the entire Magic Tree House series ordered the collection for their libraries to meet the popular demand!

 RESEARCH REPORT

Cognitive and motivational benefits of bilingual read-aloud projects

- Hearing different parts of a story each read in a different language can enhance rather than hinder students' understanding and appreciation of the story (Lyster et al., 2009).
- Alternating languages can increase students' engagement with the stories, to which students give more importance than usual as they see the involvement of two teachers rather than only one (Lyster, 2019).
- Switching between languages is considered to lead to cognitive advantages for emergent bilinguals, as they develop greater mental flexibility in the brain's executive functions (Bialystok, 2007).

Despite the many potential opportunities for students to learn new concepts along with new words in both languages, systematic collaboration between partner teachers to reinforce connections across languages was minimal. In a bilingual read-aloud project such as this one, teachers need, at the very least, to meet briefly to determine language objectives pertaining to vocabulary learning. For example, in alternating between both versions of *Vacation Under the Volcano*, teachers can decide that students will acquire vocabulary related to volcanoes in both languages (e.g., lava, pumice, eruption, etc.).

The researchers concluded that, to better exploit the potential that such a project has for facilitating teacher collaboration, more time for participating teachers to actually collaborate on planning, as well as more structured guidance regarding the language focus, would be needed. This led to another bilingual read-aloud project, this time with a more intentional focus on language and more guidance from the researchers concerning the language focus, as well as more time for teachers to plan collaboratively (Lyster et al., 2013).

The Tomi Ungerer Project

The content focus this time derived from three children's illustrated storybooks by Tomi Ungerer (*The Three Robbers, Moon Man*, and *Crictor*) and is thus referred to here as the Tomi Ungerer Project. Tomi Ungerer is an award-winning illustrator and multilingual author from Alsace, who was chosen by the Council of Europe as its Ambassador for Childhood and Education in 2003. In the spirit of counterbalanced instruction, activities were designed and implemented to shift students' attention between content and language. The content focus emerged from the themes of the illustrated storybooks, while the language focus was on derivational morphology in French and English.

Derivational morphology and morphological instruction

As explained in Chapter 3, morphology is the study of how words are formed. One type of word formation results from *inflections*, which are morphemes added to verbs to mark person (*eat* ⇒ *eats*) or tense (*walk* ⇒ *walked*) and to nouns to mark number (*child* ⇒ *children*). The Tomi Ungerer Project targeted two types of morphological units other than inflections. There was a primary focus on *derivations*, which occur when prefixes or suffixes are added to base morphemes to change their meaning or syntactic category (e.g., adding the suffix *-ous* to the noun *courage* produces the adjective *courageous*). The process of forming new words by adding prefixes and suffixes—together known as *affixes*, which also include *infixes* (e.g., *foot* ⇒ *feet*)—is called *derivational morphology*. A secondary focus in the Tomi Ungerer Project was on *compounds*—yet another way to form new words by combining two or more words to form compound words such as *sunrise*, *toymaker*, and *bedtime*.

Research has shown that morphological instruction—which focuses on inflections, derivations, and compounds—improves reading comprehension (Carlisle, 2000; Kuo & Anderson, 2006), increases vocabulary size (Bowers & Kirby, 2010), and also increases "motivation to investigate words" (Bowers, Kirby, & Deacon, 2010, p. 145). Bowers et al.'s (2010) meta-analysis of 22 studies of morphological instruction from preK to Grade 8 revealed positive effects, especially for younger learners, when the intervention was combined with other aspects of literacy instruction. They further noted, "If morphological instruction were introduced early in literacy learning, morphological knowledge would have time to become consolidated and have more opportunities to contribute to literacy learning" (p. 148). Drawing on this previous research, the Tomi Ungerer Project supported partner teachers (French and English) as they co-designed and implemented morphological instruction in their Grade 2 ImDL classrooms by means of biliteracy units based on the themes of illustrated storybooks.

Project implementation

Unlike the Magic Tree House series, the illustrated storybooks by Tomi Ungerer had no chapters, so some of the partner teachers read the storybooks at least once in each language while others alternated between languages, reading short sections in each. *Crictor* will be used first to illustrate how the biliteracy interventions were implemented.

WHO IS CRICTOR?

Crictor is a boa constrictor that was offered as a gift to a schoolteacher living in Paris named Mme. Bodot. She goes out of her way to make Crictor feel comfortable in her home, by installing a long bed for him alongside palm trees and even knitting him a long scarf. In turn, Crictor makes himself very useful in the community, by helping the children at school learn to count, read the alphabet, and tie knots, as well as serving as a slide, a skipping rope, and other playful means. At the story's climax, Crictor becomes a hero as he saves Mme. Bodot from a burglar who has gagged and tied her up. Crictor is awarded a medal for his bravery and a statue is erected in his honor.

Copyright 1958 by Jean Thomas Ungerer. Used by permission of HarperCollins Publishers.

As they read the story aloud to emphasize the theme of heroism and the heroic attributes of Crictor, English teachers drew attention to key words such as *helpful, faithful, honor*, and *respected* (see Figure 9.2), while French teachers highlighted their French equivalents: *serviable, fidèle, honneur*, and *respectè* (see Figure 9.3). The focus on these target words occurred separately in each language without side-by-side comparisons of the two languages.

The derivational relationships in reference to Crictor's heroic traits were emphasized by the words *hero* and *heroism* in the English class and *hèros* and *héroisme* in the French class. English teachers drew attention to the suffix *-ic* in *heroic* to encourage students to discover similar derivations (e.g., *science* ⇒ *scientific*; *history* ⇒ *historic*), while French teachers drew attention to the suffix *-ique* in *hèroïque* to encourage students to discover analogous derivations in French (e.g., *science*

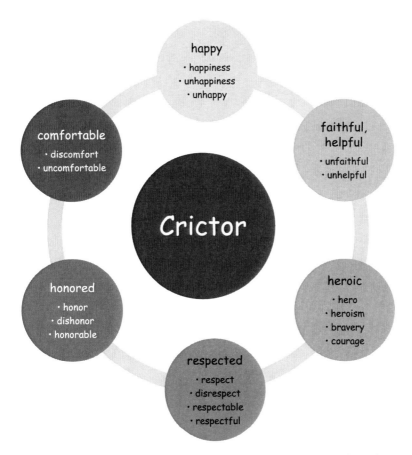

FIGURE 9.2 Graphic organizer depicting semantic and morphological connections among English words related to *Crictor*

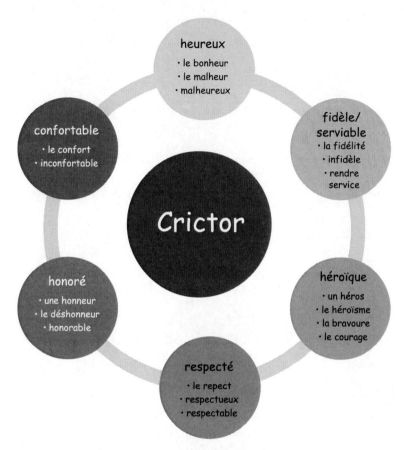

FIGURE 9.3 Graphic organizer depicting semantic and morphological connections among French words related to *Crictor*

⇒ *scientifique; histoire* ⇒ *historique*). Still other tasks focused on similar patterns of suffixation in words whose meanings were closely tied to the story (e.g., *courage* ⇒ *courageous* or *courageux; danger* ⇒ *dangerous* or *dangereux*). Teachers followed up in their respective classes with tasks or games requiring other words to be formed by analogy with the same suffixes.

The following example is a prototypical biliteracy task concerning *The Three Robbers* that began in one class and continued in the other. The English teacher read aloud *The Three Robbers*, but stopped at an important point in the story, when the protagonist wakes up only to discover the robbers' hidden treasures, which they had simply hoarded rather than spending. The teacher then asked students to make oral predictions about how they thought the money could be spent and then to illustrate their predictions along with written annotations.

In the following French class, the French teacher asked students to retell their predictions in French and then proceeded to read the rest of or all of *Les trois brigands*. The students then compared and discussed their own predictions with the actual ending: "They set off and gathered up all the lost, unhappy, and abandoned children they could find, and ... they bought a beautiful castle where all of them could live."

Within this context, the students' attention was drawn to derivational morphology—by the English teacher, who pointed out the use and meaning of the prefix *un-* in *unhappy*, and by the French teacher, who pointed out the use and meaning of the prefix *mal-* in *malheureux*. The teachers followed up in their respective classes with tasks or games requiring other words to be formed by analogy with the same prefixes. In English, this included adjectives such as *unable* and *unbelievable* and verbs such as *unfold* and *unpack*. In one class, the English teacher covertly asked individual students to mime words such as *unfold* or *unpack* for the others to guess what action was being mimed. Meanwhile, in French, teachers drew attention to adjectives such as *malhonnête* and *malpoli*, but because *mal-* is limited in its use as an adjectival prefix, they extended their focus to include the much more productive prefix *in-* in words such as *incapable* and *incroyable*.

Moon Man also served as a springboard for making theme-driven connections across the curriculum and cross-linguistic connections across languages. In terms of content objectives, *Moon Man* aligned well with one pair of partner teachers' theme of space, as they focused on planets in the English class and on the moon and its phases in the French class. In terms of language objectives, the English teacher used as her starting point the adjective *mysterious,* which appears as a key word to describe the protagonist, as she helped students to recognize the noun *mystery* as its base and to form and identify similarly formed adjectives (e.g. *courageous* from *courage*) or nouns (e.g. *disaster* from *disastrous*). The French equivalent of *courageous, courageux,* appears in the French version, so the French teacher helped students to identify the noun *courage* as its base and to generate similarly constructed adjectives (e.g. *paresseux* from *paresse*) or nouns (e.g. *mystère* from *mystèrieux*).

To conclude this section, we return to Cummins's linguistic interdependence model (Figure 9.1) to suggest that overall knowledge of word formation (i.e., affixes attach to bases) can be considered as part of an emergent bilingual's common underlying proficiency, whereas knowledge about which affixes are associated with each language and how they attach to their bases may be considered as knowledge of surface features belonging to one language but not the other. For this reason, it was important in the Tomi Ungerer Project to target not only affixes that were similar across languages but also affixes that were different. So, for example, suffixes such as *-ful* in English, which turns nouns into adjectives (e.g., *help* > *helpful, faith* > *faithful*), and *-ment* in French, which turns verbs into nouns (e.g., *hurler* > *un hurlement, dèguiser* > *un dèguisement*), were also focused on to avoid the impression that suffixation might be identical across French and English.

TEACHER SPOTLIGHT

Karin Ménard and Audrey Paquette, two partner teachers from Cedar Street Elementary School in Beloeil, Quebec, co-designed and implemented a biliteracy task related to the theme of adaptation in *Crictor*. They identified adaptation as a key theme because Mme. Bodot helped Crictor to adapt to his new home and, at the same time, Crictor was adapting to his new community by being very helpful. So, the teachers presented students with information about four other animals (giraffes, octopuses, porcupines, and bats) to pique their interest in imagining having one as a pet. After orally brainstorming various scenarios, students in the English class each created an annotated illustration depicting what they would do to help their pet adapt to its new home. Meanwhile, in the French class, they made an annotated illustration of how the same pet would adapt to its new community by being helpful. The final product was a bilingual class book portraying each student's contribution in French and English on facing pages.

Results: "Oh look! A little word inside a big word!"

The Tomi Ungerer Project included a pretest-posttest design comparing an experimental group receiving the biliteracy instruction with a comparison group not receiving the instruction. On the posttest measures of morphological awareness in French, the experimental group significantly outperformed the comparison group. In addition, participating teachers' perceptions were positive and enthusiastic. They were impressed by their students' positive reactions to the biliteracy instruction, observing that students enjoyed making connections between the two languages. As in the Magic Tree House Project, there was no evidence that use of the same storybook in both languages bored the children or created confusion. As one teacher stated, "The kids responded well to the lessons, and they saw that they were intertwined, and they liked the reading of the English book and the French book." With respect to the focus on derivational morphology, another teacher summed up her experience as follows: "They started seeing it when we were doing other activities. They would say, 'Oh look! A little word inside a big word.' So, I thought, it's really sinking in."

An especially positive result of the project, as reported by their teachers and captured on video, was the enthusiasm exhibited by the children during the instructional interventions. In the same vein, Bowers et al. (2010) reported that several of the authors of the studies included in their meta-analysis "commented on the enthusiasm children showed during morphological instruction" (p. 171). They suggested that "increased motivation and literacy skills may mutually support each other." Arguably, the enthusiasm of the young children in the Tomi Ungerer Project, as they adopted a detective-like approach to morphological derivation, contributed to their significant improvement. This fits well with Lambert and Tucker's (1972) seminal research on French immersion programs, in which they found very young students to have a "children's version of contrastive linguistics" and a linguistic "detective" capacity: "an attentive, patient, inductive concern with words, meanings, and linguistic regularities" (p. 208).

Bilingual read–aloud projects can also be combined with the CAPA (contextualization, awareness, practice, and autonomy) model (see Chapter 4) to emphasize form-focused instruction in both program languages, as illustrated in the Teacher Spotlight below.

 TEACHER SPOTLIGHT

Inspired by Lyster et al.'s (2013) bilingual read-aloud project with the Tomi Ungerer books, a team of three Grade 3 TWI teachers from Alturas Elementary School in Hailey, Idaho developed a bilingual read-aloud project. They combined it with the CAPA model in a unit on storytelling to draw students' attention to the creation of adverbs with the suffix *-ly* in English and *-mente* in Spanish. Rosalyn León, María Piña, and Gretchen Weber worked together on the project, the latter two being partner teachers. They focused on the story *Crictor* and modified the text somewhat to ensure that enough adverbs were included. They decided to focus on adverbs because students had difficulty recognizing and forming words to modify verbs and also struggled with placement of adverbs. The form was a good choice, given their focus in this unit on having students develop more description in their writing and storytelling.

During the *Contextualization* phase, Gretchen read *Crictor* in English up to the part where Mme. Bodot takes Crictor to her classroom at the school. Her students predicted what would come next. María had students summarize what they had already read in Spanish and share their predictions; then, she finished the story and engaged students in a discussion about it. The emphasis in this phase was on the meaning of the story.

For the noticing task in the *Awareness* phase, each teacher displayed different excerpts of the text on the SmartBoard in their respective languages and highlighted the adverbs in yellow, with the suffixes appearing in red font. For an awareness activity, during Spanish time, students were given cards with adjectives from the story and cards with the suffix *-mente*. They had to match the words with suffix cards. They compared their newly formed words with the highlighted words in the text and then sorted the cards based on spelling patterns they noticed (*rápido* ⇒ *rápidamente*). Together with the teacher, they co-constructed spelling rules for adding the suffix. During English time, Gretchen had created a SmartBoard activity focused on spelling changes when adding *-ly* to adjectives (e.g., *happy* ⇒ *happily*). In both classes, they discussed adverb placement and the role that adverbs play in text.

For the *Practice* phase, in English time, students played a dice game in small groups. Each were given two dice; one die had adjectives on each surface and the other verbs (all from the story). Students took turns rolling their dice, and they had to change the adjectives to adverbs to describe the verb. They could earn a point by simply changing the word to an adverb correctly, another two if they could use the adverb with the verb in a complete sentence related to the story, and three more if they could write the sentence correctly. Students kept track of points and could "steal" points if they caught another student saying, spelling, or placing the adverb incorrectly. During Spanish time, students played a partner game. Pairs were given picture cards with pictures from the story and a word bank of words that could be changed to adverbs. Partner A served as the judge. Partner B chose a picture card and a word card and then described the picture using a complete sentence with an adverb to earn a token. Partner B then had to write the sentence on an erasable sentence strip, and if the adverb was spelled and placed correctly he or she earned another five tokens. Partner A judged the sentence for accuracy, and then they switched roles.

Finally, for the *Autonomy* phase, during Spanish time, students engaged in oral storytelling. They had to choose a different, unusual animal to send to Mme. Bodot and then, with six note cards, they had to illustrate their story featuring how the animal helped others. They were instructed to include adverbs in their stories. They then practiced telling their stories orally to partners, using their pictures for support, and finally shared their stories orally with children in a kindergarten class. During English time, students wrote *Crictor* stories with different endings (using adverbs). They compiled their stories into a book to share with the other Grade 3 classes.

Finally, bilingual read-aloud projects can be used to foster cross-cultural connections and for students to develop insight into the cultural and linguistic nuances that emerge when the same story is read in different languages. This is exemplified in the Teacher Spotlight below.

 TEACHER SPOTLIGHT

Viviana Fontela and Paul Skipper, two partner teachers at Washington International School in Washington, DC, undertook a bilingual read-aloud with their Grade 5 Spanish immersion students. They read *Cajas de cartón* by Francisco Jiménez and its English version, *The Circuit*, reading a chapter in Spanish in the Spanish class followed by the next chapter in English in the

English class, and so on. The primary goal was to instill in students the pleasure of being read to aloud in alternate languages, but without having them engage specifically in related biliteracy tasks. A subsequent debriefing with the students about their experience revealed their enthusiasm for hearing the story in two languages and also their cultural insights into the differences between the Spanish and English versions:

S1:   It just has a better feel in Spanish, kind of like, I don't know what it is, but it's better to read it in Spanish.

S2:   I feel that in Spanish it might be more interesting, but hearing it in both languages you might benefit more and you made connections.

S3:   I like how we read it in Spanish and English because I liked hearing Signora Fontela having, like, emotions in the book and also how Mr. Skipper can't pronounce some words in Spanish. In Spanish, you can really feel the emotions but in English it's a little bit calmer.

These Grade 5 students' comments show that alternating between program languages to read a chapter book can be a powerful way of achieving cross-cultural objectives, as it enabled students to reflect on the impact that the different versions had on their feelings and perceptions (e.g., Spanish evoked more emotions while English seemed a bit calmer!). We speculate that hearing English L1 students express preferences for Spanish over English might be every Spanish teacher's dream come true!

Summary

In this chapter, we have defined biliteracy and offered a discussion of ways in which ImDL instruction can proceed from a biliteracy stance. We have described the bilingual read-aloud projects as an approach to establishing cross-lingual comparisons while maintaining separate spaces for instructional languages. In the final chapter that follows, we turn our attention to performance assessment.

Application activity: Developing a bilingual read-aloud project

Work with your partner teacher or with your grade-level team (if you're responsible for literacy instruction in both languages) to develop a bilingual read-aloud project. With careful review of the text in both languages, consider which linguistic feature(s) could be emphasized, and plan instructional activities collaboratively to occur in each of the languages. During and after implementing the project, reflect on the process.

Online resources for readers

Online access to texts in multiple languages

World stories

www.kidsout.org.uk/world-stories-introduction/introduction

World Stories is a growing collection of traditional and new stories representing the 21 languages most commonly spoken by children across the UK. These stories can be read, listened to, and downloaded in English and their original language.

This website is designed for easy use in the classroom, both in whole-class settings and to support guided reading. The Teachers' Area is packed with individual story guides, lesson plans, resources, and a search index for teachers. You will need to register to access this free support.

International Children's Digital Library

http://en.childrenslibrary.org/

This site provides books online in a variety of languages and many multicultural titles in English.

Storybook Canada

www.storybookscanada.ca

This site provides access to text and audio versions of 40 stories ideal for beginning readers in many languages, including English, French, Spanish, Mandarin, Arabic, Portuguese, Italian, Bengali, Cantonese, Punjabi, and more.

Teaching Heart

www.teachingheart.net/readerstheater.htm

This site provides readers with theater scripts and plays—free printables, lessons, and themes for K–3 classrooms (in English).

For Mandarin programs

www.tom61.com/huibengushi/

This online resource has many books, movies, songs, comics, textbooks, nursery rhymes, and so on that could be used in Mandarin ImDL programs:

10
PERFORMANCE ASSESSMENT

In this chapter, we turn our attention to assessment. The chapter addresses both student performance assessment—that is, ways in which immersion and dual language (ImDL) teachers can assess students' content learning and language use and development with performance tasks—and teacher performance assessment. The following questions are discussed:

- What is assessment, and why should teachers assess student performance?
- What is the difference between program-level and classroom-level assessment?
- What is the difference between formative and summative assessment?
- What are checklists and rubrics?
- What is performance assessment?
- What is the Integrated Performance Assessment, and how can it be modified for ImDL classrooms?
- How can teachers engage in the process of self-assessment of their teaching performance?

Student performance assessment

What is assessment?

Assessment involves collecting, describing, recording, grading, and interpreting information about a student's learning. It captures an episode in the learning process and, as such, forms a part of the teacher's understanding of a student's progress. Assessment allows teachers to detect gaps between *intended* learning outcomes (what the teacher planned for students to learn) and *actual* learning outcomes (what students demonstrate that they have learned).

There are different contexts and purposes for assessment. We distinguish between program-level and classroom-level assessment and emphasize the latter in this chapter. As explained in Chapter 2, well-implemented ImDL programs administer program-level academic achievement tests in both program languages. In Canada, how students' achievement is assessed varies from province to province, but some testing in French is not uncommon. Unfortunately, in the US, academic achievement is typically only measured on the basis of standardized tests given in English. Often, standardized measures are not available in languages other than English in the US, although some standardized measures are available in Spanish (see *Resources for Readers* at the end of the chapter).

As discussed in Chapter 2, well-implemented programs also assess students' minority-language development. When it comes to assessment of the minority language, program-level assessment is concerned with language *proficiency* assessment, whereas classroom-level assessment emphasizes language *performance* assessment vis-à-vis demonstration of content learning. Proficiency reflects a learner's ability to use language in spontaneous (non-rehearsed) situations. "Proficiency demonstrates what a language user is able to do regardless of where, when or how the language was acquired" (ACTFL, 2012b, p. 4). Thus, the content of a proficiency assessment may not be linked to the curriculum that was taught. In contrast, classroom-level performance assessment is closely aligned with the content of the curriculum, as it reflects the ability to use language in relation to the content that has been learned and practiced in a classroom context (ACTFL, 2012b).

Classroom-level assessment

Classroom-level assessment encompasses all the forms of assessment that a teacher uses to determine whether students have achieved the intended learning outcomes. There are two broad categories of assessment: formative and summative.

Formative and summative assessment

Formative assessments are assessments *for* learning. They indicate whether and how well a particular lesson's objective(s) have been met. Formative assessments can take on many forms and are used continuously throughout a class period. **Summative assessments** are assessments *of* learning. They indicate whether and how well the student has achieved the multiple goals of an instructional unit or course goals at the end of a grading period. Table 10.1 summarizes the characteristics of formative and summative assessment.

Formative assessment should always align with the learning objectives identified for a particular lesson. As a result, formative assessment is often built into classroom instructional activities. For example, if students are working on an experiment in small groups, their ability to explain the process and the outcomes of the experiment to the class serves as an assessment of their learning. Formative assessments also include standard classroom practices used to quickly check whether students understand an explanation, an example, or instructions. The use of red, yellow, and green cards is an example. Students have a red, a

TABLE 10.1 Characteristics of formative and summative assessment

Formative assessment	Summative assessment
• assessment *for* learning	• assessment *of* learning
• informal, not typically graded	• formal, graded
• ongoing (i.e., during every lesson)	• intermittent (i.e., at end of unit)
• gauges understanding during instructional time	• determines extent of learning after instruction
• teacher is coach, whose role is to help and provide feedback	• teacher is judge, whose role is to evaluate with feedback
• purpose is to gather information, to see if learning is on track	• purpose is to make judgments based on quality of performance
• focus is on practice	• focus is on final product/performance
• reflection is key	• rigor is key
• checklists are commonly used	• rubrics are commonly used

yellow, and a green card on their desks. Green means *go* to indicate that the student understands the explanation. Yellow means *caution* to signify that the student needs more practice and/or further explanation. Red means *stop* to show that the student doesn't understand the explanation. Students can select the card that describes their current understanding at any point during the lesson, without waiting for the teacher to ask. Visual representations, such as graphic organizers, can be used to demonstrate an understanding of a concept, a story, or the relationship between two or more items. Formative assessments can also take the form of summary learning checks at the end of a lesson to verify that the objectives have been met. One example is called *3, 2, 1*: students write down three things they learned, two things they found interesting, and one question they still have. Another summary learning check is *ticket to exit*: students respond to a question or give an example of something they learned on a "ticket" (index card or small piece of paper). They turn in their ticket as they leave class—for recess or lunch, or at the end of the day.

Checklists may be used for formative assessment. They indicate whether a student can or can't do something. They can be used to record observed performance or to keep track of progress over time. For example, a simple checklist can be used to track early learners' decoding skills:

Decoding Skills	Yes	No
Has basic sight vocabulary		
Can match letters with sounds		
Distinguishes beginning, middle, and ending sounds in words		
Can segment one-syllable words into individual phonemes		
Recognizes new words by sounding them out and/or using context clues		

Checklists can also be used for self- and peer-assessment. They are relatively easy to construct and use. They align closely with instructional activities, and they aid in making students aware of task requirements.

Summative assessments involve assessing students' achievement of many unit-level goals and lesson-level objectives at the end of a unit or course of study. It is not possible to assess every learning objective that is included in the unit, so teachers have to make decisions about which objectives should inform the design of summative assessments. Like formative assessments, summative assessments can take many forms, such as traditional paper and pencil (or computer-based) tests; final projects; essays, letters, papers, or reports; multi-media presentations; and other types of performance assessment. These assessments *of* learning evaluate a student's work by comparing his or her achievement against a specific benchmark, standard, or criterion reflected in a rubric. As mentioned in Chapter 7, traditional assessments continue to play a role in ImDL classrooms, but they tend to emphasize content learning exclusively and focus on recall of facts. ImDL classrooms assessments should offer assessment of both content learnings *and* students' ability to use language to engage with content. For this reason, we emphasize performance assessment in this chapter.

Performance assessment

Traditional tests get at the question "Do you know it?", whereas performance assessment gets at "How well can you use what you know?" (Hibbard et al., 1996, para. 3). Performance assessments involve tasks or activities that ask students to create or construct answers. They emphasize application of knowledge and skills by engaging students in real-world tasks that are worthwhile and form part of the curriculum.

Performance assessments have several advantages and limitations (Oosterhof, 2009). They (a) allow assessment of skills that cannot be evaluated with traditional forms of assessment, (b) tend to have a positive impact on classroom instruction (in other words, instruction tends to incorporate more activities that are performance based to ensure that students will succeed in the assessments), and (c) can be used to assess process as well as product. A major limitation of performance assessments is that they require a great deal of time to develop and administer. In addition, it can be difficult to grade students' performance assessments in a consistent manner; however, this limitation can be remedied if a detailed rubric and a careful scoring plan are developed.

Rubrics are typically used to assess student performance. Whereas a checklist merely provides an indication of whether a specific criterion or behavior is present, a rubric provides a measure of quality of performance based on established criteria. There are two major types of rubrics: holistic and analytic.

Holistic rubrics assess a student's performance as a whole; one integrated score is assigned to a performance. For example, a holistic rubric for assessing writing might include reference to content, organization, cohesion, clarity, sentence structure, vocabulary, grammar, and mechanics. Both the American Council on the Teaching of Foreign Languages (ACTFL) Guidelines and the Common European Framework of Reference for Languages (CEFR) (briefly described in Chapter 2) are examples of holistic rubrics. Holistic rubrics are primarily used for large-scale assessment when a relatively quick yet consistent approach to scoring is necessary. These rubrics tend to be less useful for classroom purposes because they provide little information to students about their performance.

Analytic rubrics are divided into separate categories representing different aspects or dimensions of performance. Each dimension is scored separately, and scores for each are added to determine an overall score. This configuration allows the teacher to weigh certain aspects more heavily than others (for example, content may be considered more important than mechanics). These rubrics have the advantage of providing more information to students about the strengths and weaknesses of various aspects of their performance. The rubrics included in Appendix C are examples of analytic rubrics.

🔑 KEY CONCEPTS

Rubrics measure quality of performance based on clear criteria.

- Holistic rubrics assign one score based on an assessment of the "whole" of a performance.
- Analytic rubrics divide aspects of performance into categories, each of which is scored separately.

When assessing students' performances, teachers must take care to use the rubric consistently across assessments. This can be difficult, because the use of rubrics inevitably involves subjective judgments. The more practice teachers have in using rubrics, the more comfortable they will become and the more reliable (consistent) their scoring will be.

Teachers need to share and discuss the rubric with students before they engage in the performance assessment. Whenever possible, teachers should present exemplars of performance that correspond to the different levels of the rubric. Doing so will enable students to observe what good performance looks like. Thus, we recommend that teachers keep copies of exemplars that they can use with subsequent classes.

Why assess at the classroom level?

Classroom-level assessment allows teachers to determine whether (a) instruction was effective or if a different approach is required, (b) students need more instruction, and (c) students are ready for the content of the next lesson. It is necessary for providing formative and summative feedback to learners. Learners need to know what is expected of them and what they can do to improve their performance or grade.

What is the Integrated Performance Assessment?

The Integrated Performance Assessment (IPA) was originally developed for a non-immersion foreign-language teaching context. It provides teachers with a summative assessment framework for assessing students' language performance in relation to the three communicative modes that comprise ACTFL's communication standards: interpretive mode, interpersonal mode, and presentational mode (Adair-Hauck et al., 2013). Table 10.2 summarizes the characteristics of each mode.

To implement the IPA, teachers need to design three inter-related performance assessment phases based on a central theme, with each phase corresponding to one of the three modes. IPA tasks build upon each other such that the information and interaction that occur for one task are needed to complete the next task. Teachers can use the IPA as an end-of-unit, end-of-term, or end-of-year summative assessment.

Students complete all three tasks in the language they're learning. For example, within the theme of food and nutrition, for the interpretive task, high-school students might read about and study excerpts from a website summarizing the government's nutritional recommendations. Afterwards,

TABLE 10.2 Characteristics of communicative modes

Communicative modes
Interpretive mode: • interpretation of meaning • reading and listening (viewing) • "one-way": no opportunity to interact with the writer or speaker
Interpersonal mode: • spontaneous interaction • oral and written (e.g., instant messaging) • "two-way": includes opportunity to clarify meaning and seek clarification
Presentational mode: • creation of messages for an audience • speaking and writing • "one-way": no opportunity to interact with intended audience

they would complete what Adair-Hauck et al. (2013) call a "comprehension guide," or set of activities designed to assess their comprehension (often given in English for this foreign-language teaching context). Then, for the interpersonal task, students might be asked to interact with a partner to compare their individual food diaries in the context of what they learned about the daily dietary guidelines. The teacher would then use a rubric to assess their ability to interact with a peer. Finally, for the presentational task, students might create informational posters summarizing the government's nutritional guidelines and share them with students in a younger grade, and again the teacher would use a rubric to assess their performance.

A key component of the IPA is the "feedback loop," which represents the provision of continuous feedback to learners throughout the assessment process. Adair-Hauck et al. (2013) advocate for a constructivist approach to feedback whereby students and the teacher engage in dialogic interaction to *co-construct* assessment. Feedback co-construction on students' interpretive task performance occurs before they begin the interpersonal task. After completing the interpersonal task, students again engage with the teacher around feedback on their performance before continuing on to complete the cycle with the presentational task. The presentational task provides more opportunities for co-constructed feedback as students are engaged in preparing for the task (via drafts on which students receive feedback from the teacher and possibly peers) and after they complete the task. As teachers include the modeling, practice, and feedback loop of the process, learners are developing important skills *through* the IPA, and they use those skills to perform better on the next IPA. In these ways, the IPA represents a cyclical approach (B. Adair-Hauck, personal communication, May 2019). Figure 10.1 depicts the cyclical nature of the IPA and feedback loop.

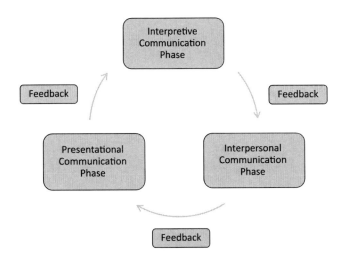

FIGURE 10.1 Cyclical nature of IPA and feedback loop

According to Adair-Hauck et al. (2013), the IPA:

- is an integrated assessment of the three communicative modes around a central theme;
- exemplifies performance-based assessment with meaningful, motivating, age-appropriate tasks that are linked to instruction;
- represents authentic assessment, as it reflects real-world tasks;
- is developmental in nature, with four levels ranging from novice to advanced; and
- includes modeling of student performance and the provision of co-constructed feedback that encourages learners to self-reflect and self-assess.

The IPA was originally designed as an assessment of *language* performance; the content theme simply serves to contextualize the three integrated tasks. It is a powerful performance-based approach to assessment, and we believe it holds tremendous potential for ImDL classrooms provided that modifications are made to align with the subject-matter content focus of ImDL settings.

Modifying the IPA for ImDL classrooms

In ImDL classrooms, the IPA needs to serve not only as a language assessment but also as a content assessment. Thus, it must be modified so that it functions as an assessment of subject-matter content learning and students' ability to use the minority language to demonstrate their content learnings. Subject-matter content underlies all the assessment tasks, which take place in a linear fashion, with feedback on the final task bringing an end to the assessment process. Figure 10.2 shows the critical role of content, which underlies all the assessment tasks. In the IPA example provided in Appendix C, the theme is *Animal Adaptations*.

In the ImDL classroom, the IPA is best used as an end-of-unit summative assessment, and as such fits well into the Autonomy phase of the CAPA (contextualization, awareness, practice, and autonomy) model. The IPA can be used annually, which has been instituted by some school districts. For example, the Minnetonka Public Schools in Minnesota have six K–5 dual-track one-way ImDL programs: four in Spanish and two in Mandarin Chinese. They administer an IPA annually in Grades 1–5 toward the end of the school year (K. Rue, personal communication, May, 2019). The IPAs are linked to curricular units. For example, Grade 2 Spanish immersion students do an IPA that is integrated into a reading unit on biography.

 TEACHER SPOTLIGHT

In Chapters 7 and 8 we introduced the unit on *Adaptations* to exemplify the components of the unit-level and lesson-level instructional design templates. Three members of the team of teachers that developed the unit were primarily responsible for creating the IPA that served as the summative performance assessment: Megon Coon, Kirsten Rue, and Amanda Zwiefelhofer. We present a modified version of their IPA in Appendix C.

The IPA begins with the interpretive task, because it provides students with the content knowledge that will be necessary to perform the subsequent tasks. As for the sequencing of subsequent tasks, ImDL teachers have a choice to make, based on their students' proficiency levels and their vision for the IPA. In non-immersion contexts, Adair-Hauck et al. (2013) recommend that the interpersonal task occur next. However, because authentic interpersonal communication requires spontaneous, unrehearsed face-to-face interaction, it can be difficult to achieve, particularly with learners having lower proficiency levels (Brown & Yule, 1983). In such cases, students can complete the presentational task after the interpretive task so that they have more content knowledge to draw on and will have practiced some of the grammatical structures and vocabulary they need to carry out

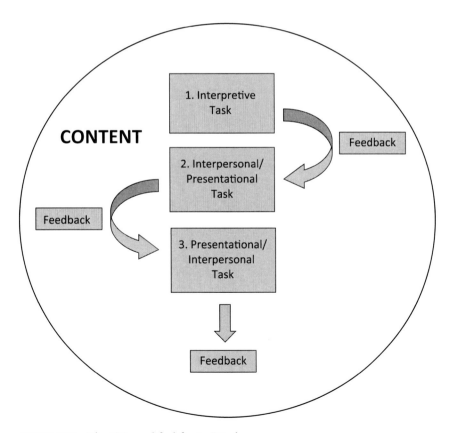

FIGURE 10.2   The IPA modified for ImDL classrooms

ImDL IPA Design Template	
Theme:	**Time Frame:**

IPA Overview	
Interpretive Task	Text (citation and description) Time frame Comprehension Guide Interpretive Rubric Feedback Loop Description Task Logistics
Task 3: Interpersonal/ Presentational	Task description Time frame Rubric Feedback Loop Description Task Logistics
Task 3: Presentational/ Interpersonal	Task description Time frame Rubric Feedback Loop Description Task Logistics
Materials	

FIGURE 10.3   ImDL IPA Design Template

the interpersonal task. Figure 10.2 illustrates the flexible nature of interpersonal and presentational task sequencing. As also depicted in Figure 10.2, the feedback loop remains a critical component of IPAs that are designed for ImDL classrooms. However, the extent to which a constructivist approach to feedback is feasible will depend upon the cognitive and proficiency level of learners.

Designing the IPA for ImDL classrooms

The IPA includes several components: a general introduction to the tasks, each of the three inter-related tasks, and the feedback loop, which includes rubrics for assessing student performance. All IPA tasks in the ImDL classroom take place in the minority language. The example in Appendix C is presented in English, but in an actual classroom, all parts of the IPA would occur in the minority language, which in this case is Spanish. Figure 10.3 presents a template for designing an IPA for the ImDL classroom. Each of the components that appear in the template is described thereafter.

IPA overview

The IPA and the template begin with a general introduction to and overview of the context and series of assessment tasks. This overview should illustrate how the three tasks are inter-related and should be written in a way that motivates learners and gets them excited about completing the tasks. In the sample provided in Appendix C, students are told that they'll have an opportunity to invent an imaginary animal based on a "mystery biome" they will be given. Each of the three inter-related tasks is described briefly to give students a clear idea of what the assessment entails. Whenever possible, students should be shown exemplars of final products that have been developed by previous students.

Interpretive task

The next part of the template focuses on interpretive communication, which involves having students either read a written text or listen to a spoken text (video, song, or podcast). The text selected should not be a text that students have already had exposure to during the unit. It may be authentic, adapted by the teacher, or created by the teacher, provided that it is content and language rich and grammatically accurate. It should be new to students but closely aligned with the content of the unit. It should be at a level that students can handle, although it should also contain some unfamiliar vocabulary. All students typically read the same text. However, it is possible to include more than one; if more than one are used they should be very similar—the same discourse type, same level of difficulty, and so on. Teachers should keep in mind that different texts will require the creation of different comprehension guides as well. In the example provided in Appendix C, the teachers chose to assign half the class one text (*Estar frescos—Keeping cool*) and the other half another text (*En el frío—In the cold*). These are two chapters from the same book, so they are constructed in much the same way, are at the same level of difficulty, and include similar visual support (pictures and drawings). The teachers elected to assign two different texts because of the way they set up the interpersonal task (described below).

Once the text is selected, teachers design the comprehension guide(s). Depending upon the proficiency level of learners, comprehension guides may only include questions that tap into literal comprehension, or they may include questions that go beyond literal comprehension and involve interpretation; that is, reading between the lines, offering personal opinions, and so on. Adair-Hauck et al. (2013) offer a template for creating comprehension guides. A completed example is provided in Appendix C. One can see that literal comprehension items involve word recognition as well as the ability to detect main ideas and supporting details. Adair-Hauck et al. suggest the following for items corresponding to interpretive comprehension: identifying the organizational features of the text, guessing meaning from context, inferring, identifying the author's perspective, comparing cultural perspectives, and reacting personally to the text. Teachers may choose among those types of items or include others that they have found to successfully capture interpretive levels of comprehension.

Drawing upon the model provided by Adair-Hauck et al. (2013), teachers create the rubric that will be used to assess students' comprehension guides. Criteria align closely with the types of items that comprise the comprehension guide; for example, word recognition, main idea detection, and guessing meaning from context. Four levels are recommended, ranging from "Exceeds Expectations" (accomplished comprehension) to "Does Not Meet Expectations" (limited comprehension). Nevertheless, teachers may simplify the rubric and include just three levels if they so choose. Once a rubric is developed it can be modified for different texts.

Finally, teachers need to think through the task logistics and plan for the feedback loop. For example, if the text used is a video, teachers must decide how many times the students will be able to view the video prior to completing the comprehension guide. If it is a written text, teachers need to determine whether students can refer to the text while completing the guide. Teachers also must decide how much time students will be given to read the text and complete the guide. If more than one text is to be used, teachers need to decide which students will be assigned each text. Teachers should also consider how the feedback loop will occur. Students should get written feedback on their work but also have an opportunity to connect individually or in small groups with the teacher to discuss their performance. They might be asked to engage in self-assessment using the rubric as well. In the example described in Appendix C, the teacher meets with small groups (based on similar performance on the task) to give oral feedback and dialogue with students about their performance. Teachers also need to decide what the other students will be doing while they meet with small groups.

For example, they might have theme-related texts for students to read (which could later be used as resources for the presentational task).

Determining the sequence of subsequent tasks

The template provides space for the development of interpersonal and presentational tasks, but, as briefly explained above, the sequencing of the two needs to be determined by the teacher as the IPA is developed. The sequence of these subsequent two tasks will be determined based on students' proficiency levels and teachers' overall conceptualization for the IPA. It's also possible for the two tasks to overlap somewhat. Students could begin their work on the presentational task and then be called aside to engage in the interpersonal task. For example, let's imagine that high-school students have completed a unit on climate change in science class. After reading about specific impacts that climate change has had in their state or province (interpretive task), for the presentational task, they are asked to write persuasive letters to politicians regarding impending legislation on climate change. Students begin developing drafts of their letters, and the following day, students could be asked to interact with a partner about their letters to give and receive feedback on accuracy of content, persuasive language, and other aspects. These interactions could serve as the interpersonal task, because they require spontaneous, face-to-face communication.

Interpersonal task

As previously explained, interpersonal communication involves spontaneous interaction that gives interlocutors the opportunity to clarify meaning and seek clarification. We find that tasks that elicit this type of language can be challenging to develop. We recommend, therefore, that interpersonal tasks involve some type of problem-solving activity, such as joint completion of a graphic organizer. Each student should come to the interaction with information that the other student doesn't have in order to create a natural information gap and thus the need for communication. Teachers should set up the task in such a way as to require approximately the same amount of language production from each student. In the example shown in Appendix C, students are paired with partners who read the opposite text during the interpretive task. That is, if Student A read "*Keeping cool*," he or she is partnered with Student B, who read "*In the cold*." Together they fill out a comparison/contrast chart. Student A completes the portion corresponding to the text he or she did not read. Student A then must ask Student B questions and write the answers in the chart. Student B does the same, focusing on learning about Student A's text.

In designing interpersonal tasks, teachers need to consider a number of task logistics. For example, how will students be paired? Teachers should take into account proficiency level. We recommend that, in general, students will benefit from being assigned a partner with a similar proficiency level. Personalities should also be considered. It's important that neither student dominate the conversation (see discussion about peer collaboration in Chapter 8). For the example displayed in Appendix C, the teachers carefully considered how students would be paired for the interpersonal task before assigning students the texts for the interpretive task. Also important is thinking through how and where the interactions can take place to maximize student language production and minimize distractions and extraneous noise. Most ImDL teachers who have developed IPAs have enlisted the help of classroom assistants or parent volunteers who can accompany assigned pairs of students to a quiet place in the media center to record their interactions. Clearly, it is not possible for teachers to observe and assess multiple pairs at once. Therefore, recording the interactions is an effective alternative. Many classrooms are equipped with iPads or other devices to facilitate recording. Teachers can then assess the interactions that evening. Again, teachers need to decide what the class will be working on while pairs of students leave the room to record their interpersonal interactions. In our example, students have already begun their work on the presentational tasks before they are called out in pairs to complete the interpersonal task.

Using templates provided by Adair-Hauck et al. (2013), teachers design the rubric to be used for assessing the interpersonal task. Adair-Hauck et al. include five criteria in the interpersonal rubrics:

- *language function*: language tasks the speaker is able to handle in a consistent, comfortable, sustained, and spontaneous manner;
- *text type*: the quantity and organization of language (word—phrase—sentence—connected sentences—paragraph—extended discourse);
- *communication strategies*: quality of engagement and interactivity (how one participates in the interaction and advances it); strategies for negotiating meaning;
- *comprehensibility*: how well the speaker can be understood;
- *language control*: grammatical accuracy, appropriate vocabulary, and degree of fluency.

For the ImDL context, criteria related to content understandings must be added. The teachers who created the IPA showcased in Appendix C added the criterion "content knowledge" (accuracy and thoroughness of content shared) to their interpersonal rubric.

Finally, teachers must think through how the feedback loop will occur. Student pairs should receive written feedback based on the rubric, but teachers also need to meet with pairs and engage them in a conversation about their performance. In our example showcased in Appendix C, these conversations take place while the class continues to work on the presentational task.

Presentational task

The presentational task involves speaking or writing to a specific audience; for example, preparing for and giving an oral presentation or writing a report.

Sometimes the tasks include both speaking and writing; for instance, preparing a written poster and then presenting it at a science fair in the school. Whenever possible, the intended audience should include someone other than the teacher. Real audiences tend to motivate learners to do their best work. In the example shown in Appendix C, the same pairs of students are assigned a "mystery biome" and are tasked with creating an imaginary animal that adapts to thrive in that biome. They prepare in writing a presentation that they will deliver orally via VoiceThread, a web-based (cloud) application that allows users to create and share dynamic conversations around a document, image, photograph, diagram, or audio or video file. These are then shared with their pen pals in Ecuador, and students there must guess the biome based on the animal's adaptations and respond orally via the VoiceThread. Students must share the workload equitably (the more structured the task is to support collaboration, the better).

Students typically have several class sessions to work on their presentational tasks, and teachers often provide some feedback along the way. In designing these tasks, teachers need to consider task logistics: how much time students will have to prepare their work, how long oral presentations will need to be, whether there will be opportunities for peer or teacher feedback during the preparation of the task, and so on. The rubric to be used to assess performance can be based on the Adair-Hauck et al. (2013) models, provided that additional criteria related to content knowledge are added. Adair-Hauck et al. recommend the same rubric criteria for presentational tasks that are stipulated for interpersonal tasks, with one exception. Instead of "communication strategies" (which correspond to interpersonal communication), they include a criterion called "impact," which refers to the clarity, organization, and depth of the presentation as well as the degree to which the presenters maintain the attention and interest of the audience.

Once again, as teachers plan the presentational task they must consider how the feedback loop will take place. Students should receive both written feedback as well as oral feedback. They may also be asked to assess their own work using the rubric or a simpler version of the rubric. What's important is ensuring that students have a clear understanding of what they did well and how they might improve their performance on similar tasks in the future.

Materials

The materials section of the template provides space for teachers to list all the materials they will need for all three tasks.

Additional considerations for ImDL IPA design

Teachers need to design IPA tasks in a way that reflects the types of tasks students do in the classroom. Students' interpersonal communication should not be assessed if they are not accustomed to interacting in pairs or small groups on a regular basis.

In developing rubrics for assessing student performance on the tasks, ImDL teachers find it helpful to draw upon rubrics already designed by Adair-Hauck et al. (2013). The generic descriptions of performance allow the rubric to be used for many different tasks. At the same time, it is advisable to include some modifications for ImDL classrooms that are specifically related to the content of the IPA (as seen in the example displayed in Appendix C). ImDL teachers that we have worked with have found it helpful to identify a checklist of "non-negotiables" (D. Clementi, personal communication, October, 2002) along with their rubrics. Non-negotiables spell out specific expectations for completing the tasks that must be met by students but are not included in the quality descriptors of the rubric itself. For example, non-negotiables for the interpersonal task in our example include:

- asking questions to elicit information;
- responding to partner's questions without sharing the text;
- interacting for at least five minutes and no more than 15;
- completing assigned portion of the graphic organizer.

The teacher must review these with students ahead of time so that expectations are clear.

It may be difficult to design an IPA for very young learners with low levels of proficiency, although some teachers have been successful in doing so. For example, Dawn Breutzman developed an IPA for kindergarten Japanese L1 students who were learning through English L2 in a small private school. The IPA was designed as a summative assessment at the culmination of a unit having the theme "I am special. You are special." Dawn had students use pictures to show their comprehension of a book read aloud. Students drew pictures rather than writing words for the interpersonal and presentational tasks. They were expected to use English with each other during the interpersonal task and during a basic oral presentation for the culminating task. Very basic rubrics were used to provide students with oral feedback. Dawn's complete IPA is provided at the Center for Advanced Research on Language Acquisition (CARLA) website (CoBaLTT Project) (see *Resources for Readers* below for link).

Finally, given its comprehensive nature, the IPA is an approach to assessment that takes time to develop and implement. Making the effort to assess students' ability to *use* language across the spectrum of communicative modes—interpretive, interpersonal, and presentation—to express their content learning is important. Doing so communicates to students that they are in ImDL programs not only to learn content but also to acquire language. Moreover, knowing that their interpersonal communication skills will be assessed may have the added benefit of helping students to realize the importance of staying in the minority language when working in pairs or small groups. They will need to practice such skills if they are to be successful on the assessments. Likewise, implementing an IPA at least once per year may also produce that positive washback effect, leading ImDL teachers to ensure that their students are engaged on a regular basis in activities that hone their interpretive, interpersonal, and presentational skills. Kirsten Rue, one of the teachers who developed the IPA showcased in Appendix C, summed up her experience by stating that "the authenticity of a performance assessment like the IPA where students are able to demonstrate their ability to communicate for real purposes makes the time and effort worthwhile."

Teacher performance assessment

Having discussed student performance assessment, we now turn our attention to teacher performance assessment. In doing so, we will introduce a self-assessment rubric that ImDL teachers can use to assess their ability to put into practice the pedagogical strategies emphasized in this book.

Teacher quality matters. It has regularly been identified as the single most important school-based factor in student achievement (e.g., Rivkin, Hanushek, & Kain, 2005; Rowan, Correnti, & Miller, 2002). Across the US, Canada, and other countries there is an ongoing search for better ways to develop and assess teacher effectiveness. Performance-based measures are being designed and instituted at both preservice and in-service levels. They indicate what a teacher should know and be able to do in real classrooms. The purpose of such measures is to strengthen the knowledge, skills, dispositions, and classroom practices of professional educators.

Scholars agree that ImDL teaching is distinct from content teaching through the L1 or language teaching. It requires a particular knowledge base and a unique pedagogical skill set (e.g., Cammarata & Tedick, 2012; Day & Shapson, 1996; Lyster, 2007, 2016; Lyster & Tedick, 2014; Tedick & Fortune, 2013). Yet, most ImDL teachers are prepared as either content teachers or as language teachers, but not both (Lyster & Ballinger, 2011). Relatively rare are teacher preparation programs designed specifically for ImDL teacher candidates. Even if such programs exist, teacher candidates are typically assessed on the basis of generic assessment tools. For example, in the College of Education and Human Development (CEHD) at the University of Minnesota, all teacher candidates (regardless of licensure type) are assessed in their student teaching placements using the generic CEHD "Evaluation of Student Teaching." This tool includes general categories of performance related to subject-matter knowledge, student learning, instructional strategies, diverse learners, and so on. Moreover, assessment of in-service teacher performance in ImDL programs tends to utilize the same assessment tools designed for non-immersion teachers. ImDL school principals are required to conduct periodic observations of teachers and provide feedback. They use observational tools and rubrics required by the state or province or a particular school district or board.

To date, few research-supported tools exist to assess ImDL teachers' knowledge and their ability to put into practice ImDL-specific pedagogical skills. To address this need, and with support from a federal grant, Tedick, along with Corinne Mathieu, a PhD candidate, developed an extensive rubric for use with preservice teachers enrolled in the CEHD licensure program in elementary education with a focus on ImDL teaching. Its title is "DLI-Specific Formative

Assessment of Teaching Rubric" (DLI = dual language and immersion, a common acronym in the US). The initial inspiration for the content of the rubric was Fortune's (2014) "Immersion Teaching Strategies Observation Checklist." Tedick and Mathieu then changed and expanded categories to describe ImDL teacher practices across several rubric levels.

 RESEARCH REPORT

Tedick and Mathieu (2018) conducted a survey study based on an initial version of the rubric to establish how well and how comprehensively the rubric described ImDL pedagogy. They were interested in assessing the construct validity of the rubric—the degree to which the assessment tool measures what it claims to be measuring.

Two separate online surveys were developed: one for practitioners (pre- and in-service teachers, clinical student teaching supervisors, and administrators) and another for academics and specialists (ImDL teacher educators, researchers, curriculum specialists, and state-level supervisors).

The online surveys included three parts:

1. brief demographic information (e.g., professional role of the survey takers and type(s) of ImDL program they are associated with);
2. Likert scales for rating the relevance of each rubric strand and sub-strand to ImDL pedagogy with space for open-ended comments after each;
3. open-ended questions inquiring about potential gaps, the applicability of the rubric to different ImDL and CLIL contexts and to pre- and in-service teaching, and suggestions for improvement.

A total of 212 practitioners were invited to complete surveys, and 60 (28%) responded. Of the 72 academics/specialists invited to participate, 57 (79%) responded. Thus, nearly equal numbers of practitioners and academics/specialists completed the surveys, although there was a much higher response rate for academics/specialists.

Tedick and Mathieu found that both groups rated most strands and sub-strands as highly relevant to ImDL teaching, although there was more variation among practitioner respondents. The strands receiving the highest ratings in terms of relevance were those related to instructional scaffolding and maintaining a language-rich learning environment.

As a result of the study findings and additional feedback, Tedick and Mathieu revised the rubric.

The current version of the "DLI-Specific Formative Assessment of Teaching Rubric" (available online – see *Resources for Readers*) includes eight strands, each of which has several sub-strands. Based on this rubric, we have developed a self-assessment tool for ImDL teachers (see Appendix D). The "Self-Assessment Rubric for ImDL Teachers" is designed to be a tool for a teacher's formative growth. It represents four developmental stages: lacking, emerging, demonstrating, and excelling. As such, it should be completed over time with input from multiple teaching reflections. It would be appropriate for a teacher to select one or a few sub-strands on which to focus for a period of time—several weeks or months. In doing so, teachers can assess themselves at one point in time using, for example, a particular color or shape to indicate the level, and then assess themselves again at a later point using a different color or shape. Connecting the two levels with an arrow will then represent progress over time. Because the rubric levels lie on a continuum representing developmental stages, it is possible for a teacher's performance to straddle two (possibly more) levels of the rubric in any sub-strand, showing their continuously evolving strengths and areas of growth. The rubric levels intentionally convey that the development of mastery in these pedagogical practices is a *process* requiring time, practice, reflection, and ongoing feedback.

The rubric is intended to be developmental and educative. Our goal is for teachers to learn from interacting with the rubric. To that end, we have included spaces for reflection at the bottom of each sub-strand. Teachers can reflect on what they've tried or what they've observed other teachers do in relation to the sub-strand. They can also identify their goals for improvement.

The self-assessment rubric could also potentially be used as a powerful professional development tool in an ImDL program. We envision the ImDL teaching staff deciding together on a sub-strand to focus on during a designated period of time with the proviso that all teachers would work to improve their practice in relationship to that sub-strand. They could read portions of this book and other resources that correspond to the sub-strand to increase their awareness and understanding of the specific practices. They could discuss their progress and offer ideas at meetings as well as observe each other and provide feedback. The school principal, curriculum specialist, or program coordinator could observe teachers and engage in dialogue about the teacher's progress vis-à-vis the practices outlined in the sub-strand. The idea would be to provide a supportive environment for teachers to openly talk about their practices, the challenges they experience as they attempt to adopt new practices, and the successes they experience as they hone their knowledge and skills. The ultimate goal, of course, is to improve student learning by improving classroom teaching.

Summary

In the first part of this chapter, we emphasized classroom-based assessment. We made a case for implementing performance-based assessments in ImDL classrooms and focused on one comprehensive approach to assessment, the IPA. We explained how to modify the IPA for the ImDL context and described how to design an IPA by using an IPA design template and following the corresponding steps illustrated in Appendix C. We then turned our attention to teacher performance assessment in the second part of this final chapter. We described the creation of a rubric for assessing the performance of preservice ImDL teacher candidates and introduced a self-assessment rubric (seen in Appendix D) that can be used by practicing teachers. Next, in the conclusion, we synthesize the instructional approaches advocated throughout this book and highlight the potential they hold to engage ImDL learners with language across the curriculum.

 ## Application activity 1: Designing an IPA

Gather together a team of teachers from the same grade level. Together, decide on an end-of-year unit for which you would like to develop an IPA. Using models from Appendix C and others available online (see *Resources for Readers* below), collaboratively develop the IPA. Carry it out in your classrooms and reflect on the process. What worked well? What aspects need revision? How did students respond to this approach to assessment?

 ## Application activity 2: Engaging in self-assessment

Using the self-assessment rubric presented in Appendix D, select a sub-strand to focus on over a period of three to six months to improve your practice. Begin by using the rubric to conduct a "pre-assessment" of your practices as they relate to that sub-strand (you might need to videotape yourself for this assessment). Then date and set it aside. Challenge yourself to work toward improvement in that sub-strand for a designated period of time. Invite colleagues and/or the school principal or director to observe you and give you feedback in relationship to the specific sub-strand you have selected. Reflect on your progress over time, and, after the designated time frame has passed, conduct the self-assessment again and compare your scores on the "post-assessment" with those on the "pre-assessment." Repeat the process with another sub-strand.

Alternatively, work together as a program community to identify one or two sub-strands to work on together over the course of a term or school year. Engage in conversations about your progress. Share ideas with one another. Observe each other and offer feedback. In this way, the self-assessment rubric can be used as a powerful professional tool for the teaching community.

Online resources for readers

Achievement testing in Spanish

Logramos: www.riversideinsights.com/solutions/logramos-tercera-edicion?tab=0
This test measures and assesses achievement in reading, language, and mathematics (Grades K–8) as well as science and social studies (Grades 1–8). It parallels the scope and sequence of the Iowa Assessments.

Aprenda 3: www.pearsonassessments.com/
This test measures reading, mathematics, language, spelling, listening comprehension, science, and social science (Grades K–12).

IPA development

http://carla.umn.edu/cobaltt/modules/assessment/ipa/index.html
A number of well-developed IPAs (some for the ImDL context) are available at the CARLA website (CoBaLTT Project) (navigate through the examples by clicking on links in the left margin).

http://carla.umn.edu/assessment/vac/index.html
The CARLA website also offers a "Virtual Assessment Center" with information about creating performance assessments (including the IPA). Although developed for non-immersion foreign-language contexts, the site offers valuable information that is applicable to ImDL settings.

Rubric development

http://rubistar.4teachers.org/index.php
Rubistar is a website that facilitates the development of rubrics for project-based learning activities. It is also available in Spanish. Teachers choose categories and then use the tool to create rubrics. It is also possible to modify or add content to the rubric text boxes:

Rubrics for ImDL teacher assessment

dliteachingrubrics.umn.edu
This website provides several rubrics that can be used to assess ImDL teaching. It includes detailed rubrics for formative assessment of both preservice and in-service ImDL teaching. It also provides the self-assessment rubric presented in Appendix D.

CONCLUSION

Years ago, a consultant for Research and Evaluation Services at the North York Board of Education in Ontario, Jean Handscombe, eloquently summed up content and language integration as follows: "No content is taught without reference to the language through which that content is expressed, and no language is taught without being contextualized within a thematic and human environment" (Handscombe, 1990, p. 185). She further elaborated, saying that "the best content teaching is also the best language teaching" (p. 185). We believe that this vision still holds true today and have aimed throughout this book to support immersion and dual language (ImDL) teachers in this ambitious endeavor to make the best content teaching and the best language teaching coalesce.

This book has focused specifically on scaffolding learners in their development of non-English languages in Canadian and US ImDL programs. We hope that that counterbalanced instruction, which gives complementary status to content and language objectives, will have implications for content-based instructional settings in other contexts as well. Some of the classroom examples we have provided do indeed come from other contexts where we've worked with teachers who consider the integration of content and language a top priority.

We began in Part I by describing in detail four distinct models of ImDL education and their foundational principles, and then identified features that characterize well-implemented programs. Part II expounded upon counterbalanced instruction and provided theoretical support from skill acquisition theory, according to which L2 development entails a gradual transition from effortful use drawing on declarative knowledge to more automatic use drawing on procedural knowledge. The CAPA (contextualization, awareness, practice, and autonomy) model was then introduced as a blueprint for designing instructional sequences integrating content and language that enable students to move forward in their language development as they transition from declarative to procedural knowledge. The transition is fostered by considerable scaffolding and curricular planning on the part of ImDL teachers. Accordingly, Part III zoomed in on the scaffolding strategies that are indispensable in ImDL classrooms. While the strategic use of teacher questions and corrective feedback serve to make classroom interaction a key source of language learning, other types of scaffolding entail instruction that helps students to fully engage with content taught through a language they are still learning.

Part IV then outlined, in detail, the recommended steps for ImDL teachers to follow in planning units, modules, and lessons that integrate content, language, and culture in ways that provide differentiated instruction to diverse learners. Also in Part IV, we introduced ways of scaffolding students' biliteracy development as a means to enhance the kind of metalinguistic awareness that is requisite for developing literacy skills in two languages. We then addressed the role of student performance assessment in ImDL pedagogy and outlined steps for its design and implementation, which aim to provide students with ideal opportunities to apply their knowledge and skills in real-world tasks. Finally, we briefly described teacher performance assessment and introduced a self-assessment rubric that ImDL teachers can use to assess their ability to put into practice the pedagogical strategies emphasized in this book.

To conclude, we illustrate the main themes addressed throughout the book as being connected by three inter-related and interdependent levels (see Figure C.1). Each level interacts with and builds on the others, moving from the foundational or philosophical level toward a planning level concerning the design of ImDL curriculum and assessment tools, and then upward to the level of the instructional practices in which ImDL teachers engage on a daily basis.

The foundational principles of ImDL education, such as the premise of additive bilingualism and its development through subject-matter instruction, comprise the "why" of ImDL education and were outlined mainly in Part I. The foundational level informs curriculum and assessment practices in ImDL education, which were addressed primarily in Part IV. This second level constitutes the "what" of ImDL education, such as the planning of instructional units designed to integrate content, language, and culture while responding to diverse learner needs. The curriculum and assessment level in turn informs the third level, which reflects the "how" of ImDL education, that is, the various instructional practices we have showcased throughout the book. Because the book is intended for preservice and in-service teachers, this third level permeates the entire book but is addressed specifically in Parts II and III.

The levels are connected by bidirectional arrows to show that the relationships among levels are fluid and not necessarily hierarchical. Whereas foundational principles are, by definition, what anchors all that follows, we wish to conclude by stressing the agency that teachers have in the dynamic field of ImDL education. That is, while the foundational principles do indeed inform curriculum, assessment, and instructional practices, it is also the case that practice can

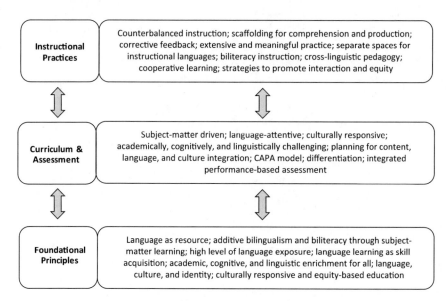

FIGURE C.1 Relationship among foundational principles, curriculum and assessment, and instructional practices

inform theory. Challenges encountered by teachers at the curricular and instructional levels might reflect that certain foundational principles were misinterpreted or misapplied during program implementation, or that there is something fundamentally wrong with some principles. This means that, as agents of change, teachers need to maintain a critical perspective that will empower them to always seek more effective ways of creating optimal learning conditions for their students. It is our hope that this book will serve as a useful resource for ImDL teachers as they strive for the high-quality instruction that all students deserve.

REFERENCES

ACTFL. (2012a). *ACTFL proficiency guidelines 2012.* Alexandria, VA: American Council on the Teaching of Foreign Languages. Retrieved from https://www.actfl.org/pub lications/guidelines-and-manuals/actfl-proficiency-guidelines-2012

ACTFL. (2012b). *ACTFL performance descriptors for language learners.* Alexandria, VA: American Council on the Teaching of Foreign Languages. Retrieved from https://www.actfl.org/publications/guidelines-and-manuals/actfl-performance-descripto rs-language-learners

ACTFL. (n.d.). *Assigning CEFR ratings to ACTFL assessments.* Alexandria, VA: American Council on the Teaching of Foreign Languages. Retrieved from https://www.act fl.org/sites/default/files/reports/Assigning_CEFR_Ratings_To_ACTFL_Assessme nts.pdf

Adair-Hauck, B., Glisan, E. W., & Troyan, F. J. (2013). *Implementing integrated performance assessment.* Alexandria, VA: American Council on the Teaching of Foreign Languages

Alberta Education. (2014). *Handbook for French immersion administrators.* Edmonton, AB: French Language Education Services. Retrieved from https://education.alberta.ca/m edia/3115178/frimmhandbook.pdf

Alexander, R. (2003). *Talk for learning: The first year.* Northallerton, UK: North Yorkshire County Council.

Aljaafreh, A., & Lantolf, J. (1994). Negative feedback as regulation and second language learning in the zone of proximal development. *The Modern Language Journal, 78,* 465–483.

Allen, P., Swain, M., Harley, B., & Cummins, J. (1990). Aspects of classroom treatment: Toward a more comprehensive view of second language education. In B. Harley, P. Allen, J. Cummins, & M. Swain (Eds.), *The development of second language proficiency* (pp. 57–81). Cambridge, UK: Cambridge University Press.

Anderson, J. (1996). *The architecture of cognition.* Mahwah, NJ: Lawrence Erlbaum.

Andersson, L., & Trudgill, P. (1990). *Bad language.* Oxford: Blackwell.

Argue, V., Lapkin, S., Swain, M., Howard, J., & Lévy, L. (1990). *Enseignement du français en immersion française : un survol de la 6e à la 8e année.* [Video cassette and user guide.] Toronto, ON: Ontario Institute for Studies in Education, University of Toronto.

August, D., & Hakuta, K. (Eds.). (1997). *Improving schooling for language-minority children: A research agenda.* Washington, DC: National Academy Press.

August, D., & Shanahan, T. (2006). *Developing literacy in second-language learners: Report of the National Literacy Panel on language-minority children and youth.* Mahwah, NJ: Erlbaum.

Baker, C., & Jones, S. P. (1998). *Encyclopedia of bilingualism and bilingual education.* Clevedon, UK: Multilingual Matters.

Baker, C., & Wright, W. E. (2017). *Foundations of bilingual education and bilingualism* (6th ed.). Bristol, UK: Multilingual Matters.

Ballinger, S. (2013). Towards a cross-linguistic pedagogy: Biliteracy and reciprocal learning strategies in French immersion. *Journal of Immersion and Content-Based Language Education, 1*(1), 131–148.

Ballinger, S. (2015). Linking content, linking students: A cross-linguistic pedagogical intervention. In J. Cenoz & D. Gorter (Eds.), *Multilingual education: New perspectives.* Cambridge, UK: Cambridge University Press.

Ballinger, S., & Lyster, R. (2011). Student and teacher oral language use in a two-way Spanish/English immersion school. *Language Teaching Research, 15*(3), 289–306.

Ballinger, S., Lyster, R., Sterzuk, A., & Genesee, F. (2017). Context-appropriate crosslinguistic pedagogy: Considering the role of language status in immersion education. *Journal of Immersion and Content-Based Language Education, 5*(1), 30–57.

Bamford, K., & Mizokawa, D. (1991). Additive-bilingual (immersion) education: Cognitive and language development. *Language Learning, 41*(3), 413–429.

Bange, P. (with Carol, R., & Griggs, P.). (2005). *L'apprentissage d'une langue étrangère : cognition et interaction.* Paris: L'Harmattan.

Bearse, C. I., & de Jong, E. J. (2008). Cultural and linguistic investment: Adolescents in a secondary two-way immersion program. *Equity & Excellence in Education, 41*(3), 325–340.

Beeman, K., & Urow, C. (2013). *Teaching for biliteracy: Strengthening bridges between languages.* Philadelphia: Caslon Publishing.

Benati, A. (2013). The input processing theory in second language acquisition. In P. García Mayo, M. Gutierrez-Mangado, & M. Martínez Adrián (Eds.), *Contemporary approaches to second language acquisition* (pp. 93–110). Amsterdam: John Benjamins.

Bialystok, E. (1994). Analysis and control in the development of second language proficiency. *Studies in Second Language Acquisition, 16*, 157–168.

Bialystok, E. (2007). Cognitive effects of bilingualism: How linguistic experience leads to cognitive change. *International Journal of Bilingual Education and Bilingualism, 10*(3), 210–223.

Bialystok, E., & Barac, R. (2012). Emerging bilingualism: Dissociating advantages for metalinguistic awareness and executive control. *Cognition, 122*, 67–73.

Bitchener, J. (2008). Evidence in support of written corrective feedback. *Journal of Second Language Writing, 17*, 102–118.

Björklund, S. (1997). Immersion in Finland in the 1990s: A state of development and expansion. In R. K. Johnson & M. Swain (Eds.), *Immersion education: International perspectives* (pp. 85–101). Cambridge, UK: Cambridge University Press.

Björklund, S., Mård-Miettinen, K., & Savijärvi, M. (2014). Swedish immersion in the early years in Finland. *International Journal of Bilingual Education and Bilingualism, 17*(2), 197–214.

Blain, S., & Painchaud, G. (1999). L'impact de la rétroaction verbale des pairs sur l'amélioration des compositions des élèves de 5e année en immersion française [The impact of peers' verbal feedback on the improvement of Grade 5 French immersion students' compositions.] *The Canadian Modern Language Review, 56*(1), 73–98.

Blanc, N., Carol, R., Griggs, P., & Lyster, R. (2012). Lexical scaffolding in immersion classroom discourse. In E. Alcón & M. P. Safont (Eds.), *Discourse and language learning across L2 instructional contexts* (pp. 31–51). Amsterdam: Rodopi.

Blaz, D. (2006). *Differentiated instruction: A guide for foreign language teachers.* Larchmont, NY: Eye on Education.

Block, D. (2003). *The social turn in second language acquisition.* Washington, DC: Georgetown University Press.

Bostwick, M. (2001). English immersion in a Japanese school. In D. Christian & F. Genesee (Eds.), *Bilingual education* (pp. 125–137). Alexandria, VA: Teachers of English to Speakers of Other Languages, Inc.

Bourdieu, P. (1986). The forms of capital. In J. Richardson (Ed.), *Handbook of theory and research for the sociology of education* (pp. 241–258). New York, NY: Greenwood.

Bowers, P. N., & Kirby, J. R. (2010). Effects of morphological instruction on vocabulary acquisition. *Reading and Writing: An Interdisciplinary Journal, 23*, 515–537.

Bowers, P. N., Kirby, J. R., & Deacon, H. (2010). The effects of morphological instruction on literacy skills: A systematic review of the literature. *Review of Educational Research, 80*, 144–179.

Broadfoot, P. M., Daugherty, R., Gardner, J., Harlen, W., James, M., & Stobart, G. (2002). *Assessment for learning: 10 principles.* Cambridge, UK: University of Cambridge School of Education.

Broner, M. (2000). *Impact of interlocutor and task on first and second language use in a Spanish immersion program* (Unpublished doctoral dissertation). University of Minnesota, Minneapolis, MN, USA.

Brown, A. (2009). Students' and teachers' perceptions of effective foreign language teaching: A comparison of ideals. *The Modern Language Journal, 93*(1), 46–60.

Brown, D. (2016). The type and linguistic foci of oral corrective feedback in the L2 classroom: A meta-analysis. *Language Teaching Research, 20*(4), 436–458.

Brown, G., & Yule, G. (1983). *Teaching the spoken language.* Cambridge: Cambridge University Press.

Bruck, M., Lambert, W. E., & Tucker, G. R. (1976). *Cognitive consequences of bilingual schooling: The St. Lambert Project through Grade 6.* Unpublished manuscript, Psychology Department, McGill University, Montreal.

Bruner, J. (1971). *The relevance of education.* New York, NY: Norton.

Bruton, A. (2009). Improving accuracy is not the only reason for writing, and even if it were .... *System, 37*, 600–613.

Burkhauser, S., Steele, J. L., Li, J., Slater, R. O., Bacon, M., & Miller, T. (2016). Partner-language learning trajectories in dual-language immersion: Evidence from an urban district. *Foreign Language Annals, 49*(3), 415–433.

Cameron, L. (2001). *Teaching languages to young learners.* Cambridge, UK: Cambridge University Press.

Cammarata, L. (2005). Instructional scaffolding with graphic organizers. *ACIE Newsletter, 8*(2), 1–12 [Bridge Insert]. Retrieved from http://carla.umn.edu/imme rsion/acie/#bridge

Cammarata, L., & Tedick, D. J. (2012). Balancing content and language in instruction: The experience of immersion teachers. *Modern Language Journal, 96*, 251–269.

Campbell, R. N. (1984). *Studies on immersion education: A collection for US educators.* Sacramento: California State Department of Education.

Canadian Association of Immersion Professionals/L'Association canadienne des professionnels de l'immersion (ACPI). (2018). Final report: Canada-wide consultation. *Immersion Journal, 40*(2), 6–31.

Canadian Parents for French. (2017). *The state of French second language education in Canada 2017.* Ottawa, ON: Canadian Parents for French.

Carlisle, J. (2000). Awareness of the structure and meaning of morphologically complex words: Impact on reading. *Reading and Writing: An Interdisciplinary Journal, 12*, 169–190.

Carpenter, H., Jeon, S., MacGregor, D., & Mackey, S. (2006). Recasts as repetitions: Learners' interpretations of native speaker responses. *Studies in Second Language Acquisition, 28*(2), 209–236.

Carroll, S. (1989). Second-language acquisition and the computational paradigm. *Language Learning, 39*, 535–594.

Cathcart, R., & Olsen, J. (1976). Teachers' and students' preferences for correction of classroom conversation errors. In J. Fanselow & R. Crymes (Eds.), *On TESOL '76* (pp. 41–53). Washington, DC: TESOL.

Cazden, C. B. (1983). Adult assistance to language development: Scaffolds, models, and direct instruction. In R. P. Parker & F. A. Davis (Eds.), *Developing literacy: Young children's use of language* (pp. 3–17). Newark, DE: International Reading Association.

Center for Applied Second Language Studies (CASLS). (2013). *What levels of proficiency do immersion students achieve?* Eugene, OR: Center for Applied Second Language Studies. Retrieved from https://casls.uoregon.edu/wp-content/uploads/pdfs/tenquestions/TBQImmersionStudentProficiencyRevised.pdf

Chandler, J. (2004). A response to Truscott. *Journal of Second Language Writing, 13*, 345–348.

Chandler, J. (2009). Dialogue. *Journal of Second Language Writing, 18*, 57–58.

Christian, D. (2011). Dual language education. In E. Hinkel (Ed.), *Handbook of research in second language teaching and learning. Vol. II* (pp. 3–20). New York, NY: Routledge.

Christian, D., & Genesee, F. (2001). Bilingual education: Contexts and programs. In D. Christian & F. Genesee (Eds.), *Bilingual education* (pp. 1–7). Alexandria, VA: Teachers of English to Speakers of Other Languages, Inc.

Christian, D., Genesee, F., Lindholm-Leary, K., &. Howard, E. (2004). *Final progress report: CAL/CREDE study of two-way immersion education.* Alexandria, VA: Center for Applied Linguistics. Retrieved from http://www.cal.org/twi/CREDEfinal.doc

Clark, S. (1995). The generation effect and the modeling of associations in memory. *Memory & Cognition, 23*, 442–455.

Cloud, N., Genesee, F., & Hamayan, E. (2000). *Dual language instruction: A handbook for enriched education.* Boston, MA: Heinle & Heinle.

Cook, G. (1989). *Discourse.* Oxford: Oxford University Press.

Cook, V. (2001). Using the first language in the classroom. *The Canadian Modern Language Review, 57*, 402–423.

Corbaz, P. (2006). Assessing the effect of foreign language immersion programs on intercultural sensitivity. *The ACIE Newsletter, 10*(1), 3, 12–13.

Corriveau, M. (1966). *Max.* Toronto: Copp Clark Pitman.

Council of Europe. (2001). *Common European Framework of Reference for Languages: Learning, Teaching, Assessment (CEFR).* Strasbourg: Council of Europe. Retrieved from www.coe.int/lang-CEFR

Covey, S. R. (1989). *The seven habits of highly effective people: Powerful lessons in personal change.* New York, NY: Free Press.

Crawford, D. (1995). Parts of a whole: Building a shared school culture in dual-track immersion schools. *Immersion Journal, 18*(3), 28–30.

Cummins, J. (1979). Linguistic interdependence and the educational development of bilingual children. *Review of Educational Research, 49*, 222–251.

Cummins, J. (1981). The role of primary language development in promoting educational success for language minority students. In California State Department of Education (Ed.), *Schooling and Language Minority Students: A Theoretical Framework* (pp. 3–49). Los Angeles, CA: Evaluation, Dissemination and Assessment Center, California State University.

Cummins, J. (1989). *Empowering minority students*. Sacramento, CA: California Association for Bilingual Education.

Cummins, J. (2000). *Language, power, and pedagogy: Bilingual children in the crossfire.* Clevedon, UK: Multilingual Matters.

Cummins, J. (2001). *Negotiating identities: Education for empowerment in a diverse society* (2nd ed.). Los Angeles, CA: California Association for Bilingual Education.

Cummins, J. (2007). Rethinking monolingual instructional strategies in multilingual classrooms. *Canadian Journal of Applied Linguistics, 10*, 221–241.

Dagenais, D. (2008). Developing a critical awareness of language diversity in immersion. In T. W. Fortune & D. J. Tedick (Eds.), *Pathways to multilingualism: Evolving perspectives on immersion education* (pp. 201–220). Clevedon, UK: Multilingual Matters.

Dalton-Puffer, C. (2006). Questions in CLIL classrooms: Strategic questioning to encourage speaking. In A. Martinez-Flor & E. Usó (Eds.), *Current trends in the development of the four skills within a communicative framework* (pp. 187–213). Berlin: Mouton de Gruyter.

Dalton-Puffer, C. (2013). A construct of cognitive discourse functions for conceptualising content-language integration in CLIL and multilingual education. *EuJAL, 1*(2), 216–253.

Dana, N. F. (2010). Teacher quality, job-embedded professional development, and school-university partnerships. *Teacher Education and Practice, 23*, 321–325.

Day, E. M., & Shapson, S. M. (1991). Integrating formal and functional approaches to language teaching in French immersion: An experimental study. *Language Learning, 41*, 25–58.

Day, E. M., & Shapson, S. M. (1996). *Studies in immersion education*. Clevedon, UK: Multilingual Matters.

de Bot, K. (1996). The psycholinguistics of the output hypothesis. *Language Learning, 46*, 529–555.

de Courcy, M., Warren, J., & Burston, M. (2002). Children from diverse backgrounds in an immersion programme. *Language and Education, 16*(2), 112–127.

de Guibert, F., & Delafon, G. (2010). *Les pirates*. Paris: Larousse.

de Jong, E. J. (2011). *Foundations for multilingualism in education: From principles to practice.* Philadelphia, PA: Caslon Publishing.

de Jong, E. J. (2014). Program design and two-way immersion programs. *Journal of Immersion and Content-Based Language Education, 2*(2), 241–256.

de Jong, E. J. (2016). Two-way immersion for the next generation: Models, policies, and principles. *International Multilingual Research Journal, 10*(1), 6–16.

de Jong, E. J., & Bearse, C. I. (2014). Dual language programs as a strand within a secondary school: Dilemmas of school organization and the TWI mission. *International Journal of Bilingual Education and Bilingualism, 17*(1), 15–31.

de Jong, E. J., & Howard, E. R. (2009). Integration in two-way immersion education: Equalising linguistic benefits for all students. *International Journal of Bilingual Education and Bilingualism, 12*(1), 81–99.

DeKeyser, R. (1998). Beyond focus on form: Cognitive perspectives on learning and practicing second language grammar. In C. Doughty & J. Williams (Eds.), *Focus on form in classroom second language acquisition* (pp. 42–63). Cambridge, UK: Cambridge University Press.

DeKeyser, R. (2005). What makes learning second-language grammar difficult? A review of issues. *Language Learning, 55*(S1), 1–25.

DeKeyser, R. (Ed.). (2007). *Practice in a second language: Perspectives from applied linguistics and cognitive psychology.* Cambridge, UK: Cambridge University Press.

DeKeyser, R. (2010). Practice for second language learning: Don't throw out the baby with the bath water. *International Journal of English Studies, 10*(1), 155–165.

Doell, L. (2011). Comparing dual-track and single-track French immersion programs: Does setting matter? *The ACIE Newsletter, 14*(2), 3, 12–15. Retrieved from http://carla.umn.edu/immersion/acie/vol14/no2/may2011_bp.html

Doughty, C. (2001). Cognitive underpinnings of focus on form. In P. Robinson (Ed.), *Cognition and second language instruction* (pp. 206–257). New York, NY: Cambridge University Press.

Doughty, C., & Varela, E. (1998). Communicative focus on form. In C. Doughty & J. Williams (Eds.), *Focus on form in classroom second language acquisition* (pp. 114–138). Cambridge, UK: Cambridge University Press.

DuFour, R., DuFour, R., & Eaker, R. (2008). *Revisiting professional learning communities at work: New insights for improving schools.* Bloomington, IN: Solution Tree.

Dutro, S., & Moran, C. (2003). Rethinking English language instruction: An architectural approach. In G. G. García (Ed.), *English learners: Reaching the highest level of English literacy* (pp. 227–258). Newark, DE: International Reading Association.

Echevarría, J., & Graves, A. (1998). *Sheltered content instruction: Teaching English-language learners with diverse abilities.* Boston, MA: Allyn & Bacon.

Echevarría, J., Vogt, M., & Short, D. J. (2008). *Making content comprehensible for English learners: The SIOP® model* (3rd ed.). Boston, MA: Pearson Education.

Egi, T. (2010). Uptake, modified output, and learner perceptions of recasts: Learner responses as language awareness. *The Modern Language Journal, 94*(1), 1–21.

Ellis, R. (1986). *Understanding second language acquisition.* Oxford: Oxford University Press.

Ellis, R. (2002). The place of grammar instruction in the second/foreign curriculum. In E. Hinkel & S. Fotos (Eds.), *New perspectives on grammar teaching in second language classrooms* (pp. 17–34). Mahwah, NJ: Lawrence Erlbaum.

Ellis, R. (2009). Corrective feedback and teacher development. *L2 Journal, 1,* 3–18.

Ellis, R. (2012). *Language teaching research and language pedagogy.* Oxford: Wiley Blackwell.

Ellis, R., Loewen, S., & Erlam, R. (2006). Implicit and explicit corrective feedback and the acquisition of L2 grammar. *Studies in Second Language Acquisition, 28*(3), 339–368.

Ericsson, A., Krampe, R., & Tesch-Römer, C. (1993). The role of deliberate practice in the acquisition of expert performance. *Psychological Review, 100*(3), 363–406.

Escamilla, K., Hopewell, S., Butvilofsky, S., Sparrow, W., Soltero-González, L., Ruiz-Figueroa, O., & Escamilla, M. (2014). *Biliteracy from the start: Literacy squared in action.* Philadelphia, PA: Caslon Publishing.

Feinauer, E., & Howard, E. R. (2014). Attending to the third goal: Cross-cultural competence and identity development in two-way immersion programs. *Journal of Immersion and Content-Based Language Education, 2*(2), 257–272.

Ferris, D. (2004). The "grammar correction" debate in L2 writing: Where we are, and where do we go from here? (and what do we do in the meantime …?). *Journal of Second Language Writing, 13,* 49–62.

Ferris, D. (2006). Does error feedback help student writers? New evidence on the short- and long-term effects of written error correction. In K. Hyland & F. Hyland

(Eds.), *Feedback in second language writing* (pp. 81–102). Cambridge, UK: Cambridge University Press.

Finocchiaro, M., & Brumfit, C. (1983). *The functional-notional approach.* New York, NY: Oxford University Press.

Fleta Guillén, M. T. (2007). The role of interaction in the young learners' classroom. *Encuentro, 17,* 6–14.

Fortune, T. W. (2001). *Understanding immersion students' oral language use as a mediator of social interaction in the classroom* (Unpublished doctoral dissertation). University of Minnesota, Minneapolis.

Fortune, T. W. (2014). *Immersion teaching strategies observation checklist.* Retrieved from http://carla.umn.edu/immersion/checklist.pdf

Fortune, T. W., & Fernández del Rey, C. (2003). Maximizing language growth through collaborative-creative writing. *ACIE Newsletter, 6*(2), 1–8 [Bridge Insert]. Retrieved from http://carla.umn.edu/immersion/acie/#bridge

Fortune, T. W., & Ju, Z. (2017). Assessing and exploring the oral proficiency of young Mandarin immersion learners. *Annual Review of Applied Linguistics, 37,* 264–287. DOI: 10.1017/S0267190517000150.

Fortune, T. W. with Menke, M. (2010). *Struggling learners and language immersion education: Research-based, practitioner-informed responses to educators' top questions.* Minneapolis, MN: Center for Advanced Research on Language Acquisition.

Fortune, T. W., & Song, W. (2016). Academic achievement and language proficiency in early total Mandarin immersion education. *Journal of Immersion and Content-Based Language Education, 4*(2), 168–197.

Fortune, T. W., & Tedick, D. J. (2003, May). *Addressing issues of language status in dual language teacher education.* Paper session presented at the Third International Conference on Language Teacher Education, Minneapolis.

Fortune, T. W., & Tedick, D. J. (2008). One-way, two-way and Indigenous immersion: A call for cross-fertilization. In T. W. Fortune & D. J. Tedick (Eds.), *Pathways to multilingualism: Evolving perspectives on immersion education* (pp. 3–21). Clevedon, UK: Multilingual Matters.

Fortune, T. W., & Tedick, D. J. (2015). Oral proficiency development of English proficient K–8 Spanish immersion students. *Modern Language Journal, 99*(4), 637–655. DOI: 10.1111/modl.12275.

Fortune, T. W., & Tedick, D. J. (2019). Context matters: Translanguaging and language immersion education in the U.S. and Canada. In M. Haneda & H. Nassaji (Eds.), *Perspectives on language as action: Festschrift in honor of Merrill Swain* (pp. 27–44). Bristol, UK: Multilingual Matters.

French, L. G. (2019). Bilingual education in Brazil: Multiple perspectives on language learning. *New Routes, 67,* 16–19.

Furneaux, C., Paran, A., & Fairfax, B. (2007). Teacher stance as reflected in feedback on student writing: An empirical study of secondary school teachers in five countries. *International Review of Applied Linguistics, 45,* 69–94.

García, O. (2009). *Bilingual education in the 21st century: A global perspective.* Malden, MA: Wiley-Blackwell.

García, O. (with Makar, C., Starcevic, M., & Terry, A.) (2011). Translanguaging of Latino kindergarteners. In K. Potowski & J. Rothman (Eds.), *Bilingual youth: Spanish in English-speaking societies* (pp. 33–55). Amsterdam: John Benjamins.

García, O., Johnson, S. I., & Seltzer, K. (2017). *The translanguaging classroom: Leveraging student bilingualism for learning.* Philadelphia, PA: Caslon Publishing.

García, O., & Wei, L. (2014). *Translanguaging: Language, bilingualism and education*. New York, NY: Palgrave Macmillan.

García-Mateus, S., & Palmer, D. K. (2017). Translanguaging pedagogies for positive identities in two-way dual language bilingual education. *Journal of Language, Identity, and Education, 16*(4), 245–255. DOI: 10.1080/15348458.2017.1329016.

Garmston, R. J., & Wellman, B. M. (2016). *The adaptive school: A sourcebook for developing collaborative groups* (3rd ed.). Lanham, MD: Rowman & Littlefield.

Gass, S. (1997). *Input, interaction, and the second language learner*. Mahwah, NJ: Lawrence Erlbaum.

Gass, S., & Mackey, A. (2007). Input, interaction, an output in second language acquisition. In B. VanPatten & J. Williams (Eds.), *Theories in second language acquisition* (pp. 175–200). Mahwah, NJ: Lawrence Erlbaum.

Gay, G. (2018). *Culturally responsive teaching: Theory, research, and practice* (3rd ed.). New York, NY: Teachers College Press.

Genesee, F. (1981). A comparison of early and late second language learning. *Canadian Journal of Behavioral Science, 13*, 115–127.

Genesee, F. (1987). *Learning through two languages: Studies on immersion and bilingual education*. Cambridge, MA: Newbury House.

Genesee, F. (1994). *Integrating language and content: Lessons from immersion*. [Educational Practice Report No. 11]. Santa Cruz, CA: National Center for Research on Cultural Diversity and Second Language Learning.

Genesee, F. (2004). What do we know about bilingual education for majority language students? In T. K. Bhatia & W. Ritchie (Eds.), *Handbook of bilingualism and multilingualism* (pp. 543–576). Malden, MA: Blackwell.

Genesee, F. (2015). Canada: Factors that shaped the creation and development of immersion education. In P. Mehisto & F. Genesee (Eds.), *Building bilingual education systems: Forces, mechanisms and counterweights* (pp. 43–57). Cambridge, UK: Cambridge University Press.

Genesee, F., & Fortune, T. W. (2014). Bilingual education and at-risk students. *Journal of Immersion and Content-Based Language Education, 2*(2), 196–209.

Genesee, F., & Lindholm-Leary, K. J. (2013). Two case studies of content-based language education. *Journal of Immersion and Content-Based Language Education, 1*(1), 3–33.

Genesee, F., Lindholm-Leary, K. J., Saunders, W., & Christian, D. (2006). *Educating English language learners*. Cambridge, NY: Cambridge University Press.

Gibbons, P. (1998). Classroom talk and the learning of new registers in a second language. *Language and Education, 12*, 99–118.

Gibbons, P. (2003). Mediating language learning: Teacher interactions with ESL students in a content-based classroom. *TESOL Quarterly, 37*, 247–273.

Gibbons, P. (2009). *English learners, academic literacy, and thinking: Learning in the challenge zone*. Portsmouth, NH: Heinemann.

Gibbons, P. (2015). *Scaffolding language scaffolding learning: Teaching English language learners in the mainstream classroom* (2nd ed.). Portsmouth, NH: Heinemann.

Goldschneider, J., & DeKeyser, R. (2005). Explaining the natural order of L2 morpheme acquisition in English: A meta-analysis of multiple determinants. *Language Learning, 55*(S1), 27–77.

González, J. M. (1979). Coming of age in bilingual/bicultural education: A historical perspective. In H. T. Trueba & C. Barnett-Mizrahi (Eds.), *Bilingual multicultural education and the professional: From theory to practice* (pp. 1–10). Rowley, MA: Newbury House.

Gort, M. (2006). Strategic code-switching, interliteracy, and other phenomena of emergent bilingual writing: Lessons from first grade dual language classrooms. *Journal of Early Childhood Literacy, 6*(3), 323–354.

Government of Canada. (2018). *Action plan for official languages—2018–2023: Investing in our future*. Retrieved from https://www.canada.ca/en/canadian-heritage/services/off icial-languages-bilingualism/official-languages-action-plan/2018-2023.html#a11

Government of Manitoba. (2016). *La langue au cœur de l'immersion française: Une approche intégrée dans la pédagogie immersive*. Winnipeg, MB: Éducation et Enseignement Supérieur Manitoba. Retrieved from http://www.edu.gov.mb.ca/m12/frpub/me/la ngue_coeur/docs/document_complet.pdf

Government of Québec. (2001). *Québec education program*. Québec, QC: Ministère de l'Éducacion.

Grabe, W., & Stoller, F. L. (1997). Content-based instruction: Research foundations. In M. A. Snow & D. M. Brinton (Eds.), *The content-based classroom: Perspectives on integrating language and content* (pp. 5–21). New York, NY: Addison Wesley. Retrieved from http://carla.um n.edu/cobaltt/modules/principles/grabe_stoller1997/SELECTION.html

Guénette, D., & Lyster, R. (2013). Written corrective feedback and its challenges for pre-service ESL teachers. *The Canadian Modern Language Review, 69*(2), 129–153.

Guimont, G. (2003). *French immersion in different settings. A comparative study of student achievement and exemplary practices in immersion centres versus dual- and multi-track schools* (Unpublished master's thesis). University of Alberta, Edmonton, Canada. Retrieved from http://www.collectionscanada.gc.ca/obj/s4/f2/dsk4/etd/MQ82226.PDF

Haj-Broussard, M. (1993). *Language, identity and the achievement gap: Comparing experiences of African-American students in a French immersion and a regular education context* (Unpublished doctoral dissertation). University of Louisiana at Lafayette.

Haj-Broussard, M. (2018). Ensuring high quality dual language immersion education: Louisiana's Certified Foreign Language Immersion Program Rubric. *Research Issues in Contemporary Education, 3*(1), 51–56. Retrieved from http://www.leraweb.net/docs/ rice-18s-v3n1.pdf

Hakuta, K. (2001, April 13). *The education of language minority students*. Testimony to the United States Commission on Civil Rights. Washington, DC. Retrieved from https ://web.stanford.edu/~hakuta/www/archives/syllabi/Docs/CivilRightsCommission .htm

Hall, K. (1993). Process writing in French immersion. *The Canadian Modern Language Review, 49*(2), 255–274.

Hamayan, E., Genesee, F., & Cloud, N. (2013). *Dual language instruction from A to Z: Practical guidance for teachers and administrators*. Portsmouth, NH: Heinemann.

Hamman, L. (2018). Translanguaging and positioning in two-way dual language classrooms: A case for criticality. *Language and Education, 32*(1), 21–42. DOI: 10.1080/09500782.2017.1384006

Han, Z-H. (2004). *Fossilization in adult second language acquisition*. Clevedon, UK: Multilingual Matters.

Han, Z-H., & Selinker, L. (1999). Error resistance: Towards an empirical pedagogy. *Language Teaching Research, 3*(3), 248–275.

Haneda, M. (2005). Functions of triadic dialogue in the classroom: Examples for L2 research. *The Canadian Modern Language Review, 62*, 313–333.

Handscombe, J. (1990). The complementary roles of researchers and practitioners in second language education. In B. Harley, P. Allen, J. Cummins, & M. Swain (Eds.), *The development of second language proficiency* (pp. 181–186). Cambridge, UK: Cambridge University Press.

Harley, B. (1986). *Age in second language acquisition*. Clevedon, UK: Multilingual Matters.

Harley, B. (1989). Functional grammar in French immersion: A classroom experiment. *Applied Linguistics, 10*, 331–359.

Harley, B. (1998). The role of form-focused tasks in promoting child L2 acquisition. In C. Doughty & J. Williams (Eds.), *Focus on form in classroom second language acquisition* (pp. 156–174). Cambridge, UK: Cambridge University Press.

Harley, B. (1992). Patterns of second language development in French immersion. *Journal of French Language Studies, 2*, 159–183. DOI: 10.1017/S0959269500001289.

Harley, B. (1993). Instructional strategies and SLA in early French immersion. *Studies in Second Language Acquisition, 15*, 245–259.

Harley, B. (1994). Appealing to consciousness in the L2 classroom. *AILA Review, 11*, 57–68.

Harley, B., & King, M. (1989). Verb lexis in the written compositions of young L2 learners. *Studies in Second Language Acquisition, 11*, 415–439.

Harley, B., Cummins, J., Swain, M., & Allen, P. (1990). The nature of language proficiency. In B. Harley, P. Allen, J. Cummins, & M. Swain (Eds.), *The development of second language proficiency* (pp. 7–25). Cambridge, UK: Cambridge University Press.

Hart, D., Lapkin, S., & Swain, M. (1991). Secondary level immersion French skills: A possible plateau effect. In L. Malavé & G. Duquette (Eds.), *Language, culture and cognition* (Vol. 69, pp. 250–265). Clevedon, UK: Multilingual Matters.

Hattie, J., & Timperley, H. (2007). The power of feedback. *Review of Educational Research, 77*(1), 81–112.

Heller, M. (1996). Legitimate language in a multilingual school. *Linguistics and Education, 8*, 139–157.

Henderson, A. T., & Mapp, K. L. (2002). *A new wave of evidence: The impact of school, family, and community connections on student achievement.* Austin, TX: Southwest Educational Development Laboratory.

Herman, R., Gates, S. M., Arifkhanova, A., Barrett, M., Bega, A., Chavez-Herrerias, E. R., … Wrabel, S. L. (2017). *School leadership interventions under the Every Student Succeeds Act: Evidence review updated and expanded.* Santa Monica, CA: RAND. Retrieved from https://www.rand.org/pubs/research_reports/RR1550-3.html

Hernández, A. M. (2015). Language status in two-way bilingual immersion: The dynamics between English and Spanish in peer interaction. *Journal of Immersion and Content-Based Language Education, 3*(1), 102–126.

Hibbard, K. M., Van Wagenen, L., Lewbel, S., Waterbury-Wyatt, S., Shaw, S., Pelletier, K., … Wislocki, J. (1996). *Teacher's guide to performance-based learning and assessment.* Alexandria, VA: Association for Supervision and Curriculum Development. Retrieved from http://www.ascd.org/publications/books/196021/chapters/What_is_Performance-Based_Learning_and_Assessment,_and_Why_is_it_Important%C2%A2.aspx

Housen, A., Pierrard, M., & Van Daele, S. (2005). Rule complexity and the efficacy of explicit grammar instruction. In A. Housen & M. Pierrard (Eds.), *Investigations in instructed second language acquisition* (pp. 235–269). Amsterdam: Mouton de Gruyter.

Howard, E. R., & Christian, D. (2002). *Two-way immersion 101: Designing and implementing a two-way immersion education program at the elementary level* (Educational Practice Report 9). Santa Cruz, CA and Washington, DC: Center for Research on Education, Diversity & Excellence. Retrieved from http://www.cal.org/twi/pdfs/two-way-immersion-101.pdf

Howard, E. R., Lindholm-Leary, K. J., Rogers, D., Olague, N., Medina, J., Kennedy, B., … Christian, D. (2018). *Guiding principles for dual language education* (3rd ed.). Washington, DC: Center for Applied Linguistics.

Howard, E. R., Olague, N., & Rogers, D. (2003). *The dual language program planner: A guide for designing and implementing dual language programs.* Washington, DC and Santa Cruz, CA: Center for Research on Education, Diversity & Excellence (CREDE).

Howard, E. R., Sugarman, J., Perdomo, M., & Temple Adger, C. (2005). *The two-way immersion toolkit*. Providence, RI: Education Alliance.

Hulstijn, J. H., & de Graaff, R. (1994). Under what conditions does explicit knowledge of a second language facilitate the acquisition of implicit knowledge? A research proposal. *AILA Review, 11*, 97–112.

Huicochea, A. (2016, June 6). Audit: TUSD's dual language program too weak to promote proficiency. *Arizona Daily Star*. Retrieved from https://tucson.com/news/local/education/audit-tusd-s-dual-language-program-too-weak-to-promote/artic le_1cf17151-549d-5414-b4a3-7e0ff2d2b1dc.html

Hunt, V. (2011). Learning from success stories: Leadership structures that support dual language programs over time in New York City. *International Journal of Bilingual Education and Bilingualism, 14*(2), 187–206.

Jean, G., & Simard, D. (2011). Grammar learning in English and French L2: Students' and teachers' beliefs and perceptions. *Foreign Language Annals, 44*(3), 465–492.

Johnson, K. (1996). *Language teaching and skill learning*. Oxford: Blackwell.

Johnson, R. K., & Swain, M. (Eds.) (1997). *Immersion education: International perspectives*. Cambridge, UK: Cambridge University Press.

Kagan, S. (1992). *Cooperative learning*. San Juan Capistrano, CA. Resources for Teachers, Inc.

Kagan, S. (2001, Fall). Kagan structures for emotional intelligence. *Kagan Online Magazine*. Retrieved from https://www.kaganonline.com/free_articles/dr_spenc er_kagan/ASK14.php

Kang, E., & Han, Z-H. (2015). The efficacy of written corrective feedback in improving L2 written accuracy: A meta-analysis. *The Modern Language Journal, 15*, 1–18.

Kim, J., & Han, Z-H. (2007). Recasts in communicative EFL classes: Do teacher intent and learner interpretation overlap? In A. Mackey (Ed.), *Conversational interaction in second language acquisition: A collection of empirical studies* (pp. 269–297). Oxford: Oxford University Press.

Koike, D., & Pearson, L. (2005). The effect of instruction and feedback in the development of pragmatic competence. *System, 33*, 481–501.

Koven, M. (1998). Two languages in the self/the self in two languages: French-Portuguese bilinguals' verbal enactments and experiences of self in narrative discourse. *Ethos, 26*(4), 410–455.

Krashen, S. (1982). *Principles and practice in second language acquisition*. New York, NY: Pergamon.

Krashen, S. (1985). *The input hypothesis: Issues and implications*. London: Longman.

Krashen, S. (1994). The input hypothesis and its rivals. In N. Ellis (Ed.), *Implicit and explicit learning of languages* (pp. 45–77). London: Academic Press.

Kucer, S. B., Silva, C., & Delgado-Larocco, E. L. (1995). *Curricular conversations: Themes in multilingual and monolingual classrooms*. York, ME: Stenhouse Publishers.

Kuo, L.-J., & Anderson, R. C. (2006). Morphological awareness and learning to read: A cross-language perspective. *Educational Psychologist, 41*, 161–180.

Lambert, W. E. (1980). The social psychology of language. In H. Giles, W. P. Robinson, & P. M. Smith (Eds.), *Language: Social psychological perspectives* (pp. 415–424). Oxford: Pergamon.

Lambert, W. E. (1984). An overview of issues in immersion education. In R. Campbell (Ed.), *Studies on immersion education: A collection for United States educators* (pp. 8–30). Sacramento, CA: California State Department of Education.

Lambert, W. E., & Tucker, G. R. (1972). *The bilingual education of children: The St. Lambert experiment*. Rowley, MA: Newbury House.

Lantolf, J., & Poehner, M. (2008). Dynamic assessment. In N. Hornberger (Ed.), *Encyclopedia of language and education* (pp. 2406–2417). New York, NY: Springer.

Lapkin, S., Hart, D., & Turnbull, M. (2003). Grade 6 French immersion students' performance on large-scale reading, writing, and mathematics tests: Building explanations. *Alberta Journal of Educational Research, 49*, 6–23.

Lapkin, S., & Swain, M. (1996). Vocabulary teaching in a grade 8 French immersion classroom: A descriptive study. *The Canadian Modern Language Review, 53*, 242–256.

Laplante, B. (1993). Stratégies pédagogiques et enseignement des sciences en immersion française: Le cas d'une enseignante. *The Canadian Modern Language Review, 49*, 567–588.

Lee, I. (2004). Error correction in L2 secondary writing classrooms: The case of Hong-Kong. *Journal of Second Language Writing, 13*, 285–312.

Lee, J. (2006). *Corrective feedback and learner uptake in english immersion classrooms in Korea* (Unpublished master's thesis). International Graduate School of English, Seoul, Korea.

Legaretta, D. (1977). Language choice in bilingual classrooms. *TESOL Quarterly, 11*, 9–16.

Legaretta, D. (1979). The effects of program models on language acquisition by Spanish speaking children. *TESOL Quarterly, 13*(4), 521–534.

Legislature of Louisiana. (2011). *ACT No. 212, Senate Bill No. 104.* Retrieved from http://www.legis.la.gov/legis/ViewDocument.aspx?d=760362

Leite, J., & Cook, R. (2015). Utah: Making immersion mainstream. In P. Mehisto & F. Genesee (Eds.), *Building bilingual education systems: Forces, mechanisms and counterweights* (pp. 83–96). Cambridge, UK: Cambridge University Press.

Leung, C. (2007). Dynamic assessment: Assessment *for* and *as* teaching? *Language Assessment Quarterly, 4*, 257–278.

Lewis, G., Jones, B., & Baker, C. (2012). Translanguaging: Origins and development from school to street and beyond. *Educational Research and Evaluation: An International Journal on Theory and Practice, 18*(7), 641–654.

Li, S. (2010). The effectiveness of corrective feedback in SLA: A meta–analysis. *Language Learning, 60*(2), 309–365.

Lightbown, P. M. (1991). What have we here? Some observations on the influence of instruction on L2 learning. In R. Phillipson, E. Kellerman, L. Selinker, M. Sharwood Smith, & M. Swain (Eds.), *Foreign/second language pedagogy research* (pp. 197–212). Clevedon, UK: Multilingual Matters.

Lightbown, P. M. (1998). The importance of timing in focus on form. In C. Doughty & J. Williams (Eds.), *Focus on form in classroom second language acquisition* (pp. 177–196). Cambridge, UK: Cambridge University Press.

Lightbown, P. M. (2008a). Transfer appropriate processing as a model for class second language acquisition. In Z. Han (ed.), *Understanding second language process* (pp. 27–44). Clevedon, UK: Multilingual Matters.

Lightbown, P. M. (2008b). Easy as pie? Children learning languages. *Concordia Working Papers in Applied Linguistics, 1*, 5–29.

Lightbown, P. M. (2014). *Focus on content-based language teaching.* Oxford: Oxford University Press.

Lightbown, P. M., & Spada, N. (1990). Focus on form and corrective feedback in communicative language teaching: Effects on second language learning. *Studies in Second Language Acquisition, 12*, 429–448.

Lightbown, P. M., & Spada, N. (2013). *How languages are learned* (4th ed.). Oxford: Oxford University Press.

Lindholm, K. J. (1987). *Directory of bilingual immersion programs: Two-way bilingual education for language minority and majority students*. Los Angeles: University of California Center for Language Education and Research (CLEAR). ERIC ED 291–241.

Lindholm-Leary, K. J. (2001). *Dual language education*. Clevedon, UK: Multilingual Matters.

Lindholm-Leary, K. J. (2012). Success and challenges in dual language education. *Theory into Practice, 51*(4), 256–262. DOI: 10.1080/00405841.2012.726053.

Lindholm-Leary, K. J., & Genesee, F. (2014). Student outcomes in one-way, two-way, and indigenous language immersion education. *Journal of Immersion and Content-Based Language Education, 2*(2), 165–180.

LinguaHealth (Producer). (2012). *Myths about bilingual children* (video). Available from https://www.youtube.com/watch?v=LVYhpCprtzQ&t=10s.

Llinares, A., & Lyster, R. (2014). The influence of context on patterns of corrective feedback and learner uptake: A comparison of CLIL and immersion classrooms. *The Language Learning Journal, 42*(2), 181–194.

Llinares, A., Morton, T., & Whittaker, R. (2012). *The roles of language in CLIL*. Cambridge, UK: Cambridge University Press.

Loewen, S. (2011). Focus on form. In E. Hinkel (Ed.), *Handbook of research in second language teaching and learning* (Vol. 2, pp. 576–592). New York, NY: Routledge.

Loewen, S., & Philp, J. (2006). Recasts in the adult English L2 classroom: Characteristics, explicitness, and effectiveness. *The Modern Language Journal, 90*, 536–555.

Long, M. (1991). Focus on form: A design feature in language teaching methodology. In K. de Bot, R. Ginsberg, & C. Kramsch (Eds.), *Foreign language research in cross-cultural perspective* (pp. 39–52). Amsterdam: John Benjamins.

Long, M. (1996). The role of the linguistic environment in second language acquisition. In W. C. Ritchie & T. K. Bhatia (Eds.), *Handbook of second language acquisition* (pp. 413–468). San Diego, CA: Academic Press.

Long, M. (2007). *Problems in SLA*. Mahwah, NJ: Lawrence Erlbaum.

Loschky, L., & Bley-Vroman, R. (1993). Grammar and task-based methodology. In G. Crookes & S. Gass (Eds.), *Tasks and language learning: Integrating theory and practice* (pp. 123–167). Clevedon, UK: Multilingual Matters.

Lyster, R. (1994). The effect of functional-analytic teaching on aspects of French immersion students' sociolinguistic competence. *Applied Linguistics, 15*, 263–287.

Lyster, R. (1998a). Recasts, repetition, and ambiguity in L2 classroom discourse. *Studies in Second Language Acquisition, 20*, 51–81.

Lyster, R. (1998b). Negotiation of form, recasts, and explicit correction in relation to error types and learner repair in immersion classrooms. *Language Learning, 48*, 183–218.

Lyster, R. (1998c). Form in immersion classroom discourse: In or out of focus? *Canadian Journal of Applied Linguistics, 1*, 53–82.

Lyster, R. (1998d). Immersion pedagogy and implications for language teaching. In J. Cenoz & F. Genesee (Eds.), *Beyond bilingualism: Multilingualism and multilingual education* (pp. 64–95). Clevedon, UK: Multilingual Matters.

Lyster, R. (2004). Differential effects of prompts and recasts in form-focused instruction. *Studies in Second Language Acquisition, 26*, 399–432.

Lyster, R. (2007). *Learning and teaching languages through content: A counterbalanced approach*. Amsterdam: John Benjamins.

Lyster, R. (2016). *Vers une approche intégrée en immersion* [Towards an integrated approach in immersion]. Montreal: Les Éditions CEC.

Lyster, R. (2017, August). Corrective feedback in second language learning and teaching. *Keynote address at the 2nd International Conference on New Trends in English Language Teaching and Testing.* Ardabil, Iran.

Lyster, R. (2018). *Content-based language teaching.* [The Routledge E-Modules on Contemporary Language Teaching edited by B. VanPatten & G. Keating.] New York, NY: Routledge.

Lyster, R. (2019). Making research on instructed SLA relevant for teachers through professional development. *Language Teaching Research, 23*(4), 494–513.

Lyster, R., & Ballinger, S. (2011). Content-based language teaching: Convergent concerns across divergent contexts. *Language Teaching Research, 15*, 279–288.

Lyster, R., Collins, L., & Ballinger, S. (2009). Linking languages through a bilingual read-aloud project. *Language Awareness, 18*(3–4), 366–383.

Lyster, R., & Izquierdo, J. (2009). Prompts versus recasts in dyadic interaction. *Language Learning, 59*, 453–498.

Lyster, R., & Mori, H. (2006). Interactional feedback and instructional counterbalance. *Studies in Second Language Acquisition, 28*, 269–300.

Lyster, R., Quiroga, J., & Ballinger, S. (2013). The effects of biliteracy instruction on morphological awareness. *Journal of Immersion and Content-Based Language Education, 1*(2), 169–197.

Lyster, R., & Ranta, L. (1997). Corrective feedback and learner uptake: Negotiation of form in communicative classrooms. *Studies in Second Language Acquisition, 19*, 37–66.

Lyster, R., & Rebuffot, J. (2002). Acquisition des pronoms d'allocution en classe de français immersif. *Acquisition et Interaction en Langue Étrangère, 17*, 51–71.

Lyster, R., & Saito, K. (2010). Oral feedback in classroom SLA: A meta-analysis. *Studies in Second Language Acquisition, 32*, 265–302.

Lyster, R., Saito, K., & Sato, M. (2013). Oral corrective feedback in second language classrooms. *Language Teaching, 46*(1), 1–40.

Lyster, R., & Sato, M. (2013). Skill Acquisition Theory and the role of practice in L2 development. In P. García Mayo, M. Gutierrez-Mangado, & M. Martínez Adrián (Eds.), *Contemporary approaches to second language acquisition* (pp. 71–92). Amsterdam: John Benjamins.

Lyster, R., & Tedick, D. J. (2014). Research perspectives on immersion pedagogy: Looking back and looking forward. *Journal of Immersion and Content-Based Language Education, 2*(2), 210–224.

Mackey, A. (2006). Feedback, noticing, and second language development: An empirical study of L2 classroom interaction. *Applied Linguistics, 27*, 405–430.

Mackey, A., Gass, S., & McDonough, K. (2000). How do learners perceive interactional feedback? *Studies in Second Language Acquisition, 22*(4), 471–497.

Mackey, A., & Oliver, R. (2002). Interactional feedback and children's L2 development. *System, 30*, 459–477.

MacSwan, J. (2017). A multilingual perspective on translanguaging. *American Educational Research Journal, 54*(1), 167–201.

Mady, C. (2015). Examining immigrants' English and French proficiency in French immersion. *Journal of Immersion and Content-Based Language Education, 3*(2), 268–284.

Manchón, R. M., & Vasylets, O. (2019). Language learning through writing: Theoretical perspectives and empirical evidence. In J. W. Schwieter & B. Alessandro (Eds.), *The Cambridge handbook of language learning* (pp. 341–362). Cambridge, UK: Cambridge University Press.

May, S. (2013). Indigenous immersion education: International developments. *Journal of Immersion and Content-Based Language Education, 1*(1), 34–69.

McCarty, T. L., & Lee, T. S. (2014). Critical culturally sustaining/revitalizing pedagogy and Indigenous education sovereignty. *Harvard Educational Review, 84*, 101–124.

McCarty, T. L., & Watahomigie, L. J. (1999). Indigenous community-based language education in the USA. In S. May (Ed.), *Indigenous community-based education* (pp. 79–94). Clevedon, UK: Multilingual Matters.

McCollum, P. (1999). Learning to value English: Cultural capital in a two-way bilingual program. *Bilingual Research Journal, 23*(2–3), 113–134.

McHoul, A. (1990). The organization of repair in classroom talk. *Language in Society, 19*, 349–377.

McLaughlin, B. (1987). *Theories of second language learning.* London: Edward Arnold.

McLaughlin, B. (1990). Restructuring. *Applied Linguistics, 11*(2), 113–128.

McLaughlin, B., & Heredia, R. (1996). Information-processing approaches to research on second language acquisition and use. In W. Ritchie & T. Bhatia (Eds.), *The handbook of second language acquisition* (pp. 213–228). San Diego, CA: Academic Press.

McLaughlin, M. (2012). *Guided comprehension for English learners.* Newark, DE: International Reading Association.

Mehisto, P. (2015). Estonia: Laying the groundwork for bilingual education. In P. Mehisto & F. Genesee (Eds.), *Building bilingual education systems: Forces, mechanisms and counterweights* (pp. 59–82). Cambridge, UK: Cambridge University Press.

Menken, K. (2017). *Leadership in dual language bilingual education.* A National Dual Language Forum White Paper. Alexandria, VA: Center for Applied Linguistics. Retrieved from http://www.cal.org/ndlf/resources/

Met, M. (2008). Paying attention to language: Literacy, language and academic achievement. In T. W. Fortune & D. J. Tedick (Eds.), *Pathways to bilingualism and multilingualism: Evolving perspectives on immersion education* (pp. 49–70). Clevedon, UK: Multilingual Matters.

Minnesota Mandarin Immersion Collaborative. (n.d.). *Engineering is Elementary® units.* Center for Advanced Research on Language Acquisition (CARLA). Minneapolis, MN: University of Minnesota. Retrieved from http://carla.umn.edu/immersion/MMIC/index.html

Miville, M. L., Gelso, C. J., Pannu, R., Liu, W., Touradji, P., Holloway, P., & Fuertes, J. (1999). Appreciating similarities and valuing differences: The Miville-Guzman Universality-Diversity Scale. *Journal of Counseling Psychology, 46*(3), 291–307.

Mohan, B., & Beckett, G. H. (2001). A functional approach to research on content-based language learning: Recasts in causal explanations. *The Canadian Modern Language Review, 58*, 133–155.

Moll, L. C., Amanti, C., Neff, D., & González, N. (1992). Funds of knowledge for teaching: Using a qualitative approach to connect homes and classrooms. *Theory into Practice, 31*(2), 132–141.

Muñoz, C. (2008). Symmetries and asymmetries of age effects in naturalistic and instructed L2 learning. *Applied Linguistics, 24*, 578–596.

Muñoz, C., & Spada, N. (2019). Foreign language learning from early childhood to young adulthood. In A. de Houwer & L. Ortega (Eds.), *The Cambridge handbook of bilingualism* (pp. 233–249). Cambridge, UK: Cambridge University Press.

Musumeci, D. (1996). Teacher-learner negotiation in content-based instruction: Communication at cross-purposes? *Applied Linguistics, 17*, 286–325.

Nakatsukasa, K. (2016). Efficacy of recasts and gestures on the acquisition of locative prepositions. *Studies in Second Language Acquisition, 38*(4), 771–799.

Nakatsukasa, K., & Loewen, S. (2017). Non-verbal feedback. In H. Nassaji & E. Kartcheva (Eds.), *Corrective feedback in second language teaching and learning: Research, theory, applications, implications* (pp. 158–173). New York, NY: Routledge.

Nassaji, H., & Wells, G. (2000). What's the use of "triadic dialogue"?: An investigation of teacher-student interaction. *Applied Linguistics, 21,* 376–406.

National Academies of Sciences, Engineering, and Medicine. (2017). *Promoting the educational success of children and youth learning English: Promising futures.* Washington, DC: The National Academies Press. Retrieved from https://www.nap.edu/catalog/24677/promoting-the-educational-success-of-children-and-youth-learning-english

National Governors Association Center for Best Practices, Council of Chief State School Officers. (2010). *Common core state standards.* Retrieved from http://www.corestandards.org/

National Standards Collaborative Board. (2015). *World-readiness standards for learning languages* (4th ed.). Alexandria, VA: National Standards Collaborative Board. Summary retrieved from https://www.actfl.org/publications/all/world-readiness-standards-learning-languages/standards-summary

Naughton, D. (2006). Cooperative strategy training and oral interaction: Enhancing small group communication in the language classroom. *The Modern Language Journal, 90,* 169–184.

Netten, J. (1991). Towards a more language oriented second language classroom. In L. Malavé & G. Duquette (Eds.), *Language, culture and cognition* (pp. 284–304). Clevedon, UK: Multilingual Matters.

Netten, J., & Spain, W. (1989). Student-teacher interaction patterns in the French immersion classroom: Implications for levels of achievement in French language proficiency. *The Canadian Modern Language Review, 45,* 485–501.

Nicholas, H., Lightbown, P. M., & Spada, N. (2001). Recasts as feedback to language learners. *Language Learning, 51*(4), 719–758.

Nunan, D. (1989). Hidden agendas: The role of the learner in programme implementation. In R. K. Johnson (Ed.), *The second language curriculum* (pp. 176–186). Cambridge, UK: Cambridge University Press.

Oliver, R. (2000). Age differences in negotiation and feedback in classroom and pairwork. *Language Learning, 50*(1), 119–151.

Oliver, R., & Mackey, A. (2003). Interactional context and feedback in child ESL classrooms. *The Modern Language Journal, 87*(4), 519–543.

Olivos, E. M. (2006). *The power of parents: A critical perspective of bicultural parent involvement in public schools.* New York, NY: Peter Lang.

Olivos, E. M., Ochoa, A. M., & Jiménez-Castellanos, O. (2011). Critical voices in bicultural parent engagement: A framework for transformation. In E. M. Olivos, O. Jiménez-Castellanos, & A. M. Ochoa (Eds.), *Bicultural parent engagement: Advocacy and empowerment* (pp. 1–17). New York, NY: Teachers College Press.

O'Malley, J. M., & Chamot, A. U. (1990). *Learning strategies in second language acquisition.* New York, NY: Cambridge University Press.

Oosterhof, A. (2009). *Developing and using classroom assessments* (4th ed.). Upper Saddle River, NJ: Pearson Education.

Otheguy, R., García, O., & Reid, W. (2015). Clarifying translanguaging and deconstructing named languages: A perspective from linguistics. *Applied Linguistics Review, 6*(3), 281–307.

Ovando, C. J. (2003). Bilingual education in the United States: Historical development and current issues. *Bilingual Research Journal, 27*(1), 1–24. DOI: 10.1080/15235882.2003.10162589.

Palmer, D. K. (2007). A dual immersion strand programme in California: Carrying out the promise of dual language education in an English-dominant context. *International Journal of Bilingual Education and Bilingualism, 10*(6), 752–768.

Palmer, D. K., & Martínez, R. A. (2013). Teacher agency in bilingual spaces: A fresh look at preparing teachers to educate Latina/o bilingual children. *Review of Research in Education, 37*, 269–297.

Palmer, D. K., Martínez, R. A., Mateus, S. G., & Henderson, K. (2014). Reframing the debate on language separation: Toward a vision for translanguaging pedagogies in the dual language classroom. *Modern Language Journal, 98*(3), 757–772.

Paradis, J., Genesee, F., & Crago, M. (2011). *Dual language and development disorders: A handbook on bilingualism & second language learning* (2nd ed.). Baltimore: Brookes Publishing.

Pasquarella, A., Chen, X., Lam, K., & Luo, Y. C. (2011). Cross-language transfer of morphological awareness in Chinese-English bilinguals. *Journal of Research in Reading, 34*(1), 23–42.

Penner, S. (1987). Parental responses to grammatical and ungrammatical child utterances. *Child Development, 58*, 376–384.

Perfetti, C. A., & Dunlap, S. (2008). Learning to read: General principles and writing system variations. In K. Koda & A. M. Zehler (Eds.), *Learning to read across languages: Cross-linguistic relationships in first- and second-language literacy development* (pp. 13–38). New York, NY: Routledge.

Philp, J., Walter, S., & Basturkmen, H. (2010). Peer interaction in the foreign language classroom: What factors foster a focus on form? *Language Awareness, 19*(4), 261–279.

Poirier, J., & Lyster, R. (2014). Les pronoms objets directs de la 3e personne et leur apport aux indices du genre grammatical dans le discours oral des enseignants en immersion. [Third-person direct object pronouns as clues to grammatical gender in immersion teacher talk.] *The Canadian Modern Language Review, 70*(2), 246–267.

Porras, D. A., Ee, J., & Gándara, P. C. (2014). Employer preferences: Do bilingual applicants and employees experience an advantage? In R. M. Callahan & P. C. Gándara (Eds.), *The bilingual advantage: Language, literacy and the US labor market* (pp. 234–257). Bristol, UK: Multilingual Matters.

Potowski, K. (2004). Student Spanish use and investment in a dual immersion classroom: Implications for second language acquisition and heritage language maintenance. *Modern Language Journal, 88*(1), 75–101.

Potowski, K. (2007). *Language and identity in a dual immersion school.* Clevedon, UK: Multilingual Matters.

Purpura, J. (2004). *Assessing grammar.* Cambridge, UK: Cambridge University Press.

Quinn, G. P., & Nakata, T. (2017). The timing of oral corrective feedback. In H. Nassaji & E. Kartchava (Eds.), *Corrective feedback in second language teaching and learning: Research, theory, applications, implications* (pp. 35–47). London: Routledge.

Ranta, L., & Lyster, R. (2007). A cognitive approach to improving immersion students' oral language abilities: The Awareness-Practice-Feedback sequence. In R. DeKeyser (Ed.), *Practice in a second language: Perspectives from applied linguistics and cognitive psychology* (pp. 141–160). Cambridge, UK: Cambridge University Press.

Ranta, L., & Lyster, R. (2018). Form-focused instruction. In P. Garrett & J. Cots (Eds.), *The Routledge handbook of language awareness* (pp. 40–56). New York, NY: Routledge.

Rao, M. (2019, March 17). Looking for books that reflect diverse students, Minnesota teachers publish their own. *Star Tribune.* Retrieved from http://www.startribune.com/looking-for-books-that-reflect-diverse-students-minnesota-teachers-publish-their-own/507279402/

Rehner, K. (2018). *The classroom practices of DELF teacher-correcteurs: A pan-Canadian perspective.* Ottawa, ON: Canadian Association of Immersion Professionals (ACPI). Retrieved from http://www.acpi.ca/documents/documents/Rehner_Report_20 18_final_mars_2018_EN_final.pdf

Rivkin, S. G., Hanushek, E. A., & Kain, J. F. (2005). Teachers, schools, and academic achievement. *Econometrics, 73,* 417–458.

Rolstad, K. (1997). Effects of two-way immersion on the ethnic identification of third language students: An exploratory study. *Bilingual Research Journal, 21*(1), 43–63.

Ronfeldt, M., Farmer, S., McQueen, K., & Grissom, J. (2015). Teacher collaboration in instructional teams and student achievement. *American Educational Research Association, 52*(3), 475–514.

Roothooft, H., & Breeze, R. (2016). A comparison of EFL teachers' and students' attitudes to oral corrective feedback. *Language Awareness, 25*(4), 318–335.

Rowan, B., Correnti, R., & Miller, R. J. (2002). What large-scale survey research tells us about teacher effects on student achievement. Insights from the Prospects study of elementary schools. *Teachers College Record, 104,* 1525–1567.

Salomone, A. (1992a). Immersion teachers' pedagogical beliefs and practices: Results of a descriptive analysis. In E. Bernhardt (Ed.), *Life in language immersion classrooms* (pp. 9–44). Clevedon, UK: Multilingual Matters.

Salomone, A. (1992b). Student-teacher interactions in selected French immersion classrooms. In E. Bernhardt (Ed.), *Life in language immersion classrooms* (pp. 97–109). Clevedon, UK: Multilingual Matters.

Sánchez, M. T., García, O., & Solorza, C. (2018). Reframing language education policy in dual language bilingual education. *Bilingual Research Journal, 41,* 37–51.

Santamaria, L. J. (2009). Culturally responsive differentiated instruction: Narrowing gaps between best pedagogical practices benefiting all learners. *Teachers College Record, 111*(1), 214–247.

Santibañez, L., & Zárate, M. E. (2014). Bilinguals in the US and college enrollment. In R. M. Callahan & P. C. Gándara (Eds.), *The bilingual advantage: Language, literacy and the US labor market* (pp. 211–233). Bristol, UK: Multilingual Matters.

Sato, M. (2017). Interaction mindsets, interactional behaviors, and L2 development: An affective-social-cognitive model. *Language Learning, 67*(2), 249–283.

Savignon, S. (1997). *Communicative competence: Theory and classroom practice* (2nd ed.). New York, NY: McGraw-Hill.

Scanlan, M., & López, F. (2012). ¡Vamos! How school leaders promote equity and excellence for bilingual students. *Educational Administration Quarterly, 48*(4), 583–625.

Schleppegrell, M. J. (2012). Academic language in teaching and learning: Introduction to the special issue. *The Elementary School Journal, 112*(3), 409–418.

Schmidt, R. (1990). The role of consciousness in second language learning. *Applied Linguistics, 11,* 129–158.

Schmidt, R. (2001). Attention. In P. Robinson (Ed.), *Cognition and second language instruction* (pp. 3–32). New York, NY: Cambridge University Press.

Schulz, R. (2001). Cultural differences in student and teacher perceptions concerning the role of grammar instruction and corrective feedback: USA-Columbia. *The Modern Language Journal, 85,* 244–258.

Seedhouse, P. (1997). The case of the missing "no": The relationship between pedagogy and interaction. *Language Learning, 47,* 547–583.

Segalowitz, N. (2000). Automaticity and attentional skill in fluent performance. In H. Riggenbach (Ed.), *Perspectives on fluency* (pp. 200–219). Ann Arbor, MI: University of Michigan Press.

Selinker, L. (1972). Interlanguage. *International Review of Applied Linguistics in Language Teaching, 10*(1–4), 209–232.

Shannon, S. (2011). Parent engagement and equity in a dual language program. In E. M. Olivos, O. Jiménez-Castellanos, & A. M. Ochoa (Eds.), *Bicultural parent engagement: Advocacy and empowerment* (pp. 83–102). New York, NY: Teachers College Press.

Sharwood Smith, M. (1993). Input enhancement in instructed SLA. *Studies in Second Language Acquisition, 15*, 165–179.

Sharpe, T. (2006). "Unpacking" scaffolding: Identifying discourse and multimodal strategies that support learning. *Language and Education, 20*(3), 211–231.

Sheen, Y. (2011). *Corrective feedback, individual differences and second language learning.* New York, NY: Springer.

Sheen, Y., & Ellis, R. (2011). Corrective feedback in language teaching. In E. Hinkel (Ed.), *Handbook of research in second language teaching and learning* (Vol. 2, pp. 593–610). New York, NY: Routledge.

Shiffrin, R. M., & Schneider, W. (1977). Controlled and automatic human information processing: II. Perceptual learning, automatic attending, and a general theory. *Psychological Review, 84*, 127–190.

Shohamy, E., & Ghazaleh-Mahajneh, A. (2012). Linguistic landscape as a tool for interpreting language vitality: Arabic as a "minority" language in Israel. In D. Gorter, H. F. Marten, & L. Van Mensel (Eds.), *Minority languages in the linguistic landscape* (pp. 89–106). London: Palgrave Macmillan.

Siekmann, S., Webster, J. P., Samson, S. A., & Moses, C. K. (2017). Teaching our way of life through our language: Materials development for Indigenous immersion education. *Cogent Education, 4*, 1–13.

Sinclair, J., & Coulthard, R. M. (1975). *Towards an analysis of discourse: The English used by teachers and pupils.* Oxford: Oxford University Press.

Skehan, P. (1998). *A cognitive approach to language learning.* Oxford: Oxford University Press.

Slaughter, H. (1997). Indigenous language immersion in Hawai'i: A case study of Kula Kaiapuni Hawai'i. In R. K. Johnson & M. Swain (Eds.), *Immersion education: International perspectives* (pp. 105–129). Cambridge, UK: Cambridge University Press.

Snow, M. A. (1990). Immersion education: An overview and comparison of three programs. In A. Padilla, H. Fairchild, & C. Valadez (Eds.), *Foreign language education: Issues and strategies* (pp. 109–126). Newbury Park, CA: Sage Publications.

Snow, M. A., Met, M., & Genesee, F. (1989). A conceptual framework for the integration of language and content in second/foreign language instruction. *TESOL Quarterly, 23*, 201–217.

Soanes, C., & Hawker, S. (Eds.) (2008). *Compact Oxford English dictionary of current English* (3rd ed., revised). Oxford: Oxford University Press.

Södergård, M. (2008). Teacher strategies for second language production in immersion kindergarten in Finland. In T. W. Fortune & D. J. Tedick (Eds.), *Pathways to bilingualism and multilingualism: Evolving perspectives on immersion education* (pp. 152–173). Clevedon, UK: Multilingual Matters.

Spada, N., & Lightbown, P. M. (1993). Instruction and the development of questions in L2 classrooms. *Studies in Second Language Acquisition, 15*, 205–224.

Spada, N., & Lightbown, P. M. (2008). Form-focused instruction: Isolated or integrated? *TESOL Quarterly, 42*(2), 181–207.

Spada, N., Lightbown, P. M., & White, J. (2005). The importance of form/meaning mappings in explicit form-focused instruction. In A. Housen & M. Pierrard (Eds.),

302 References

Investigations in instructed second language acquisition (pp. 199–234). Amsterdam: Mouton de Gruyter.

Spada, N., & Tomita, Y. (2010). Interactions between type of instruction and type of language feature: A meta-analysis. *Language Learning, 60*(2), 263–308.

Statistics Canada. (2017). *English, French and official language minorities in Canada.* Retrieved from http://www12.statcan.gc.ca/census-recensement/2016/as-sa/98-200-x/2016 011/98-200-x2016011-eng.cfm

Steele, J. L., Slater, R. O., Zamarro, G., Miller, T., Li, J., Burkhauser, S., & Bacon, M. (2017). Effects of dual-language immersion programs on student achievement: Evidence from lottery data. *American Educational Research Journal, 54*(1S), 282S–306S.

Stern, H. H. (1990). Analysis and experience as variables in second language pedagogy. In B. Harley, P. Allen, J. Cummins, & M. Swain (Eds.), *The development of second language proficiency* (pp. 93–109). Cambridge, UK: Cambridge University Press.

Stern, H. H. (1992). *Issues and options in language teaching.* Oxford: Oxford University Press.

Stevens, F. (1983). Activities to promote learning and communication in the second language classroom. *TESOL Quarterly, 17*, 259–272.

Swain, M. (1985). Communicative competence: Some roles of comprehensible input and comprehensible output in its development. In S. Gass & C. Madden (Eds.), *Input in second language acquisition* (pp. 235–253). Rowley, MA: Newbury House.

Swain, M. (1988). Manipulating and complementing content teaching to maximize second language learning. *TESL Canada Journal, 6*, 68–83.

Swain, M. (1993). The output hypothesis: Just speaking and writing aren't enough. *The Canadian Modern Language Review, 50*, 158–165.

Swain, M. (1995). Three functions of output in second language learning. In G. Cook & B. Seidlhofer (Eds.), *Principle and practice in applied linguistics: Studies in honour of H. G. Widdowson* (pp. 125–144). Oxford: Oxford University Press.

Swain, M. (2005). The output hypothesis: Theory and research. In E. Hinkel (Ed.), *Handbook of research in second language teaching and learning* (pp. 471–484). Mahwah, NJ: Lawrence Erlbaum.

Swain, M., & Johnson, R. K. (1997). Immersion education: A category within bilingual education. In R. K. Johnson & M. Swain (Eds.), *Immersion education: International perspectives* (pp. 1–16). Cambridge, UK: Cambridge University Press.

Swain, M., & Lapkin, S. (2013). A Vygotskian sociocultural perspective on immersion education: The L1/L2 debate. *Journal of Immersion and Content-Based Education, 1,* 101–129.

Swain, M., Lapkin, S., Rowen, N., & Hart, D. (1990). The role of mother tongue literacy in third language learning. *Language, Culture, and Curriculum, 3*(1), 65–81.

Swan, M. (2018). Applied linguistics: A consumer's view. *Language Teaching, 51*(2), 246–261.

Tedick, D. J. (2015). United States of America: The paradoxes and possibilities of bilingual education. In P. Mehisto & F. Genesee (Eds.), *Building bilingual education systems: Forces, mechanisms and counterweights* (pp. 1–21). Cambridge, UK: Cambridge University Press.

Tedick, D. J., & Fortune, T. W. (2013). Bilingual/immersion teacher education. In C. A. Chapelle (Ed.), *The encyclopedia of applied linguistics* (pp. 438–443). Hoboken, NJ: Wiley-Blackwell. DOI: 10.1002/9781405198431.wbeal0096.

Tedick, D. J., & Mathieu, C. (2018, May). Validating a rubric for immersion teacher assessment. In T. J. Ó Ceallaigh (Chair), *Developing Teaching and Leadership Capacity in*

Immersion. Symposium conducted at The Second All-Ireland Research Conference on Immersion Education, Limerick, Ireland.

Tedick, D. J., & Wesely, P. M. (2015). A review of research on content-based foreign/second language education in US K-12 contexts. *Language, Culture and Curriculum, 28*(1), 25–40.

Tedick, D. J., & Young, A. I. (2016). Fifth grade two-way immersion students' responses to form-focused instruction. *Applied Linguistics, 37*(6), 784–807.

Tedick, D. J., & Zilmer, C. (2018). Teacher perceptions of immersion professional development experiences emphasizing language-focused content instruction. *Journal of Immersion and Content-Based Language Education, 6*(2), 271–297.

Tharpe, R., & Gallimore, R. (1988). *Rousing minds to life: Teaching, learning, and schooling in social context.* New York, NY: Cambridge University Press.

The National Standards Collaborative Board. (2015). *World-readiness standards for learning languages* (4th ed.) Alexandria, VA: The National Standards Collaborative Board.

Thomas, W. P., & Collier, V. P. (2012). *Dual language education for a transformed world.* Albuquerque, NM: Dual Language Education of New Mexico and Fuente Press.

Thomas, W. P., & Collier, V. P. (2017). *Why dual language schooling.* Albuquerque: Dual Language Education of New Mexico and Fuente Press.

Tomlinson, C. A. (2003). *Fulfilling the promise of the differentiated classroom: Strategies and tools for responsive teaching.* Alexandria, VA: Association for Supervision and Curriculum Development.

Truscott, J. (1996). The case against grammar correction in L2 writing classes. *Language Learning, 46*, 327–369.

Truscott, J. (1999). What's wrong with oral grammar correction. *The Canadian Modern Language Review, 55*, 437–456.

Truscott, J. (2009). Dialogue. *Journal of Second Language Writing, 18*, 59–90.

Truth and Reconciliation Commission of Canada. (2015). *Report of the Truth and Reconciliation Commission of Canada.* Retrieved from http://caid.ca/DTRC.html

Turnbull, M., Lapkin, S., & Hart, D. (2001). Grade 3 immersion students' performance in literacy and mathematics: Province-wide results from Ontario (1998–1999). *The Canadian Modern Language Review, 58*(1), 9–26

Unger, M. (2001). Equalizing the status of both languages in a dual immersion school. *The ACIE Newsletter, 5*(1), 1–3, 8, 12–13. Retrieved from http://carla.umn.edu/immersion/acie/vol5/Nov2001_EqualStatus.html

Utah Dual Language Immersion. (2018). *Utah Dual Language Immersion.* Retrieved from http://utahdli.org/index.html

Valdés, G. (1997). Dual-language immersion programs: A cautionary note concerning the education of language-minority students. *Harvard Educational Review, 67*(3), 391–429.

VanPatten, B. (2017). Processing instruction. In S. Loewen & M. Sato (Eds.), *The Routledge handbook of instructed second language acquisition* (pp. 166–180). New York, NY: Routledge.

Vygotsky, L. (1978). *Mind and society.* Cambridge, MA: Harvard University Press.

Weber, S., & Tardif, C. (1991). Assessing L2 competency in early immersion classrooms. *The Canadian Modern Language Review, 47*, 916–932.

Weiner, S. L., & Goodenough, D. R. (1977). A move toward a psychology of conversation. In R. Freedle (Ed.), *Discourse production and comprehension* (pp. 213–225). Norwood, NJ: Ablex.

Weininger, E. B., & Lareau, A. (2003). Translating Bourdieu into the American context: The question of social class and family-school relations. *Poetics, 31*, 375–402.

Wells, G. (2001). The development of a community of inquirers. In G. Wells (Ed.), *Action, talk, and text: Learning and teaching through inquiry* (pp. 1–22). New York, NY: Teachers College Press.

Wesche, M. (1993). French immersion graduates at university and beyond: What difference has it made? In J. Alatis (Ed.), *Georgetown University Round Table on Languages and Linguistics 1992: Language, communication and social meaning* (pp. 208–240). Washington, DC: Georgetown University Press.

Wesely, P. M. (2010). Language learning motivation in early adolescents: Using mixed methods research to explore contradiction. *Journal of Mixed Methods Research, 4,* 295–312.

Wiggins, G., & McTighe, J. (2005). *Understanding by design* (2nd ed.). Alexandria, VA: Association for Supervision and Curriculum Development.

Williams, C. (1996). Secondary education: Teaching in the bilingual situation. In C. Williams, G. Lewis, & C. Baker (Eds.), *The language policy: Taking stock* (pp. 39–78). Llangefni, UK: CAI.

Williams, C. (2002). *Ennill iaith: Astudiaeth o sefyllfa drochi yn 11–16 oed* [A language gained: A study of language immersion at 11–16 years of age]. Bangor, UK: School of Education. Retrieved from http://www.bangor.ac.uk/addysg/publications/Ennill_Iaith.pdf

Williams, M., & Burden, R. (1997). *Psychology for language teachers: A social constructivist approach.* Cambridge, UK: Cambridge University Press.

Wilson, W. H., & Kamanā, K. (2001). "Mai loko mai o ka 'i'ini: Proceeding from a dream." The 'Aha Pūnana Leo connection in Hawaiian language revitalization. In L. Hinton & K. Hale (Eds.), *The Green Book of Language Revitalization in Practice* (pp. 147–76). San Diego, CA: Academic Press.

Wilson, W. H., & Kamanā, K. (2011). Insights from Indigenous language immersion in Hawai'i. In D. J. Tedick, D. Christian, & T. W. Fortune (Eds.), *Immersion education: Practices, policies, possibilities* (pp. 36–57). Bristol, UK: Multilingual Matters.

Wood, D., Bruner, J., & Ross, G. (1976). The role of tutoring in problem solving. *Journal of Child Psychology and Psychiatry, 17,* 89–100.

Wood, L., & Bauman, E. (2017). *How family, school, and community engagement can improve student achievement and influence school reform: Literature review.* Washington, DC: American Institutes for Research. Retrieved from https://www.nmefoundation.org/getattachment/67f7c030-df45-4076-a23f-0d7f0596983f/Final-Report-Family-Engagement-AIR.pdf?lang=en-US&ext=.pdf

Wong, J., & Waring, H. Z. (2009). "Very good" as a teacher response. *ELT Journal, 63*(3), 195–203.

Wong-Fillmore, L. (1982). Instructional language as linguistic input: Second language learning in classrooms. In L. C. Wilkinson (Ed.), *Communicating in the classroom* (pp. 283–294). New York, NY: Academic Press.

Wray, A. (2002). *Formulaic language and the lexicon.* Cambridge, UK: Cambridge University Press.

Wright, R. (1996). A study of the acquisition of verbs of motion by grade 4/5 early French immersion students. *The Canadian Modern Language Review, 53,* 257–280.

Yoshida, R. (2008). Learners' perception of corrective feedback in pair work. *Foreign Language Annals, 41*(3), 525–541.

Young, A. I. (2016). Facilitating functional complexity: Differentiated linguistic scaffolding in two-way Spanish-English immersion. *Journal of Immersion and Content-Based Language Education, 4*(2), 251–273.

Young, A. I., & Tedick, D. J. (2016). Collaborative dialogue in a two-way Spanish/English immersion classroom: Does heterogeneous grouping promote peer linguistic scaffolding? In M. Sato & S. Ballinger (Eds.), *Peer interaction and second language learning: Pedagogical potential and research agenda* (pp. 135–160). Amsterdam: John Benjamins.

Zehrbach, G. (2006). Paradigms of participation. *The ACIE Newsletter, 10*(1), 1–2, 15. Retrieved from http://carla.umn.edu/immersion/acie/vol10/nov2006_bestpractice_paradigms.html

Zwiers, J. (2008). *Building academic language: Essential practices for content classrooms.* San Francisco, CA: Jossey-Bass.

APPENDIX A: ImDL UNIT DESIGN EXAMPLE

Adaptations Unit Plan

Context

Program Particulars

- ImDL program model: 90:10 TWI
- Minority/partner language: Spanish
- Grade level(s): Grade 3 (specifically the 3rd quarter)

Student Characteristics

- *Ethnic and Linguistic Background and Gender*
    - 24 students total, 14 girls and 10 boys
    - 10 Latinx students (4 boys, 6 girls), 8 Mexican, 1 Honduran, 1 Ecuadoran
        - 3 simultaneous bilinguals
        - 7 sequential bilinguals (Spanish-dominant)
    - 14 English-dominant sequential bilinguals (8 girls, 6 boys), 2 African American, 1 Asian, 11 White
- *Special Needs*
    - One Mexican boy and one English-dominant White girl have IEPs (individualized education program).

- *Minority/Partner Language Proficiency and Literacy Level* (2 students with IEPs still at "Entering" level in some modalities)
    - Oral proficiency (WIDA performance descriptors)
        - Bilinguals and students learning through L1
            - Listening range: Level 2 Emerging to Level 5 Bridging
            - Speaking range: Level 2 Emerging to Level 4 Expanding
        - Students learning through L2
            - Listening range: Level 2 Emerging to Level 4 Expanding
            - Speaking range: Level 1 Entering to Level 3 Developing

- Literacy (WIDA performance descriptors)
  - Bilinguals and students learning through L1
    - Reading range: Level 1 Entering to Level 4 Expanding
    - Writing range: Level 1 Entering to Level 4 Expanding
  - Students learning through L2
    - Reading range: Level 1 Entering to Level 4 Expanding
    - Writing range: Level 1 Entering to Level 3 Developing

Unit Particulars

Unit Theme/Big Idea: Adaptations	*Time Frame:* 6 weeks (including summative assessment)
Key Generalization: All living things adapt to their environment.	*Subject Matters Targeted:* Science Social Studies Language Arts/Literacy

Students' Background Knowledge and Skills

Knowledge/Understandings   Students have developing understanding of …

- how a food chain works;
- the life cycles of different living things;
- map literacy skills;
- basic parts of speech: verbs, nouns, adjectives, adverbs, and conjunctions;
- some verb tenses in Spanish (present, some understanding of preterite and imperfect) and how conjugations work;
- how to organize paragraphs and longer texts in some genres (e.g., reports).

Essential Skills   Students are able to …

- use non-fiction text features (table of contents, index, diagrams, etc.) to locate important information and use dictionaries;
- retain a limited number of facts and share them in their own words with visual aid support;
- use developing digital literacy skills (keyboarding, Google searches);
- locate places on simple maps;
- collaborate effectively with group members;
- comprehend grade-level oral and written text in Spanish;
- ask and answer questions;
- paraphrase information from a written or oral text;
- recognize cognates and use some contextual clues to learn new words.

Key Concepts (by subject) and Module Topics

Key concepts:

- Science—adaptation, heredity, classification, habitat, climate, survival
- Social studies—maps, geographical features of environments, human impact
- Language arts/literacy—informational text genre, fiction versus non-fiction

(left margin labels: Context / Desired Results)

Module topics:

- What are heredity and adaptation?
- How and why are different living things classified?
- Are approaches to animal classification the same across cultures?
- What are habitats?
- Why do living things adapt? What happens when they don't adapt?
- What do adaptations look like for different living things?
- What is a climate map?
- How does location affect adaptation? How do adaptations help living things survive in their environment?

Standards/Outcomes

Content (by subject):

Literacy and Language Arts: (CCSS)

CCSS.ELA-Literacy.RI.3.10 By the end of the year, read and comprehend informational texts, including history/social studies, science, and technical texts, at the high end of the grades 2–3 text complexity band independently and proficiently.

CCSS.ELA-Literacy.W.3.2 Write informative/explanatory texts to examine a topic and convey ideas and information clearly.

CCSS.ELA-Literacy.SL.3.4 Report on a topic or text, tell a story, or recount an experience with appropriate facts and relevant, descriptive details, speaking clearly at an understandable pace.

CCSS.ELA-Literacy.SL.3.6 Speak in complete sentences when appropriate to task and situation in order to provide requested detail or clarification.

Science: (Minnesota)

3.4.1.1.1 Compare how the different structures of plants and animals serve various functions of growth, survival, and reproduction.

3.4.1.1.2 Identify common groups of plants and animals using observable physical characteristics, structures, and behaviors.

Language and Culture:

Communication:

1.1: Learners interact and negotiate meaning in spoken, signed, or written conversations to share information, reactions, feelings, and opinions.

1.2: Learners understand, interpret, and analyze what is heard, read, or viewed on a variety of topics.

1.3: Learners present information, concepts, and ideas to inform, explain, persuade, and narrate on a variety of topics using appropriate media and adapting to various audiences of listeners, readers, or viewers.

Cultures:

2.2: Learners use language to investigate, explain, and reflect on the relationship between the products and perspectives of the cultures studied.

Connections:

3.1: Learners build, reinforce, and expand their knowledge of other disciplines while using the language to develop critical thinking and to solve problems creatively.

Desired Results

3.4.3.2.1 Give examples of likenesses between adults and offspring in plants and animals that can be inherited or acquired. *Social Studies: (Minnesota)* *3.3.1.1.1* Use maps and concepts of location (relative location words and cardinal and intermediate directions) to describe places in one's community, the state of Minnesota, the United States, or the world. *3.3.1.1.2* Create and interpret simple maps of places around the world, local to global; incorporate the "TODALS" map basics, as well as points, lines, and colored areas to display spatial information.	*Comparisons:* *4.1:* Learners use the language to investigate, explain, and reflect on the nature of language through comparisons of the languages studied and their own. *Communities:* *5.1:* Learners use the language both within and beyond the classroom to interact and collaborate in their community and the globalized world.

Unit-Level Goals

(Desired Results)

Knowledge/Understandings: *Students will understand that …*	*Skills:* *Students will be able to …*
• form is connected to function; • key characteristics are used to classify living things; • living things inherit traits; • adaptation is necessary for survival; • biodiversity is worth preserving; • location affects adaptation; • environment impacts the need for adaptation; • maps have elements (legends) that help people find locations and interpret the information on the map; • there are a variety of ways to express cause and effect and compare/contrast in Spanish; • preterite and imperfect tenses in Spanish are used to express different events/descriptions in the past; • the informational genre has specific characteristics.	• gather information from provided resources; • use non-fiction text features to draw information from a text; • summarize information from a variety of sources; • identify adaptations of living things; • compare and contrast the adaptations of different living things; • speculate about alternative classification methods to Western science based on criteria specific to folk cultures; • use a map to identify specific locations; • locate similar habitats in different parts of the world; • explain how adaptations help living things survive in their environments;

Desired Results		• explain cause and effect in relation to adaptations; • correctly use academic language related to adaptations; • recount information to peers using content-related language; • use word-formation strategies and cognates (cross-lingual connections) to identify the meaning of new words in Spanish (drawing upon knowledge of English and vice versa); • formulate questions related to content of informational texts and adaptations; • interact with and work collaboratively with peers.
Evidence	**Unit-Level Summative Performance Assessment and Other Assessment Activities**	
	IPA tasks *Interpretive:* Students will read different sections from the *¿Cómo se adaptan?* text (Kalman, 2007) and complete a reading comprehension task. *Interpersonal:* Pairs of students will engage in an information gap activity (completion of a graphic organizer) to share the information they learned during the Interpretive task. *Presentational:* Pairs of students will collaborate to create a living creature that is well adapted to an assigned environment (biome). The pairs will present their designs to their pen pals in Ecuador in a VoiceThread presentation.	*Other assessments* • close observation with use of checklists as students complete lesson activities; • checking of individual science notebooks/journals; • completion of graphic organizers; • completion of a handout to accompany climate map reading; • homework assignments; • written summaries; • written reflections; • small-group and whole-class discussions about informational texts.

Unit References and Resources

Ciudad 17 (2011). *Animales salvajes*. Retrieved from http://www.ciudad17.com/
Naturaleza/

Conklin, W. (2017). *Características de supervivencia*. Huntington Beach, CA: Teacher
Created Materials Publishing.

Galapaguide. *Animales de las Islas Galápagos*. Retrieved from http://www.galapagui
de.com/islas_galapagos_fauna_esp.htm

Gibbons, P. (2015). *Scaffolding language scaffolding learning: Teaching English language
learners in the mainstream classroom* (2nd ed.). Portsmouth, NH: Heinemann.

Hamayan, E., Genesee, F., & Cloud, N. (2013). *Dual language instruction from A to Z:
Practical guidance for teachers and administrators*. Portsmouth, NH: Heinemann.

Heller, R. (1994). *How to hide a polar bear & other mammals*. New York, NY: Scholastic
Inc.

Kalman, B. (2007). *¿Cómo se adaptan los animales?* New York, NY: Crabtree
Publishing Company.

Kids Do Ecology. (2004). *Biomas del mundo*. Retrieved from http://kids.nceas.ucsb.ed
u/sp/biomesspan/index.html

Met, M. (2008). Paying attention to language: Literacy, language and academic
achievement. In T. W. Fortune & D. J. Tedick (Eds.), *Pathways to bilingualism and
multilingualism: Evolving perspectives on immersion education* (pp. 49–70). Clevedon,
UK: Multilingual Matters.

Punchard, I. (2002, November). Improving immersion student oral proficiency by
fostering the use of extended discourse. *The ACIE Newsletter*. Retrieved from http:
//carla.umn.edu/immersion/acie/#bridge

The National Standards Collaborative Board. (2015). *World-readiness standards for
learning languages* (4th ed.) Alexandria, VA: Author.

WIDA Consortium. (2012). *Performance definitions*. Madison, WI: Wisconsin Center
for Education Research, University of Wisconsin.

Web-based resource:

https://cva4cca.wordpress.com/2015/03/20/adaptaciones-de-los-animales/

APPENDIX B: ImDL MODULE AND LESSON DESIGN EXAMPLE

Module Number: 7 **Module Topic:** How do geographic location and climate affect adaptation? **Time Frame:** 5 lessons over 5 days (approximately 5 hours total)	

<table>
<tr><td rowspan="1">Desired Results</td><td>Learning Objectives</td></tr>
<tr><td></td><td>

Content: Students will …

Social Studies:

1. identify geographic locations on a climate map to show where certain animals live;
2. use a map legend to determine the climate of an area.

Science:

3. identify different types of animal adaptations, providing examples of both structural and behavioral adaptations in relationship to the underlying reason for the adaptation;
4. explain how certain animals have adapted to survive in their environment;
5. compare and contrast key characteristics of specific animals.

Literacy/Language Arts:

6. demonstrate comprehension of animal cards describing geographic location and physical characteristics of animals;
7. answer questions, provide detail, and share information and opinions;
8. write an informative paragraph comparing two animals from different climates to report on how adaptations help living things survive.

</td></tr>
</table>

<table>
<tr>
<td rowspan="1">Desired Results</td>
<td>

Language:
Content obligatory

All students

1. Dialogue: ask simple questions to check the partner's prior knowledge about a given animal using the following verbs:
   - present tense of the verb *to know (conocer):* Do you know this animal? (*¿Conoces a este animal?*)
   - present perfect tense of verbs such as *to see (ver)* and *to hear (oír)*: Have you seen this animal (*¿Has visto a este animal?); * Have you heard of this animal? (*¿Has oido hablar de este animal?*)
2. Report: identify animal characteristics using the following nouns and verbs:
   - animal names such as *giraffe (la jirafa), el koala, desert rabbit (el conejo desér- tico), camel (el camello), gnu (el ñu),* etc.;
   - body part names such as *feet (las patas), wings (las alas), tail (la cola), neck (el cuello), beak (el pico), feathers (el plumaje), fur (el pelaje),* etc.;
   - behaviors with the present tense of verbs such as *to be (ser), to have (tener, poseer),* and *to eat (comer, alimentarse), to drink (beber),* and *to sleep (dormir)*: Giraffes eat leaves from the branches of trees. (*La jirafa se alimenta de hojas y ramas de árboles.*)
3. Report: identify climates on the climate map using phrases with:
   - climate terms: *tropical wet and dry (tropical lluvioso y tropical seco), continental (continental), arid/desert (desértico), mountains/highlands (alta montaña), polar (polar),* etc.;
   - map legend words: *equator (el ecuador), legend (la leyenda), compass rose (la brújula), scale (la escala).*
4. Explanation: justify which animal characteristics are examples of *structural or behavioral adaptations (adaptaciones estructurales o de comportamiento)* of animals with *because* clauses and present tense forms of *to be (ser)* and the following nouns and phrases:
   - *camouflage (el camuflaje), horns (los cuernos), physiological mechanism (el mecan- ismo fisiológico), fat layer (la capa de grasa), migration (la migración), hibernation (la hibernación), herd (la manada, el rebaño), flight (el vuelo),* etc.); e.g., The giraffe's neck is an example of a structural adaptation because it is a body part. (*El cuello de la jirafa es un ejemplo de adaptación estructural porque es una parte del cuerpo.*)

Differentiated for L2 learners and bilinguals/L1 learners:

5. Dialogue: ask questions about and identify where animals live in the world indicating geographic locations (*África, La Antártida, Asia, Australia, Europa; Norteamérica, Sudamérica*) and climatic conditions using question words *in what, what, where (en qué, qué, dónde)* and present tense verbs such as:
   [L2 learners]
   - *to live (vivir)*: It lives in Africa, it lives in a desert climate. (*Vive en África, Vive en un clima desértico.*)
   [Bilinguals/L1 learners]
   - *inhabit (habitar)* and reflexive verbs such as *to find (hallarse o encontrarse).* It is found (lives) in Africa ... *se encuentra en África ...*

</td>
</tr>
</table>

6. Explanation: explain the reason for the adaptation of a given animal with:
[L2 learners]

- prepositions such as *with* (*con*) to introduce prepositional phrases, the verb *to be able* (*poder, ser capaz de*), and familiar adjectives such as *long* (*largo/a*), *tall* (*alto/a*), and *big* (*grande*) with gender and number agreement: With a long neck the giraffe can eat leaves on tall trees. (*Con un cuello largo, la jirafa puede comer las hojas de los árboles altos.*)

[Bilinguals/L1 learners]

- the preposition *para* and the infinitive of the verb *to be able* (*poder, ser capaz de*): The giraffe has a long neck to be able to reach the leaves of tall trees and feed itself. (*La jirafa tiene un cuello largo para poder alcanzar las hojas de los árboles altos y así alimentarse.*)

7. Report: compare and contrast two animals in a coherent paragraph in science journals, drawing upon language that appears in content-obligatory objectives 2, 3, 4, 5, 6, and content-compatible objective 4.

Content compatible

All students

1. Dialogue: express (dis)agreement respectfully using the present tense of the verb *to be* (*estar*); e.g., I (don't) agree because … yes, agreed. (*No*) *estoy de acuerdo porque … Sí, de acuerdo.*

Differentiated for L2 learners and bilinguals/L1 learners:

2. Dialogue: explore other perspectives by first writing down and then sharing ideas and thoughts related to animal adaptations with present tense verbs (1st and 3rd person singular and 1st person plural) such as:
[L2 learners]

- I think, I believe (*pienso, creo*); s/he thinks/believes (*piensa, cree*); we think/believe (*pensamos, creemos*), and the prepositional phrase in my/his/her/our opinion (*en mi/su/nuestra opinion …*): I think the white fur of the polar bear serves as camouflage because it lives in the Arctic where there's a lot of snow. *Pienso que el pelaje blanco del oso polar le sirve de camuflaje porque vive en el Ártico donde hay mucha nieve.*

[Bilinguals/L1 learners]

- I, s/he, we opine/s,[1] maintain/s, propose/s, suppose/s that (*opino, mantengo, propongo, supongo, afirmo que; opina, mantiene, propone, supone que; opinamos, mantenemos, proponemos, suponemos, afirmamos que*) or it seems to me/us that (*me/nos parece que*); e.g., I/s/he/we propose(s) that … *Propongo/propone/proponemos que el pelaje blanco del oso polar le sirve de camuflaje porque vive en el Ártico donde hay mucha nieve.*

3. Survey: elicit classmates' ideas related to animal adaptations by asking questions with verbs in the present tense (2nd person singular and plural or 3rd person plural):
[L2 learners]

- What do you think? What ideas do you have? Do you have another idea? (*¿Qué piensas/pensáis/piensan? ¿Qué ideas tienes/tenéis/tienen? ¿Tienes/tenéis/tienen otra idea?*)

[Bilinguals/L1 learners]

- What do you opine/propose/suppose/maintain? Would you like to share your idea with me/us or tell me/us your idea? (*¿Qué opinas/opináis/opinan? ¿Quisieras/Quisiérais/Quisieran decirme/decirnos tu/vuestra/su idea?*)

Desired Results

---

[1] A rarely used formal variant in English, "opine" is the literal translation of "opinar," a high-frequency verb in Spanish.

Desired Results	4. Report: compare and contrast structural and behavioral adaptations of animals from different climates with the following features: [*L2 learners*] • determiners such as *both* (*tanto ... como, los dos, ambos*) and conjunctions such as *and, but* (*y, pero*) and the adverb *however* (*sin embargo*): Both polar bears and giraffes have four legs. (*Tanto los osos polares como las jirafas* [*o, ambos animales*] *tienen cuatro patas.*) The giraffe has a long neck and tongue to be able to eat the leaves of high trees. However, polar bears have large teeth to eat seals. (*La jirafa tiene un cuello largo y una lengua larga para poder comer las hojas de los árboles altos. Sin embargo, los osos polares tiene dientes grandes para comer las focas.*) [*Bilinguals/L1 learners*] • determiners such as *both* (*tanto ... como, los dos, ambos*) and conjunctions such as *whereas* (*mientras que*), adverbs such as *in contrast* (*por el contrario*), and adjective phrases such as *are the same/similar/different in that ...* (*son iguales/semejantes/diferentes en que ...*). Giraffes and polar bears are similar in that they both have four legs. (*Las jirafas y los osos polares* [*o, ambos animales*] *son semejantes en que los dos tienen cuatro patas.*) *Cross-Linguistic:* 1. Identify cognates and demonstrate understanding of spelling rules and connections between Spanish and English. *Learning Strategies:* 1. Activate prior knowledge to complete learning tasks. 2. Monitor understandings and ask for clarification as needed. 3. Summarize main learnings from the module in science journals. *Social/Affective:* 1. Remain attentive during whole-class instruction and modeling of tasks. 2. Work collaboratively in pairs and small groups, contributing actively (not dominating or remaining passive). 3. Practice listening and responding to others' ideas and thoughts respectfully. 4. Resolve conflicts and disagreements in respectful ways.
Learning Experiences/Instruction	**Materials** • large climate map; • copies of the graphic organizer for modified think-pair-share activity (1 per student) (attachment 1); • chart for summarizing types of and reasons for adaptations (attachment 2); • teacher-created animal adaptation cards with pictures of selected animals (same as information cards)—1–2 for each pair of students; • completed animal adaptation card for the giraffe—1 normal size and 1 enlarged to display (attachment 3); • teacher-created information cards about selected animals—1–2 for each pair of students (13 copies of the information card about the giraffe, 1 for the teacher and 1 for each pair) (attachment 4); • index cards for "exit tickets;" • Venn diagrams from CoBaLTT website with additional language task; http://carla.umn.edu/cobaltt/modules/strategies/gorganizers/index.html; • science journals for each student.

Learning Experiences/Instruction	**Learning Activities (with pair/grouping and differentiation strategies)**
	Links to learning objectives are indicated in parentheses: C = content, L–CO = language content obligatory, L–CC = language content compatible, CL = cross-linguistic, LS = learning strategies, S/A = social/affective.
	Contextualization Phase
	Lesson 1—55 minutes
	1. Students sit next to partners (preassigned according to similar proficiency). Direct students to open their science journals to the climate map they studied the day before. Ask students, "What information does this map provide us? What do the different colors on this map show?" Students whisper-talk about the different climates in the world. After 2–3 minutes, call on students randomly (using popsicle sticks with names) to share their thoughts (C 2, S/A 1). Draw attention to academic vocabulary introduced previously, such as *climate (el clima)*, and its descriptors: *desert (desértico)*, *rainy tropical (tropical lluvioso)*, *polar (polar)*, etc. Remind students that even though *clima* ends in an "a" it is a masculine noun, so the climate descriptions need to end in "o". [10 minutes]
	2. Tell students, "Our question for today is: How do adaptations help animals survive in their environment? Our focus is on how geographic location and climate affect adaptation."
	3. Guide students through Met's Modified Think-Pair-Share (Met, 2008) (Graphic Organizer attachment 1) to engage their prior knowledge and thoughts on the question: "How does geographic location and climate affect an animal's characteristics?" Generate one example from the group as a model. For example, "Polar bears have white fur because they live in the Arctic where there is lots of snow and ice. It serves as camouflage so they blend into the environment." *Los osos polares tienen el pelaje blanco porque habitan en el Ártico donde hay mucha nieve y mucho hielo. Les sirve de camuflaje para pasar desapercibidos en el medio ambiente.* (C 3, 4, 7; S/A 1)
	a. **Think** about the question and jot down what you think and some examples you can think of. (L–CO 2, 3; L–CC 2; LS 1) [5 minutes]
	b. Share with your **partner** what you are thinking, and ask your partner what his or her ideas are. Place a check mark by anything you both said. Add at least one of his or her thoughts to your graphic organizer (L–CO 2, 3; L–CC 2, 3, LS 2, S/A 2, 3). [10 minutes]
	c. Form a **group of two pairs**. [Teacher directs pairs so that a higher-proficient pair is partnered with a lower-proficient pair.] Each pair shares their responses and asks questions. Place a check mark by any statement written by both sets of pairs. Add at least one new thought or idea to the graphic organizer (L–CO 2, 3; L–CC 2, 3; LS 2, S/A 2, 3). [10 minutes]
	d. **Share** your thoughts with the class. [Teacher documents ideas on chart paper or whiteboard.] Each group shares one idea, and sharing rotates among groups until all ideas have been noted. Teacher provides corrective feedback as needed (C 7; L–CO 2, 3; L–CC 2; S/A 1). [15 minutes]
	4. Teacher collects each student's graphic organizer and explains: "Over the next couple of days we are going to create an interactive map that will enable us to compare key characteristics that animals have developed over a long time. We'll display our interactive map to teach other students in our school what we discover. First, we'll need to figure out where each animal lives. Then, we'll identify each animal's key characteristics that make it well adapted to its environment."

	Awareness Phase
	Lesson 2—80 minutes

Learning Experiences/Instruction

Awareness Phase

Lesson 2—80 minutes

1. Move to common gathering place in the classroom where large climate map of the world is posted. Direct students' attention to list of ideas shared the day before for review. Ask students to identify on map where they believe the animals mentioned live and to name the climate. Have individual students point on the map and share their statements: "The polar bear lives in the Arctic. It's a polar climate." *El oso polar vive en el Ártico. Es un clima polar.* (C 1; L-CO 5) [5 minutes]

2. Review different types of animal adaptations in relationship to the four primary reasons introduced in a module earlier in the unit. Present the first column of the chart (attachment 2) with headings for the other 2 columns. Fill in the 2 columns, eliciting as many examples as possible from students (e.g., *camouflage*; *big, sharp teeth*; *fur*; *fat layers*; *living/moving together in herds/colonies*; *hibernation*, etc.). (C 3, 7; L-CO 4, 6; L-CC 2; S/A 1) [10 minutes]

3. Place the enlarged version of the giraffe card on the wall or board (attachment 3). (The teacher also has a fully completed giraffe card of the normal size to use at the end of the next activity.) Show students the animal adaptation card that is displayed and explain that they will be developing these. [1–2 minutes]

4. Assign pairs (one more proficient with one less proficient) and distribute the sample animal information card about the giraffe (attachment 4) to all pairs. The two special needs students are paired together so that the teacher and special education specialist can assist them. With a student helper, model the steps each pair will take with their assigned animal information and animal adaptations cards (S/A 1). [3 minutes]

   a. First, model looking at the picture and whisper-reading the name of the animal together. Ask the student helper if he or she has ever seen or heard of this animal before (L-CO 1). "Do you know this animal?" *¿Conoces a este animal?* "Have you seen this animal?" *¿Has visto a este animal?* "Have you heard about this animal?" *¿Has oído hablar de este animal?* Bring students' attention to the expression *has oído hablar de.* Have the student helper write the name of the animal on the enlarged sample animal adaptations card (LS 1, 2). [2 minutes]

   b. Second, read aloud the description of the location and model a conversation with student helper showing how to find the location and continent on the map and to determine the climate of that location by using the map's legend (C 1, 2; L-CO 3, 5). "On which continent does it live?" *¿En qué continente vive?* "Do you know where Africa is on the map?" *¿Sabes dónde se encuentra África en el mapa?* "Can you point to it with your finger?" *¿Puedes señalarlo con el dedo?* "Now let's find the climate by looking at the legend." *Ahora vamos a buscar el clima con la ayuda de la leyenda.* "In what type of climate does it live?" *¿En qué tipo de clima vive?* Be sure also to model these phrases or sentence starters: *I do [not] agree with … because…* *(No) Estoy de acuerdo con … porque…* (L-CC 1, 2, 3). Direct student helper to write name of continent and type of climate in blank spaces on card. [5 minutes]

Learning Experiences/Instruction

  c. Third, model taking turns to read aloud description of the animal (C 6). Model simple sentences to describe characteristics (L–CO 2). "The giraffe has a long neck." (*La jirafa tiene un cuello largo.*) Model compound sentences with *because* clauses (L–CO 2): "The giraffe's neck is an example of a structural adaptation because it is a body part." (*El cuello de la jirafa es un ejemplo de adaptación estructural porque es una parte del cuerpo.*) Invite students to have their own whisper-talk conversation with their partner to identify the key characteristics of the animal in relationship to the two kinds of adaptations, structural and behavioral (C 3). Direct students to use classroom scaffolds and word wall for expressions and vocabulary (LS 2). [5 minutes]

  d. Ask student volunteers to share what they determined was a key characteristic related to the two kinds of adaptations (C 3, L–CO 2). List key characteristics in the blank spaces on the front of the card, being sure to leave space below each one. [10 minutes]

  e. Finally, model asking questions and sharing answers related to reasons for adaptations. (C 3, 7) "Why does the giraffe have a long neck?" (*¿Por qué tiene la jirafa un cuello largo?*) Bring students' attention to different ways of responding to this question—with simple present and with *para* + infinitive (L–CO 6). Write the reason directly below the adaptation on the card. [10 minutes]

    Con un cuello largo, la jirafa puede comer las hojas de los árboles altos.
    La jirafa tiene un cuello largo para poder alimentarse.

  f. Once the animal adaptation card for the giraffe is complete, explain to students that they will place their completed cards onto the climate map using a piece of tape. Have the student helper place the completed giraffe card the teacher had prepared onto the map with tape (C 1). [2–3 minutes]

5. Review and number the steps (*a–f* = 6) that were just modeled on chart paper or whiteboard. [5 minutes]

6. Gather students on floor in front of large completed card about giraffe that is posted on wall. Ask them to look for cognates (just look and keep thoughts to themselves). Call on students randomly (using popsicle sticks with names) to come up to board. First, students whisper to the teacher the word that they think is a cognate, and if it's accurate, the teacher directs the student to circle it on the displayed card with a big red marker. After all cognates have been identified, the teacher asks students to *think* about the English equivalents and visualize how they are spelled. She briefly discusses some spelling connections and rules—e.g., *-ción* = *-tion*, *-es* + *consonante* = *-s* + *consonant* (*estructural, structural*) (CL 1). [10 minutes]

7. "Ticket to exit"—distribute index cards and ask students to write three things that they learned in this lesson about animal adaptations (emphasize that a bulleted list with phrases is acceptable). [5 minutes]

Practice Phase
Lesson 3—60 minutes

1. Have students join partners that were assigned the day before. Review the steps that were modeled (Day 2 #4/5), and review some of the language that was modeled to remind students of sentence frames and questions they are to use. [10 minutes]

<table>
<tr>
<td rowspan="2" style="writing-mode: vertical-lr;">**Learning Experiences/Instruction**</td>
<td>

2. Tell students, "Now it's your turn!" Student pairs receive an animal adaptation card (attachment 2) and its accompanying information card (attachment 3) and move to their own space in the classroom. The special needs students are given an animal information card that includes glossed words and phrases. It is written in a way that shows clear links between types of adaptations and reasons and provides some illustrations. These scaffolds should help these two students to be successful with the activity. Elicit examples from students of previously learned words and phrases they can use to disagree respectfully and offer encouragement (S/A 3, 4). Also review what it means to collaborate, and remind students that both partners need to work in tandem on the activity (S/A 2). [5 minutes]

3. Remind students to use a whisper-voice to follow steps 1–6 (a–f under Awareness Phase). While students are working together, circulate around the classroom to listen to student conversations, assist, clarify, provide corrective feedback (on content, language, and collaborative behaviors), and address misconceptions as needed. Check the cards that are posted on the map for accuracy. Students who finish early should first check appropriate science vocabulary, spelling, subject-verb-adjective agreement, verb conjugations, etc. Then they may choose another animal card to complete (C 1, 2, 3, 4, 6, 7; L-CO 1, 2, 3, 4, 5, 6; L-CC 1, 2, 3; LS 2). [40 minutes]

4. Admire the map with the cards posted and explain that they will be using it the next day. (5 minutes) The teacher removes cards from map and provides written feedback on the back of students' animal adaptations cards for them to review the following day.

Autonomy Phase
Lesson 4—45 minutes

1. Students are given 5 minutes with their partners to review the feedback provided by the teacher and then return cards to climate map. [5 minutes]

2. Turn students' attention to large climate map on which they posted their cards the previous day. Assign new partners representing different animals and climates from the previous day's work. Be sure to pair students representing animals that are somewhat similar (e.g., *birds* or *mammals*) but from different climates (proficiency levels are mixed as much as possible). Each pair gets a Venn diagram that asks them to compare and contrast the animals in terms of their structural and behavioral adaptations (C 3, 4, 5, 6, 7; LS 2; L-CO 2, 3, 4, 5; L-CC 1, 2, 3; S/A 2, 3, 4). It includes an additional language task at the end that asks them to write simple and compound sentences to compare and contrast the two animals and provides models (L-CC 4). As a review, the teacher asks students to share expressions that they can use to disagree respectfully (L-CC 1) and to ask each other for more information (L-CC 3). While students are working, mingle to observe pairs and give feedback (on Post-its) about their content understandings, language use, and collaborative behaviors. After they have finished, ask students to write their names on the Post-its they received during the Venn diagram activity and turn them in. [20 minutes].

</td>
</tr>
</table>

<table>
<tr><td rowspan="1">**Learning Experiences/Instruction**</td><td>

3. Have pairs report to the whole-class about the types of structural and behavioral adaptations that they have discussed. Make sure each person has an opportunity to share one idea. Engage the whole class in further discussion, asking questions to get them to describe the kinds of characteristics that align with different climates and sharing compare/contrast sentences (L-CO 2, 3, 4, 5; L-CC 2, 4; S/A 1). [20 minutes]
4. Collect completed Venn diagrams. Provide written feedback overnight and prepare whole-class feedback on compare/contrast sentences.

Autonomy Phase (continued)
Lesson 5—30 minutes

1. Ask students to pair with the same partner from the day before (Venn diagram activity). Return completed Venn diagrams with written feedback and ask students to review. [5 minutes]
2. Give whole-class feedback on construction of compare/contrast sentences in the additional language task that was part of the Venn diagram activity. [5 minutes]
3. Instruct individual students to take out their science journals and write a paragraph comparing and contrasting the two animals they focused on during the Venn diagram activity the day before. For special needs learners, prepare a handout that acts as a scaffold and gives students key vocabulary and sentence frames. Ask all students to address the following question at the end of the paragraph: "How do adaptations help animals survive in their environment?" (C 3, 4, 8; L-CO 2, 3, 4, 5, 6, 7; L-CC 4; LS 3). If students need more time, have them complete paragraphs as homework and return the science journals the next day. [20 minutes]
4. While students are writing, enlist student volunteers to help move the map with the posted cards to the hallway for the school community to see.

</td></tr>
<tr><td rowspan="1">**Evidence**</td><td>

Lesson-Level Formative Assessment Procedures

Formative assessment is embedded in most of the activities. The teacher assesses students'

- participation in whole-class activities through observation;
- graphic organizers (completed in contextualization phase Lesson 1) by reviewing them;
- "tickets to exit" by reviewing them (Lesson 2);
- animal adaptations cards (practice phase Lesson 3) and their placement on the climate map for accuracy and thoroughness of content as well as language use, specifically language reflected in content-obligatory objectives. The teacher gives students feedback in writing;
- interactions during the Venn diagram activity in the autonomy phase (Lesson 4) by collecting the Post-it notes that were distributed with feedback during the activity. The teacher uses them to assess students' collaborative behaviors with a checklist used on a regular basis—the checklist includes students' names and 2 columns for checkmarks—"good collaboration" and "needs improvement." A column for comments is also provided;

</td></tr>
</table>

Evidence	• completed Venn diagrams to check students' understandings and their ability to produce accurate compare/contrast sentences. The teacher provides written feedback and offers whole-class feedback on students' sentences before the writing task the next day. • science journal paragraphs (Lesson 5) with a simple rubric (exceeds expectations, meets expectations, or needs improvement) in terms of content accuracy and thoroughness, language accuracy (in relationship to L-CO objectives), and coherence.

Attachments

Note that students would receive these in Spanish only.

Attachment #1: Prior knowledge graphic organizer

¿Cómo afectan la ubicación geográfica y el clima a las características de un animal? How does geographic location and climate affect an animal's characteristics?	
Mis ideas ... My ideas ...	*Las ideas de mi compañero/a ... (agrega por lo menos una nueva idea)* My partner's ideas ... (add at least one new idea)
Las ideas de nuestros nuevos compañeros ...(agrega por lo menos una nueva idea) Our new partners' ideas ... (add at least one new idea)	

Attachment #2: chart for review of previously learned content

Motivo de adaptación **Reason for adaptation**	*Adaptaciones estructurales* **Structural Adaptations** **(body parts and body coverings)**	*Adaptaciones de comportamiento* **Behavioral Adaptations**
Para protegerse de los depredadores For protection from predators		
Para la conservación de recursos For resource conservation		
Para protegerse de la temperatura For protection from temperatures		
Para el tipo de alimento For type of food		

Attachment 3: Animal adaptations card

Nombre: Name:	*Continente:* Continent:	*Clima:* Climate:
Adaptaciones estructurales **Structural Adaptations** 1. 2. 3.	*Adaptaciones de comportamiento* **Behavioral Adaptations** 1. 2. 3.	

Attachment 4: Animal information card

La Jirafa
Vive en África cerca del ecuador en climas desérticos.
Es el animal más alto del mundo, y puede llegar a tener unos seis metros de altura y dos toneladas de peso. Se distingue por las manchas de la piel que le sirven de camuflaje con el fin de pasar desapercibida para los depredadores (como los leones y las hienas). Suele vivir en manadas o rebaños con otras 10 a 15 jirafas.   Tiene patas muy largas y fuertes, y las puede usar para protegerse de los depredadores. Puede matar a un león o una hiena con una patada en la cabeza.   Prefiere alimentarse de hojas de acacias, unos árboles muy altos. Es capaz de pasar largos períodos de tiempo sin tomar agua, lo cual le conviene porque le resulta difícil beber debido a su gran altura. Cuando bebe necesita separar sus patas delanteras para que llegue su cabeza al agua. Así se queda indefensa en una situación peligrosa. Para protegerse las otras jirafas del rebaño se turnan para que haya siempre una vigilando.   Adapted from http://www.ciudad17.com/Naturaleza/animales/mamiferos/jirafa.html

APPENDIX C: ImDL IPA EXAMPLE

	Adaptations IPA
	IPA theme: How do animals adapt? *Time frame: Approximately 7 hours over 6 days*
IPA Overview	Have you ever heard of the aguimono, the scaly green creature that has a long, flexible tail and flaps of skin that look like wings? No? Perhaps because it doesn't exist! But if it did, it might be well adapted to life in a jungle environment with tall trees. Soon you will have an opportunity to invent a new animal of your own! First, you will read one of two texts: 1) *En el frío*, a text about how animals have adapted to live in very cold places, or 2) *Estar frescos*, a text about how animals are able to survive in very hot places. Next, you will share the information you learned from the text with a partner who read the opposite text. Finally, you will be given a "mystery biome" and you and your partner will create and draw an imaginary animal with adaptations that would allow it to thrive in that biome. You will share these new, well-adapted creatures with your pen pals in Ecuador in a VoiceThread presentation.
Interpretive Task—Days 1 and 2	**Text:** Kalman, B. (2007). *¿Cómo se adaptan los animales?* [How do animals adapt?] New York, NY: Crabtree Publishing. *Summary:* This book contains 14 sections that identify and describe ways in which animals adapt to their surroundings. The sections entitled *Estar frescos* (Keeping cool) and *En el frío* (In the cold) address climatic adaptations. The text is grade-level appropriate with photographs, drawings, and textual supports that make it interesting and accessible yet challenging for Grade 3. The *En el frío* text is two pages with sections having subheadings such as *Grasa para calentarse* (Body Fat for Keeping Warm) and *La tundra ártica* (The Arctic Tundra). The *Estar frescos* text is also two pages having sections with subheadings such as *Almacenar agua* (Storing Water) and *Hibernar en el calor* (Hibernating in the Heat).

Interpretive Task—Days 1 and 2	**Task—Day 1:** Divide class into 2 groups and assign each group a different text to read—either *Estar Frescos* or *En el frío*. Students are instructed to read the text and complete the comprehension guide (Attachment 1). They can refer to the text as they complete it. Students submit their assigned texts and comprehension guides to teacher for evaluation and feedback. [45 minutes] As an informal assessment, teacher will observe students as they complete the interpretive task to note which questions and which aspects of the text appear challenging.
	Feedback loop—Day 2: Teacher distributes the written feedback using the interpretive task assessment rubric (Attachment 2). Teacher meets briefly with small groups (organized based on similar performance) to give oral feedback and engage learners in dialogue about their performance. Teacher can address confusions or misunderstandings about the text content and features as well as any issues that arose in the assessment of comprehension guides [5–8 minutes per group]. Note: the final section on the comprehension guide (making predictions) serves as a preview to the next task and is not formally assessed. [~60 minutes]
	Logistics: Teacher should divide the class into 2 groups based on how students will be paired for the interpersonal task (by proficiency). In other words, each text should be read by students with a range of proficiency levels so that teacher can pair students with similar levels of proficiency for subsequent tasks. Teacher uses the rubric to assess students' comprehension guides, making sure to have all feedback prepared by the following day. Teacher should make available theme-related texts for students to read if they finish the comprehension guide early and as they wait while teacher meets with groups during feedback loop.
Interpersonal Task—Days 2 and 3	**Task—Day 2:** Students are paired with partners having similar proficiency who have read the opposite text. Together they complete a "comparison/contrast chart" (Attachment 3) by asking each other questions and responding to them. To introduce the task, teacher shows a model (video-recorded the previous year). Students watch video and use Interpersonal Task rubric (Attachment 4) to assess how successful the interaction was and become familiar with rubric expectations. [20 minutes] Teacher should remind students that this task involves having a conversation and that they should ask their partners to repeat if they don't understand and be sure to answer their partner's questions completely. Students can refer to their respective texts but are instructed not to share them with their partners. Their interactions are video-recorded to facilitate teacher assessment.
	Feedback loop—Day 3: Each pair of students meets with the teacher for a short conference about their performance on Interpersonal Task. Teacher shares written feedback using rubric and, time permitting, may have students view short excerpts from their video-recorded interaction to illustrate successful interaction or areas where they might improve. Together, students and teacher discuss ways in which students might improve their performance in future pair and small-group activities (and other interpersonal assessment tasks). [5–8 minutes per pair] [~90 minutes]

Interpersonal Task—Days 2 and 3	**Logistics:** For Day 2: Teacher needs to enlist a parent volunteer or classroom assistant to accompany pairs to a quiet space in the media center to record their interactions on iPad or other device. Teacher should have a schedule prepared so that it's clear when student pairs need to go to be recorded. As students await their turn to engage in the Interpersonal Task they read their assigned texts (for Interpretive Task) again to prepare for the task. They may also read other theme-related texts or do other work (not related to the assessment tasks) that teacher has assigned. For Day 3: Teacher begins providing feedback *after* introducing the Presentational Task and assigning pairs of students their biomes. Students will begin their work on the Presentational Task as teacher calls pairs to receive feedback on the Interpersonal Task. Teacher will have reviewed the recorded interactions and prepared feedback the previous day. Teacher can use different highlighter colors for each student when providing feedback on rubric for each pair.
Presentational Task—Days 3–6	**Task—Day 3:** Students remain in the same pairs as in previous task. They receive a "mystery biome" (descriptions of actual biomes without the name of the biome associated with it; see Attachment 5) and are instructed to name and create a drawing of a new animal that has adapted to this environment. Together they prepare (in writing) an oral presentation to describe the animal and its adaptations. They must include at least four structural characteristics (ways the animal has adapted physically to survive in its environment) and at least two behavioral characteristics. They are instructed not to name the biome itself in oral presentation. They have one 90-minute session on Day 3 (while teacher gives feedback on Interpersonal Task performance) to work on the task and another 45-minute session on Day 5 to finalize their presentations. Teacher informally observes students as they work to create their animal drawings and prepare their presentations to provide guidance and corrective feedback as needed. **Day 4:** Teacher assigns 2 pairs to work together. They practice giving their oral presentations and get feedback from each other as teacher circulates to provide guidance and feedback. **Day 5:** Students have approximately 45 minutes to finalize their oral presentations. Finally, students take a photograph of the animal drawing. They upload the picture to VoiceThread and record their oral presentations (using the oral comment feature). Each student is responsible for half of the presentation. VoiceThread presentations are shared with their pen pals in Ecuador (those students play "guess the biome" based on pictures and oral presentations, and they record their responses on the VoiceThread, indicating specifically which biome they believe the animal has adapted to and why). [90 minutes]
	About a week later students receive feedback from their pen pals in Ecuador, and the teacher engages students in a whole-class discussion.
	Feedback loop—Day 6: Prior to Day 6, teacher uses the Presentational Task rubric (Attachment 6) to assess students' final VoiceThread presentations. Teacher shares written feedback with students and meets with student pairs to engage in dialogue about what went well and what aspects could be improved [5 minutes per pair]. Meanwhile, other students are working on math homework or another activity that they can complete independently. [60 minutes]

Presentational Task—Days 3–6	**Logistics:** For Days 3–5: Teacher needs to provide materials for students to create visual models or drawings of their animals. For Day 4: Teacher assigns pairs to work together to share presentations and offer feedback. The teacher goes over the rubric with students beforehand so that they can use rubric criteria to offer feedback. For Day 5: Teacher creates a schedule for 2–3 pairs at a time to go to the media lab to record their VoiceThread presentations. Teacher enlists the help of a parent volunteer or classroom assistant to provide assistance to students in media lab. Teacher can use different highlighter colors for each student when providing feedback on rubric for each pair.
Materials	• 12 copies of each text (*Estar frescos* and *En el frío*) • 12 copies of each comprehension guide (Attachment 1) • 24 copies of Interpretive Task rubric (Attachment 2) • 12 copies of Interpersonal Task graphic organizer (Attachment 3) • 12 copies of Interpersonal Task rubric (Attachment 4) • 12 "mystery" biome descriptions (Attachment 5) • 12 copies of Presentational Task rubric (Attachment 6) • iPads or digital camera • Computers in media center lab with VoiceThread application

Attachment 1: Comprehension Guide for Interpretive Task*

***Estar frescos* (Keeping Cool)**

I. Key word recognition. *Find the names of 5 animals that have adapted to a hot and dry environment and list them below.*

1. _____
2. _____
3. _____
4. _____
5. _____

II. Main idea(s). *Write the main idea(s) of the text.*

_____

_____

_____

_____

III. Supporting details.

- *Read the statements below. Circle the letter of each statement that is mentioned in the text (**Watch out! Some of the statements below ARE NOT IN THE TEXT.**)*
- *Write the letter of the statement next to where it appears in the text you read.*
- *List one detail from the text that supports each statement you circled.*

A. Animals that live in dry climates get the majority of their water that they need from the food they eat.

_____

B. All the animals that live the desert are reptiles.

_____

C. Many desert animals hide from the sun during the day.

_____

D. For some animals, many deserts are too hot and dry in the summer.

_____

E. Deserts are warm places that get a lot of rain.

_____

F. In deserts there aren't any lagoons or rivers for animals to drink from.

_____

IV. Guessing meaning from context. *Based on the sentences given, draw what the following three words/expressions probably mean and explain what the word means.*

1. **burrow**—They sleep in <u>burrows</u> or subterranean shelters to keep cool.

My definition of burrow is:
_____

2. **to store**—To survive, animals must <u>store</u> all the moisture they can in their bodies.

My definition of "to store" is:
_____

3. **to estivate**—Desert turtles and frogs dig burrows and <u>estivate</u> during the hottest and driest summer months.

My definition of "to estivate" is:
_____

V. Inferences. *Decide if each statement is true or false. Circle true or false. Then support your answer by listing two pieces of evidence from the text.*

1. True or false? *All animals that live in hot and dry places have adapted in the same ways.*

   _____

   _____

2. True or false? *To be able to survive in a hot and dry climate, animals need special adaptations.*

   _____

   _____

VI. Making predictions based on the text. *Based on what you know about animals that have adapted to hot and dry environments, what adaptations do you think animals in cold environments might have?*

   _____

   _____

   _____

   _____

* Similar guide created for other text. Note also that students' comprehension guides are presented in Spanish only.

Attachment 2: Interpretive Task Rubric*

Non-negotiables:

_____ On-task while reading and completing comprehension guide
_____ Task comprehension guide is completed neatly and thoroughly

Accomplished comprehension (A-comp)	complete, thorough responses supported with complete, relevant evidence from text; able to infer with complete accuracy
Strong comprehension (S-comp)	mostly complete responses supported with some relevant evidence from text; mostly able to infer with accuracy
Minimal comprehension (M-comp)	somewhat complete responses with some attempts to support with evidence from text (but limited, lacking relevance); able to infer with some accuracy
Limited comprehension (L-comp)	limited responses with no evidence from text; unable to infer with accuracy

Literal Comprehension	A-comp	S-comp	M-comp	L-comp
Word recognition: Identifies names of 5 animals that have adapted to the environment.				
Main idea detection: Identifies complete main idea.				
Supporting detail detection: Identifies 4 supporting details and accurately provides evidence from text to explain details.				
Interpretive Comprehension	A-comp	S-comp	M-comp	L-comp
Guessing meaning from context: Infers meaning of unfamiliar words. All 3 picture inferences are accurate. All written explanations are reasonable and coincide with pictures.				
Inferences (Reading between the lines): Correctly identifies 2 statements as true or false and lists complete and relevant evidence from text to support each statement.				

* Adapted from Adair-Hauck et al., 2013.

Attachment 3: Comparison/Contrast Chart for Interpersonal Task

Without showing your partner your text, share what you have learned about animal adaptations in hot or cold climates. Ask and answer questions to learn from your partner and make sure your partner learns from you. Complete the graphic organizer that corresponds to your partner's text with information from your partner. You have 10 minutes.

	En el frío (Complete this half if you read *Estar frescos*)	*Estar frescos* (Complete this half if you read *En el frío*)
Ways animals conserve or release heat		
Ways animals adapt their behavior to extreme temperatures (2 examples)		
Ways animals' physical features help them survive		

Attachment 4: Interpersonal Task Rubric*

Non-negotiables:

_____ Asks questions to elicit information

_____ Responds to partner's questions and requests without sharing the text

_____ Interacts with partner for at least 5 and no more than 15 minutes

_____ Completes assigned section of graphic organizer based on partner's shared information

CRITERIA	Exceeds Expectations	Meets Expectations (Strong)	Meets Expectations (Minimal)	Does Not Meet Expectations
Content knowledge Accuracy and thoroughness of content shared	Provides accurate responses about animal adaptations and completes graphic organizer with accurate information.	Provides mostly accurate responses about animal adaptations and completes graphic organizer with mostly accurate information.	Provides somewhat accurate responses about animal adaptations and completes graphic organizer with somewhat accurate information.	Has difficulty responding with accurate information about animal adaptations. Struggles to gain information from partner to complete graphic organizer.
Language function Language tasks speaker is able to handle in consistent, comfortable, sustained, and spontaneous manner	Creates with language; is able to express own meaning clearly and in varied ways. Successfully handles all task demands.	Creates with language by combining/recombining known elements; is mostly able to express own meaning in somewhat varied ways. Successfully handles most task demands.	Creates somewhat with language by combining/recombining known elements; is able to express meaning in a basic way. Handles somewhat successfully portions of the task.	Has difficulty creating meaning with language; requires frequent prompting to express meaning. Demonstrates little functional ability. May resort to use of English.
Text type Quantity and organization of language (word – phrase – sentence – connected sentences – paragraph – extended discourse)	Uses mostly connected sentences and some paragraph-like discourse.	Uses strings of sentences with some complex constructions (dependent clauses).	Uses simple sentences and some strings of sentences.	Struggles to produce sentences. Produces some phrases and some very simple sentences but falters frequently.

CRITERIA	Exceeds Expectations	Meets Expectations (Strong)	Meets Expectations (Minimal)	Does Not Meet Expectations
Communication strategies Quality of engagement and interactivity; how one participates in conversation and advances it; strategies for negotiating meaning in face of communication breakdown.	Converses with ease and confidence when discussing animal adaptations. Asks varied questions to obtain detailed information. May clarify by paraphrasing.	Responds clearly and directly to direct questions and requests for information about animal adaptations. Asks a variety of questions to obtain basic information. May clarify by restating.	Responds somewhat to direct questions and requests for information about animal adaptations. Asks a few appropriate questions, but tends to function reactively. May try to restate in the face of miscommunication.	Makes some attempts to respond to basic direct questions and requests for information about animal adaptations. Attempts to ask a few formulaic questions, but is primarily reactive. If prompted, attempts to clarify by repeating and/or substituting different words.
Comprehensibility How well student is understood by others.	Is easily understood.	Is generally understood, although gaps in communication may occur.	Is mostly understood, although repetition or rephrasing may be required.	Is understood with some difficulty, and repetition or rephrasing are frequently required.
Language control Grammatical accuracy, appropriate vocabulary, degree of fluency	Produces grammatically accurate and sufficiently complex language based on task demands. Uses wide range of appropriate vocabulary. Communicates with fluency.	Produces mostly grammatically accurate and complex language based on task demands. Errors don't impede communication. Uses appropriate vocabulary. Communicates with fluency, although hesitates at times.	Produces somewhat grammatically accurate and complex language based on task demands, but some errors lead to confusion or communication breakdown. Uses somewhat appropriate vocabulary. Communicates with fluency sometimes, although hesitates with some frequency.	Produces minimal language or produces language that is so grammatically inaccurate that it is difficult to understand. Uses limited vocabulary and hesitates frequently when trying to communicate.

* Adapted from Adair–Hauck et al., 2013.

Attachment 5: Example "Mystery Biome" for Presentational Task*

This biome can be found along the coastal regions of the arctic (northern hemisphere) and is extremely cold and dry. These biomes have very long winters that are cold and harsh. The summer is short (6–8 weeks) and mild, not even considered a real summer by some. Air temperatures are very low in this biome. In the winter they can be as low as −58 degrees F (−50 °C). In the summer it hardly ever gets above 54 degrees F (12 °C). It is usually very dark in the winter months. Even the summer doesn't offer much sunlight because it is often cloudy. There isn't much rainfall in this biome, less than 30 inches (76 cm) each year. Most of the moisture comes from the ice and the snow pack.

* Adapted from https://www.bioexpedition.com/types-of-biomes-in-the-world/

Attachment 6: Presentational Task Rubric*

Non-negotiables:

___ The presentation is entirely in Spanish

___ A visual model or drawing is included

___ Student pairs upload visual to and record oral presentation on VoiceThread

___ Oral presentations are no longer than 5–6 minutes

___ Oral presentations are divided equally between partners

CRITERIA	Exceeds Expectations	Meets Expectations (Strong)	Meets Expectations (Minimal)	Does Not Meet Expectations
Content knowledge Accuracy of scientific terms and understanding of scientific concepts	Animal characteristics and behaviors are clear examples of adaptations that would help the animal thrive in given environment. Demonstrates solid understanding of adaptation through use of expanded range of relevant scientific vocabulary.	Animal characteristics and behaviors are mostly clear examples of adaptations that would help the animal thrive in given environment. Demonstrates good understanding of adaptation through consistent use of relevant scientific vocabulary.	Most animal characteristics and behaviors are examples of adaptations that would help the animal thrive in given environment, although some may be questionable. Demonstrates acceptable understanding of adaptation through some use of relevant scientific vocabulary.	Several animal characteristics and behaviors may not be examples of adaptations or may not serve to help the animal thrive in given environment. Relevant scientific vocabulary is rarely, if ever, used.
Language function Language tasks the speaker is able to handle in a consistent, comfortable, sustained, and spontaneous manner	Successfully describes the animal's characteristics and behaviors and explains how those adaptations would help the animal survive by using appropriate sentence constructions. Informs the audience in a consistent, comfortable, and sustained manner.	Successfully describes the animal's characteristics and behaviors and explains how those adaptations would help the animal survive by using mostly appropriate sentence structures. Informs the audience in a consistent and comfortable manner.	Describes the animal's characteristics and behaviors somewhat and states how those adaptations would help the animal survive by using somewhat appropriate sentence structures. May struggle to maintain a consistent flow of speech.	Has difficulty creating meaning with language. Demonstrates little functional ability. May resort to use of English.

Text type Quantity and organization of language (word – phrase – sentence – connected sentences – paragraph – extended discourse)	Uses mostly connected sentences and some paragraph-like discourse to describe in detail at least 4 structural characteristics and 2 behavioral characteristics and how those adaptations would help the animal survive.	Uses strings of sentences with some complex sentences (dependent clauses) to describe 4 structural characteristics and 2 behavioral characteristics and how those adaptations would help the animal survive.	Uses simple sentences and some strings of sentences to adequately describe at least 3 structural characteristic and how those adaptations would help the animal survive.	Uses some simple sentences and memorized phrases that may or may not adequately describe some of the animal's structural and behavioral characteristics and how those adaptations would help the animal survive.
Impact Clarity, organization, and depth of presentation; degree to which presentation maintains attention and interest of audience	Presentation is clear and organized. Presentation illustrates originality, depth of thought about adaptations, rich details, interesting visual, and clear organization to maintain audience's attention and interest.	Presentation is mostly clear and organized. Presentation illustrates some depth of thought about adaptations, features sufficient details and visuals, and organization of the presentation maintains audience's attention and/or interest.	Presentation is somewhat clear and organized. Some thought about adaptations is apparent. There is some effort to maintain audience's attention through visuals, organization of text, and/or details.	Presentation may be either unclear or unorganized. Demonstrates shallow thought about adaptations. There is minimal to no effort to maintain audience's attention. Visuals may be missing or poorly done.
Comprehensibility How well student is understood by others.	Is easily understood.	Is generally understood, although gaps in communication may occur.	Is mostly understood, although repetition or rephrasing may be required.	Is understood with some difficulty, and repetition or rephrasing are frequently required.
Language control Grammatical accuracy, appropriate vocabulary, degree of fluency	Produces grammatically accurate and sufficiently complex language based on task demands. Uses wide range of appropriate vocabulary. Communicates with fluency.	Produces mostly grammatically accurate and complex language based on task demands. Errors don't impede communication. Uses appropriate vocabulary. Communicates with fluency, although hesitates at times.	Produces somewhat grammatically accurate and complex language based on task demands, but some errors lead to confusion or communication breakdown. Uses somewhat appropriate vocabulary. Communicates with fluency sometimes, although hesitates with some frequency.	Produces minimal language or produces language that is so grammatically inaccurate that it is difficult to understand. Uses limited vocabulary and hesitates frequently when trying to communicate.

* Adapted from Adair-Hauck et al., 2013.

APPENDIX D: SELF-ASSESSMENT RUBRIC FOR ImDL TEACHERS

This self-assessment rubric is designed specifically for ImDL educators. The comprehensive categories focus on pedagogical methods and knowledge that are specific to ImDL teaching and necessary for promoting high levels of academic achievement and language development. The term *target language* is used throughout the rubric to refer to the expected language of instruction at any given time.

The rubric represents four developmental stages: lacking, emerging, demonstrating, and excelling.

- *Lacking*: at this stage, the practice described is not evident in the teacher's performance, and the teacher lacks awareness of the practice.
- *Emerging*: at this stage, the teacher has achieved a level of awareness about the practice. He or she seeks to make the practice a part of his/her own teaching repertoire. The teacher is beginning to make some attempts to apply their understandings in practice, but the attempts are not often successful.
- *Demonstrating*: at this stage, the teacher not only understands the importance of the practice for successful ImDL teaching but also makes frequent attempts to make it a part of his/her own teaching repertoire. Many, although not all, attempts are successful.
- *Excelling*: at this stage, the practice has become a part of the teacher's daily repertoire. It is in action, live, and at play in the classroom on a consistent basis. The teacher is adept and confident in implementing the practice.

Self-Assessment Rubric for ImDL Teachers

1A. Language and content integration in curricular planning

I integrate language-focused and content-focused instruction in curricular planning.

Lacking		Emerging		Demonstrating		Excelling	
1	2	3	4	5	6	7	8

I plan varied language-focused activities within content-based instruction (e.g., CAPA model).

Lacking		Emerging		Demonstrating		Excelling	
1	2	3	4	5	6	7	8

What I've tried/What I've observed.	*My goals for improvement.*

1B. Language objectives: discourse type + function + grammatical feature + vocabulary

I write language objectives that are developmentally and contextually appropriate for students.

Lacking		Emerging		Demonstrating		Excelling	
1	2	3	4	5	6	7	8

I write clear objectives that can be assessed and that include discourse type, language function, grammatical feature, and vocabulary.

Lacking		Emerging		Demonstrating		Excelling	
1	2	3	4	5	6	7	8

I write both content-obligatory and content-compatible language objectives.

Lacking		Emerging		Demonstrating		Excelling	
1	2	3	4	5	6	7	8

I differentiate objectives for a range of proficiency levels and learner characteristics.

Lacking		Emerging		Demonstrating		Excelling	
1	2	3	4	5	6	7	8

What I've tried/What I've observed.	*My goals for improvement.*

1C. Classroom assessment: performance (i.e., real-life tasks) and other assessments that require students to demonstrate their content knowledge and their ability to use the language to express their understandings

I differentiate formative and summative assessments for different learner groups.

Lacking		Emerging		Demonstrating		Excelling	
1	2	3	4	5	6	7	8

I use different ways to assess student content learning and language development.

Lacking		Emerging		Demonstrating		Excelling	
1	2	3	4	5	6	7	8

I use assessment data to select target features/functions and content for future instruction and to identify areas in which academic language development is needed.

Lacking		Emerging		Demonstrating		Excelling	
1	2	3	4	5	6	7	8

I design and implement performance assessments (such as the IPA) to assess both content learning and language development.

Lacking		Emerging		Demonstrating		Excelling	
1	2	3	4	5	6	7	8

What I've tried/What I've observed.	*My goals for improvement.*

1D. Culture integration throughout the curriculum

I plan activities that promote identity development, cross-cultural awareness, and multicultural appreciation.

Lacking		Emerging		Demonstrating		Excelling	
1	2	3	4	5	6	7	8

I weave culture-related activities throughout the content curriculum as appropriate.

Lacking		Emerging		Demonstrating		Excelling	
1	2	3	4	5	6	7	8

I plan for the use of authentic resources (literature, songs, artifacts, and people) that are appropriate for students' cognitive and linguistic levels to promote cross-cultural awareness.

Lacking		Emerging		Demonstrating		Excelling	
1	2	3	4	5	6	7	8

I include family and community knowledge and assets in planning in ways that empower learners.

Lacking		Emerging		Demonstrating		Excelling	
1	2	3	4	5	6	7	8

What I've tried/What I've observed.	*My goals for improvement.*

Strand 2: Teaching for Biliteracy Development

I understand the fundamental principles of biliteracy development and use a variety of effective instructional strategies that promote vocabulary and biliteracy development across a range of genres/text types.

2A. Biliteracy instruction

My approach to literacy instruction accounts for students who are developing biliteracy rather than literacy in only one language.

Lacking		Emerging		Demonstrating		Excelling	
1	2	3	4	5	6	7	8

I can articulate and use research-based approaches to (bi)literacy instruction (e.g., balanced literacy, phonological awareness, guided reading, shared reading and writing, comprehension strategies, etc.).

Lacking		Emerging		Demonstrating		Excelling	
1	2	3	4	5	6	7	8

I use literacy instruction that is specific to the program language(s) I teach.

Lacking		Emerging		Demonstrating		Excelling	
1	2	3	4	5	6	7	8

What I've tried/What I've observed.	*My goals for improvement.*

2B. Vocabulary development, word knowledge, and text types

I use a variety of effective, grade-level appropriate strategies to build students' vocabulary.

Lacking		Emerging		Demonstrating		Excelling	
1	2	3	4	5	6	7	8

I use varied word-learning strategies (e.g., teaching parts of speech, word parts such as affixes, cognates, etc.).

Lacking		Emerging		Demonstrating		Excelling	
1	2	3	4	5	6	7	8

I draw attention to how different genres/text types are constructed.

Lacking		Emerging		Demonstrating		Excelling	
1	2	3	4	5	6	7	8

What I've tried/What I've observed.	My goals for improvement.

2C. Cross-lingual connections

I incorporate cross-linguistic instruction in some of the lessons I plan.

Lacking		Emerging		Demonstrating		Excelling	
1	2	3	4	5	6	7	8

When appropriate, I draw students' attention to cross-linguistic connections, focusing on metalinguistic knowledge, to support biliteracy development across program languages.

Lacking		Emerging		Demonstrating		Excelling	
1	2	3	4	5	6	7	8

I remain exclusively (or primarily) in the target language while making cross-lingual connections explicit.

Lacking		Emerging		Demonstrating		Excelling	
1	2	3	4	5	6	7	8

When appropriate, I model how students can draw on cross-lingual connections to support their biliteracy development.

Lacking		Emerging		Demonstrating		Excelling	
1	2	3	4	5	6	7	8

What I've tried/What I've observed.	My goals for improvement.

Strand 3: Maintaining a Linguistically Rich Learning Environment
I maintain a linguistically rich learning environment and use that environment to enhance students' language development and content learning.

3A. Visual language scaffolds

I display a variety of social and curriculum-related words, phrases, and written scaffolds throughout the classroom that evolve over time.

Lacking		Emerging		Demonstrating		Excelling	
1	2	3	4	5	6	7	8

I refer to displayed language to enhance content learning and facilitate language production.

Lacking		Emerging		Demonstrating		Excelling	
1	2	3	4	5	6	7	8

I model how to use classroom scaffolds and lead students to independently use the resources as tools for learning.

Lacking		Emerging		Demonstrating		Excelling	
1	2	3	4	5	6	7	8

What I've tried/What I've observed.	My goals for improvement.

3B. Target language use

I expose learners to accurate and appropriately complex oral and written language input.

Lacking		Emerging		Demonstrating		Excelling	
1	2	3	4	5	6	7	8

I use the target language while teaching and communicate clear expectations for students to remain in the target language exclusively (or primarily).

Lacking		Emerging		Demonstrating		Excelling	
1	2	3	4	5	6	7	8

I employ numerous strategies and routines to support consistent student use of the target language.

Lacking		Emerging		Demonstrating		Excelling	
1	2	3	4	5	6	7	8

What I've tried/What I've observed.	My goals for improvement.

Strand 4: Scaffolding for Student Comprehension
I understand and use a variety of techniques to promote student comprehension in the target language.

4A, Verbal scaffolding: using language and non-verbal cues to support comprehension

I modify my teacher-talk (speed, intonation, repetition, etc.) as appropriate for students' ages and abilities.

Lacking		Emerging		Demonstrating		Excelling	
1	2	3	4	5	6	7	8

I include other verbal discourse strategies such as paraphrasing and using cognates.

Lacking		Emerging		Demonstrating		Excelling	
1	2	3	4	5	6	7	8

I use body language and facial expressions to support comprehension.

Lacking		Emerging		Demonstrating		Excelling	
1	2	3	4	5	6	7	8

I adjust the above strategies over time as students develop.

Lacking			Emerging		Demonstrating		Excelling
1	2	3	4	5	6	7	8

What I've tried/What I've observed.	*My goals for improvement.*

4B. Procedural scaffolding: organizing activities and routines to support comprehension

I use instructional routines (e.g., think-pair-share) to ensure predictability and facilitate comprehension.

Lacking			Emerging		Demonstrating		Excelling
1	2	3	4	5	6	7	8

I ensure predictability in instructional routines and use clear boundary markers between activities to facilitate classroom management.

Lacking			Emerging		Demonstrating		Excelling
1	2	3	4	5	6	7	8

I pair/group students systematically and in various arrangements to scaffold their comprehension.

Lacking			Emerging		Demonstrating		Excelling
1	2	3	4	5	6	7	8

What I've tried/What I've observed.	*My goals for improvement.*

4C. Instructional scaffolding: using tools within instructional activities to support comprehension

I incorporate a variety of instructional tools to support comprehension (graphic organizers, props, word walls, etc.).

Lacking			Emerging		Demonstrating		Excelling
1	2	3	4	5	6	7	8

I use instructional tools that are appropriate to students' ages and abilities.

Lacking			Emerging		Demonstrating		Excelling
1	2	3	4	5	6	7	8

I intentionally remove or modify scaffolds when necessary to promote student growth.

Lacking		Emerging		Demonstrating		Excelling	
1	2	3	4	5	6	7	8

What I've tried/What I've observed.	My goals for improvement.

Strand 5: Scaffolding for Student Production
I understand and use a variety of instructional strategies to promote extended student discourse and academic language production.

5A. Verbal scaffolding: questioning techniques and follow-up moves to support student language use and development

I use different questioning techniques and follow-up moves to improve student production and to move beyond Initiation-Response-Evaluation (IRE) sequences.

Lacking		Emerging		Demonstrating		Excelling	
1	2	3	4	5	6	7	8

I use follow-up moves, such as prompts for clarification, precision, or elaboration to elicit academic language and student thinking and to extend student discourse.

Lacking		Emerging		Demonstrating		Excelling	
1	2	3	4	5	6	7	8

I make effective use of wait time during classroom interaction.

Lacking		Emerging		Demonstrating		Excelling	
1	2	3	4	5	6	7	8

What I've tried/What I've observed.	My goals for improvement.

5B. Procedural scaffolding: grouping strategies, routines, and activities to support student language use and development

I use activities and routines (such as think-pair-share, learning centers, and cooperative learning) that promote independent student production and student-student interaction.

Lacking		Emerging		Demonstrating		Excelling	
1	2	3	4	5	6	7	8

I use a variety of organized interactive groupings (dyads and cooperative groups) to promote student language production.

Lacking		Emerging		Demonstrating		Excelling	
1	2	3	4	5	6	7	8

I review the language that students need to carry out interactive activities in the target language.

Lacking		Emerging		Demonstrating		Excelling	
1	2	3	4	5	6	7	8

What I've tried/What I've observed.	My goals for improvement.

5C. Instructional scaffolding: print and multi-media resources to support student language use and development

I use a range of print and multi-media resources related to instructional activities to support and facilitate language production.

Lacking		Emerging		Demonstrating		Excelling	
1	2	3	4	5	6	7	8

I teach familiar language "chunks" effectively and post them as reminders to use these scaffolds (as developmentally appropriate).

Lacking		Emerging		Demonstrating		Excelling	
1	2	3	4	5	6	7	8

I provide students with scaffolds to elicit sustained, academic oral and written language (such as sentence starters or frames and graphic organizers to support content learning and language development).

Lacking		Emerging		Demonstrating		Excelling	
1	2	3	4	5	6	7	8

I use modeling to prepare students to use such scaffolds as resources.

Lacking		Emerging		Demonstrating		Excelling	
1	2	3	4	5	6	7	8

What I've tried/What I've observed.	My goals for improvement.

Strand 6: Teaching for Language and Content Integration
I understand and use a variety of instructional practices to attend to students' language development and improve proficiency.

6A. Integrating language and content: instructional choices that intentionally bring attention to language during content instruction

I shift attention between content and language in natural ways.

Lacking		Emerging		Demonstrating		Excelling	
1	2	3	4	5	6	7	8

I look for and take advantage of opportunities to teach language and to clarify linguistic misconceptions in relation to content.

Lacking			Emerging		Demonstrating		Excelling	
1	2	3	4	5	6	7	8

I clearly communicate language objectives to students in student-friendly terms.

Lacking			Emerging		Demonstrating		Excelling	
1	2	3	4	5	6	7	8

I model and elicit specific language structures and functions.

Lacking			Emerging		Demonstrating		Excelling	
1	2	3	4	5	6	7	8

My focus on language is contextualized within content instruction.

Lacking			Emerging		Demonstrating		Excelling	
1	2	3	4	5	6	7	8

What I've tried/What I've observed.	*My goals for improvement.*

6B: Corrective feedback

I use a range of developmentally and contextually appropriate corrective feedback types to improve students' language proficiency.

Lacking			Emerging		Demonstrating		Excelling	
1	2	3	4	5	6	7	8

Many of the types of corrective feedback that I use encourage student uptake and repair.

Lacking			Emerging		Demonstrating		Excelling	
1	2	3	4	5	6	7	8

I provide feedback that clearly distinguishes a focus on language from a focus on content.

Lacking			Emerging		Demonstrating		Excelling	
1	2	3	4	5	6	7	8

What I've tried/What I've observed.	*My goals for improvement.*

Strand 7: Supporting Diverse Learners

I support diverse learners by differentiating instruction, maintaining high expectations, and promoting equitable classroom dynamics.

7A. Differentiated instruction and assessment

I differentiate by content, instructional processes, and student products according to students' language proficiencies as well as readiness, exceptionalities, and interests.

Lacking		Emerging		Demonstrating		Excelling	
1	2	3	4	5	6	7	8

I employ appropriate strategies to differentiate instruction and assessment (e.g., flexible grouping, leveled texts, and tiered activities and assessments).

Lacking		Emerging		Demonstrating		Excelling	
1	2	3	4	5	6	7	8

What I've tried/What I've observed.	My goals for improvement.

7B. Maintaining high expectations for students of all language backgrounds

I have appropriately high learning, language use/development, and behavioral expectations for all students.

Lacking		Emerging		Demonstrating		Excelling	
1	2	3	4	5	6	7	8

I support students in meeting those expectations.

Lacking		Emerging		Demonstrating		Excelling	
1	2	3	4	5	6	7	8

I leverage students' "funds of knowledge" and work to promote parent/family involvement and engagement.

Lacking		Emerging		Demonstrating		Excelling	
1	2	3	4	5	6	7	8

What I've tried/What I've observed.	My goals for improvement.

7C. Equitable classroom dynamics

I respond to instances in which the societal and institutional dominance of and preference for English affect minority-language use and development as well as social status in the classroom.

Lacking		Emerging		Demonstrating		Excelling	
1	2	3	4	5	6	7	8

*I employ inclusive pedagogical practices that position **all** students as knowledgeable and capable in the classroom and that promote equitable classroom discourse.*

Lacking		Emerging		Demonstrating		Excelling	
1	2	3	4	5	6	7	8

What I've tried/What I've observed.	*My goals for improvement.*

Strand 8: Advocacy

I am an active advocate for immersion and dual language education in general and as a potential educational option for any and all learners.

8A. Advocacy for exceptional learners

When appropriate, I advocate for students with disabilities, language delays, and other exceptionalities to be supported within the ImDL program rather than exited.

Lacking		Emerging		Demonstrating		Excelling	
1	2	3	4	5	6	7	8

I use research evidence to support these arguments.

Lacking		Emerging		Demonstrating		Excelling	
1	2	3	4	5	6	7	8

What I've tried/What I've observed.	*My goals for improvement.*

8B. Program model knowledge and commitment

I understand the goals and outcomes of my school's ImDL program model and communicate them to parents and other stakeholders.

Lacking		Emerging		Demonstrating		Excelling	
1	2	3	4	5	6	7	8

I understand and support practices and policies that represent commitment to the program model.

Lacking		Emerging		Demonstrating		Excelling	
1	2	3	4	5	6	7	8

I am comfortable and knowledgeable in giving accurate answers to common questions from other teachers, district personnel, parents, and the community at large.

Lacking		Emerging		Demonstrating		Excelling	
1	2	3	4	5	6	7	8

What I've tried/What I've observed.	*My goals for improvement.*

APPENDIX E: ANSWER KEYS

Chapter 6

Application activity 1: Oral feedback coding exercise

1. recast
2. metalinguistic clue
3. recast
4. repetition of error
5. recast
6. recast
7. elicitation
8. elicitation; recast
9. clarification request
10. elicitation
11. elicitation
12. recast
13. repetition of error + metalinguistic clue
14. explicit correction; metalinguistic clue
15. repetition + metalinguistic clue
16. recast

Application Activity 2: What's wrong with this prompt?

Line 2:   *The house that my grandparents live inside of* [repetition of error], *we don't say it like that* [metalinguistic clue]. *How are you going to say it?* [elicitation]
         What's wrong? There are three CF moves here. Combining CF types is not necessarily ineffective, but here they all target a rather complex error and none of them helps the young student to identify the actual error.

Line 4: *If they live there, are they inside of it?* [This could be considered either a metalinguistic clue or a clarification request].

What's wrong? The question is too abstract in its attempt to react to the literal meaning of what the student said.

Line 6: *So, you don't have to say "inside of it"* [Metalinguistic clue]. *The house where my grandparents live* [recast]. *In which my grandparents live* [recast]. *Very good.*

What's wrong? The three CF moves together draw on logic in an attempt to convey to this young student why his utterance was wrong. But the error seems to stem from following English rules for relative pronouns and the possibility of ending a sentence with a preposition in English (i.e., "The house that my grandparents live in"). Because in French a sentence can't end with a preposition, it's best to change the relative pronoun to *où* (*where*) or *dans laquelle* (*in which*) as the teacher did in her recasts, but this is hard to convey through indirect hints on the spur of the moment to a young learner. A simple recast would suffice.

Chapter 8

Application activity 1: What's wrong with this objective?

Examples of "good" objectives: 1, 7, 8, 10, 12

Examples of "bad" objectives: Explanations:

2. Describes an activity. It should get at the what/why that underlies the activity; e.g., Students will name and describe animals that are native to Ecuador.
3. Lacks focus—it embeds multiple objectives (recognize numbers, identify numbers, and trace/write the numbers).
4. Too vague. It should be more specific. A lot happens in one lesson—will students predict while reading a text? As part of a KWPL (What I know, What I want to know, What I predict, What I learned) activity?
5. Framed with respect to what teacher will do. Objectives should always be framed in terms of what students will do.
6. Written at the macro level. It only specifies the function. Language objectives need to identify the discourse type, function, grammatical feature, and vocabulary.
9. Too broad (students can't learn the alphabet in one lesson). Objectives should be written at the lesson level.
11. Doesn't get at aspects related to social/affective development. Social/affective objectives should incorporate words that reflect development of social skills and affect, such as collaboratively, respectfully, etc.

INDEX

Made in United States
North Haven, CT
01 March 2022

16613341R00209